e Peschio

Share Schemes for Directors and Employees

'The shares are a penny, and ever so many are taken by Rothschild
and Baring,
And just as a few are allotted to you, you awake with a shudder
despairing.'

W S Gilbert: *Iolanthe*

Share Schemes for Directors and Employees

David F. Williams MA (Cantab), FCA, FCCA, FTII, FRSA

London
Butterworths
1989

United Kingdom	Butterworth & Co (Publishers) Ltd, 88 Kingsway, LONDON WC2B 6AB and 4 Hill Street, EDINBURGH EH2 3JZ
Australia	Butterworths Pty Ltd, SYDNEY, MELBOURNE, BRISBANE, ADELAIDE, PERTH, CANBERRA and HOBART
Canada	Butterworth & Co (Canada) Ltd, TORONTO and VANCOUVER
Ireland	Butterworth (Ireland) Ltd, DUBLIN
Malaysia	Malayan Law Journal Sdn Bhd, KUALA LUMPUR
New Zealand	Butterworths of New Zealand Ltd, WELLINGTON and AUCKLAND
Singapore	Butterworth & Co (Asia) Pte Ltd, SINGAPORE
USA	Butterworth Legal Publishers, ST PAUL, Minnesota, SEATTLE, Washington, BOSTON, Massachusetts, AUSTIN, Texas and D & S Publishers, CLEARWATER, Florida

A CIP Catalogue record for this book is available from the British Library.

First edition 1985

ISBN 0 406 50334 6

Typeset by Phoenix Photosetting, Chatham
Printed and bound by Mackays of Chatham PLC, Chatham, Kent

To Hilary, Helen and Peter

Preface

Since the first edition of this work was published, a number of refinements have been made to the legislation governing the three types of Inland Revenue approved share schemes, mostly to deal with specific points of difficulty; in particular, provision has been made to allow the replacement of options on a company takeover.

Various changes have also been made to the treatment of unapproved share options and to the 'growth in value' charge under ICTA 1988, s 138 (formerly FA 1972, s 79), principally to close loopholes, but also (in the case of the 'growth in value' charge) to prevent a liability arising on company takeovers.

The FA 1972 rules, however, now apply only to shares acquired before 26 October 1987. For shares acquired on or after that date the provisions of FA 1988, ss 77 to 89 impose an income tax charge, broadly, only on growth in value arising from manipulation of share rights in favour of employees, rather than, as previously, on all increases in the value of relevant shares. The charge on shares in 'dependent subsidiaries', however, continues to make no distinction between 'natural' and 'artificial' growth in value.

This considerable relaxation may be expected to bring about a revival of interest in unapproved share schemes. Even more significantly, the alignment of income tax and capital gains tax rates in the Finance Act 1988 affects fundamentally the balance of advantage between unapproved share option schemes and Inland Revenue 'selective' schemes, considerably diminishing the overwhelming tax advantages previously enjoyed by the latter.

Statutory references in the second edition have been revised to take account of the consolidation of the previous legislation into the Income and Corporation Taxes Act 1988. The law is stated as at 31 November 1988.

DFW
Hatch End, Middlesex
December 1988

Preface to the first edition

The last ten years have seen a significant increase in share ownership by employees, encouraged by the favourable tax treatment for Inland Revenue approved 'profit-sharing' and savings-related share option schemes introduced in the Finance Acts of 1978 and 1980.

With the advent of the new approved share option scheme rules contained in the Finance Act 1984, the emphasis of the legislation changed in favour of a 'selective' approach, allowing share options to be made available to directors and senior executives as desired, rather than to the workforce as a whole. The value of the benefits which could be offered was also significantly increased. Whereas the intention of the two earlier schemes was to encourage 'worker participation', the 1984 legislation was designed, by contrast, to provide a (potentially very valuable) incentive to senior management. FA 1984 schemes were, however, intended to complement, rather than replace, the existing arrangements, as the present government remains committed to the principle of wide share ownership, whether through employee schemes or other measures. Moreover, in larger companies, irrespective of government policy, industrial relations considerations may demand the introduction of 'worker share schemes' in conjunction with 'senior management' schemes, where the former do not already exist.

The result is that managers in industry who have to make decisions on remuneration policy, and those in the professions who have to advise on such matters, must be familiar, to a greater or lesser extent, with all three existing statutory schemes, and Chapters 4, 5 and 6 of the present work therefore begin by setting out briefly, for easy reference, the salient features of each scheme, before going on to consider the legislation in detail, highlighting planning opportunities, points of practical difficulty, and the relative advantages and disadvantages of each arrangement. Appendices also give illustrative rules for each of the statutory schemes.

It should not be forgotten, however, that in many cases Inland Revenue approved schemes are not appropriate (or were not an available option when existing arrangements were implemented). Larger companies may have 'unapproved' share option or incentive schemes set up under detailed rules for the benefit of senior executives, but in smaller companies much less formal arrangements may exist, fashioned (often without thought to the tax consequences) to meet individuals needs—to reward or retain key personnel, to regulate the ultimate control of the company, or to fulfil personal obligations between shareholders. The tax regime governing such 'unapproved' schemes has emerged piecemeal through the legislation of successive Finance Acts since 1966, coupled with decisions of the courts. The result is what the Institute of Chartered Accountants in England and Wales, in representations to the Chancellor of the Exchequer in 1984, described as a 'minefield' of complex and interacting provisions, spread haphazardly across the Taxes Acts.

Chapters 2 and 3 of the present work aim to bring together and explore the implications of the statutory and case law provisions relating to unapproved schemes in order to illustrate, both by narrative and example, how they apply to the multifarious share transactions involving employees and directors which may be undertaken or contemplated. They also highlight traps which may impose an unnecessary tax burden on the unwary, and suggest the most effective ways of planning for and implementing such arrangements.

Just as the 1984 share option schemes have not eliminated the need for the earlier Inland Revenue approved schemes, so neither have they eradicated unapproved schemes. Commercial realities and personal circumstances, particularly in smaller companies, will always necessitate arrangements between persons entering into business together which do not fit into the straitjacket of any approved scheme—often because they are not designed to provide 'executive perks', but are an integral part of a company's financing arrangements, or are intended to redress the balance between the supplier of initiative and the supplier of capital.

In summary, then, it is hoped that this book will provide the necessary information for businessmen and professional advisers to judge which, if any, of the three 'approved schemes' meets their needs, and, in those cases where none is appropriate, will enable them to pass through the 'minefield' of the remaining statutory provisions with as much expedition and as little damage as possible.

DFW
Hatch End, Middlesex
September 1985

Contents

Acknowledgements

The author and publishers would like to thank the following bodies, who have given permission for the reproduction of material included in the text and appendices:

The Association of British Insurers
The National Association of Pension Funds Limited
The Council of The International Stock Exchange of the United Kingdom and the Republic of Ireland Limited
The Controller of Her Majesty's Stationery Office
The Consultative Committee of Accountancy Bodies

Table of cases

Table of statutes

1 Introduction

GENERAL

1.1 It is a commonplace of financial planning that the tax tail should not be allowed to wag the commercial dog. In a sense this is true: it can easily be overlooked in the excitement of the chase through the taxing statutes that a profit, even if it is taxed at 40%, is a better thing than a loss, even if it is relieved at 40%. The distinction between commercial and tax considerations, however, is in many ways a false dichotomy. Tax may represent an appropriation of profits when looked at from the point of view of the Inspector of Taxes. To the businessman, however, it is an expense like any other. Tax considerations *are* commercial considerations.

1.2 In determining an employee's 'remuneration package', tax and other commercial considerations are inextricably linked, although where employee share schemes are concerned, whether they take the form of 'share option' or 'share incentive' arrangements, the tax factors are by far the most complicated, even if not ultimately the most important, of the points to be considered—and that complexity is the justification for the present work. Before the tax considerations can be examined, however, it is necessary to have some idea of the mechanics of the arrangements involved, and the way in which they are structured from a legal and financial point of view.

THE MECHANICS OF A SHARE OPTION SCHEME

General

1.3 Under a share option arrangement, the company concerned grants to the employee, not shares, but the *right to subscribe* for shares in the company at a specified price. The right may be exerciseable without any restriction as to time or, more usually, on specified occasions or between given dates. The exact conditions will depend upon the prevailing circumstances, the object in view and, in large measure, the tax considerations. Essential to the concept of the option, and implicit in its name, is the fact that while the employee has rights as against the company, the company has no rights as against him. He is not obliged to take up the shares over which his option extends. (Such an arrangement is not inconceivable, of course, but is outside the scope of the present work.)

The exercise price

1.4 The price at which the holder is entitled to exercise his option may be the market value of the shares at the time the option is granted; a higher figure; or even, on occasions, a lower figure.

1.5 Where the 'exercise price' is equal to the market value at the time of the grant of the option, the intention will be to enable the employee to acquire an interest in the shares of the company, with all the potential for gain of an immediate investment, at a time when he is unable, or unwilling, to make an outright purchase of the underlying shares.

1.6 An option with an exercise price higher than market value at the time it is granted will not only reflect the expectation of growth (as indeed will any option), but may also represent, in effect, a rather more sophisticated variation of the restriction on the time of exercise. Acquisition of the shares is deferred, not for some arbitrary period of years, but (at least) until such time as the company reaches a specific stage in its financial development (as measured by the share price), irrespective of the length of time required to achieve this objective.

1.7 An option to purchase at less than market value at the time of grant, though rare, is a possibility to be considered where the company wishes to increase the financial benefit to the employee beyond that which would arise from the use of market value, but does not wish to commit itself to passing control of the number of shares which would be required in order to achieve the same financial benefit to the employee at such an exercise price. While the proportion of a company's share capital involved in share option arrangements is unlikely to be large, 1% or 2% may nevertheless serve to dilute existing majority interests below the critical 75% or 50% mark. A 75% holding is required (in the tax arena) to establish the necessary relationship for group relief of losses, or for the passing of assets between group companies without a charge to corporation tax on capital gains, and (in the company law field) to obtain the necessary majority for the passing of a special or extraordinary resolution in general meeting, for example, to change the company's name, reduce its capital, or initiate a voluntary liquidation. A '51%' holding (by which term the Income and Corporation Taxes Act (ICTA) 1988, s 838(1)(a) designates any holding in excess of 50%) is required for a group income election (allowing the payment of intra-group dividends without advance corporation tax, and of annual interest and other charges without the deduction of income tax) and, as far as company law is concerned, provides the necessary majority for the passing of a simple resolution.

1.8 Such a right to purchase shares at less than their current market value is even less likely than most options to be exerciseable immediately. Certainly, if immediate exercise were the intention, it would be more straightforward simply to issue shares at an undervalue. However, the recipient of such an option which imposes no time limit on its exercise will by no means necessarily wish to exercise it to realise an immediate gain. If further substantial growth in the share value is expected, it will obviously be wiser to delay any action in order to reap even greater rewards in the future.

The time of exercise

1.9 While there may be no restrictions on the time at which an option can be exercised, such arrangements are unusual. Normally a company will wish to defer exercise for one reason or another (most often, to provide an incentive for employees to remain with the company and work to build up its value).

Similarly, it will not wish to have a completely 'open-ended' liability, so there will usually be a date after which the option, if not exercised, will lapse. Typically, therefore, an option arrangement might provide for exercise at any time between the third and seventh anniversaries of its grant, or (for administrative convenience) on stated dates between those anniversaries, perhaps at six-monthly or annual intervals.

The option consideration

1.10 Monetary consideration may be given by the employee for the grant of the option, as well as for the later purchase of the shares when the option is exercised. The amount of such consideration may be commercially determined, so that an employee will, for example, willingly pay £1,000 for an option to purchase at £5,000 in three years' time shares which he confidently expects by then to be worth £10,000. In the vast majority of cases, however, the monetary consideration is non-existent or purely nominal (£1 for the total rights under the option, for example; or 1p per share). Consideration of some sort is necessary before the option agreement can constitute a legally enforceable contract between the company and the employee (*Rann v Hughes* (1778) 7 Term Rep 350, 4 Bro Parl Cas 27; *Eastwood v Kenyon* (1840) 11 Ad & El 438; *Dunlop Pneumatic Tyre Co Ltd v Selfridge & Co Ltd* [1915] AC 847, 84 LJ KB 1680), although it is not necessary to establish the adequacy of the consideration, so that a purely nominal figure will suffice (*Sturlyn v Albany* (1587) Cro Eliz 67; *Haigh v Brooks* (1839) 10 Ad & El 309, 2 Per & Dav 477; *Thomas v Thomas* (1842) 2 QB 851, 2 Gal & Dav 226; *Alexander v Rayson* [1936] 1 KB 169). While many companies no doubt honour obligations gratuitously undertaken (and indeed do not realise that they have any choice in the matter), it is always advisable to put the point beyond any doubt. Management or ownership of the company, or personal relationships within it, may change, and the benevolence which inspired promises to the workforce of benefits in future years may evaporate when the company sees just how advantageous the arrangements have proved to be.

1.11 Consideration will normally take a pecuniary form, but need not necessarily do so: where an individual is engaged on the basis of a 'remuneration package' which includes the grant of options, the work he performs under his contract of employment may equally well provide the necessary consideration. This will not be the case, however, where, as commonly happens, the option agreement is superimposed on existing employment arrangements, and the work carried out by the employee subsequent to the grant of the option forms part of the agreed consideration under his original contract of employment.

1.12 Under English law an obligation undertaken for no consideration is enforceable if made by a document under seal (*Fletcher v Fletcher* (1844) 4 Hare 67, 14 LJ Ch 66; *Xenos v Wickham* (1867) LR 2 HL 296, 36 LJCP 313; *Lady Naas v Westminster Bank Ltd* [1940] AC 366, [1940] 1 All ER 485), and this is a possible, but more cumbersome, way of dealing with the grant of options if there is to be no consideration. Different rules apply in Scotland.

Documentation

1.13 Share option arrangements may be employed in a wide variety of situations, ranging from the small company, where the agreement relates to one employee and is set out in an informal letter from the sole shareholder and managing director, to the multinational public limited company where thousands of employees are involved. In the latter case, standardised documentation will be required which might typically include:

(a) An introductory letter to eligible employees setting out the salient points of the scheme: such a letter might well be construed as forming part of the contract, notwithstanding the subsequent issue of more formal documentation, and care should therefore be taken to ensure either that any such informal letter correctly conveys the sense of the scheme rules (which is evidently desirable in any case), or that (where the scheme rules have not yet been finalised) such letters clearly state their provisional nature.
(b) The formal rules of the scheme: the features which need to be incorporated in such rules as a result of tax considerations are set out in Chapters 5 and 6 for Inland Revenue approved schemes and, to a lesser extent, for unapproved schemes in Chapter 3. In addition, examples are given in Appendices 6 and 7. Apart from those items dictated by tax considerations, the rules will largely be determined by the commercial objectives of the scheme: whether the aim is to reward past service or to provide an incentive for future efforts; to spread share ownership widely or to restrict it to senior executives; to provide an early return, or to encourage a long term interest in the company; and other similar factors. Regard may also have to be had to requirements imposed by institutional investors (see further 1.14).
(c) A resolution adopting the scheme, for the formal approval of the company in general meeting (by ordinary resolution).
(d) Minutes of the meeting at which the scheme was adopted.
(e) A letter of invitation to apply for options, to be issued to those persons eligible under the scheme or, in the case of a selective scheme, to those individuals to whom the Board of Directors (or other nominated body) may choose to offer options. Such invitations will normally be issued soon after the establishment of the scheme and at intervals thereafter, and will specify the date by which an application must be made, the number of shares over which options may be acquired, the consideration to be given for the grant of the option, and the price at which shares may be acquired on its exercise.
(f) An application form, which will accompany the letter of invitation, and will be returned to the company on completion.
(g) A certificate of the option held, to be issued on receipt and processing of the application.
(h) A form of exercise of the option, to be submitted to the company on the appropriate occasion, together with the option certificate. Alternatively, such a form may be incorporated in the option certificate, or its purpose may be fulfilled by a simple letter. Provision will also need to be made for the issue of new certificates in respect of any balance of the option which remains unexercised.

Institutional requirements

1.14 Sophisticated schemes may be governed by detailed rules on a variety of matters which are unrelated to the requirements for obtaining Inland Revenue approval. These are a matter of commercial preference, and are not examined further here. They may also be affected by the requirements of the Investment

Committees of various bodies representing institutional investors, such as the Association of British Insurers, whose guidelines are set out at Appendix 1, or the National Association of Pension Funds, whose statement is reproduced at Appendix 2. Essentially, these are designed to prevent excessive dilution of the interests of non-employee shareholders, by restricting the proportion of the equity which may be used in employee share schemes, and to prevent such shares as are available for allocation to employees being issued to only a small group. Following revision in 1987, they now, also, link the exercise of 'selective' share options to growth in the company's earnings per share. There are many further detailed regulations for which reference should be made to the Appendices. These guidelines and statement have no statutory force, but institutions which are members of the bodies concerned are advised by them to vote in the company's general meeting against the adoption of any scheme which does not comply with their recommendations. The Stock Exchange also imposes various requirements as regards the establishment of employee share schemes by listed companies, details of which are given in Appendix 3.

Example

1.15 A simple example may serve to illustrate the mechanics, and the financial effects for the employee, of a share option scheme:

> On 15 January 1989, Woodhouse is invited by his employer, Taylor Ltd, to apply for an option to purchase 1,000 shares in the company at their then market value of £2. He makes the application, and the option is granted on 1 February 1989 for a total nominal consideration of £1. Under the terms of the relevant scheme, he may exercise his rights under the option, in whole or in part, on the third anniversary of its grant, and on any subsequent anniversary up to the seventh.
>
> On 1 February 1992, the shares have fallen in value to £1.75, and there is, obviously, no question of Woodhouse exercising his option. A year later they have risen to £2.25, but he does not choose to make a purchase then. On 1 February 1994, the shares are valued at £3.50. Woodhouse exercises his option to purchase 1,000 shares at £2, and makes a profit as follows:

Value of shares on acquisition:		
1,000 × £3.50		£ 3,500
Cost:		
1,000 × £2	£ 2,000	
Option consideration	1	(2,001)
Profit		£ 1,499

> Woodhouse may choose to sell his shares and realise the gain, or to retain them in the hope of further appreciation in their value. If he expects the price to continue to rise, however, and he intends to retain the shares, he would have been wiser to delay the exercise until the latest possible opportunity, in 1996.

The tax effects of such a series of transactions are dealt with in Chapter 3.

THE MECHANICS OF A SHARE INCENTIVE SCHEME

General

1.16 Any employee share scheme, whether or not it involves the use of options, is intended to provide an 'incentive' to employees—as indeed is the provision of any benefit in kind, or the payment of a salary. The term 'share incentive' scheme, therefore, is not a particularly helpful one. It is, however, generally applied to any arrangement, other than a share option scheme, under which an employee is given the opportunity to acquire shares on favourable terms. These may involve the outright gift of shares to employees, or the opportunity to purchase them below market value or on deferred payment terms. Alternatively, there may be no direct monetary advantage in the terms offered, but the employee may be given preference in an over-subscribed share issue, or the employing company may make him a loan (perhaps at a preferential rate of interest), or guarantee a loan by a third party such as a bank, in order to enable him to subscribe for shares offered to him, or perhaps so that he may purchase shares on the open market.

1.17 As in the case of share options, discussed above, the arrangements may range from the informal ad hoc offer of shares to one employee, in particular circumstances, to a formal scheme where all employees, or certain categories of employees, are offered shares at a price, and in a quantity, determined according to a set formula based on such factors as length of service, earnings, and productivity. In such a case there will often be restrictions on the transferability of the shares, or a minimum period for which they must be retained, in order to encourage the employee's identification of his interests with those of the company.

Documentation

1.18 In the case of a a formal scheme, standard documentation will be required, which will typically include:

(a) The rules of the scheme, setting out which employees are entitled to shares; the extent of that entitlement; and the appropriate purchase price, together with administrative details. Such rules will normally be less complex than the rules for a share option scheme, as once the shares are issued the company's involvement is at an end (except for monitoring any restrictions on subsequent dealings in the shares). The detailed rules which are necessary to regulate all the preliminary features of a share option scheme (by which shares are effectively issued in two stages over a period of several years) are not required.
(b) Letters of invitation to apply for shares: as explained in connection with options at para (a) of 1.13, such letters may well form part of the eventual contract between the company and the employee, even where they merely purport to summarise the rules of the scheme in laymen's terms, and care should be exercised in their drafting.
(c) Forms of application for shares.

The remaining formalities and documentation will not be peculiar to an employee share incentive scheme, but will in general follow the pattern of any normal share issue.

1.19 The exact rules adopted will be determined by tax and commercial considerations, and, in the case of those companies to which they apply, by the restrictions imposed under the Investment Committee guidelines and statement (see 1.14).

Example

1.20 A simple example may help to illustrate the principles involved in a typical share incentive scheme where the preferential terms on which the shares are offered involve a discount to market value. As already indicated, however, while all share option arrangements essentially represent variations of one basic idea, the concepts underlying share purchase schemes are much more varied, and a discount will not necessarily form an essential feature of every scheme.

> On 1 June 1989, Weston receives an invitation to apply for 500 shares in Knightley Ltd, his employer company, at a preferential price of £2, as compared to their then market value of £3. Under the terms of the offer, he may not dispose of the shares within 18 months after their allotment, except by sale back to the company at the original subscription price of £2. He makes the necessary application and payment, and shares are allotted to him on 15 June 1989. On 31 December 1991, the share price has risen to £5, and he sells his shares, realising a profit as follows:

Sale proceeds:	
500 × £5	£ 2,500
Cost:	
500 × £2	(1,000)
Profit	£ 1,500

The tax consequences of such a series of transactions are examined in Chapter 2.

THE COMMERCIAL APPLICATION OF EMPLOYEE SHARE SCHEMES

General

1.21 Having looked at the mechanics of employee share option and share incentive schemes, it is instructive to consider the circumstances in which they are likely to be employed, and the motivation underlying their use.

1.22 'Non-approved' arrangements and 'selective' share option schemes approved by the Inland Revenue are commonly used as executive 'perks'. They enable management and directors to be offered an additional benefit in kind which costs the company nothing, and which will, indeed, bring in further capital if options are granted for more than a nominal consideration, or if shares are issued either in pursuance of a share incentive or a share option scheme. While there is no cost to the company, as a legal entity, (other than administrative expenses) there will, of course, be a dilution of the equity interests of existing shareholders, although this is often so small as to have no effect on the market value of their shares. Such schemes are attractive to the recipients because unlike other benefits, such as the provision of cars, accommodation or cheap loans, they are (theoretically) of potentially unlimited value (although it follows that they may also prove to be of no value at all). In addition, they foster a sense of identity of interests between the employee and the company: his endeavours contribute towards its success, and this is reflected in the value of the shares which he owns, or which he has rights to acquire.

1.23 The use of employee benefits other than straightforward cash remuneration increased in its attractiveness to employers with the abolition from 6 October 1985 of the 'upper earnings limit' for employers' Class 1 national insurance contributions. This effectively imposed a 'payroll tax' of 10.45% for highly paid employees, but non-cash benefits are, in general, excluded from this charge.

1.24 In general, continuity of staff will be of benefit to a company, and any improvement in an individual's salary or benefits will have the effect of making him less likely to seek alternative employment elsewhere. More specifically, the possession of an option which cannot be exercised for a period of years, and which lapses on leaving the company's employment, or the ownership of shares which must be sold back to the company if the holder leaves its employ, will act as an incentive to the employee to remain where he is. Even where he has held options for the requisite period, there may still be a disincentive to leave the company if the options lapse in that eventuality, as in order to take advantage of the scheme he must exercise his options immediately, and forfeit the benefit of any expected future growth. Thus, if an individual has acquired an option to purchase shares in his employer company at their then market value of £2 at any time between the third and seventh anniversaries of the grant of the option, and the shares have risen (and are expected to continue to rise) in value by £1 per year, the combination of the rules that options lapse on leaving the company, and that they cannot be exercised within three years of grant, will effectively tie him to the company for that three year period. Even after the expiry of that period, an exercise of his option would yield a profit of £3 per share, but he would forfeit the expectation of a further £4 of profit per share in the future.

1.25 The corollary of this argument, of course, is that if the company is performing badly, and employees have low expectations of its future prosperity, share schemes will provide no incentive to remain. Indeed, the feeling of community of interest referred to above may well generate a disillusion and dissatisfaction which would not have arisen, or would have been less marked, had the scheme never been established.

1.26 As well as having the general effect of encouraging staff loyalty, a share option or share incentive arrangement may be used specifically, as part of their contract of employment, to attract or retain key personnel; not only because of the expectation of financial gain, but in view of the natural desire of a successful manager with entrepreneurial flair to be working for a company of which he is part-owner rather than merely paid servant—to feel that (whatever the strict legal position) he is in some sense in business on his own account.

1.27 It must be recognised that, in perhaps the majority of cases, any direct correlation between an individual's efforts or his value to the company and the rewards provided by an employee share scheme is illusory. Equally, it must be recognised that the absence of any such correlation need in no way diminish the psychological value of the arrangements.

The family company

1.28 Just as special arrangements may be made for key personnel, family relationships, particularly in the smaller company, may dictate that a shareholding should be transferred to certain individuals. All the points made above concerning identity of interest between the individual and the company are of relevance in these circumstances too, but in addition there may simply be a feeling that it is only right and proper that a family director or employee should have a shareholding in the company. Alternatively, shares may be transferred to a family member or close business associate through the mechanism of an employee share scheme, out of completely gratuitous motives, or in order to meet some obligation, or to rearrange some aspect of family finances, completely unconnected with the affairs of the company. In such a case, where a close company is involved, consideration will have to be given to the inheritance tax implications, and these are discussed further at 2.346 to 2.348.

1.29 There are a variety of reasons why a share option or share incentive scheme might be preferred in such a context to a straightforward sale or gift of shares between the parties, or to a subscription for new shares without reference to the subscriber's status as employee or director.

1.30 First, a share option or incentive scheme may provide an alternative to a gift of shares by a major shareholder which could precipitate a significant inheritance tax charge (subject, again, to the points made at 2.346 to 2.348). An outright sale would also avoid this problem, of course, but this would involve the provision of funds by the new shareholder which he might be unable or unwilling to commit to such an arrangement. An option scheme would postpone this necessity, while a purchase of shares on preferential terms would reduce the scale of the difficulty (or increase the benefit obtainable for a given outlay). Any income tax charge on the purchase of shares at a discount (see 2.13 to 2.28) could be reduced or eliminated by the imposition of restrictions on their transferability or on the rights attaching to them, in order to bring about a diminution in the value of the shares (see 2.22 to 2.24), although consideration would also need to be given to the possibility of an income tax charge arising from an increase in the value of the shares on the subsequent lifting of such restrictions.

1.31 Second, an option to purchase a substantial number of shares in the future may be perceived as a much more valuable benefit than the gift of a small number of shares now, even if an expert valuation would put the same price on the current value of either set of rights. (As to the valuation of options, see further 3.6 to 3.8.) Even where the recipient is well aware of the value of the rights involved, it may well suit him, as a matter of personal preference in the light of all his circumstances, to opt for the larger shareholding provided by an option arrangement, even at the expense of considerable delay before the shares are actually obtained.

1.32 Third, an existing shareholder may be much more willing to see his interest diluted by an option which does not take effect for a number of years than by a gift of shares, particularly as the eventual exercise of the option will only take place if the company enjoys a certain degree of financial success, in which the existing shareholder will share.

1.33 Fourth, an option, like a gift of deferred shares, may be used to give a promise of a worthwhile shareholding in the future while giving away little or nothing of substance immediately. It may therefore be well suited to the situation in a family company where a major shareholder wishes to encourage a younger member of the family who is involved in the business by an expression of confidence (which he may not necessarily feel), secure in the knowledge that the recipient will not be in a position to sell, or to use the votes attaching to, the relevant shares until he is older and of more mature judgment.

The larger company

1.34 Share schemes are also used, particularly in larger companies, not as an executive 'perk', but as a means of encouraging widespread share ownership by employees (although typically the numbers of shares held in each case will not be large). The Inland Revenue approved 'profit-sharing' schemes and savings-related share option schemes are particularly suitable for use in this context. A company's motives for entering into such schemes will normally be to encourage staff morale and a sense of 'worker participation' which will ultimately work for the benefit of the company, although the incidence of arrangements entered into out of philanthropic or political conviction should not be overlooked. Such widespread share ownership schemes may be very effective in generating employee goodwill towards the company, but the size of the organisations concerned usually precludes any direct correlation between individual effort and increases in the share price, and the sums involved are not normally large enough to assist in the retention of employees for whom other factors point to a change of employment. Neither, of course, is the loss of a single employee in a large company, for whom no special provisions have been made, likely to represent a major blow to the employer.

'Turn-round' situations

1.35 Neither the grant of options nor the issue of shares (whether on the exercise of an option or under a 'share gift' or 'share purchase' scheme) actually costs the company anything. Its profit is not reduced; nor does it suffer any adverse cash flow effect. While there is a cost to existing shareholders in the form of the dilution of their holdings, this will often be minimal in view of the figures involved. This 'lack of cost' of employee share schemes may make them particularly attractive to companies which cannot currently afford to pay salaries at market rates, but hope to retain staff, and particularly key personnel, by the promise of an exceptional reward in the future. Such an approach may be particularly appropriate in new, expanding companies, or in 'turn-round' situations, where an existing and ailing company comes under new management which has the confidence of the workforce. It is of particular relevance to the remuneration of the new management team themselves, who may effectively swap the present enjoyment of a normal rate of salary for the hope of exceptional rewards in the future, based on their own efforts.

Inland Revenue approved schemes

1.36 The Inland Revenue approved 'profit-sharing' or share appropriation schemes, which were introduced by FA 1978, and the savings-related approved share option schemes which followed in FA 1980, aimed at spreading share ownership widely (but fairly thinly) among the workforce. The 'selective' share option schemes introduced by FA 1984 stand in contrast to these earlier schemes in being designed not to spread wealth but:

> to attract top calibre company management and to increase the incentives and motivation of existing executives and key personnel by linking their rewards to performance.
>
> [Rt Hon Nigel Lawson MP, Chancellor of the Exchequer, Budget Statement, 13 March 1984 (56 HC Official Report (6th series) col 299).]

As the preface to the first edition of the present work indicates, however, many companies have perceived the 'old' and 'new' schemes as complementary rather than mutually exclusive, and as enabling them to provide benefits for all sectors of the workforce within a statutory framework.

SHARE OPTION *v* SHARE INCENTIVE SCHEMES

General

1.37 As discussed at 1.21 to 1.36, any share scheme is entered into (barring exceptional personal considerations) with the objective of motivating and retaining staff. This is good for staff, and, provided the returns are commensurate with the cost, is good for the company also. It remains, however, to consider the relative merits of the two basic variants: the share option and the share incentive (or share purchase/gift) scheme.

The company

1.38 From the point of view of the company, the grant of share options has no immediate effect on its financial position (apart from any nominal consideration received). A gift of shares to employees, as under an Inland Revenue approved profit-sharing scheme (see Chapter 4), similarly does not cost the company anything, (although prior to 16 March 1988 capital duty at 1% was payable on the value of the shares issued). Indeed, in the case of an Inland Revenue approved scheme, the company will be better off to the extent of any corporation tax relief obtained (see 4.75–4.77). Its existing share capital is, however, diluted, so that there is a cost to the shareholders, although not to the company itself. In practice, such an effect is likely to be so small as to have no effect on the share price or on dividends. A more usual incentive scheme involving the sale of shares to employees at a discount has the advantage to the company that it produces an immediate influx of funds (albeit with a slight dilution of the value of existing equity capital), and from this point of view at least it is to be preferred to a share option scheme which (depending on the fortunes of the company) produces its influx of funds considerably later, or not at all; which may well involve, on exercise of the options, a larger discount and correspondingly increased dilution of existing shareholders' interests; and which may well see the exercise of options closely followed by a sale of the relevant shares, with (theoretically at least) a depressing effect on the share price.

1.39 For the company, a share purchase scheme also has the advantage over a gift of shares or the grant of an option in that the employee has put his own money at risk, and committed himself financially to the future success of the company. While the other schemes may offer equal benefit, an employee may prize less that which has cost him nothing.

The employee

1.40 From the employee's point of view, obviously, the most advantageous arrangement is one which gives him an immediate full beneficial interest in shares at no cost, and enables him to enjoy all the benefits of such a holding including the receipt of dividends, the exercise of voting power (although this is unlikely to be significant in the context of the small shareholdings normally involved), and (subject to any restrictions) the possibility of realising his shares by a sale for cash. A gift of shares by the company, however, will either have a high income tax cost to the employee (see 2.13 to 2.28) or will be made under the terms of the approved 'profit-sharing' legislation, which provides strictly limited benefits. Normally, therefore, the employee's preference will be for the other 'no cost' route of share option arrangements. Such a scheme has many advantages for the employee and ostensibly, as considered above, none for the company. In practice, however, as the company's aim is to provide a benefit which will please and motivate its employees, this route will often be the company's own preferred alternative.

1.41 Options, unlike a share purchase scheme, do not require the employee to put up any finance; yet his potential gain is as great as if he purchased shares outright. His investment is 'geared up' as the following example illustrates:

Mitchell is granted an option, a price of £0.10 per share, to purchase 2,000 shares in three years' time at £2, which is their market value at the time of the grant. After three years have elapsed the share price is £3. Mitchell exercises his option and sells the shares immediately. His profit is as follows:

Sale proceeds: 2,000 × £3	£ 6,000
Exercise price: 2,000 × £2	(4,000)
	2,000
Option consideration: 2,000 × £0.10	(200)
Profit	£ 1,800

Mitchell's profit of £1,800 represents a return of 900% on his investment of £200. Had the consideration merely been a nominal £1 for the option to purchase the entire holding of 2,000 shares, his return would have been 180,000%, and had there been no consideration (see 1.10), the profit of £1,800 would have represented a windfall in return for no investment at all.

By contrast, if Mitchell had bought the shares outright originally, at a discount of, for example, £0.25 each, his return would have been as follows:

Sale proceeds:	
2,000 × £3	£ 6,000
Purchase price:	
2,000 × £1.75	(3,500)
Profit	£ 2,500

This represents a return of 71%; ie only 8% of the return with a £0.10 per share option consideration, or 0.04% of the return with a merely nominal option consideration.

The figures chosen for illustration are arbitrary, and could have been made to produce a more or a less striking result. The essential point is that the returns on options are of a completely different order from those on share purchase schemes. The return is not, of course, to be looked at by normal investment criteria, as it is received by way of reward for the employee's services.

1.42 The 'investment' is 'geared up' in the example above, where a £0.10 per share option consideration is used, by a multiple of 20 as compared to the then market price of the shares. However, it is only relevant to consider options in terms of 'gearing up' where there is no limit, or a very high limit, on the options which the employee may purchase; where, for example, he could have chosen to invest the £3,500 with which he bought shares in the second example above in purchasing options over 35,000 shares at £0.10, each, which would have produced a profit of £31,500. Such a situation is unlikely to arise in practice.

1.43 Of more general relevance than the possibility of 'gearing up' an investment is the fact that an option arrangement may enable an employee to acquire an interest in shares when he has no funds available to invest in a share purchase scheme, however potentially profitable, and would be unable or unwilling to borrow for the purpose.

1.44 It should be noted also that the employee is not prevented from exercising his option, if it is showing a profit, by the absence of liquid funds. There should be no problem in borrowing from a bank until the shares acquired on exercise of the option are sold, although this may not be so where the shares are in a small private company and there is no ready market for them, or where it is a condition of the scheme that the shares should be retained for a certain period by the employee, or there are other restrictions on transfer. Even in the case of readily marketable quoted company shares, an arrangement for a loan such as that envisaged will not enable the employee to retain the shares and participate in the future growth of the company, as he might have wished, but he will at least have realised his profit from the options.

1.45 It follows also from the fact that an option arrangement does not normally require any significant investment, that there is no 'downside risk' for employees. If the company fares well, they exercise their options and realise a profit; if not, they simply allow their options to lapse and they have lost nothing, or virtually nothing, although of course they are disappointed in their hopes. In the worst possible situation for the company, where it fares so badly that it eventually goes into liquidation, and the employees lose their jobs, then at least with an option arrangement they do not lose their savings as well. In the less drastic situation, where the share value falls, so that the option holders do not exercise their rights, and thus make no gain or loss, staff discontent is minimised, as compared to the position where employees have invested directly in shares. This is of advantage to the company as well as the employees.

Summary

1.46 In summary, then, from the employee's point of view the option arrangement is almost always to be preferred to a share purchase incentive scheme, although in the final analysis all must depend on the particular terms which are on offer. For the company, a share purchase scheme may have certain advantages, although these are unlikely to be major considerations. As, however, the object of the arrangements on the company's part is to provide an attractive package to the workforce, or to certain elements of it, it is the considerations affecting employees which are likely to be given prominence, and thus the choice is normally made (leaving aside Inland Revenue approved schemes) in favour of an option arrangement. The tax considerations affecting 'unapproved' incentive or option schemes are considered at 1.48 and 1.49 and in Chapters 2 and 3, but, broadly speaking, the choice between the two is neutral from the tax perspective as whatever benefit is gained by the employee, by whichever route, will be taxed as income. If a share option scheme can be brought within the rules for Inland Revenue approval, in particular, it will gain a considerable tax advantage (provided the shares are to be retained—see 1.57), thus adding further weight to the arguments in favour of an option, rather than a share purchase arrangement.

THE TAX TREATMENT OF EMPLOYEE SHARE SCHEMES

General

1.47 Chapters 2 to 6 deal in detail with the tax treatment of 'unapproved' share option and share incentive schemes, and with the various statutory schemes which are subject to particularly favourable tax regimes. The following brief descriptions are intended simply to provide an overview of the various arrangements and their tax effects, to assist the reader in seeing how each particular scheme fits into the overall pattern. In addition, each of Chapters 2 to 6 begins with a resumé of its contents, before going on to discuss the statutory provisions in detail. Action should not be taken on the basis of the following brief outlines alone, which are subject to many qualifications and exceptions.

Share incentives

1.48 Where shares are sold to employees at a discount (or, indeed, transferred free of charge, other than under an Inland Revenue approved 'profit-sharing' scheme) the discount given is taxable as an emolument. In addition, in certain circumstances a charge to income tax will arise on any subsequent growth in value of the shares arising from an alteration in share rights. In the case of shares in a 'dependent subsidiary', the charge is on any growth in value, however arising, and crystallises, broadly, after seven years or on earlier disposal. For shares acquired prior to 26 October 1987, the income tax charge (subject to transitional provisions) is on any growth in value between acquisition and disposal, or, if the shares are still held after seven years, on the increase in value over that period. The charge may also be crystallised by the lifting of certain restrictions on the shares.

Share options

1.49 A charge to tax on the value of an 'unapproved' share option only arises on its grant if it is capable of being exercised more than seven years later. Otherwise, there is no charge until the option is exercised, when the amount taxable is the market value of the shares at that time, less any consideration given for them under the terms of the option, or paid originally for its grant. A 'growth in value' charge as described in 1.48 may also arise in certain circumstances on increases in the value of the shares after the option is exercised.

Share option and incentive schemes under FA 1972

1.50 For shares or options acquired on or after 6 April 1972 and before 27 March 1974, no charge arose as described at 1.48 or 1.49 on share incentive or share option schemes approved by the Inland Revenue as meeting certain conditions, the only liability being the capital gains tax (CGT) charge on ultimate disposal of the shares. Options granted before 27 March 1974 and exercised on or after that date were, however, caught by the withdrawal of the legislation providing for such approved schemes, so that on exercise they became subject to the income tax charge described at 1.49.

Savings-related share option and incentive schemes under FA 1973

1.51 From 1 December 1973 to 26 March 1974, arrangements existed for the approval by the Inland Revenue of option or incentive schemes under which employees or directors could purchase a company's shares out of the proceeds of a contractual savings scheme without any liability to tax other than the normal CGT charge on disposal of the shares. Again, this favourable tax treatment was withdrawn for options obtained, but not exercised, before 27 March 1974.

Inland Revenue approved 'profit sharing' (share appropriation) schemes

1.52 Under a 'profit-sharing' scheme approved by the Inland Revenue in accordance with the provisions originally introduced by FA 1978, a company may provide trustees with funds for the purchase of shares in that company (or another related company) to be held on behalf of employees. The provision of such funds is a tax allowable expense to the employing company. There is no charge to income tax on the acquisition of the shares, nor any 'growth in value' charge as mentioned at 1.48. CGT arises on a sale in the normal way, and in addition there is a tapering income tax charge on a sale within five years of acquisition. Broadly speaking, the scheme must be open to all employees, and the maximum value of shares allocated to any individual in a year cannot exceed £5,000 (or in some cases considerably less).

Inland Revenue approved savings-related share option schemes

1.53 Under an Inland Revenue approved savings-related share option scheme (the legislation for which was introduced by FA 1980), there is no charge on the grant or exercise of the option nor a 'growth in value' charge as described at 1.48 and 1.49. Again, the only tax charge arising is to CGT on the eventual disposal of the shares. To obtain approval the scheme must be linked to a contractual savings ('SAYE') scheme run by the Department for National Savings or a building society, with the shares being acquired out of the proceeds of the SAYE contract on its maturity after five or seven years. All employees, broadly speaking, must be eligible to join, and monthly contributions to the savings scheme may not exceed £100, or be subject to a minimum in excess of £10.

Inland Revenue approved 'selective' share option schemes

1.54 Under an Inland Revenue approved 'selective' share option scheme (the legislation for which was introduced by FA 1984), again, there is no income tax charge on the grant or exercise of the option, nor on subsequent increases in value of the shares acquired, as described at 1.48 and 1.49, so that CGT on the sale of the shares is the only liability which arises. The two main distinguishing features of such schemes are that options may be granted to employees on a selective basis, rather than to the entire workforce; and that the limit on the benefits which may be provided for any one individual is considerably higher than that applying under either the 'profit-sharing' or savings-related schemes. The value (at the time of grant) of the shares over which an employee or director may hold options is the greatest of: £100,000; four times his emoluments for the current year; or four times his emoluments for the previous year.

Approved *v* unapproved schemes

1.55 The tax treatment of share schemes may therefore be summarised as follows: in unapproved arrangements, any benefit accruing is effectively taxed as income. In the three forms of approved scheme currently operating, the income tax charge is removed, leaving only a charge to CGT on the ultimate sale of the shares. The benefits under a 'profit-sharing' or savings-related scheme, however, are strictly limited, and must be provided to all employees, while under a selective scheme the benefits may be considerably greater, and restricted to chosen employees.

1.56 Prior to 6 April 1988 it was virtually axiomatic that an approved selective share option scheme was to be preferred to an unapproved scheme wherever possible, as far as tax considerations were concerned. If an unapproved scheme was chosen, this was because its commercial benefits outweighed its tax disadvantages: a participant would prefer £500,000 less income tax at 60% to £10,000 less capital gains tax at 30%. It was possible for a situation to arise, where options were exercised and the shares sold shortly thereafter, in which an unapproved scheme would give rise to an income tax charge at 27%, while an approved scheme would result in a 30% CGT charge in the same year, so that the unapproved scheme was more advantageous. This advantage disappeared as soon as the taxpayer entered the higher rates of income tax (which was inevitable where there was any significant gain on exercise), and in any case the effective rate of capital gains tax, particularly in the case of basic rate taxpayers who were not wealthy individuals, was often well below 30% if the annual exemption was available, not having been utilised elsewhere.

1.57 The balance of advantage was shifted radically by the provisions of FA 1988 under which capital gains are taxed from 6 April 1988 at either the basic rate of income tax or the single higher rate, as if they formed the top slice of the taxpayer's income. Subject to a number of qualifications arising from the individual's particular circumstances, there is now nothing to choose between an unapproved and an approved scheme if (as is common) the shares are sold immediately after the exercise of the option: one gives an income tax charge and the other a capital gains tax charge, but both at the same rate. Clearly, if the shares are retained the capital gains tax charge is deferred indefinitely, and in such a case the approved scheme offers a major advantage. In the longer term, the gain can be held over under FA 1980, s 79 on a gift of the shares, and will be eliminated if they are still held on death (at the cost of a possible inheritance tax charge).

1.58 Even where the tax charge arises immediately, capital gains tax treatment will be preferable if there are capital losses arising on other assets in the year, or brought forward from previous years, which can be set against the gain, or if the annual exemption is available. The indexation allowance will not be a relevant factor, where the shares are sold immediately after acquisition. Income tax treatment may be more advantageous where there are unutilised reliefs in the year, such as those for interest paid or for investment under the Business Expansion Scheme, but in practice these are unlikely to exceed other income. Neither is it likely that significant trading losses will be sustained by employed individuals in receipt of share options, although income tax relief is also available for a wife's losses (until the introduction of the independent taxation of husband and wife on 6 April 1990).

1.59 The decision as to whether to establish an approved or an unapproved scheme must be made, normally, some years before the options are exercised, and at a time when the individual's tax position for that year will not be known. If an unapproved scheme is established he will be 'locked in' to an income tax treatment. If an approved scheme is established, by contrast, income tax treatment can still be secured by exercising an option within three years after a previous exercise (if necessary, after a minimal previous exercise undertaken solely for this purpose), so that the relevant income tax exemptions cease to be available (see 6.7). This will not prejudice the availability of the exemption on a later exercise. It should not be overlooked, however, that exemption from the 'growth in value' charge under FA 1988, ss 78 and 79 (see 2.53 to 2.121) for the shares acquired is forfeited in these circumstances; nor that, if it had been known that the gain on exercise was in the event to be charged to income tax, the restrictions and limitations imposed by an approved scheme could have been avoided.

2 Unapproved share incentive schemes

THE SCOPE OF UNAPPROVED SHARE OPTION AND INCENTIVE SCHEMES

2.1 As explained in Chapter 1, share option and share incentive schemes which do not have Inland Revenue approval include not only formally constituted schemes in large companies, but also informal and ad hoc arrangements tailored to meet the particular circumstances and needs of individual companies and employees. Prior to 1984, when the legislation dealing with approved 'selective' schemes was introduced, a large number of companies had 'executive share schemes', operating under carefully defined rules, which were intended to provide significant benefits to a fairly wide class of directors and senior managers, rather than to one or two key individuals, and which accepted as inevitable the tax charges described briefly at 1.48 and 1.49, and examined in more detail in this chapter and the following chapter. Since 1984, schemes of this sort have almost invariably been set up in such a way as to come within the rules for Inland Revenue approval, with the considerable advantages which that may entail (see 1.54 and Chapter 6), and many existing formal schemes have been amended to come within those rules, or wound up and replaced by approved schemes.

2.2 Increasingly, therefore, the general rules discussed in this chapter and in Chapter 3 apply to the informal arrangements of the smaller company, or to the arrangements made by the larger company for one particular individual, which cannot be brought within the rules for approval (although it should be noted that the usefulness of approved schemes is by no means restricted to larger concerns). There still exist, in addition, a large number of 'unapproved' schemes which remain so because their members are not prepared to alter their rules; because they have only a short period to run until all options are exercised or expire; or simply because the companies concerned do not realise the benefits which would accrue from bringing the scheme within the rules for approval, or underestimate the latitude and flexibility which would be allowed them under those rules. In addition, as a result of the changes in tax rates made by FA 1988, the balance of advantage has to some extent shifted back towards unapproved schemes (see 1.55 to 1.59).

2.3 The rules discussed in these two chapters apply not only to those arrangements for which Inland Revenue approval is not sought, but also to those schemes whose original approval is withdrawn through their failure to comply with the necessary conditions, and to those cases where individual members act in such a way as to forfeit the relevant exemptions without prejudicing the standing of the scheme as a whole. It is important, therefore, that they be understood even by those who are not contemplating any arrangement other than one with Inland Revenue approval, so that they may appreciate the effect of any departure from the rules of the chosen scheme, whether this takes place as part of a calculated strategy, or by mistake, or is forced on the individual or the company as a result of external pressures.

UNAPPROVED SHARE INCENTIVE SCHEMES: A SUMMARY

The general Schedule E charge

2.4 The decision of the House of Lords in *Weight v Salmon* (1935) 19 TC 174, HL established that where shares in a company were made available to its employees at a price below market value, the 'discount' constituted money's worth taxable under the general rules of Schedule E (now contained in ICTA 1988, s 19).

The 'growth in value' charge: FA 1988, ss 77 to 89

2.5 In addition, specific provisions in FA 1988, ss 77 to 89 impose a Schedule E charge in certain circumstances where an individual has acquired shares in a company 'in pursuance of a right conferred on him or an opportunity offered to him by reason of his office as a director of, or his employment by, that or any other company', and not in pursuance of an offer to the public. This wording covers not only acquisitions under an incentive scheme which enables employees to subscribe for shares on preferential terms, but also acquisitions as a result of the exercise of an option, and in a variety of other situations in which there may be no question of the employees concerned having received any immediate financial benefit.

2.6 Except where the shares are in a 'dependent subsidiary' a liability under these rules arises on any increase in their value brought about by a 'chargeable event'; that is, a variation in the rights or restrictions attaching to the shares, or to other shares in the company, which increases the value of the employee shares (see 2.54 to 2.81). An event is not a 'chargeable event' if it affects all shares of a particular class and:

(a) the majority of the shares of that class are held otherwise than by directors or employees, or associated companies, or directors and employees of associated companies (see 2.73);
(b) the company is employee-controlled by virtue of holdings of shares of that class (see 2.74); or
(c) the company is a subsidiary with shares of only one class (see 2.75).

2.7 Different rules apply where the company is a 'dependent subsidiary' (broadly, a company which does not carry on substantially the whole of its business with persons who are not members of the same group of companies—see 2.85 to 2.106). In such a case there is a charge to tax on the earlier of the disposal of the shares and the expiry of seven years from their acquisition, on the increase in their value since that time. Where the company was not a dependent subsidiary when the shares were acquired, but subsequently became so, the charge arises on the increase in value from that later time until the earliest of the disposal of the shares, the expiry of seven years from the company's becoming a dependent subsidiary, and its ceasing to be so (see 2.107 to 2.121).

2.8 Any amount chargeable to tax under either set of rules is treated as additional expenditure for CGT purposes on any subsequent disposal of the shares.

The 'growth in value' charge: shares acquired before 26 October 1987

2.9 For shares acquired prior to 26 October 1987, different rules apply, on broadly the same pattern as the current rules for dependent subsidiaries, under ICTA 1988, s 138 (formerly FA 1972, s 79). The Schedule E charge is based on the increase in market value of the shares between acquisition and disposal or, if the shares are still held after seven years, the increase over that period. The charge may also be crystallised by the removal of certain restrictions attaching to the shares (see 2.190 and 2.201 to 2.217). The amount brought into charge is treated as additional acquisition expenditure for CGT purposes on any subsequent disposal of the shares.

2.10 Exemptions from the charge are provided in three main circumstances:

(a) where employees receive shares as part of their emoluments to an extent determined, in advance, by reference to profits, and certain other conditions are met (see further at 2.232 to 2.241). In such cases, while the 'growth in value' charge does not apply, a tax liability will arise on receipt of the shares, based on their then market value, under the normal rules of Schedule E;
(b) where the shares concerned are 'normal' shares; ie, in looking at the position immediately after the acquisition in question, the majority of the shares of the relevant class (other than those held by associated companies) was acquired otherwise than under share incentive or share option arrangements, and the shares so acquired are not subject to special restrictions (see further 2.252 to 2.260);
(c) where the incentive or option is provided to an employee or director of an 'employee-controlled company'; ie where, looking at the position immediately after the acquisition concerned, the majority of the shares of the relevant class (other than those held by associated companies) was acquired by present or former employees or directors who, as holders of the shares of that class, could control the company, and, again, the shares acquired under the share incentive or share option scheme are not subject to special restrictions (see further at 2.261 to 272).

2.11 Where a charge arises under these rules after 26 October 1987, other than on shares in a dependent subsidiary, the market value at 26 October 1987 (if lower) is substituted for the disposal value or the value on expiry of seven years from acquisition. Any growth in value after October 1987 is subject to the new rules outlined in 2.6 (ie, a tax liability will only arise if there is a 'chargeable event').

The 'notional loan' charge: ICTA 1988, s 162

2.12 A further charge to tax may arise in respect of share acquisitions by a director or 'higher paid' employee (broadly, an individual earning in excess of £8,500 pa), under ICTA 1988, s 162 (formerly FA 1976, s 67). This section applies, generally speaking, whenever such a director or employee acquires shares in any company in pursuance of a right or opportunity available by reason of his employment and those shares are acquired at an undervalue. An acquisition is at an undervalue for this purpose if either no payment is made for the shares at the time of acquisition or the amount paid *at that time* is less than the then market value of fully paid-up shares of that class. The provisions therefore apply to the issue of 'partly paid' shares, as well as to shares issued at a permanent 'discount'. The amount of the undervalue is treated as though it were an interest-free loan to the employee, and the benefit conferred is therefore charged to income tax under the beneficial loan provisions of ICTA 1988, s 160. No charge arises, however, to the extent that the undervalue is chargeable to tax as an emolument under general Schedule E rules, or on the exercise of an option, under ICTA 1988, s 135, as discussed in Chapter 3, so the major application of the section is to the issue of shares for full value but on deferred payment terms. The application of these 'notional loan' provisions is considered in greater detail at 2.303 to 2.343.

THE GENERAL SCHEDULE E CHARGE

General

2.13 As indicated at 2.4, the general principle that any discount given on the sale of shares to an employee is taxable under Schedule E as 'money's worth' was established by the decision in *Weight v Salmon* (1935) 19 TC 174, HL. In that case, the managing directors of a large publicly quoted company were given the opportunity in each of the seven years for which assessments were under appeal to subscribe for shares at par. This opportunity was offered to them by the remainder of the Board from year to year, rather than being a standing entitlement, and in the relevant minutes of directors' meetings for years before those in question (which were presumably out of time before the Inland Revenue came to make their assessments) was originally expressed as being made available 'having regard to the eminent and special services involving an abnormal amount of work rendered' by them. The documentation was modified before the years in question to omit the reference to services, not because the motive for the benefit provided had changed, but because, to adopt the words of Lord Atkin (at 192) 'no doubt by that time the value of the services was well ingrained in the minds of the directors of the company'.

2.14 The market price of the existing quoted shares of the same class was well above par at the time in each year when the offer of shares was made to the individuals in question, as was also the value of the new shares allotted, although this was marginally below that of the existing shares because: they were not entitled to the dividend paid shortly after their allotment; they were not immediately quoted on The Stock Exchange (for reasons which are not apparent from the stated case); and for 'other reasons'.

2.15 The Special Commissioners found in favour of the taxpayer on the ground that a different body of Special Commissioners had previously so found in another case the facts of which were indistiguishable from those in Mr Salmon's appeal. The report of that earlier case was, presumably, not a matter of public record, although it was obviously available to both parties in the present case. The Special Commissioners conceived it to be their 'duty' to follow this precedent, and did so without any consideration of the merits of the case before them. As Slesser LJ said in the Court of Appeal at 190:

> . . . [the Commissioners] have not favoured us with the materials in that case, nor do we really know anything about it, and therefore Mr Justice Finlay had himself to come to a conclusion as to the nature of this transaction, and so have we, without any assistance to be derived from any finding of the Commissioners.

In view of their decision, the Commissioners did not have occasion to determine the values of the shares allotted, but it appears from the speech of Lord Atkin in the House of Lords that they were worth, in the different years concerned, between £3 and £4 compared to their £1 par value.

2.16 The facts were summarised by Finlay J in the High Court as follows:

> Mr Salmon received a right to apply for shares at par, which were very much more valuable than that, and the effect of what happened was to give him a valuable thing, to give it to him for a payment indeed, but for a payment which was much below its real value.

The judge also identified two questions which arose: whether there was a 'profit' within Schedule E, rule 1 (see now the definition of 'emoluments' in ICTA 1988, s 131(1) as including 'all salaries, fees, wages, perquisites and *profits* whatsoever'); and whether it was paid to Mr Salmon as 'having or exercising an office or employment of profit' (in terms of current legislation, whether it was 'from' any 'office or employment' within ICTA 1988, s 19(1), para 1). As regards the latter he had no doubt; as regards the former, he considered it to be an assessable 'profit' if, to adopt the wording of Lord Halsbury LC in *Tennant v Smith* [1892] AC 150, 3 TC 158, HL (at 164), it constituted 'money or money's worth'.

2.17 For the taxpayer it was argued that the benefit he received was similar to the free occupation of living accommodation granted to the bank manager in *Tennant v Smith*, in that it was a non-transferable privilege; while evidently a thing of value, it was not money, nor could it be turned into money; indeed, the taxpayer had himself to find money from his own resources to take advantage of the offer made to him.

2.18 Finlay J rejected this approach (at 185):

> Here in substance the thing can be turned into money . . . In *Tennant v Smith* the man could not get money . . . there are, so to speak, two stages in the acquisition of the money [ie the taking up of the shares and their subsequent sale], but I cannot think that that makes any difference.

He considered that this principle applied even where, as in the particular circumstances of this case, the director had not in fact sold any of the shares acquired by him. The justification for this approach was that (at 185):

> . . . one must have regard, I think, in a case of this sort to the substance of what is done. Numerous passages might be cited to justify that view;

providing a reminder that the doctrine of 'substance over form' did not begin with *WT Ramsay Ltd v IRC* (see 7.79 to 7.82).

2.19 The House of Lords (where the only judgment was given by Lord Atkin, with whom the other Lords of Appeal concurred), together with Slesser and Romer LJJ in the Court of Appeal, also found for the Crown on the same ground, that the privilege granted to Mr Salmon could be turned to pecuniary account. Slesser LJ, again, referred to the 'substance of the matter' (at 190 and 191), and, answering the point that the recipient could not take advantage of the privilege without making use of additional funds from his own resources said (at 191):

> I cannot conceive that anyone obtaining this privilege to obtain these shares could possibly have the slightest difficulty, however impecunious or embarrassed he was, in finding means to turn such a very valuable asset to pecuniary account.

2.20 Lord Hanworth MR, in the Court of Appeal, while accepting the argument that the benefit given constituted 'money's worth', upheld the decision at first instance on the somewhat wider ground that the opportunity offered to Mr Salmon (at 187):

> . . . [made] him year by year a richer man in the sense that he had got into his hands something which, if so minded, he could have turned into a profit.

He also referred (at 189) to:

> . . . the profit which arose from these constant and successive allotments of shares which enured to his advantage and increased the [i e his] estate at the end of each year.

The difference between this case and *Tennant v Smith*, on this analysis, would presumably be that while the bank manager had an improved standard of living during the year as a result of the accommodation provided without charge, he was not a richer man at the end of the year, as Mr Salmon undoubtedly was. Admittedly, the bank manager would be richer to the extent of any rental costs saved, but it might be argued that such a result was too remote from the benefit provided, and depended on extraneous factors, such as whether the bank manager already owned his own house, which he was obliged to maintain. The benefit of living accommodation would now be taxable under ICTA 1988, s 145. See also 7.104 re CGT.

Example

2.21 A simple example may illustrate the income tax charge arising from the application of the principle of *Weight v Salmon*.

> Eton is given the opportunity to subscribe for 1,000 shares in his employer company, Churchill Ltd, for £2.50 per share, at a time when they are being traded on the open market at £3.25 per share. An income tax charge arises as follows:

Market value of shares:	
1,000 × £3.25	£ 3,250
Actual price paid:	
1,000 × £2.50	(2,500)
Taxable under ICTA 1988, s 19	£ 750

Shares subject to restrictions

2.22 In *Ede v Wilson, Ede v Cornwall* [1945] 1 All ER 367, 26 TC 381, the facts were broadly similar to those in *Weight v Salmon* except that certain restrictions were imposed on resale of the shares by the employees concerned, and in remitting the case to the Commissioners to determine the quantum of the assessment, the High Court instructed them to take account of those restrictions in reaching their valuation.

Example

2.23 The decision in *Ede v Wilson* is illustrated by the following example:

> Perry is given the opportunity to subscribe for 750 shares in his employer company, Bates Ltd, at £5 each, when the shares are changing hands on the open market at £10. The offer is, however, conditional upon an undertaking that Perry will not dispose of the shares, except on death or bankruptcy, for three years, and during that period he will have no right to exercise a vote or receive dividends. Perry's accountants agree with the Shares Valuation Division of the Inland Revenue that the effect of these restrictions is to reduce the market value of the shares to £8, a discount of £2 from the value of the unrestricted shares. The amount chargeable to income tax is calculated as follows:

Market value of shares:	
750 × £10	£ 7,500
Discount for restrictions:	
750 × £2	(1,500)
	6,000
Actual price paid:	
750 × £5	(3,750)
Amount chargeable under ICTA 1988, s 19	£ 2,250

2.24 In valuing the shares subject to the restriction the problem arises that there can *ex hypothesi* be no open market value of an asset which the shareholder is prohibited from selling on the open market. In such a case the value is established on the basis of an hypothetical open market in which the purchaser would obtain the shares subject to the same restrictions on sale as apply to the present holder (*IRC v Crossman* [1936] 1 All ER 762, HL).

Other cases

2.25 Prior to the decision in *Weight v Salmon*, a director had also been found taxable in a more straightforward case where he was remunerated, in part, in the form of commission which was credited to him in the accounts of the company but not immediately drawn as cash. During a period of financial difficulties for the company, he agreed to apply the amount standing to his credit in purchasing new shares in the company, and was held to be liable to income tax on the amount of commission credited to him, even though this had not been received in cash form (*Parker v Chapman* (1927) 13 TC 677, 138 LT 729, CA).

2.26 Following *Weight v Salmon*, *Patrick v Burrows* (1954) 35 TC 138, [1954] TR 73 dealt with the situation where shares were held on trust for transfer to such employees as the directors might select, 'in consideration of past or future services', and such transfers were held to be assessable under Schedule E notwithstanding the interposition of the trust between the company and the employees. By contrast, in *Bridges v Bearsley*; *Bridges v Hewitt* [1957] 2 All ER 281, 37 TC 289, CA, shares transferred to directors were held, in the exceptional circumstances of that case, to be gifts or testimonials, and not assessable remuneration.

2.27 In *Bentley v Evans* (1959) 39 TC 132, [1959] TR 117 an employee took up an offer to purchase shares at a discount, with the price to be paid in instalments, and the appropriate number of shares to be issued as each instalment was paid. The benefit of the discount was held to be assessable when he took up the offer to purchase the shares, and by reference to the market value at that time, rather than in the years in which, or by reference to the value at the time when, the shares were actually issued.

2.28 In *Tyrer v Smart* [1979] 1 All ER 321, [1979] STC 34, HL, a company offered shares to the public, by tender, with a minimum 'striking price' of £1. On the close of the offer, the price was fixed at £1.5s.0d, and dealings on The Stock Exchange commenced a few days later at £1.6s.0d. In conjunction with the public offer, shares were offered to employees at a preferential price of £1, and the taxpayer subscribed for 5,000 shares. The Special Commissioners held that the benefit he obtained (which they valued at 4s 0d per share) was assessable as arising from his employment, while the High Court and Court of Appeal regarded the gain as the result of a commercial investment decision. The House of Lords, however, restored the determination of the Commissioners, as one which could be justified on the evidence, even though a different body of Commissioners might have reached a different decision (see 7.3).

Priority share allocations

2.29 A charge to tax under the general rules of Schedule E also arises, following the decision in *Weight v Salmon*, where an employee or director obtains shares on terms which are preferential, not as to price, but insofar as the individual concerned is given priority in the allocation of shares at a price which applies to all subscribers; for example, under the 'pink form' procedure in a privatisation issue. The value of this opportunity is not always easy to quantify, but is normally the amount of the premium at which the shares are first traded, multiplied by the number of the additional shares allocated to the individual because he was an employee or director. The number of additional shares is itself difficult to quantify if, for example, allocations to the public are by ballot, or by a scaling down which is not directly proportionate to the numbers applied for, and in practice the Inland Revenue has not normally attempted to assess such benefits.

2.30 For offers of shares made on or after 23 September 1987 a statutory exemption applies, so that any benefit derived by a director or employee from his preferential entitlement to shares (whether under general rules or under ICTA 1988, s 162: see 2.303 to 2.339) is not treated as an emolument of his office or employment if (FA 1988, s 68(1) and (2)):

(a) there is an offer to the public of shares in a company, at a fixed price, or by tender;

(b) he is entitled by reason of his office or employment (as to which see 2.41 to 2.48), whether as a director or employee of that company or of any other company or person, to an allocation of the shares, in priority to members of the public, at the fixed price or at the lowest price successfully tendered;
(c) the aggregate number of shares which can be allocated to any person under such priority applications is 10% or less of the shares subject to the offer (including the priority shares);
(d) all the persons entitled to such a priority application are entitled on similar terms; and
(e) the persons so entitled are not restricted wholly or mainly to persons who are directors, or whose remuneration exceeds a particular level.

2.31 For the purposes of para (d) in 2.30 above, the fact that different provision is made for individuals according to the level of their remuneration, the length of their service, or similar factors, is not regarded as meaning that their entitlement is not on similar terms (FA 1988, s 68(3)). For a discussion of the same wording as it occurs in the context of Inland Revenue approved 'profit-sharing' schemes, see 4.97.

2.32 Where the income tax charge is removed under these provisions, the shares are treated for capital gains tax purposes as acquired at the issue price and not at their market value, as would otherwise be the case for assets acquired in recognition of services in an office or employment (FA 1988, s 68(4); CGTA 1979, s 29A(1)(b)).

2.33 A 'director' or 'employee' for the purposes of 2.30 above includes a person who is to be, or has ceased to be, a director or employee respectively (FA 1988, s 68(5)). See also 7.36.

2.34 The major application of the extension in para (b) of 2.30 to employees and directors of other companies is to the case where employees of a number of group companies are entitled to apply for shares in the parent company. The 10% restriction in para (c) ensures that the benefit is merely incidental to a public offer, and that such an offer is not made primarily to pass shares into the hands of employees. Similarly, under paras (d) and (e) the benefit must, broadly, extend to the workforce as a whole, and not simply to favoured individuals. For prospective legislation announced on 11 October 1988, see Appendix 13.

THE 'GROWTH IN VALUE' CHARGE UNDER FA 1988, ss 77 to 89: GENERAL

General

2.35 FA 1988, ss 77 to 89 impose two specific charges to income tax in respect of shares acquired under share incentive schemes, or otherwise by reason of employment: a charge on growth in value of the shares, under s 78 (or s 79 in the case of a dependent subsidiary: see 2.53 to 2.121), and the 'special benefits' charge under s 80, which is discussed further at 2.122 to 2.137. These provisions apply where shares are acquired on or after 26 October 1987 (the date on which the Government's intention to legislate was announced, and a draft of the provisions was issued for consultation). Transitional rules (explained more fully at 2.180 and 2.181) also apply the charge under s 78 on the variation of rights (see 2.53 to 2.83) to shares held at that date, other than shares in a dependent subsidiary. Prior to 26 October 1987 the more onerous rules of ICTA 1988, s 138 (formerly FA 1972, s 79) applied, and these may still give rise to an income tax charge on the disposal of shares which were held at that date, or on the seventh anniversary of their acquisition (or in certain other circumtances—see 2.190), subject to transitional provisions which limit the growth in value charge, other than for shares in a dependent subsidiary, by reference to the market value at the date from which the new legislation took effect (see further at 2.180). The old rules therefore remain relevant, and are discussed in detail in paragraphs 2.183 to 2.189.

Acquisition of shares 'by reason of' an employment or directorship

General

2.36 The growth in value charge applies where, on or after 26 October 1987, a person acquires shares, or an interest in shares, in a company (but not, as for the purposes of ICTA 1988, s 138, in any other form of body corporate—see 2.184), and the acquisition is made in pursuance of a right conferred on him, or an opportunity offered to him, by reason of his office as a director of, or his employment by, the company issuing the shares, or any other company (FA 1988, s 77(1)). No charge arises where the acquisition is made in pursuance of an offer to the public (FA 1988, s 77(3)).

Shares and interests in shares

2.37 The term 'shares', as used in 2.36 above, includes stock, and also securities as defined in 7.97 (FA 1988, s 87(1); ICTA 1988, s 254(1)), and an 'interest in shares' includes an interest in the proceeds of sale of part of the shares; for example, where the shares are held in trust (FA 1988, s 87(1)). See also 7.101.

Directors and employees

2.38 For the purposes of the legislation governing the growth in value charge, the terms 'director' and 'employee' include, respectively, a person who is to be, or who has ceased to be, an employee or director (FA 1988, s 87(1)). Strangely, however, there is no provision that the word 'employment' (which is the term used in s 77(1), rather than 'employee') is to be construed accordingly, so that the scope of the legislation as regards employees is, apparently, not as wide as for directors. The difference would not appear to be intentional; in the case of the legislation under ICTA 1988, s 138 both categories are extended, without distinction, to cover persons who 'are to be' employees or directors, but not those who have ceased to be such (see 2.184). It is considered unlikely, however, that the extended definition of 'employee' could be held to apply also to the definition of 'employment', without specific provision to that effect, as the word 'employee' occurs elsewhere in the legislation (see, for example, 2.77), and the extended definition therefore has a straightforward application without straining its wording to cover s 77(1). For the interpretation of the phrase 'is to be', see 7.36.

2.39 Alternatively, as the extended definition of FA 1988, s 87(1) applies 'except where the context otherwise requires', it might be argued that in a context where it would otherwise introduce a distinction between employees and directors it has no relevance. Other provisions of the Taxes Acts, however, bear more hardly on directors than on employees, so the point cannot be free from doubt.

The company

2.40 As stated at 2.36 the charge extends to cases where the shares acquired (or an interest in which is acquired) are in a different company from that in which the individual concerned holds his directorship or employment. The most common case where this will occur is where a share incentive scheme is operated on a group basis, and the only shares issued under the scheme are those of the parent company. Less commonly, shares of a subsidiary or other associated company might be employed for the same purpose, and the wording of s 77(1) is also apt to cover any arrangement whereby employees might be given the opportunity of acquiring shares in an unrelated company in which their employer, or employing group, had acquired a small stake, either as a portfolio investment, or through a take-over, and of which it subsequently wished to divest itself. Such circumstances would be unusual, however. The legislation also covers the situation where shares of the employer company or any other company are made available, not by the company itself, but by a controlling (or other) shareholder, out of his existing holding.

'By reason of office or employment'

2.41 In order for the growth in value charge to arise, the right to acquire the shares (or interest therein) must be conferred on the director or employee, or the opportunity to do so be offered to him 'by reason of' his office or employment (FA 1988, s 77(1)). It is not sufficient simply that the recipient should *be* an employee or director. By contrast, in the benefits in kind legislation of ICTA 1988, ss 153 to 168 *any* provision made for a director or higher-paid employee by a corporate employer is deemed to be made by reason of the employment, irrespective of the actual motive (ICTA 1988, s 168(3)). No similar rule applies in the case of the growth in value charge, and it is therefore crucial to establish in what capacity an employee obtains the right or opportunity given to him. In practice, though not in law, there tends to be a presumption that it arises to him by reason of his office or employment, so that the onus is on the individual to displace this.

2.42 An opportunity to acquire shares may be given as a result of 'domestic, family, or personal relationships' (to adopt the wording of ICTA 1988, s 168(3), referred to in 2.41), but this may be difficult to establish, particularly as, in the nature of the case, the motives underlying family and personal dealings are rarely as well documented (or, indeed, as well understood by those involved) as those governing relations between employer and employee. The Inland Revenue may therefore be expected to argue that, while an appointment with the company may originally have been procured for an individual by virtue of his family connections, any subsequent benefits flow from the employment itself and not from the initial, or any subsequent, access of family goodwill.

2.43 Shares may also be acquired by an employee in his capacity as an existing shareholder. If the existing shareholding was itself acquired, in whole or in part, otherwise than by reason of office, then it will follow that the same applies to the new shares, or to the appropriate portion thereof. Clearly, the fact that the new shares are acquired by reason of the existing holding, and not by virtue of office, will be easier to establish in the case of a formal bonus or rights issue than when new shares are placed selectively with existing shareholders, some or all of whom are employees, and the exact criteria for the selection may be open to question.

2.44 Where shares are acquired by virtue of an existing holding, the acquisition of which fell within s 77(1) (or which would have fallen within that sub-section had it been operative at that time), special rules apply, broadly, to treat the new shares as themselves having been acquired by reason of office (see 2.146 to 2.154). These apply most obviously to rights or bonus issues, but also to other, perhaps less formal, arrangements where shares are offered to some or all of the existing shareholders, by reason of their status as such. Just as there will be cases where it is unclear whether an original acquisition is 'by reason of' employment, so there will be cases where it is difficult to determine whether a subsequent acquisition is 'by virtue of' the original employee holding or is a completely independent transaction. All will depend on the particular circumstances of the case. While the fact that other shareholders have not been treated in the same way may be an argument for the independence of the transaction, it is still open to the Inland Revenue to look one stage further back and maintain that, while the new acquisition is not 'by virtue of' the original holding, it is (like that first holding) made in pursuance of a right or opportunity which is available by reason of office or employment.

2.45 The most common situation where it may be argued that an employee (or more often a director) has acquired shares otherwise than in that capacity is where he is a founder of the business. A company will normally be acquired, perhaps with a £2 or a £100 issued share capital, and the individual will become a director and shareholder. He will then inject (alone or with others) the share capital required to carry on the trade, and at the time the bulk of his shareholding is thus acquired he will already be a director. Clearly, however, his acquisition is made as founder, entrepreneur, or existing shareholder, rather than as employee or director. The point is much less clear where existing owner/directors are joined by an additional 'entrepreneur' at a later stage. If such a person makes a large investment in shares in order to protect the company from financial collapse, or to enable further expansion, and takes a seat on the Board, even perhaps as an executive director, in order to safeguard his investment, it may well be that the opportunity for him to acquire his shares does not arise 'by reason of' his directorship. If, by contrast, he is appointed primarily in order to strengthen the management team, and because of that appointment he is permitted, or even required, to take up shares in order to tie his fortunes more strongly to those of the company, then clearly he will acquire those shares in the capacity of director rather than investor. Between these two extremes lies a multitude of possible different arrangements, and the effects of each one must be judged in the light of its particular facts.

2.46 The term 'opportunity offered to him [by reason of office]' in FA 1988, s 77(1) was clarified in *Cheatle v IRC* [1982] STC 376, [1982] 1 WLR 834, where the point at issue was the similar wording in the legislation now appearing in ICTA 1988, s 138(1) (see 2.184). In 1971, a group of companies of which the taxpayer's employer was a member introduced a scheme under which interest-bearing loans were made to senior managers to enable them to acquire loan stock in the parent company. In 1974 the stock, which had not appreciated in value, was redeemed, and to compensate participating employees for the lack of success of this scheme, they were given the opportunity to use the proceeds of redemption to acquire ordinary shares in the company, in which case their original loans would cease to bear interest and would not be repayable for seven years. The shares were acquired, through a normal purchase on The Stock Exchange, by a group company which managed the scheme and acted as nominee for the investors concerned. In 1979, the taxpayer sold some of his shares, and was assessed to income tax on the growth in value under what is now ICTA 1988, s 138(1)(a). In appealing against the assessment, it was argued on his behalf that the acquisition of the shares was not:

> . . . in pursuance of . . . [an] opportunity offered to him as . . . employee of that or any other body corporate, and not in pursuance of an offer to the public . . .

within the terms of s 138(1). As far as the opportunity offered to him by the company was concerned, it was claimed that this was an opportunity to borrow money, rather than to buy shares. This argument was rejected by the court: the renewal of the loan was conditional upon its use for the specified purpose of acquiring shares, and even though it was not the company itself which made the shares available, its loan had provided the relevant opportunity.

2.47 It was also claimed for the taxpayer that the acquisition was 'in pursuance of an offer to the public' as the shares were bought under normal Stock Exchange procedures, via a stockbroker, from a jobber who was offering the shares to all comers on the market. It was held, however, that in this context an 'offer to the public' referred only to an invitation to subscribe for shares made by the publication of a prospectus, or through an issuing house, or by similar means.

2.48 It will be seen that the terms of s 77(1) cover not only 'standard' share incentive schemes, such as those involved in *Weight v Salmon* (see 2.13 to 2.21) or *Ede v Wilson* (see 2.22 to 2.24), where shares are offered to employees at a discount to market value, but also cases where shares are acquired under share option schemes (see 1.3 to 1.15 and 1.49) and a charge has already arisen under ICTA 1988, s 135 (see Chapter 3) on the exercise of the option. The subsection also covers many other situations where employees or directors acquire shares on terms which are preferential in a non-financial sense; for example, where shares are made available, at full market value, to employees but not to the public at large, or where, in an issue which is oversubscribed preference is given to applications for allotment from employees (see also 2.29 to 2.34). The legislation may apply in a number of cases where there is, on the issue of the shares, no 'benefit in kind' or 'perk' as those terms are generally understood. For example, the offer of shares at market value only to employees may be intended, not to provide them with privileged access to a stake in the future growth of the company, but to protect the existing shareholders' position by excluding potential investors who are not already known to them and involved with the company; or, indeed, to exclude particular non-employees who are considered undesirable as shareholders for commercial or personal reasons.

Assignment of rights

2.49 If a right to acquire shares or an interest in shares in a company is assigned to an individual, and the right was originally conferred on some other person (whether a company or an individual) by reason of the assignee's office as a director of, or his employment by, that company or any other company, the assignee is treated as acquiring those shares or that interest in shares in pursuance of a right conferred on him by reason of his office or employment (FA 1988, s 87(4)). This prevents a simple avoidance manoeuvre, whereby shares would be issued first to another party (perhaps as a result of reciprocal arrangements) on the understanding that they were subsequently to be transferred to the employee or director himself.

UK residence status

2.50 No growth in value charge can arise in relation to an acquisition by a person who is not chargeable to tax under Case I of Schedule E in respect of the office or employment in question (FA 1988, s 77(2)). As to Schedule E, Case I, see 7.89 to 7.93. The effect of this provision (subject to paragraph 2.51) is that an individual can only be within the scope of the charge if he is UK resident and ordinarily resident at the time he acquires his shares; the fact that he may subsequently become so before the event which would otherwise give rise to a charge does not bring him within the scope of the provisions. See also 7.91.

2.51 The interpretation of s 77(2) given in paragraph 2.50 above takes the words 'an acquisition by a person who is not chargeable to tax under Case I of Schedule E' to mean 'an acquisition by a person who is not *at the time of that acquisition* chargeable to tax . . .'. While this is the most natural reading of the statute in the normal case, it cannot be the correct one where the terms 'director' and possibly 'employee' (see the discussion at 2.38 and 2.39) bear the extended meaning of persons who are to, or have ceased to, occupy such positions, as such individuals are clearly not chargeable to tax in respect of their employment or directorship at the time of the acquisition, under any Case of Schedule E. While it would appear sensible to apply the test immediately before the time at which the appointment was relinquished (for the ex-employee) or immediately after it was taken up (for the prospective employee) there is no particular warrant for this approach in the statute, and a case could, alternatively, be made for the interpretation that the charge applies if the individual is, at the time the charge crystallises (or, indeed, is or has been at any time) taxable under Case I of Schedule E in respect of the office or employment. If such an interpretation is adopted here, however, the effect must be to cast a certain doubt on the more restricted interpretation adopted, for current employees and directors, in 2.50 above.

2.52 Even where the individual concerned is UK resident and ordinarily resident at the time he acquires his shares (or at such other time as is relevant for the purposes of s 77(2)—see 2.51) he will not, under general principles of Schedule E, be liable to tax at the time when a growth in value charge would otherwise crystallise (see 2.53 to 2.81 and 2.107 to 2.121) unless either he remains UK resident and ordinarily resident at that time (and thus taxable under Case I) or, although not UK resident (or, if resident, not ordinarily resident) he performs the duties of his employment in the UK at that time (rendering him liable to tax under Schedule E Case II: see 7.94). A charge could also possibly arise under Case III (see 7.95) on an individual who was UK resident but either not domiciled in the UK or not ordinarily resident, where the right or opportunity to acquire the shares arose in relation to duties performed overseas (but within Case I at the relevant time for the purposes of s 77(2)—see 2.50 and 2.51 and 7.89 to 7.93). This would, however, require the taxable amount to be remitted to the UK, and could therefore have no application in the many cases where the growth in value charge crystallises without a disposal of the shares (see 2.53 to 2.81 and 2.107 to 2.121). It is open to doubt whether the disposal of shares in relation to which a charge had previously arisen, and the remittance of the proceeds to the UK, would be sufficient to bring the individual within the Case III charge. Even where the disposal is itself the occasion of charge (see 2.107 to 2.116), the doubt remains as, while the 'chargeable increase' is measured by reference to the market value of the shares at the time of the disposal, the disposal *proceeds* do not enter into the calculation of the amount chargeable to tax (although they may, in practice, be used as an indicator of market value), and it may be questioned, therefore, whether they can be said to 'contain' the growth in value which must be remitted if a charge is to arise.

THE CHARGE ON VARIATION OF RIGHTS IN EMPLOYEE SHARES: FA 1988, s 78

General

2.53 A person who has acquired shares or an interest in shares by reason of his employment or directorship (as discussed in 2.36 to 2.49 above) is chargeable to income tax under FA 1988, s 78 if a 'chargeable event' (see 2.54 to 2.81) occurs in relation to those shares before he has disposed of them or otherwise ceased to have a beneficial interest in them (FA 1988, s 78(1)(a)). If, however, either at the time he acquired the shares or interest in question, or at the time of the chargeable event, the company which issued the shares was a 'dependent subsidiary' (see 2.85 to 2.106), no charge arises under s 78 (FA 1988, s 78(1)(b)), but the (more far reaching) provisions of FA 1988, s 79 apply to impose an alternative income tax charge (see 2.107 to 2.121).

Chargeable events

General

2.54 Subject to the exceptions set out in 2.72 to 2.81, any of the following events is a 'chargeable event' in relation to shares in a company if it increases, or but for the occurrence of some other event would increase, their value (FA 1988, s 78(2)):

(a) the removal or variation of a restriction to which the shares are subject;
(b) the creation or variation of a right relating to the shares;
(c) the imposition of a restriction on other shares in the company or the variation of a restriction to which such other shares are subject; or

(d) the removal or variation of a right relating to other shares in the company.

2.55 Events within (a) of 2.54 might include the removal of restrictions on the right to receive dividends, to vote on specified subjects (or on any subject), or to transfer the shares. Alternatively the restrictions could be varied by allowing participation in dividends at a different rate from that applying to other classes of shares; by allowing a vote on a wider range of issues than previously; or by permitting the transfer of the shares to specified additional categories of transferee, such as other employees or existing shareholders. Depending on the particular circumstances, the increased income, or the increased marketability of the shares, could be expected to produce a corresponding increase in their value. Changes in voting rights are less likely to do so, unless the 'employee shares' represent a significant proportion of the share capital, and those shareholders' interests are opposed to those of the remaining members of the company; if their interests coincide, there will be little value in a vote which simply adds to the size of an existing majority.

2.56 The creation or augmentation of rights, within (b) of 2.54, may increase the value of the shares in exactly the same way as the removal or alleviation of restrictions, within (a). Both will increase the 'bundle of rights' attaching to the shares; the difference is simply in the base from which they start. Similarly, changes affecting other shares in the company, as at points (c) and (d) of 2.54, may effectively vary the rights attaching to the 'employee shares', relative to other interests in the company, even where those rights, viewed in isolation, have not changed.

2.57 A chargeable event arises not only where the variation of rights or restrictions increases the value of the 'employee shares', but also where it would do so 'but for the occurrence of some other event'. This provision ensures that a charge to tax is not avoided if, for example, all the company's shares fall in value as a result of other extraneous factors, but the shares in question retain their value, or suffer a smaller fall in value, as a result of the chargeable event. Similarly, if action is specifically taken to reduce the value of the shares by an amount corresponding to the increase which would otherwise have occurred, for example by declaring a large dividend, or by granting an option or other right over the shares in question to a third party, this will not avoid the charge. Where the fall in value which would otherwise reduce or eliminate the chargeable increase occurs as a result of general trading conditions for shares in that company or for the stock market as a whole, there is a certain difficulty in attributing it specifically to 'some other event'. Nevertheless, given that all market movements have their origin in some aspect of investor sentiment or behaviour, however lacking in foundation, it is considered that these words would be apt to cover the elimination or reduction of the growth in value by general market movements. The point will not arise frequently, if at all, as the chargeable increase is measured by comparing the value of the shares at two points in time which are separated only by the moment in which the event is effected. If the increase is brought about by a series of events taking place over a period of time then, strictly, it would seem that each must be looked at separately, although unless there are extraneous factors influencing the share price in the meantime the same result will be achieved by considering the series as one transaction. The short time scale involved in the comparison means that general market movements will rarely be relevant; compensating events would normally be artificial arrangements designed to take effect at the same time as the variation of the relevant rights or restrictions (although the wording of the legislation in this way means that such arrangements, because ineffective, are unlikely to be made).

2.58 The 'value' of shares for this purpose is defined as the amount which the person holding them might reasonably expect to obtain from a sale in the open market (FA 1988, s 87(1)). The term 'market value' is defined and discussed at 7.56 to 7.64. Although the legislation referred to there is not imported into the present context (and the relevant term here is 'value' rather than 'market value'), in practice many of the same principles will apply.

Restrictions and rights

2.59 the term 'restrictions' is defined widely for the purposes of the 'old' growth in value charge under ICTA 1988, s 138 (see 2.205 to 2.217), and includes also 'constructive restrictions' by which the shareholder is not prevented from exercising the relevant rights in connection with the shares, but he, or others connected with him, will suffer a disadvantage if he does so. That extended definition does not apply for the present purposes, but the word nevertheless has a wide meaning, as it is provided that references to restrictions to which shares are subject include references to restrictions imposed by any contract or arrangement or in any other way (FA 1988, s 78(7)).

2.60 Many factors, such as an individual's personal circumstances, may restrict 'in any other way' his ability to transfer his shares or otherwise exercise the rights attaching to them, but it is unnecessary to determine whether they constitute 'restrictions' for the present purpose because they do not, in any case, affect the value which he might reasonably expect to realise on a sale in the open market.

2.61 The restrictions contemplated by the legislation are those imposed by the terms of issue of the shares, by the company's Articles of Association, by agreement between the shareholder and the company, or by agreement between an individual and the remaining shareholders, and the abuse which is in view is the manipulation of the rights attaching to a particular employee's shares, or to a class of shares held by employees, in such a way as to transfer value to them in a capital form, chargeable to capital gains tax only if the shares are disposed of at some time in the future. In the absence of the growth in value legislation such a manoeuvre would avoid the income tax charge which would otherwise arise if the desired reward to the employee took the form of straightforward remuneration.

2.62 As discussed at 6.52, where a loan is taken out to finance the exercise of an option, and it is intended subsequently to sell the shares so acquired in order to repay the loan, then (in the absence of the special provisions applying to Inland Revenue approved 'selective' share option schemes) any charge given over the shares as security for the loan will constitute a restriction. This is only one example of the many circumstances where restrictions may arise as a result of arrangements entered into between the shareholder and a third party, most commonly involving the giving of security of loans, where the company and other shareholders are neither party to the arrangement nor necessarily even aware of it. These are clearly not within the mischief at which the legislation is aimed, as explained at 2.61, but it is not immediately apparent why their removal (or, indeed, their imposition on other shares in the company) should not give rise to a growth in value charge. The answer would appear to lie in the determination of the resulting increase in value of the shares. Such restrictions will normally relate to the transfer of the shares, so that they cannot be traded on the open market. 'Value' is defined, however (see 2.58) by reference to a hypothetical sale on the open market. The adoption of the open market hypothesis does not, however, mean that any restriction on transferability can be ignored; the value is the price obtainable in a hypothetical open market on the understanding that the purchaser would be subject to the same restrictions on transferability as the vendor (*CIR v Crossman and others*, [1936] 1 All ER 762, [1937] AC 26, (1926) 52 TCR 415, HL). If the relevant restriction was an agreement that the shares could not be transferred until all indebtedness of the shareholder to a third party was discharged, this would arguably have no relevance to the hypothetical purchaser, who would have no such indebtedness, and the value for the purposes of the legislation would therefore be unaffected by such a restriction.

2.63 Similarly, a restriction on voting or other rights, apart from the right of transfer, which was imposed neither by the company nor by other shareholders (unlikely as it is in practice) would normally be imposed only for the period of some continuing personal benefit to the shareholder, in consideration of which the restriction was accepted, and which would be eliminated by the hypothesis of sale. However, a permanent agreement not to exercise voting rights (for example), and to transfer the shares only subject to such a continuing restriction, binding successors in title, would not be eliminated on a hypothetical sale, and would therefore appear to constitute an effective restriction for the purposes of the legislation. Such an arrangement would be both unlikely in itself, and extremely difficult to enforce, and may not be expected to be seen in practice.

2.64 Where the shares in question were acquired before 26 October 1987 (but a charge arises under the FA 1988 legislation under the transitional provisions dealt with at 2.180 to 2.181), certain restrictions which were not deemed to be so for the purposes of the 'old' growth in value charge under ICTA 1988, s 138 are not treated as being so for the purposes of the FA 1988 legislation (see 2.181).

2.65 While 'rights' relating to shares are defined in very similar terms to restrictions, as 'rights conferred by any contract or arrangement or in any other way' (FA 1988, s 78(7)) the definition in fact gives rise to considerably less difficulty, as no third party (excluding the company and other shareholders) would normally wish to confer any right 'in relation to' the shares. If such an arrangement were made (for example, the receipt of a benefit being dependent on the individual's continued ownership of the shares) then (as discussed in 2.62 above) this would normally have no effect as it would be personal to the shareholder concerned, and would not therefore be reflected in the price obtained in a sale on the open market. In such a case it would also be necessary to consider the application of the charge on special benefits from shares (see 2.122 to 2.137). If a growth in value charge did arise as a result of the conferring of such a right, and also under the special benefits provisions, no credit would be given for either one against the other, nor would either taxable amount be deducted in the computation of the other, despite the fact that the growth in value would merely represent the net present value of the future stream of benefits.

Equity ratchets

2.66 Following the publication of the FA 1988 growth in value and special benefits legislation in draft form for consultation, on 26 October 1987, concern was expressed in representations to the Inland Revenue that the provisions might catch certain performance-related rights or restrictions (sometimes known as 'equity ratchets') which are common in management buy-outs. Under such arrangements the proportion of the company's equity represented by the managers' shares is increased on a predetermined basis by reference to the company's performance; for example, they might subscribe for 'A' shares which carried a right to subscribe for further shares at par in each of the next five years, the number of such further shares being determined by reference to profit, or (less likely) to some other measure of performance such as turnover or the price-earnings ratio of the existing shares. Alternatively the same effect might be achieved by imposing restrictions *ab initio* on rights which were latent in the shares, such restrictions being lifted automatically when prescribed performance criteria were met.

2.67 A press release issued on 14 April 1988, to coincide with the publication of the Finance (No 2) Bill (which became the Finance Act 1988) made it clear that, in the view of the Inland Revenue, a charge will not normally arise under FA 1988, s 78 (subject to the precise facts in each particular case) when a right such as that described in 2.66 is triggered, (ie, in the example given, where the manager becomes entitled to subscribe for the further shares), provided the right attached to the shares from the outset. This accords with the view that the right has not been 'created or varied' within the terms of the legislation, but has merely come to fruition in its existing form; it is not the rights attaching to the shares which have varied but the surrounding circumstances. If, for example, shares give no entitlement to vote until the year 1995, the advent of that year does not alter the rights, but merely crystallises them; they were 'post 1995 voting shares' when they were issued, and they remain so. Latent rights such as this are already reflected in the value of the shares. As their crystallisation comes nearer or grows more likely, with the passing of time or the growth in profits, so that value increases; there is not the sudden shift in value which results from an arbitrary change in rights, at which the growth in value legislation is aimed. Even if, in the Inland Revenue view, the circumstances are not covered by the exclusion set out in the press release, it may still be that the shift in rights brings about no appreciable change in value, because it would have been correctly anticipated in valuing the shares prior to its occurrence. In practice, no doubt, the Inland Revenue would consider the two points together in determining whether to make a charge, but an unfavourable decision would still be subject to negotiation over the 'before' and 'after' share prices and, for the reason given, the resulting increase might not be as large as would at first appear.

2.68 The press release, which is reproduced at Appendix 12, refers to employee shares and to the 'triggering of such a right or restriction'. It is assumed, although the point is not made specifically, that the same principles apply if the event in question is the triggering of a restriction on other shares, increasing the relative value of the employee shares, or if the meeting of the performance criteria, or other event in question, results in the removal of an existing restriction on the employee shares. Indeed, it would only be in the most unusual circumstances that the imposition of a restriction on employee shares themselves could increase their value.

Other special situations

2.69 The danger of imposing temporary restrictions on employee shares should be noted. If, for example, they are issued with a value of £5 per share, and restrictions are subsequently imposed which reduce that value to £3, the removal of those restrictions at a later date, restoring the value to £5, would give rise to a charge on that £2 per share increase, without any credit for the preceding, and corresponding, fall in value, even if the ownership of the shares had not changed over the relevant period. It remains to be seen whether the Inland Revenue will take the point in practice.

2.70 A chargeable event is one which *increases* the value of shares, not one which *alters* them. Not unexpectedly, an alteration in share rights cannot create a tax-allowable loss. Nor, in theory at least, can changes affecting a number of classes of shares be considered on a global basis. Care should therefore be taken to avoid arrangements which bring about a growth in the value of one class of shares held by an individual, at the expense of a diminution in the value of other shares which he holds; the growth will be chargeable, but the loss will not be allowable.

Former employees and directors

2.71 An individual cannot avoid the charge by leaving his employment when the change in rights is in prospect, perhaps to resume it at a later date. Broadly, however, he will not be liable to tax if he left his employment seven years or more previously. This result is achieved by qualifying the definition of a 'chargeable event' so that an event is not a chargeable event in relation to shares in a company unless the person who acquired the shares or interest in shares by reason of his employment or directorship (see 2.36 to 2.49) has, at some time in the seven year period ending with the date on which the event occurs, been a director or employee of (FA 1988, s 78(4)):

(a) the company in which the shares are held; or
(b) (if different) the company as a director or employee of which he acquired the shares or interest; or
(c) an associated company of a company within (a) or (b).

'Associated company' for this purpose is as defined in 7.10 (FA 1988, s 87(1); ICTA 1988, s 416). Clearly, this is a context in which the extended definition of 'employee' or 'director' as including someone who has ceased to hold that position is not relevant (see 2.38 and 2.39).

Exclusions from the charge

General

2.72 An event is not a chargeable event if it consists of one of the following, and any of the three conditions set out in 2.73 to 2.75 is satisfied (FA 1988, s 78(5)):

(a) the removal of a restriction to which all shares of a class are subject, from all those shares;
(b) the variation of a restriction to which all shares of a class are subject, in the case of all those shares;
(c) the creation of a right relating to all shares of a class;
(d) the variation of a right relating to all shares of a class, in the case of all those shares;
(e) the imposition of a restriction on all shares of a class; or
(f) the removal of a right relating to all shares of a class from all those shares.

The three conditions

2.73 The first of the three conditions, one of which must be met if an event within (a) to (f) of 2.72 above is not to be a chargeable event, is that at the time of the event the majority of the company's shares of the relevant class (see 2.76) is held otherwise than by the following categories of person, and otherwise than by another person for the benefit of persons within those categories (for example, through the medium of a trust). The categories are: directors or employees of the company; associated companies of the company (see 7.10: FA 1988, s 87(1)); and directors or employees of any such associated company (FA 1988, s 78(6)(a)). The terms 'director' and 'employee' include, respectively, persons who are to be, or have ceased to be, directors and employees (FA 1988, s 87(1)). For the interpretation of the phrase 'is to be' in the context of rights or opportunities conferred 'by reason of' employment or directorship, see 7.36. In the present context, the most natural reading (as at 7.36) is that it covers only those cases where the subsequent holding of the office or employment is intended at the time of the (potentially) chargeable event, but the point is slightly less certain. There, an adventitious subsequent employment could not be a factor 'by reason of which' a benefit was given. Here the test is, arguably, a more objective one. In practice, it is thought unlikely that the Inland Revenue would take the point, and in any case it could normally only arise for consideration if the employment or directorship was taken up, or had become intended, before the expiry of the time limit for the making of an assessment; that is, six years from the end of the year of assessment in which the chargeable event occurs.

2.74 The second of the three conditions, one of which must be satisfied if an event within 2.72 is not to be a chargeable event, is that at the time of the event the company is employee-controlled (see 2.77) by virtue of holdings of shares of the relevant class—see 2.76 (FA 1988, s 78(6)(b)).

2.75 The third of the alternative conditions is that at the time of the event the company is a subsidiary which is not a dependent subsidiary, and its shares are of a single class. A 'subsidiary' for this purpose is a company more than 50% of the ordinary share capital of which (see 7.72) is owned directly or indirectly by another company (FA 1988, s 87(1); ICTA 1988, s 838(1)(a)). For dependent subsidiaries a separate, more stringent, set of rules applies to calculate the growth in value charge (see 2.107 to 2.121), and the term 'dependent subsidiary' is defined at 2.85 to 2.106 (FA 1988, s 78(6)(c)).

2.76 The relevant class of shares for the purpose of 2.73 and 2.74 is the class of shares to which belong those acquired by the individual whose liability is in question, or to which belong those shares in which he has acquired an interest.

2.77 It should be noted that, for the purpose of 2.74 above, it is not sufficient that the company as a whole should be employee-controlled, or that a majority of the relevant class of shares should be controlled by employees. To meet the condition, the company as a whole must be employee-controlled, by virtue of holdings of shares of that class. This condition is met if (FA 1988, s 87(2)):

(a) the majority of the shares of that class (other than any held by or for the benefit of an associated company—see 7.10; FA 1988, s 87(1)) are held by or for the benefit of employees or directors (see 2.73) of the company or of a company controlled (see 2.78) by the company; and
(b) those directors and employees are together able as holders of the shares (rather than by virtue of any other factor, such as their holdings of other classes of shares) to control the company.

2.78 The term 'control' for the purposes of 2.77 (whether in the context of directors and employees controlling the company, or for the purposes of identifying employees and directors of a company controlled by the company, is defined as in 7.23 (FA 1988, s 87(3); ICTA 1988, s 840).

2.79 In 2.77 the relevant legislation (FA 1988, s 87(2)(a)) refers to 'the majority of the company's shares [being] held by or for the benefit of employees or directors of the company or [of] a company controlled by the company. The word 'of' before 'a company controlled by the company' is not included, and out of its context the most natural reading would be to take the words as referring to shares held by employees etc, or shares held by a company controlled by the company in question. Company law prohibits the holding of shares in a company by its subsidiary, but (quite apart from the fact that prohibiting a situation does not render it impossible) the test of 'control' is wider than that of the ownership of equity capital or the control of the composition of the Board of Directors which establishes a parent-subsidiary relationship for company law purposes (see 4.134), so it remains possible for shares in one company to be held by another which it controls (where control is given by factors other than the ownership of share capital or the composition of the Board). Although this is perhaps the most natural meaning of the words taken in isolation, in the context it seems clear that any ambiguity should be resolved, as it has been in 2.77, by reading the legislation as referring to shares 'held by . . . employees . . . of the company or [of] a [controlled company].

2.80 The effect of including employees and directors of a controlled company within the definition of employee control (if the legislation is so understood) is that a company can carry on its activities through a number of subsidiaries, and still fall within the 'employee-controlled' definition provided it is controlled by employees or directors of the group.

Summary

2.81 The combined effect of the provisions discussed in 2.72 to 2.80 is that no chargeable event arises, notwithstanding a variation in share rights which increases the value of employee shares and all other shares of the same class, if

(a) the majority of the shares of the class in question are held by normal shareholders, so that an artificial advantage cannot be given to employees alone. Associated companies are not 'normal' shareholders for this purpose as the shifting of value between associated companies is often a matter of commercial indifference, or can be compensated for in other ways, so that an advantage accruing to employees and associated companies could in practice amount to a benefit to employees alone. The exclusion from 'normal' shareholder status of employees or directors of an associated company similarly prevents manipulation, most obviously by the transferring of individuals' employment from one company to another;
(b) the company is employee-controlled by virtue of holdings of shares of that class. In such a case it is impossible to distinguish between advantages obtained by shareholders *qua* employee and *qua* shareholder, but action taken by shareholders in altering share rights is clearly taken by them in that capacity, and it is sensible to regard any advantage flowing from that action as accruing to them in the same capacity; or
(c) the company is a (non-dependent) subsidiary and its shares are of a single class. In such a case, there is no potential for the parent company to shift value from shares which it holds to the employee shares, as this would only be possible if those shares had different class rights attaching to them. Value cannot be shifted to the company from elsewhere in the group without a risk of bringing it within the definition of 'dependent subsidiary' (see 2.85 to 2.106).

The charge

2.82 The charge, where a chargeable event does occur, is made under Schedule E, the appropriate case thereof being determined by the residence status of the individual, and the place where the duties of the employment are carried on (see 2.50 to 2.52 and 7.88 to 7.96). It arises in the year of assessment in which the chargeable event occurs, on the amount by which the value of the shares is increased as a result of the chargeable event, or the amount by which it would be increased but for the occurrence of another event (see 2.57). If the interest which the person chargeable has in the shares is less than full beneficial ownership (see 2.37), then the charge is on an appropriate part of that amount (FA 1988, s 78(3)).

2.83 The corresponding provisions under the 'old' growth in value charge of ICTA 1988, s 138 refer not to an 'appropriate part' of the total charge, where an interest in shares is held amounting to less than full beneficial ownership, but to such part of the chargeable amount 'as corresponds to' the interest in question. As suggested in 2.192, the most natural reading of these words is that the chargeable amount is simply calculated arithmetically from the value of the underlying shares; thus, if an individual has a 50% interest in the shares, he will be chargeable on half their growth in value, not on the growth in value of his interest, if different. The use of the term 'appropriate part' in the present legislation, however, suggests that it is the increase in the value of the interest itself which must be considered, although it is the value of the underlying shares rather than of the individual's interest which must be looked at in determining whether or not there is a chargeable event.

THE GROWTH IN VALUE CHARGE FOR DEPENDENT SUBSIDIARIES: FA 1988, s 79

General

2.84 Where the shares acquired by reason of an individual's directorship or employment (see 2.36 to 2.49) are shares in a 'dependent subsidiary', a 'growth in value' charge may arise under the provisions of FA 1988, s 79, rather than the (less far reaching) provisions of FA 1988, s 78.

Definition of dependent subsidiary

General

2.85 A company which is a subsidiary (ie, a 51% subsidiary—see 2.75) is a dependent subsidiary throughout a period of account (of the subsidiary) unless each of the conditions set out in 2.86 to 2.89 is satisfied (FA 1988, s 86(1)).

2.86 The first of the conditions referred to in 2.85 above is that the whole, or substantially the whole, of the company's business during the period of account (taken as a whole) is business carried on with persons who are not members of the same group as the company (FA 1988, s 86(1)(a)).

2.87 The second condition is that during the period of account either there is no increase in the value of the company as a result of intra-group transactions, or any such increase in value does not exceed 5% of the value of the company at the beginning of the period (or a proportionately greater or smaller percentage in the case of a period which is longer or shorter than a year) (FA 1988, s 86(1)(b)).

2.88 The third condition is that the directors of the principal company of the group (see 2.95) give to the Inspector of Taxes, not later than two years after the end of the period of account, a certificate to the effect that in their opinion the conditions in 2.86 and 2.87 are satisfied in relation to that period of account (FA 1988, s 86(1)(c)).

2.89 The final condition is that there should be attached to the directors' certificate mentioned in 2.88 a report addressed to those directors by the auditors of the subsidiary to the effect that (FA 1988, s 86(1)(d)):

(a) they have enquired into the state of affairs of the company with particular reference to the two conditions in 2.86 and 2.87; and
(b) they are not aware (either as a result of those enquiries or for any other reason) of anything to indicate that the opinion expressed by the directors in their certificate is unreasonable in all the circumstances.

Periods of account

2.90 It will be seen from the above that the company's status is determined for the whole of its period of account: it is a dependent subsidiary 'throughout' the period unless the conditions of 2.86 to 2.89 are met (see 2.85), and the 'independent business test' (see 2.86) applies to the period of account taken as a whole. A 'period of account' is the period for which the company makes up its accounts (FA 1988, s 86(3)). This must be distinguished from a corporation tax 'accounting period' which, broadly, begins when the company first comes within the charge to corporation tax, or when the previous period ceases, and ends at the earlier of the expiry of twelve months and the end of the period of account. Normally a company's period of account and its accounting period will be coterminous, but not where accounts are made up for a period longer than twelve months. For all practical purposes the period of account will be the same as an 'accounting reference period' under CA 1985, s 224.

2.91 Various restrictions are imposed by company law on the distributions which may be made by companies, and in certain circumstances interim accounts must be prepared in order to establish whether these restrictions would be contravened in a particular case (CA 1985, s 272). Although these are prepared under statutory provisions, it would not appear that they bring a period of account to an end for the present purpose, given that they are prepared only for use in a particular context, and that the requirement to draw up accounts at the accounting reference date remains. A partial parallel is provided by *Jenkins Productions Ltd v IRC* [1944] 1 All ER 610, 29 TC 142, CA, where six monthly management accounts were held not to have been 'made up' for the purposes of excess profits tax. See also *Revenue Comrs v R Hilliard & Sons Ltd* (1948) 2 ITC 410, SC(I) and *BFP Holdings Ltd v IRC* (1942) 24 TC 483, KB.

2.92 If the conditions of either 2.86 or 2.87 cannot be met for the whole of a period of account, but could be met for a shorter period at the beginning or end of the period, it might in extreme cases be worthwhile to alter the company's accounting reference date (although company law formalities would have to be complied with), and make up accounts for two separate periods. The present legislation would also be a matter to take into account if the accounting reference date were being shifted for other reasons by, for example, six months, and it was necessary to decide whether to make up accounts for a six or an eighteen month period (see CA 1985, s 225(4)).

The non-group business test

2.93 Under the provision set out at 2.86 the company's business must be carried on with persons who are not group members. The term 'business' is wider than 'trade', and would extend, for example, to the activities of an investment company, as regards the identity of the other parties to its share sale and purchase transactions, or the parties from whom it purchased management services. Where a transaction, such as the borrowing of funds to finance the business (and thus the regular payment of interest) is not undertaken in the *course* of the business activities, but as a prerequisite of them, it is arguable that it should not be taken into account for this purpose. Although such an arrangement is a business transaction, as opposed to a personal or other non-commercial matter, it is suggested that the company could not be said to be 'carrying on business' with the lender in that respect. The point is not free from doubt, however.

2.94 Such transactions, and other small trading transactions, or purchases of minor services through a group co-ordinating company, may in any case be covered by the fact that only 'substantially the whole' of the company's business need be carried on with non-members of the group. 'Substantially' is not defined, and the question of whether the test is met can only be answered in all the circumstances of any particular case. Any attempt to apply a set percentage 'de minimis' limit would require the resolution of such matters as whether it applied to turnover or profit; to the number of transactions or to their value; and the relative weights to give to very diverse matters.

2.95 A 'group' for this purpose is a principal company and all its subsidiaries (FA 1988, s 86(3)). 'Subsidiary' is defined at 2.75, and 'principal company' means a company of which another company is a subsidiary and which is not itself a subsidiary of another company (FA 1988, s 86(3)). The condition in 2.86 does not therefore prohibit transactions with companies under the control of the same individuals, with other associated companies, or with individual shareholders.

2.96 Business carried on with a subsidiary of the company in question is treated as carried on with a person who is not a member of the same group unless the whole or substantially the whole (see 2.94) of the business of that, or any other, subsidiary of the company during the company's period of account (taken as a whole) is carried on with members of the group other than the company and its subsidiaries (FA 1988, s 86(2)). The effect is that business with the company's parent company or fellow subsidiaries falls foul of the condition in 2.86, but business with its own subsidiaries is, broadly, permissible, because the sub-group forms a commercial unit, and any shift in value between the companies within it will not affect the value of the sub-holding company. The exception arises where the sub-group has within it any subsidiary which during the sub-holding company's period of account (taken as a whole) carried on the whole (or substantially the whole) of its business with members of the group outside the sub-group. In such a case there is a 'window' to the remainder of the group, enabling value to be passed into (or out of) the sub-group, and thus of the sub-holding company. If this exception applies, the carrying-on of business by the sub-holding company with *any* of its subsidiaries, not only with the 'offending' subsidiary, will fall outside the exclusion for sub-groups, and will therefore be treated as business carried on with a member of the same group.

2.97 The exception detailed in 2.96 above to the exclusion for sub-groups is expressed to apply 'unless the whole or substantially the whole of the business of . . . any . . . subsidiary of the [sub-holding] company during the company's period of account (taken as a whole) is carried on with members of the group other than the company and its subsidiaries' (FA 1988, s 86(2)). The question arises as to which of the terms of the legislation are qualified by the phrase 'during the company's period of account (taken as a whole)'. If it qualifies the words 'unless the whole . . . of the business . . . is carried on with members of the group . . .' it would more naturally be inserted after 'unless'.

Nevertheless, it is thought that it has that meaning, rather than qualifying (somewhat obscurely) the period for which the parent-subsidiary relationship must exist (see 2.102), as the provision does not otherwise give any indication as to the period to be examined in determining whether the 'group business' condition of the exception is met. (The instruction in 2.86 to have regard to the sub-holding company's period of account applies only to the test of its own business, and not to business carried on by its subsidiary with other group members.)

2.98 The effect of the provisions discussed in 2.96 is that the existence of substantial business with other group members by any member of the sub-group does not prevent any business by the company in question (the sub-holding company) with its own subsidiaries being treated as non-group business for the purpose of the first of the four tests of independence, given in 2.86. It is only prevented from being so treated if the *whole* or substantially the whole of the business of any one sub-group company is carried on with other members of the group. Business between the sub-holding company and its subsidiary would, of course, remain group business if it were the status of the latter company, rather than of the sub-holding company, which was under consideration.

The 5% increase in value test

2.99 For the purposes of 2.87 there must not be an increase in the value of the company, as a result of intra-group transactions, of more than 5%. The term 'intra-group transactions' is specifically defined, to mean transactions which are not only between members of the same group, but are also made on terms which are not such as might be expected to be agreed between persons acting at arm's length. Payments for group relief are specifically excluded from the definition, so that they may be made without affecting the company's status (FA 1988, s 86(3)). A payment for group relief is a payment by a company claiming group relief, made to the surrendering company, in pursuance of an agreement between them in respect of an amount surrendered by way of group relief, where the payment does not exceed the amount of the loss passing between them (ICTA 1988, s 402(6)). Strangely, payments for the surrender of advance corporation tax, under ICTA 1988, s 240(8), are not excluded.

2.100 The 'growth in value' legislation defines 'value' not for all purposes, but only in relation to shares or a benefit received (see 2.58 and 2.122). In the present context the point at issue is the extent to which the 'value of the company' is increased as a result of intra-group transactions, but it is considered that the 'value of the company' can only mean 'the value of a 100% holding of shares in the company'. In practice, the value of the company's undertaking, after taking account of any tax charges on its realisation, could only in the most unusual circumstances have a value different from that of the shareholding, and it is difficult to see what definition of value could be employed other than that at 2.58, so the point is of no moment.

2.101 Group relief payments are specifically excluded from the definition of 'intra-group transactions' in 2.99, presumably because however commercial their motivation, they could not be excluded on the general principle of being 'such as might be expected to be agreed between persons acting at arm's length' as it is only the special relationship between the companies which makes them possible. The result of the specific exclusion is, however, that they, do not constitute 'intra-group transactions' for this purpose even where they are clearly 'non-commercial'; ie, when up to £1 is paid for £1 of loss, which can only save the claimant company 35p of tax, or 25p where it is taxable at the small companies rate (or 37.5p where it is taxable at the marginal rate on profits between £100,000 and £500,000 per annum).

Charges in group relationships

2.102 Where group relationships change during the period of account under consideration it will be necessary for the purposes of the conditions in 2.86 and 2.87 to consider transactions with any other company only for that part of the period for which the group relationship existed, as the tests relate to business (2.86) or transactions (2.87 and 2.99) with 'members of the same group' (at, presumably, the time the business or transaction was effected). However, for the purposes of the sub-group exclusion (see 2.96) the wording of the legislation is somewhat obscure (as discussed at 2.97). The exclusion applies 'unless the whole or substantially the whole of the business of that or any other subsidiary of the company during the company's period of account (taken as a whole) is carried on with members of the group other than the company and its subsidiaries'. The placing of the phrase 'during the company's period of account' has already been referred to at 2.97. It is possible to interpret this as indicating that the business to be considered is that of any company which is a subsidiary at any time during the period of account of the company whose status is at issue, whether that business is carried on during the time it is such a subsidiary or during the remainder of the period (at which time it may still be a member of, and carrying on business with, the main group). Such an interpretation, however, rather strains the phrase 'during the company's period of account', which is made to qualify both the time at which the parent-subsidiary relationship must exist, and the business to be considered. If, then, as in 2.97, the phrase is interpreted as qualifying only the latter point (an argument which is strengthened by the addition of the words 'taken as a whole', which are more appropriate to a consideration of the business than of the parent-subsidiary relationship), then the question remains as to how changes in the group structure are to be treated; it would appear that 'business of . . . any . . . subsidiary . . . during the . . . period of account' must mean 'business undertaken by a subsidiary while it was such'.

Interaction of the non-group business and 5% increase in value tests

2.103 Both the conditions in 2.86 and 2.87 must be satisfied if the company in question is not to be a dependent subsidiary. Thus if 'intra-group' (ie, non-arm's length) transactions raise its value by more than 5% in the year it is caught (2.87), but even if it does not fall foul of this test, any significant measure of group trading (even at arm's length) will prevent substantially the whole of its business being with non-members of the group, so it will fall foul of the first test, in 2.86. While the 5% test is aimed at actual manipulation of share values, any company which fell foul of it would almost certainly already be caught by the first test, which is aimed, effectively, at companies where there is the potential for manipulation, whether it actually takes place or not.

Directors' certificate and auditors' report

2.104 The directors' certificate referred to in 2.88 must be given to the Inspector of Taxes by 'the directors'. It is unclear whether this means 'all the directors' (on the basis that 'the directors' must be a wider term than 'some of the directors'), or whether the requirement of the legislation would be met if the certificate were adopted by the directors as a body (ie, by a majority decision of the company's Board). While the latter is perhaps the more likely, the question will rarely arise in practice as any divergence of view is likely to be eliminated in discussion with the auditors, and perhaps with the Inland Revenue in difficult cases. Any certificate which has less than full support from the Board—a matter which would no doubt be drawn to the attention of the Inland Revenue in the auditors' report if in no other way—could be expected to result in careful enquiry by the Inland Revenue, with a view to challenging whether the conditions in 2.86 and 2.87 were in fact fulfilled.

2.105 The question also arises as to whether 'the directors' and 'the auditors' are the persons occupying those positions for the year in question or at the time of the report, if different. The most natural reading of the legislation is that it is the office holders at the time of the report who are responsible (indeed, the practical difficulties were it otherwise could be insuperable). In practice, where a change of auditors has taken place, the giving of a report by the new auditors could involve considerable duplication of work done by their predecessors, and it is thought that a report by the auditors for the period in question would normally be equally acceptable to the Inland Revenue.

2.106 It will be noted that the report required from the auditors is a 'negative confirmation' that enquiries have not proved the directors' certificate to be unreasonable. The responsibility for making the initial decision as to the company's status lies with the directors, although they may well wish to consult with the auditors on any point of difficulty before reaching their opinion.

The 'chargeable increase'

General

2.107 Where an individual has acquired shares or an interest in shares (see 2.37), by reason of his employment or directorship, as explained at 2.36 to 2.49, a charge to income tax arises if there is a 'chargeable increase' in their value and they are shares in a company which was a dependent subsidiary (see 2.85 to 2.106) at the time of the acquisition, or which was not a dependent subsidiary at that time, but becomes so before he ceases to have any beneficial interest in the shares (FA 1988, s 79(1)). If the right to acquire the shares arose (eg, an option was granted) at a time when the company was a dependent subsidiary, but it had ceased to be such by the time the shares were acquired on exercise of the option, then no charge can arise under these provisions (unless it becomes a dependent subsidiary once more, before the individual has disposed of his shares or interest in shares).

2.108 If the company was a dependent subsidiary at the time the shares were acquired, there is a chargeable increase if the value of the shares at the earlier of:

(a) the expiry of seven years from the acquisition; and
(b) the time when the employee or director ceases to have any beneficial interest in the shares

exceeds their value at the time of acquisition (FA 1988, s 79(2)). As to 'value', see 2.58. The condition in (b) covers the disposal of the shares, or of the interest in shares, but not, for example, the conversion of full beneficial ownership of the shares into an indirect interest (for example, through the interposition of a trust). It is not, therefore, possible to crystallise the charge by such a manoeuvre before seven years have elapsed in order to eliminate the liability on future increases in value while effectively retaining the shares.

Company becoming a dependent subsidiary

2.109 Where the company was not a dependent subsidiary at the time the shares were acquired, but becomes so before the employee or director has ceased to have any beneficial interest in the shares, the chargeable increase (if any) is measured by comparing the value of the shares at the time the company becomes a dependent subsidiary with their value at the earliest of (FA 1988, s 79(3)):

(a) the expiry of seven years from that time;
(b) the time when the employee or director ceases to have any beneficial interest in the shares; and
(c) if the company ceases to be a dependent subsidiary, the time when it does so.

It should be noted that such a charge can arise even if the individual concerned has held the shares for twenty or thirty years before the company becomes a dependent subsidiary, provided he has remained an employee or director (see 2.110). The crystallisation of a charge under (c) has no parallel in the charge under s 79(2), see 2.108.

2.110 Where the company was not a dependent subsidiary at the time of the acquisition of the shares, and the chargeable increase would therefore be determined as in 2.109, no such increase arises unless the individual otherwise liable to the charge has, at some time during the seven year period ending when the company became a dependent subsidiary, been a director or employee of (FA 1988, s 79(7)):

(a) that company; or
(b) if different, the company as a director or employee of which he acquired his shares or interest in shares; or
(c) an associated company (see 7.10) of a company within (a) or (b).

Thus, broadly, if an individual's connection with the company, or a related company, as employee or director, has ceased more than seven years before it becomes a dependent subsidiary, he will not be liable to a charge on any growth in value of shares he still holds: at that stage the connection between his employment and any benefit arising from possible manipulation of the company's share price is too remote.

2.111 Until the company becomes a dependent subsidiary the shareholder is potentially liable to a charge under FA 1988, s 78, on the occurrence of a 'chargeable event', and this liability revives if the company ceases to be a dependent subsidiary, whether that is itself an occasion of charge or occurs after a 'seven year' charge under para (a) of 2.109 above. No such liability arises, by contrast, after a company which was a dependent subsidiary at the time of the acquisition ceases to be so. These consequences follow from the provisions of FA 1988, s 78(1) discussed at 2.53.

2.112 If a company is not a dependent subsidiary at the time of the acquisition, but subsequently becomes so, a charge will arise when it ceases to be so, (if it has not already arisen on the expiry of seven years). If it again becomes a dependent subsidiary, the potential liability under FA 1988, s 78 will cease, and any growth in value will again be liable under s 79, on the earliest of the three occasions set out in 2.110.

The mechanics of the charge

2.113 A charge under these provisions is made under Schedule E (see 7.88 to 7.96) for the year of assessment which includes the end of the period for which the chargeable increase is determined under 2.108 or 2.109, and is on an amount equal to the chargeable increase or, if the person chargeable has an interest less than full beneficial ownership, on an appropriate part of that amount (FA 1988, s 79(4)). As to what constitutes an appropriate part of that amount, see 2.83. As with the charge on the growth in value of shares in companies other than dependent subsidiaries (2.53 to 2.83), it is the value of the underlying shares, rather than of the individual's interest in them, which is the relevant factor in determining whether there is a chargeable increase, before any consideration is given to the question of what part of that increase relates to the particular interest of the individual concerned.

Examples

2.114 A number of examples may serve to illustrate the charge:

(a) By reason of his employment, Walpole is given the opportunity to purchase 2,000 shares in his employer company Wilmington Ltd, which is a dependent subsidiary of another company, at their then market value of £2 each. He still holds the shares seven years later, at which time their value has risen to £6. An income tax charge arises in the year of assessment in which that seventh anniversary falls, as follows:

Value on seventh anniversary:	
2,000 × £6	£12,0(
Value on acquisition:	
2,000 × £2	4,0(
Amount chargeable under FA 1988, s 78(2)	£ 8,0(

The example could equally well illustrate the charge under (b) of 2.108 if £6 were taken to be the value on disposal.

(b) Pelham is granted an option in June 1989 to purchase 1,000 shares in his employer company at their then market value of £3. In July 1990 when the shares have a value of £4, he exercises that option, acquiring the shares and becoming liable to an income tax charge under ICTA 1988, s 135 (see chapter

3). In August 2011, when the shares are worth £5, the company becomes a dependent subsidiary, and in September 2012 Pelham sells his shares at their market value of £10 each. An income tax charge arises for 2012/13 as follows:

Value on disposal:	
1,000 × £10	£10,00
Value when company became a dependent subsidiary:	
1,000 × £5	5,00
Charge under FA 1988, s 78(3)	£ 5,00

The example could equally well illustrate the charge under paragraph (a) or (c) of 2.109, if £10 were taken to be the value of the shares on the expiry of seven years from the time when the company became a dependent subsidiary, or their value when it ceased to be a dependent subsidiary.

If Pelham had ceased to be employed by the company at any time before August 2004 (ie, more than seven years before it became a dependent subsidiary) he would be excluded by s 79(7) from the charge under s 79(3) (see 2.110).

Summary

2.115 The effect of s 79, therefore, is to charge to tax any sums directed by an employer toward an employee or director, not in the way of direct remuneration, but by manipulation of the value of shares which he has acquired as a result of his office. The legislation does not differentiate, however, between 'natural' and 'artificial' growth in value: both are charged, because in the circumstances of a dependent subsidiary it is virtually impossible to distinguish between them (by contrast to the position under s 78, where the charge is effectively limited to the artificial increase). Clearly, the time at which the benefit is realised, on a sale of the shares, is an appropriate time at which to charge the growth in value if it is to charged at all, but if the disposal is by way of gift there will in fact be no funds made available to meet the charge, and no opportunity to 'hold over' the liability as may be done with a capital gains tax charge on a gift. A disposal by way of gift is, however, within the control of the shareholder, and need not be undertaken unless he knows that he has funds available from another source to meet the tax liability. The charge after seven years, or (in the case of s 79(3)) when the company ceases to be a dependent subsidiary, simply reflects the intention that the tax liability on the growth in value should not be deferred indefinitely, by retention of the shares. There is no particular reason for the choice of seven years as the appropriate limit, although it may be noted that the same period is used in ICTA 1988, s 135(2) in determining whether a charge to tax arises on the grant (as opposed to the exercise) of a share option (see 3.38), and for the purposes of the 'old' growth in value legislation of ICTA 1988, s 138 (see 2.190 to 2.286). It is, of course, always open to the shareholder to effect a sale of some or all of his shares in order to put himself in funds to pay the tax, and to that extent the charge is not inequitable, although a sale may be forced on him at a time which, judged by normal investment management criteria, is inauspicious. If shares in the company concerned are not actively traded, a sale may not always be easy to effect but, broadly speaking, the more difficult it is to sell the shares, the lower will be their market value and, accordingly, the lower will be the growth in value charge.

2.116 The crystallisation of a charge, under s 79(3), when the company ceases to be a dependent subsidiary, applies only if it was not such a subsidiary when the shares were acquired. Assuming the shares will continue to grow in value, it works to the benefit of the taxpayer, in limiting the amount of the charge, although, on the other hand, it is brought forward from the time when it would otherwise arise, on disposal of the shares, or expiry of seven years from the time when the company became a dependent subsidiary. The rationale would appear to be that the employee who acquires shares in a dependent subsidiary, knowing it to be such, must expect to see all his growth in value, 'natural' and 'artificial', charged to tax. By contrast, the employee with shares in a company which *becomes* a dependent subsidiary, very possibly not of his volition, must suffer the charge only so long as it remains dependent and it is impossible to distinguish 'natural' and 'artificial' growth; once this ceases to be the case, so that all growth is 'natural' (or caught by s 78 if it is the result of a 'chargeable event', see 2.111) his exposure to income tax under s 79 on future growth may be removed.

Increases in consideration for shares

2.117 Where, under the terms on which the shares were, or the interest in shares was, originally acquired, the acquisition consideration is subsequently increased, the 'amount' on which the tax charge arises is reduced by the amount of that increase in consideration (FA 1988, s 79(5)). Such a circumstance would arise where the purchase price included an amount to be ascertained according to a formula set out in the purchase agreement. Most commonly, this would be a 'performance related' element, depending on the profitability of the company or, less frequently, on the movement in the price of the shares on the open market. It could, however, be linked to a factor which had no direct connection with the company or the shares (for example, an indicator such as the retail prices index or a general stock market index), or to the employee's personal circumstances.

2.118 The reduction effectively limits the 'growth in value' charge to the 'growth in wealth' of the employee as a result of his shareholding, taking account of additional amounts he has had to disburse in respect of his shares. To the extent that the subsequent payment was an unexpected cost, it would otherwise go to increase the value of the shares on disposal or expiry of seven years, thus artificially inflating the growth in value charge. To the extent that it was an expected cost, it would have reduced the market value on acquisition, again inflating the charge; hence the need for an adjustment.

Example

Newcastle purchases 100 shares in his employer, Devonshire Ltd, a dependent subsidiary, at £6 each, when their market value is £10. Under the terms of the agreement a further amount may or may not become payable in two years time, dependent upon the amount of the company's profits. In the event, this amount proves to be £2. Six years after his purchase Newcastle sells the shares, at their then market value of £15.

On purchase an immediate Schedule E charge arises on the discount as follows (see 2.13 to 2.24):

Market value of shares on acquisition:		
100 × £10		£1,000
Consideration given:		
100 × £6		600
Chargeable under ICTA 1988, s 19		£ 400

On sale, a growth in value charge arises as follows:

Value on sale:		
100 × £15		£1,500
Value on acquisition:		
100 × £10		(1,000)
		500
Additional consideration (FA 1988, s 79(5))		
100 × £2		(200)
Growth in value chargeable under FA 1988, s 79(3)		£ 300
Total amount liable to tax		£ 700

The total amount chargeable to tax is equal to the economic gain, as follows:

Proceeds		£1,500
Given on acquisition:		
100 × £6	£ 600	
Subsequent additional consideration:		
100 × £2	200	800
		£ 700

2.119 A second example illustrates the position where a fixed amount is payable subsequent to the purchase; ie, where the consideration, although payable in instalments, is not subsequently increased, and it is considered that s 79(5) accordingly has no application.

Example

Bute purchases 5,000 part-paid shares in his employer company, Grenville Ltd, a dependent subsidiary, for £2 each, with a second instalment of £1 being payable in 18 months' time. This represents their market value. Seven years later the market value of the shares is £10, and a growth in value charge arises as follows:

Market value at end of seven years:	
5,000 × £10	£50,000
Market value on acquisition:	
5,000 × £3	15,000
Growth in value chargeable	£35,000

There will also be a 'notional loan' charge under ICTA 1988, s 162 on the amount of £5,000 left outstanding for eighteen months (see 2.303 to 2.343). If, alternatively, this amount were regarded as additional consideration, and the shares valued on acquisition, in the light of this known obligation attaching to them, on a part-paid basis, the net effect would be exactly the same.

Sales at an undervalue

2.120 Where the employee or director ceases to have a beneficial interest in the 'employee shares' by a disposal made for a consideration which is less than the value of the shares or interest disposed of, then if this is done in accordance with the terms of acquisition, the amount chargeable under s 79 is reduced so that it equals the excess of the consideration received over the value of the shares or interest at the time of the acquisition (FA 1988, s 79(6)).

2.121 Such a situation would arise, for example, where it was a condition of a share incentive scheme that, if sold within a specified period, the shares could only pass into the ownership of other existing shareholders, or be repurchased by the company, and the price at which the transfer should take place was predetermined, either in absolute terms, or according to a formula. An example may illustrate the point:

> Rockingham is given 200 shares in his employer Chatham Ltd, a dependent subsidiary, without charge, when their market value is £2.50, under a scheme which provides that on any sale within the next four years the shares must first be offered to other specified shareholders, at the lower of £3 and their then market value. An immediate charge arises on this benefit under ICTA 1988, s 19. Three years later, when the market value is £5, Rockingham sells his shares, as required, at £3. The growth in value charge under s 79 is calculated as follows:

Sale proceeds (as opposed to market value):	
200 × £3	£600
Market value on acquisition:	
200 × £2.50	500
Chargeable increase under FA 1988, s 79(6)	£100

It should be noted that if Rockingham had sold his shares at £3, not because the scheme required him to do so, but because he wished to confer a gratuitous benefit on the purchaser, or simply through ignorance or misunderstanding, the charge would still be based on market value, not sale proceeds, although in the case of unquoted shares a price negotiated at arm's length between independent parties is strong prima facie evidence of market value.

THE 'SPECIAL BENEFITS' CHARGE

General

2.122 An employee or director who acquires shares or an interest in shares by reason of his employment (see 2.36 to 2.49) on or after 26 October 1987 is chargeable to income tax if he receives a 'special benefit' by virtue of his ownership of or interest in the shares (FA 1988, s 80(1)). For the 'special benefits' charge on benefits arising (at whatever time) on shares or interests in shares acquired before that date, see 2.287 to 2.294. The charge is made under Schedule E (see 7.88) for the year of assessment in which the benefit is received, on an amount equal to its value (FA 1988, s 80(4)). 'Value' is defined for this purpose as the amount which the person receiving the benefit might reasonably expect to obtain from a sale on the open market (FA 1988, s 87(1)). In many cases, therefore, depending on the nature of the benefit, this might differ from both the cost to the employer and the amount that the employee would have had to pay if he had provided the benefit for himself. The employer company may have the benefit of bulk discounts, or may itself manufacture goods which are given as benefits, in which case its cost will be lower than 'value'. Alternatively, the goods may be 'personalised' (eg, by engraving with the employee's name) in a way which increases their cost, but which reduces their open market value.

Exceptions from the charge

2.123 A benefit is a 'special benefit' unless it is received in respect of all shares of the same class as those which, or an interest in which, the employee or director has acquired by reason of his office or employment, and one or more of the conditions set out in 2.124 below is satisfied (FA 1988, s 80(2)).

2.124 The conditions referred to in 2.123 are (FA 1988, s 80(3)):

(a) that when the benefit is received the majority of the company's shares of the class concerned are held otherwise than by or for the benefit of: directors or employees of the company; associated companies (see 7.10); or directors or employees of such an associated company. As regards the definition of 'employee' and 'director' see 2.38 (FA 1988, s 87(1));
(b) that when the benefit is received the company is employee-controlled by virtue of holdings of shares of the class concerned; or
(c) that when the benefit is received the company is a subsidiary which is not a dependent subsidiary, and its shares are of a single class.

2.125 The term 'employee-controlled' as used in paragraph (b) of 2.124 above is considered in more detail in 2.77, in connection with the growth in value charge (FA 1988, s 87(2)). As there, it should be noted that it is not sufficient for the company to be employee-controlled, or for the class of shares to be employee-controlled; the company must be employee-controlled by virtue of holdings of shares of that particular class.

2.126 The effect of the provision set out in 2.123 is that a 'special benefit' arises if the benefit is given to certain employee-shareholders who are singled out from other shareholders of the same class. Such benefits might include 'gifts' of the company's products, or any other goods or services which as 'shareholder perks' would not normally be taxable. The intention is to prevent the provision to individuals, as shareholders, of benefits which would be taxable as emoluments if they were received by the individuals concerned as employees. Such benefits would often, in any case, be taxable under the benefit in kind provisions of ICTA 1988, ss 153 to 168, which apply to directors and 'higher-paid employees' (see 7.41 to 7.44; broadly, those earning £8,500 pa or more), and which lay down that any benefit provided to such an individual by a corporate employer is deemed to be paid by reason of the employment (ICTA 1988, s 168(3)), irrespective of the actual motive or the manner in which it is given, and is taxable accordingly. Unlike the 'special benefits' charge, however, the charge under ICTA 1988, ss 153 to 168 does not cover individuals who are to be, or have ceased to be, directors or employees.

2.127 The effect of paragraph (a) in 2.124, in conjunction with 2.123, is, broadly, that no charge arises if the majority of the benefit is received by 'normal' shareholders; employees cannot be singled out for special treatment, by virtue of their holdings of shares of a special 'employee class'. Associated companies are not 'normal' shareholders for this purpose, as the shifting of value between associated companies by means of a shareholder benefit would often be a matter of commercial indifference, or could be compensated for in other ways, so that a benefit given to employees and associated companies could in practice amount to a benefit for employees alone. The exclusion from 'normal' shareholder status of employees or directors of an associated company similarly prevents manipulation, most obviously by transferring individuals' employment from one company to another.

2.128 Similarly, no charge arises on a benefit, provided it goes to all shareholders of the same class, if (paragraph (b) of 2.124) the company is employee-controlled by virtue of holdings of shares of that class. In such a case it is impossible to distinguish between benefits obtained by shareholders *qua* employee and *qua* shareholder, but any decision to confer a benefit on shareholders can only be taken by them in that capacity (as employees have no control over such matters), and it is therefore reasonable to regard any benefit flowing from such a decision as accruing to them in the same capacity.

2.129 Under paragraph (c) of 2.124 no charge arises (provided the benefit is given to all shareholders of the same class) if the company is a (non-dependent) subsidiary and its shares are of a single class. In such a case there is no potential to confer a benefit solely on employee-shareholders as this would be possible only if the employee shares and the shares held by the parent company had different class rights attaching to them. The value of the benefit given to the parent company cannot be shifted back into the subsidiary from the parent company or elsewhere in the group without a risk of bringing it within the definition of 'dependent subsidiary' (see 2.85 to 2.106). While *prima facie* it is a matter of indifference to employee shareholders whether or not the parent company receives the same benefit as they do, such a benefit, if universal, will decrease the value of the shares in respect of which it is paid (and will thus, effectively, cease to be a benefit). A real benefit only arises if its cost is ultimately borne by the parent company.

Special situations

2.130 The restrictions in 2.123 and 2.124 would initially appear to be circumvented if a benefit were made contingent simply on being a shareholder, and were not proportionate to the size of the shareholding; in this case a parent company (in the case of paragraph (c) of 2.124) or a small number of shareholders holding the majority of shares (in the case of paragraph (a)) need only receive the same benefit as each of the employee-shareholders. The benefits which could be given in this way without causing dissatisfaction among employees with larger shareholdings would in practice normally be fairly limited, and in any case it may be questioned whether non-proportionate benefits could be said to be received 'in respect of *all* shares of the same class' as required by FA 1988, s 80(2) (see 2.123).

2.131 The question arises, also, as to whether the requirement of the legislation for the benefit to be given to all shareholders (of the same class) can be circumvented by giving an opportunity to take advantage of a benefit, rather than the benefit itself. That opportunity would be given to all shareholders of the class, including the parent company (in a case within paragraph (c) of

2.124), but that company would not take advantage of the benefit (eg, would not exercise the option, or redeem the voucher, etc). It would appear, however, that the subsequent benefit, although received, immediately, by virtue of the option or voucher, would nevertheless, ultimately, remain receivable by virtue of the ownership of the shares within FA 1988, s 80(1), so that, as not given to all shareholders of the (only) class, it would constitute a special benefit.

2.132 Arrangements which relied on other shareholders not taking up the opportunity would not, of course, be effective for the purposes of paragraph (a) of 2.124, where independent 'normal' shareholders could not be expected to co-operate. The required effect might be achieved by offering (if such a thing could be identified) a benefit which was of no interest other than to employees. This would, however, be subject to attack under the same argument as in 2.131, as well as to the practical problem that 'normal' shareholders might object.

Time of charge

2.133 Both for the purpose of the seven year test in 2.134 and for the purpose of determining the year of assessment in which the charge falls, it is necessary to establish when the benefit is received. The legislation makes no specific provision on this point, but general principles would suggest that a benefit is received when the employee or director becomes beneficially entitled to it. Thus if the shares give, for example, entitlement to two tickets each month to use sports facilities, so long as they are held, the benefit crystallises (it is suggested) when the tickets are received (or when the shareholder would be entitled to sue for them). If, alternatively, an annual membership of a sports club is made available, which would remain in force for the current year even if the shares were disposed of, then the benefit would accrue at the time the membership took effect. Although the advantages of membership would not be enjoyed until later, the rights inherent in it would become the property of the shareholder immediately. All will depend, however, on the particular arrangements in question.

Former employees and directors

2.134 A charge does not arise under the 'special benefit' provisions unless, at some time during the period of seven years ending with the date on which the benefit is received, the person receiving the benefit has been a director or employee of (FA 1988, s 80(5)):

(a) the company in which the relevant shares are, or interest in shares is, held;
(b) if different, the company as a director or employee of which he acquired the shares or interest; or
(c) an associated company (see 7.10) of a company within (a) or (b).

Thus, broadly, if an individual's connection with the company, or with a related company, has ceased more than seven years before he receives the benefit, no charge will arise; at that stage any connection between his employment and benefits arising from his shares is considered too remote.

2.135 'Employee' and 'director' are defined for the purposes of the FA 1988 'growth in value' and 'special benefits' legislation as including individuals who are to be, or have ceased to be, employees or directors (FA 1988, s 87(1), see

2.38). This definition applies, 'except where the context otherwise requires', and 2.134 is clearly one such case. The seven year rule would have no effect if it were necessary for seven years to have passed since the individual in question had been a person who had (at any time previously) ceased to be an employee or director.

2.136 The reference in paragraph (a) of 2.134 to the company in which the shares are held reflects a reference in FA 1988, s 80(5)(a) to 'the company referred to in that subsection' (ie, FA 1988, s 80(1)). That subsection, however, does not refer to a company, but only to 'shares or an interest in shares'. 2.134 therefore reflects an interpretation of s 80(5)(a) as meaning 'the company [the shares of which are] referred to in that subsection'.

Benefits chargeable under other provisions

2.137 A benefit is not chargeable under this legislation if it is chargeable to income tax under other provisions (FA 1988, s 80(6)). This might arise, for example, under the 'higher-paid employment' benefit in kind provisions of ICTA 1988, ss 153 to 168.

'GROWTH IN VALUE' AND 'SPECIAL BENEFITS' CHARGES UNDER FA 1988, ss 77 to 89: SUPPLEMENTARY PROVISIONS

Changes in interest

Part disposals and further acquisitions

2.138 Where a person's interest in shares is increased or reduced, he is treated for the purposes of the 'growth in value' charge and the 'special benefits' charge under FA 1988, ss 77 to 89 as acquiring or disposing of a separate interest proportionate to the increase or reduction (FA 1988, s 81). The most common application of the provision (subject to the reservation in 2.139) is the sale of part of a holding, or the acquisition of additional shares of the same class as the existing holding. So, for example, an employee who acquires 3,000 shares in a dependent subsidiary and subsequently disposes of 1,000 of them will incur a charge on the increase in value, equal to one third of the liability which would have arisen on disposal of the entire holding, assuming, as will be usual, that the quantities of shares are such that the number sold will not affect the value. In the unlikely event that the numbers concerned are such as to affect the value, the growth in value charge will be calculated by reference to the market value of the smaller holding sold and the value of those shares on acquisition (presumably as a proportion, by quantity, of the total value of the acquisition, rather than by reference to the value which the smaller holding would have had if it had been acquired at that time). This method of determining the market value on acquisition would appear to be the correct one, as it pays regard to what was actually acquired (albeit as part of a larger acquisition), rather than to a purely hypothetical purchase. It might be argued, alternatively, that the concept of market value requires regard to be had to a hypothetical purchase in any event (between a willing buyer and a willing seller on the open market) and that it is therefore right to consider a hypothetical purchase of the actual number of shares subsequently disposed of. In practice, the number of occasions where the quantities involved will be sufficient to affect the price is very small (given that the point is relevant only to dependent subsidiaries, where employee holdings must, by definition, be less than 50%, and are likely to be considerably smaller).

2.139 It might be argued, contrary to 2.138, that the reference in FA 1988, s 81 to the situation where an interest in shares is increased or reduced refers, not to part disposals or additions to existing holdings, but only to the transition from full beneficial ownership to a reduced interest (or vice versa), or to a diminution or increase of such an existing interest. This interpretation (excluding part disposals etc) would be justified on the ground that the employee's interest in his remaining shares is undiminished by a part disposal; he still has (unreduced) beneficial ownership of those shares. Similarly, if he acquired additional shares his interest in the original shares would not be increased. On this interpretation a disposal of part of a holding is, in effect, a disposal of a complete holding which is 'carved out' for this purpose from the total number of the employee's shares, and an additional acquisition forms a new distinct holding. Whichever view is strictly correct, however, the net effect (subject to 2.140) is exactly the same.

Variations of indirect interests

2.140 Whether or not it applies to the disposal of part of a holding, or the increase of an existing holding (as discussed in 2.139), the provision of FA 1988, s 81 that 'when a person's interest in shares is increased or reduced he shall be treated . . . as acquiring or disposing of a separate interest proportionate to the increase or reduction' certainly applies where an individual who has, for example, a 50% interest in 6,000 shares through a trust reduces that interest to 33⅓% by consenting to the variation of the trust so as to include an additional beneficiary. In such a case he is treated, in effect, as having sold 1,000 out of 3,000 shares, leaving him with a holding of 2,000. Similarly, a variation of the trust increasing his interest from 33⅓ to 50% would be treated as an acquisition of 1,000 shares. It is not, of course, necessarily the case that a 50% interest in a certain number of shares is worth exactly the same as a full beneficial interest in half the number of shares, but it would appear that this assumption is effectively made in the wording of s 81. Alternatively, the section could be read as indicating that an increase or reduction in an employee's interest should be treated as the acquisition or disposal of a separate interest proportionate to the *value* of the increase or reduction, so that in the case of a reduction from a 70% interest (worth, for example, 65% of the underlying share value) to a 20% interest (worth, for the purposes of illustration, 10% of the total value of the shares) the charge would be based on a notional disposal of a 55% interest in the shares (65% less 10%) rather than 50% (70% less 20%). Presumably, if this interpretation were adopted, the quantification, and thus the valuation, of this notional interest at the time of acquisition (or at the time the company became a dependent subsidiary), as well as at the time of disposal, would be by reference to the proportion of the underlying shares which its value represented at the date of disposal (ie, 55%) rather than at any earlier time, but problems would then arise as to the acquisition value to be attributed to the remaining shares on a subsequent charge (see the example in 2.141 below). Fortunately, in view of the complexity of the calculations which would be necessary, this interpretation of the legislation does not appear to be the more natural reading of the statutory wording. In the case of a part disposal of a full beneficial interest—if, indeed, these provisions apply, see 2.139—it could result in a notional disposal of a different number of shares from that actually disposed of, where the value of shares varied according to the quantity (see example at 2.141). In practice, the point will rarely be of significance, because in the vast majority of cases the individual concerned will hold shares directly, rather than an indirect interest and, even where this is not the case, any differences between the value of such an interest and of a direct holding in an equivalent proportion of the underlying shares are likely to be minimal, particularly in the case of the small holdings which are characteristic of share incentive schemes.

2.141 Because small quantities are usually involved, the value of shareholdings or interests in shares will normally increase directly in proportion to their size. This will not necessarily be so, however, where larger holdings are involved, particularly in the (admittedly exceptional) case where the limit of 25% of total share capital is exceeded (see 1.7). The higher limits of 50% and 75% mentioned at 1.7 will not apply because, as mentioned at 2.138, an employee, by definition, cannot hold more than 50% of the shares in a dependent (51%) subsidiary. Where a holding over 25% has a disproportionately higher value it may be advantageous to make a disposal in stages, as illustrated in the following example:

> If 400 shares in a dependent subsidiary, out of a total share capital of 1,000, have a value of £6 each (total £2,400) and were originally acquired with a value of £2 each (total £800), the charge on their disposal would be based on a growth in value of £1,600 (£2,400 less £800). If, however, a holding below 25% is worth only £5 per share, a disposal in two stages would produce a result as follows (adopting the preferred interpretation of the phrase 'treated . . . as . . . disposing of a separate interest proportionate to the . . . reduction' discussed in 2.140).

Disposal: 151 shares @ £6	£ 906	
Less acquisition value: 151 @ £2	(302)	
		£ 604
Disposal: 249 shares @ £5	1,245	
Less acquisition value: 249 @ £2	(498)	
		747
Amount subject to growth in value charge		£1,351

The alternative interpretation of 'proportionate reduction', as at 2.140, would apparently produce no benefit, as follows:

Disposal 151 shares:		
Value of 400 shares @ £6	£2,400	
Value of 249 shares @ £5	(1,245)	
Value of notional interest disposed of: (current equivalent 231 shares @ £5)		£1,155
Acquisition value of deemed disposal (notional 231 shares @ £2)		(462)
		693
Disposal 249 shares @ £5	£1,245	
Remaining acquisition value (£800–462)	338	
		907
Amount subject to growth in value charge		£1,600

It is by no means clear, however, that it would be correct to attribute the remaining acquisition value of £338 to the disposal of the remaining 249 shares, rather than a value of 249 × £2 (total 498), which would reduce the total amount subject to the growth in value charge to £1,440. Indeed, the whole calculation is fraught with uncertainties.

2.142 A disposal in stages, as in the example in 2.141 would, of course, be commercially disadvantageous, producing proceeds of only £2,151 (ie, £906 plus £1,245) as opposed to £2,400 on a sale of the complete holding. If, however, the disposal was by way of gift it would be beneficial (although it should be noticed, in passing, that the inheritance tax rules for valuing a transfer by reference to the diminution in the donor's estate would prevent any corresponding advantage being obtained for the purposes of that tax).

2.143 An increased shareholding will not always command a higher price per share. It may be that the placing of a substantial holding in the market at one time will reduce the value. If the shares are actually disposed of on the open market, then the (reduced) sale price will constitute the value for the purposes of calculating the growth in value charge. If the charge arises on the expiry of seven years (see 2.108 and 2.109) or when a company which was not a dependent subsidiary at the time of the acquisition (but subsequently became so) ceases to be so (see 2.109), it will be possible to make an allowance for a similar reduction in arriving at the value (although there may be practical problems in determining its amount). This is in contradistinction to the position under the 'old' growth in value charge of ICTA 1988, s 138, where the capital gains tax valuation rules are adopted, preventing a reduction on account of any assumption that the whole of the asset in question is to be put on the market at one time (see 2.197 and 7.56).

Identification of shares or interests disposed of

2.144 Where a holding of employee shares has been acquired in stages, or an individual's total holding consists both of shares acquired by reason of his employment and other 'non-employee' shares, then it will be necessary, on any disposal other than a disposal of the entire holding, to identify the shares disposed of. The legislation provides no rules for this purpose, and the pooling rules which apply for capital gains tax purposes have no application in this context. It is suggested, therefore, that identification should be made using the general legal principles applying to the tracing of cash and other fungible assets; ie, a first-in first-out basis (*Devaynes v Noble, Clayton's Case* 1816 1 Mer 572; *Deeley v Lloyd's Bank Ltd* [1912] AC 756, HL). Where (exceptionally), trading is by reference to numbered shares it is thought that this would overule the general principle; and the same effect, giving flexibility as to which shares were disposed of, might also be achieved by holding parcels of shares through different nominee companies. This would, for example, enable a disposal to be identified with a more recent acquisition which had a higher acquisition value, reducing the immediate charge.

2.145 Where distinct interests representing less than full beneficial ownership are held through a number of trusts, identification of the shares concerned would be by reference to the individual interests concerned, rather than on a global FIFO basis incorporating all shares in which the individual was interested. However, where an interest is increased or reduced as discussed at 2.140 the statutory provisions treat the transaction as the acquisition or disposal of a separate interest, and such notional interests within an actual interest, it is suggested, would be identified on a FIFO basis. Thus if an individual acquired a 25% interest in 1,000 shares in year 1, which was increased to a 50% interest in year 3, and subsequently reduced to 20% in year 6, the notional disposal of a 30% interest (the reduction from 50% to 20%) would be identified as to 25% with the original acquisition in year 1, and as to 5% with part of the 25% acquisition in year 3 (subject to any complexities arising from the points discussed in 2.140 and 2.141.

Bonus and rights issues

Acquisition 'by reason of' office or employment

2.146 The legislation contains detailed rules governing the application of the growth in value charge and the 'special benefits' charge under FA 1988, ss 77 to 89 in cases where the company makes a bonus issue or a rights issue of shares.

2.147 Specifically, these rules apply where an individual has acquired shares or an interest in shares by reason of his office or employment, as discussed at 2.36 to 2.49, and by virtue of his holding of those shares or the interest in them he acquires additional shares or an interest in additional shares (whether or not additional consideration is payable (FA 1988, s 82(1)). Clearly, bonus issues and formal rights issues are caught by this wording, but it will extend also to offers of additional shares (not necessarily of the same class, although see 2.154) which are made to existing shareholders without conferring upon them transferable rights to subscribe for new shares (see 2.33 and 2.44).

2.148 The additional shares (or the interest in them) are (or is) treated as having been acquired by reason of office or employment, in the same way as the original shares or interest, and at the same time as the original acquisition (FA 1988, s 82(2)(a)). Once this statutory hypothesis is established it follows that a subsequent issue of shares in respect of the new combined holding will also be treated as constituting 'employee shares', and their acquisition will be backdated in full to the time of the first acquisition, rather than partly to the time of the second acquisition.

Deemed time of acquisition

2.149 The relevance of the deemed time of acquisition for the purposes of FA 1988, s 78 (the growth in value charge for companies other than dependent subsidiaries) is only to determine whether the shares are within the provisions of that section at all: if they are, it does not affect the quantum, or the application, of the charge. The section applies only where the company concerned is not a dependent subsidiary at the time of the chargeable event, and was not so at the time of the acquisition. Thus, if a company was a dependent subsidiary at the time of the acquisition of the original shares, but ceased to be so before the bonus or rights issue (and before the event which would otherwise be a chargeable event under s 78) both the original and the additional shares are outside the scope of s 78, and within the dependent subsidiaries charge of s 79 (FA 1988, ss 78(1)(b) and 79(1)(a)).

2.150 The deemed time of acquisition is relevant for the dependent subsidiaries growth in value charge of FA 1988, s 79 not only for the purpose of determining whether the shares are, or interest in shares is, within the charge at all (which they will be if the company is a dependent subsidiary at the time of the deemed acquisition, or if it subsequently becomes so before the individual concerned ceases to have any beneficial interest in the shares), but also in determining the time at which the charge crystallises (which in turn affects the amount of the charge). The charge on the additional shares will arise at the same time as that on the original shares; i e, in the absence of a disposal or a change in status of the company, where relevant, seven years from the deemed acquisition (see 2.108) or seven years from the company's becoming a dependent subsidiary, even if that took place before the actual acquisition of the additional shares (see 2.109; FA 1988, s 74(2)(a) & (3)(a)).

2.151 It is not considered, however, that the deemed *acquisition* of the additional shares (which in the case of a rights issue will not necessarily be held proportionately to the original shares) should be seen as giving rise to a deemed *holding* before the time they are actually acquired, which might affect such questions as whether a company was employee-controlled (see 2.74 and 2.124), was associated with another company (see 2.73 and 2.124), or even whether it was a dependent subsidiary. The acquisition, once made, is treated for the future as having been made earlier than it in fact was, but not (it is suggested) so as to affect the position obtaining prior to the actual acquisition.

2.152 For the purposes of identifying shares disposed of, when a holding has been built up in two or more stages as discussed at 2.144, the FIFO principle there suggested would apply to the additional shares on the basis of the deemed acquisition date.

Valuation and additional consideration

2.153 For the purpose of the dependent subsidiaries charge under FA 1988, s 79 the additional shares and the original shares are treated as one holding, and the value of the shares in that holding at any time is determined accordingly (the value of the original shares at the time of acquisition being attributed proportionately to all the shares in the holding); i e, not as the aggregate of the values of two smaller holdings, with perhaps a smaller value (FA 1988, s 82(2)(b)). Any consideration given for the acquisition of additional shares or of the interest in them is treated as an increase in the consideration for the original acquisition, within s 79(5), so that it reduces the amount of any charge under the section, see 2.117 (FA 1988, s 82(2)(c)).

Issues involving shares in a different company

2.154 The wording of FA 1988, s 82(1) (see 2.147) would appear to cover also bonus and rights issues involving the issue of shares in a different company (unless the use of the word 'additional' is taken to mean shares of the same class, as opposed to 'other' shares). The deemed acquisition date under s 82(1)(a) (see 2.148), will apply to determine whether the 'new' company was a dependent subsidiary on acquisition, and to determine when seven years have expired from acquisition (see 2.150). The question whether seven years have expired from the company's becoming a dependent subsidiary, for the purposes of FA 1988, s 79(3)(a) (see 2.109) would presumably be determined by reference to the time it became so, even if this was before the actual (as opposed to the deemed) acquisition of the additional shares. Its ceasing to be so, prior to the actual acquisition, would presumably have no consequence (although it might be argued that it would crystallise a charge under s 79(3)(c): see 2.109), and its ceasing to be so after the actual acquisition would certainly crystallise a charge under that provision, where applicable (ie, where the company was not a dependent subsidiary at the time of the deemed acquisition). It is difficult, however, to see how the two classes of shares could be treated as 'one holding' within FA 1988, s 82(2)(b), except for the purposes of valuation.

Company reorganisations

General

2.155 Detailed provisions apply where, on ceasing to have a beneficial interest in any shares, an individual acquires other shares or an interest in other shares, and the circumstances are such that for the purposes of CGTA 1979, ss 78 to 81, dealing with company reorganisations etc, the shares in which he ceases to have a beneficial interest constitute 'original shares', and the other shares constitute a 'new holding' (FA 1988, s 82(3)). The circumstances in which these capital gains tax provisions apply are set out in 4.42 to 4.45. Rights and bonus issues (see 2.146 to 2.154) are within their scope for capital gains purposes, but are not brought within the employee shares provisions of FA 1988, s 82(3) (having been dealt with in s 82(1) & (2)), as these provisions apply only where, as stated above, the individual concerned ceases to have a beneficial interest in the original shares. They accordingly apply where an individual's holding of shares is replaced by a holding of different shares, or where an interest in shares is replaced by an interest in different shares (eg, where a trust in which he is a beneficiary holds shares in a company which is taken over). They do not extend in any way to the replacement of a direct holding of shares by an interest in shares, or to the substitution of one interest in shares for another interest in the same shares.

2.156 Where these provisions are in point, CGTA 1979, s 78 applies for the purposes of the growth in value charge under FA 1988, ss 78 and 79, and the special benefits charge under s 80 (FA 1988, s 82(3)(a)). Under CGTA 1979, s 78, a reorganisation is not treated as involving any disposal of the original shares or any acquisition of the new holding or any part of it, but the original shares (taken as a single asset) and the new holding (taken as a single asset) are treated as the same asset, acquired as the original shares were acquired. The effect is that the new shares are treated as acquired by reason of employment if the original shares were so treated, and remain within the scope of ss 78 to 80, and that the disposal of the original shares does not crystallise charge under s 79. The acquisition value used in calculating the charge under s 79 is also that of the original shares. It would appear also that the test of employment within the last seven years (see detailed discussion at 2.71, 2.110 and 2.134) is made by reference to the new company rather than the old company, in respect of periods after the reorganisation.

2.157 The charge on the expiry of seven years from acquisition under FA 1988, s 79(2)(a) (see 2.108) will arise seven years from the acquisition of the original shares. As to the charge under s 79(3)(a) & (c), seven years from when the company becomes, or at the time when it ceases to be, a dependent subsidiary (see 2.109), it is suggested that the company whose status must be considered is that company in which the shares were, or are, held at the time in question, so that if the first company becomes a dependent subsidiary on or after the takeover, but the new company is not such a subsidiary, the shares will not come within the s 79 charge. If one company is a dependent subsidiary both before and after the takeover, and the other is not, then it is suggested that for the purposes of the charge under s 79 the (notional) company in which the deemed continuous holding exists has become, or ceased to be, a dependent subsidiary at the time of the takeover, even though neither of the two companies concerned has itself become, or ceased to be, such a subsidiary, but both retain their earlier status. Any alternative interpretation would either mean that a reorganisation could interfere with the whole structure of the charge, preventing the triggering of the relevant events (since, for example, the company in point would no longer be a dependent subsidiary, but would not have 'ceased to be' one), or that regard should be had to changes in the status of companies with which employees had nothing to do at the times in question.

2.158 The first-in first-out identification rules suggested in 2.144 are unaffected by a reorganisation as described in 2.155. Shares in the new holding would simply take the place of the original shares.

2.159 These provisions concerning reorganisations will carry through any number of subsequent reorganisations which meet the necessary conditions.

Additional consideration

2.160 If, on the reorganisation, any consideration is given for the new holding, it is treated as an increase in the consideration for the (deemed continuous) holding of shares, within FA 1988, s 79(5) (see 2.117). Accordingly, it will go to reduce any chargeable amount when a charge on a dependent subsidiary crystallises under s 79 (FA 1988, s 82(3)(b)).

2.161 If, on the reorganisation, any consideration is received for the disposal of the original shares (perhaps in the form of securities other than shares), it is apportioned among the shares in the new holding, and the amount which would otherwise be the value of any of those shares at any subsequent time is taken to be increased by the amount of the consideration apportioned to them, thus increasing any charge under s 79, on dependent subsidiaries, but not under the 'independent company' provisions of s 78, as the amount in question will increase the value both before and after any chargeable event (FA 1988, s 82(3)(c)).

Connected persons

Acquisitions by a connected person

2.162 Where a person (whether an individual or a company) acquires shares or an interest in shares in a company in pursuance of a right conferred on him or an opportunity offered to him 'as' a person connected with a director or employee of that or any other company, the shares are, or interest is, deemed to be acquired by the director or employee (FA 1988, s 83(1)). Where the acquisition is by the director or employee himself, the test is whether the right or opportunity arises to him 'by reason of' his office or employment, rather than 'as' an employee or director, but it is thought that in substance the test for connected persons is the same as the 'by reason of' test discussed more fully at 2.36 to 2.49.

2.163 The effect of the FA 1988, s 83(1) provisions, as set out in 2.162, is that the charge under s 78 or 79 on the growth in value of the shares arises on the director or employee rather than on the connected person, on the happening of a chargeable event (see 2.53), the expiry of seven years (see 2.108 and 2.109) or the company's ceasing to be a dependent subsidiary (see 2.109). Though not stated explicitly, it is assumed that the cessation of any (deemed) beneficial interest by the employee (see 2.108 and 2.109) arises when the connected person ceases to have such an interest. The legislation refers to the cessation of beneficial interest by 'the person making the acquisition'. Although the employee or director is deemed to have made the acquisition, he is not deemed to do so to the exclusion of the person actually making the acquisition, and it therefore appears that a disposal by that person will crystallise a charge. The special benefits charge under FA 1988, s 80 (2.122 to 2.137), similarly, arises on the employee or director in respect of any benefit received by the connected person (FA 1988, s 83(4)). It would appear that the severing of the connection subsequent to the acquisition does not alter this position.

2.164 The term, 'connected person' as it applies for these purposes is defined in 7.22 (FA 1988, s 87(3); ICTA 1988, s 839). The effect of the provisions is to prevent the growth in value charge being circumvented by the issue of shares, for example, to the spouses of employees, or to companies owned by employees, rather than to the employees themselves.

2.165 The anomalies which may arise when one person is taxed on a benefit accruing to another are self-evident but, in practice, if that other person is acting independently of the employee or director, and is retaining the benefit without his consent, there may be a strong argument that the acquisition was not made by reason of the latter's employment. This will not cover all 'hard cases', however, particularly where personal relationships change, for example on marital breakdown. In the case of divorce, an ex-spouse will no longer be a 'connected person'. The legislation, however, only addresses itself to the question of whether the right or opportunity is offered to the recipient 'as a connected person' (i e, to whether the connection exists at the time the offer is made), so that any growth in value arising on shares owned by the spouse, after the date of divorce and up to the time when the charge crystallises, or special benefits arising up to seven years after the cessation of employment, will still be taxable on the employee. Problems will seldom arise in practice, however, as because of the existence of s 83(1) it is only rarely that shares provided by virtue of an employment will be made available to a connected person rather than to the employee himself.

2.166 Arguably, the words 'as a person connected with a director or employee' in FA 1988, s 83(1) extend also to cases where a connection, though not existing at the time the right or opportunity is granted, is the motive for its being made available. This might arise where the connection is in prospect (as on marriage), or where it has been broken; for example, by the amicable dissolution of a business partnership.

2.167 'Connection' does not pass through a chain. So, for example, it would appear that an individual is not necessarily connected with a company controlled by his wife (see 7.22). The definition of control (see 7.25) is such, however, that he may very well be held indirectly to control such a company himself, with the result that it becomes 'connected' with him for that reason.

Disposals to a connected person

2.168 Where a person who has acquired shares or an interest in shares disposes of the shares or interest otherwise than by a bargain at arm's length with a person who is not connected with him, he is deemed to continue to have a beneficial interest in the shares until there is a disposal of the shares or interest by 'such a bargain' (FA 1988, s 83(2)). The original acquiror therefore remains the person liable to the charges under ss 78 and 79, until there is a disposal by the connected person. His deemed beneficial ownership will then cease, crystallising a charge, where appropriate, under s 79(2)(b) or (3)(b) (see 2.108 and 2.109). It will be seen that to avoid this provision the disposal must be both at arm's length *and* to a non-connected party. Thus a disposal within the family, at arm's length, will not take the employee or director out of the charge, nor a disposal to a friend who is not a connected person, if it is made otherwise than at arm's length.

2.169 The employee's beneficial ownership of the shares (or interest) is deemed to continue, as stated in 2.168 above, until there is a disposal 'by such a bargain'; ie, a disposal to an unconnected party at arm's length. It is not absolutely clear from the wording of s 83(2) whether this must be to a person unconnected with the employee, or unconnected with the vendor (the connected person to whom the original disposal was made), though it is thought that the former is the more natural reading. In practice, many individuals who are connected with the employee are likely also to be connected with the vendor, but a 'connection' does not pass through a chain (see 7.22), so this is not necessarily so.

2.170 When the shares are acquired in the first place by a connected person (see 2.162 to 2.167) any non-arm's length transfer back to the employee will have the effect that they are treated as having been in his ownership throughout.

2.171 Where shares in a company are, or an interest in such shares is, disposed of to the company in accordance with the terms on which the acquisition was made (for example, where under the terms of an employee share scheme the shares must be sold back to the company on leaving its employment), then FA 1988, s 83(2) (2.168 and 2.169) does not apply to treat the employee's beneficial interest as continuing, even if the company is a person connected with him (FA 1988, s 83(3)).

2.172 Where a person's beneficial interest is deemed to continue under 2.168, then the legislation provides that 'where . . . another person receives a benefit in such circumstances, the benefit shall be treated for those purposes as received by *him*' (FA 1988, s 83(4)). It is not clear grammatically whether 'him' refers to the deemed or the actual owner, although it is clearly consistent with the scheme of the legislation that the charge under FA 1988, s 80 on the special benefit should arise on the employee. If the alternative, less likely, interpretation were adopted, this would remove the charge from the employee, but could not impose it on the connected person, who had not acquired the shares or interest by reason of employment.

Capital gains tax considerations

2.173 Where a 'growth in value' or 'special benefits' charge arises on an individual under the provisions discussed in 2.53 to 2.137, then on the first disposal of the shares (whether by him or another person) after his acquisition, the amount chargeable is treated for capital gains tax purposes as if it had formed part of the consideration given by the person making the disposal for his acquisition of the shares (FA 1988, s 84; CGTA 1979, s 32(1)(a)). The amount chargeable to income tax therefore reduces the capital gain, or increases the allowable loss. As it is deemed to have been given for the acquisition of the shares, rather than to enhance their value, indexation allowance is presumably available from the time of acquisition rather than from the time of the Schedule E charge. It should be noted that this allowance is not available on the disposal of an interest in shares, but only on the disposal of the shares themselves. It applies, however, whether the disposal is by the Schedule E taxpayer or another person; eg, by the trustees of a settlement through which he has an interest in the shares. The effect of the section is that the same growth in value of the shares does not become liable to both a Schedule E and a capital gains tax charge.

2.174 FA 1988, s 84 (2.173 above) applies 'with the appropriate modifications' in a case to which s 83 (connected persons, etc) applies. Thus if a connected person who has acquired shares by reason of the employee's or director's office disposes of the shares, any Schedule E charge arising on the employee or director as a result of that disposal, or earlier, is an allowable deduction for capital gains tax purposes. The section is less likely to apply on a disposal by the employee to a connected person, within s 83(2) (see 2.168), because at that stage no Schedule E charge under s 79 will arise, as there is treated as having been no disposal. There may, however, have been a special benefits charge, or a chargeable event under s 78. It will often be the case that no immediate capital gains tax charge arises on such a disposal as 'hold-over' relief is available under FA 1980, s 79. It is possible that a Schedule E charge could be carried back to offset against a previous capital gains tax disposal, if the assessment had not been finalised, as the legislation does not stipulate that it must arise before the capital gains disposal. The point is by no means free from doubt, however.

2.175 It should be borne in mind that the identification of the shares disposed of for capital gains tax purposes and for the purposes of the employee shares legislation will not necessarily be the same (see 2.144).

Information

Acquisitions of shares

2.176 Where in any year of assessment a person acquires shares, or an interest in shares, in a company in the circumstances described in FA 1988, s 77(1) (ie, by reason of employment, as discussed at 2.36 to 2.49), that company and (if different) the company as a director or employee of which he acquires the shares or interest must give written particulars of the acquisition to the Inspector of Taxes within thirty days of the end of the year (FA 1988, s 85(1). See also 2.162.). It should be noted that the exclusions from the charge under s 77(2) & (3) where the employee is not taxable under Case I of Schedule E, and where the acquisition is made in pursuance of an offer to the public (see 2.50 and 2.36) do not apply to this requirement to give information. Neither is there any restriction to information which the company has or can reasonably obtain. The shareholders' register will not necessarily provide all relevant information to the company whose shares are involved, as it will not disclose indirect or nominee holdings, and the employing company (if different) will not necessarily be aware of any opportunity offered to its employees by a third party. In practice, however, such difficulties will seldom arise.

Chargeable events and special benefits

2.177 Where there occurs in relation to shares in a company a 'chargeable event' for the purposes of FA 1988, s 78 (see 2.54 to 2.81) or a person receives a 'special benefit' within the meaning of FA 1988, s 80(1) (see 2.122 to 2.137) in respect of shares, or an interest in shares, in a company, then the company and (if different) the company as a director or employee of which the person who acquired the shares or interest made the acquisition, must give the Inspector of Taxes written particulars of the event or benefit, and of the shares concerned, within sixty days of that occurrence (FA 1988, s 85(2)). While in theory the employing company may not know of a chargeable event affecting the shares in another company and, indeed, either company may be unaware of changes in agreements between shareholders and third parties (such as other shareholders) which impose restrictions on shares, in practice, again, difficulties in complying with this requirement will arise only rarely.

Penalties

2.178 Where a company fails to furnish any information required under FA 1988, s 85(1) and (2) (2.176 and 2.177), it becomes liable to a penalty of up to £50 and, if the failure continues after it has been declared by the court or Commissioners before whom proceedings for the penalty have been commenced, to a further penalty of up to £10 for each day on which the failure continues (TMA 1970, s 98(1), as amended by FA 1988, s 85(3)).

2.179 Where the company fraudulently or negligently furnishes, gives, produces, or makes any incorrect information, certificate, document, record or declaration as regards the information required to be supplied as discussed in 2.176 and 2.177, it is liable to a penalty of up to £250 and, in the case of fraud, £500 (TMA 1970, s 98(2), as amended by FA 1988, s 85(3)).

Transitional provisions

General

2.180 The 'old' growth in value and special benefits charges discussed in 2.183 to 2.302 do not apply to an acquisition of shares, or of an interest in shares, made on or after 26 October 1987 (FA 1988, s 88(1)). The new rules of FA

1988 apply to such acquisitions, as discussed at 2.35. The old rules continue, however, to apply after that date to shares or interests acquired beforehand. Where tax is charged under ICTA 1988, s 138(1)(a) (see 2.190), ie, on disposal, expiry of seven years from acquisition or lifting of restrictions, by reference to the market value, after 26 October 1987, of shares in a company which is not a dependent subsidiary on that date, and that market value is greater than the market value on 26 October 1987, the amount chargeable (and the question whether any amount is chargeable) are determined by reference to the market value (as defined in 7.56) on 26 October 1987 (FA 1988, s 88(2)). The result is that the growth in value which is charged is limited to that arising prior to the introduction of the new legislation, but allowance is made for any diminution in value after that date. The old charge is 'arrested', because a chargeable event on or after that date applies to impose a charge under FA 1988, s 78 on an 'old' (pre-October 1987) holding or interest in the same way as on a new holding (FA 1988, s 88(3)). As far as pre-October 1987 shares or interests in a dependent subsidiary are concerned, the old charge is not arrested, and no charge arises under the new provisions.

Restrictions

2.181 In relation to shares or interests acquired before 26 October 1987, the removal or variation of a restriction is not a chargeable event for the purposes of FA 1988, s 78 if it would not have been regarded as a restriction for the purposes of FA 1972, s 79(2)(c) (now ICTA 1988, s 138(3)(a)) by virtue of FA 1973, Sch 8, para 7 (now ICTA 1988, s 139(9)) (an arrangement providing for the disposal of the shares, when the shareholder ceases to hold the office or employment by virtue of which he obtained the right or was given the opportunity to acquire the shares): see 2.253 (FA 1988, s 88(4)).

Approved share schemes

2.182 No growth in value charge arises under FA 1988, s 78 or 79 in respect of shares the beneficial interest in which is acquired under an Inland Revenue approved 'profit-sharing' scheme (ICTA 1988, s 186(2)(b); FA 1988, s 89(a): see 4.7); or when the shares are acquired under an approved 'selective' or savings-related share option scheme, provided certain additional conditions are satisfied beyond the mere approval of the scheme (ICTA 1988, s 185(3)(a); FA 1988, s 89: see 5.9 and 6.11). A special benefits charge may still arise, however.

THE 'OLD' GROWTH IN VALUE AND SPECIAL BENEFITS CHARGES: ICTA 1988, s 138 (formerly FA 1972, s 79)

General

2.183 ICTA 1988, s 138 (formerly FA 1972, s 79) imposes two distinct charges to income tax on 'employee shares' acquired before 26 October 1987, subject to transitional provisions where the charge arises after that date (see 2.180 and 2.181).

Acquisition of shares 'as' an employee or director

2.184 The charges under ICTA 1988, s 138 apply where, on or after 6 April 1972 and before 26 October 1987, a person acquires shares (including stock, and securities as defined in 7.97: ICTA 1988, ss 139(11), 140(3) and 254(1)), or an interest in shares (including an interest in the proceeds of sale of part of the shares held, for example, through a trust: ICTA 1988, s 139(11) and see 7.101), in a company or other body corporate, and the acquisition is made in pursuance of a right conferred on him, or opportunity offered to him, as a director or employee of the body issuing the shares, or of any other body corporate, and not in pursuance of an offer to the public (ICTA 1988, s 138(1) & (12)). The terms 'director' and 'employee' include a person who 'is to be' a director or employee (ICTA 1988, s 139(11)). For the interpretation of the phrase 'is to be', see 7.36. The most common case where an employee or director is given the opportunity to acquire shares in a company other than that for which he works is where a share incentive scheme is operated on a group basis, and the only shares issued under the scheme are those of the parent company. Less commonly, shares of a subsidiary or other associated company might be employed for the same purpose, and the wording of the section is also apt to cover any arrangement where employees might be given the opportunity of acquiring shares in an unrelated company in which their employer, or employing group, had acquired a small stake, either as a portfolio investment, or through a take-over, and of which it subsequently wished to divest itself. Such circumstances would be rare, however. The section also covers the situation where shares of the employer company or any other company are made available, not by the company itself, but by a controlling shareholder, out of his existing holding.

2.185 In order for s 138 to apply, the right or opportunity to acquire the shares must be conferred on, or offered to, the recipient 'as' an employee (or director). It is not sufficient simply that the recipient *is* an employee. By contrast, in the benefits in kind legislation of ICTA 1988, ss 153 to 168 *any* provision made for an employee by a corporate employer is deemed to be made by reason of the employment, irrespective of the actual motive (ICTA 1988, s 168(3)). No similar rule applies in the case of s 138, and it is therefore of crucial importance to establish in what capacity an employee obtains the right or opportunity given to him. In practice, though not in law, there is a presumption that it arises to him 'as employee', and the onus is on the individual to displace this.

2.186 Specifically, the legislation provides that a right to acquire shares is obtained by an individual 'as' director or employee of a company (ICTA 1988, s 140(1)):

(a) if it is granted to him by reason of his office or employment as a director or employee of that company who is chargeable to tax in respect of that office or employment under Schedule E, Case I (see 7.89), even if he has by then ceased to hold the appointment (provided that he was taxable under Schedule E Case I in the last period in which he did hold it); or
(b) if the right is assigned to him, and was granted by reason of any such office or employment of his to some other person.

Prior to their consolidation into ICTA 1988, s 140(1) the relevant provisions applied these criteria not only to the *grant* of a right, but to its being obtained in whatever way, and also to the acquisition of shares or an interest in shares. This adaptation of the share option provisions of ICTA 1970, s 186(9) by FA 1972, s 79(12) and Sch 12 Pt VII, para 7 was excluded on consolidation, presumably unintentionally, and may be expected to be reinstated in due course if the effect of the legislation is perceived as having been altered. Strangely, even prior to consolidation these provisions laid down when a right was conferred on an individual, or shares (or an interest in shares) were acquired by an individual 'as' an employee, but did not make any reference to an 'opportunity offered to him' as an employee within the terms of s 79(1) (now ICTA 1988, s 138(1)) (see 2.184). Nevertheless, in practice, the point raised no difficulty: if shares were acquired by an individual 'as' an employee, then the opportunity so to do must have been offered to him in the same capacity.

2.187 Paragraph (b) in 2.186 prevents a simple avoidance manoeuvre, whereby shares would be issued to another party on the understanding that they were to be transferred to the employee himself. The effect of para (a) is that an individual can only be within the scope of the 'growth in value' charge under s 138(1)(a), (or the 'special benefits' charge under s 138(1)(b)), if he is UK-resident and ordinarily resident at the time he acquired his shares (or was so during the last year for which he held the appointment in question). Even then, when the charge crystallises (or would otherwise crystallise), as explained at 2.190–2.204, he will not be liable unless he remains resident and ordinarily resident (and thus taxable under Case I), or, although he is not UK-resident (or, if resident is not ordinarily resident) the duties of the employment are performed in the UK at that time (rendering him liable under Case II: see 7.94), or he is UK-resident, and the relevant emoluments arise from overseas duties and are remitted here, giving rise to a liability under Case III (see 7.95). Such a remittance cannot be made when the 'growth in value' charge crystallises without a disposal of the shares (see paras (a) and (c) of 2.190) as there are then no proceeds to deal with. See also the discussion of this point at 2.52 in connection with the 'new' growth in value and special benefits charges under FA 1988, ss 77 to 89.

2.188 Shares may be acquired by an employee in his capacity as an existing shareholder rather than as an employee. While this argument may be put forward in a variety of circumstances, depending on the particular facts of the case, it is obviously at its most persuasive when the shares are allocated by means of a bonus or rights issue, and the entitlement clearly flows from the shares already held. For rights and bonus issues made on or after 19 March 1986, however, detailed rules apply as set out at 2.222. Even prior to that date a rights issue resulting in increased holdings by all shareholders would normally be inappropriate where the object was to provide a benefit only to employees, and the problem could not be overcome simply by having a separate class of shares for employee holdings, with rights being granted only to shareholders of that class, because, while the opportunity of acquiring shares would follow immediately from the recipient's status as a shareholder, that status would in turn follow directly from his standing as an employee, with the net effect that he acquired shares in the latter capacity. Where a given class of shareholder included employees and others, the question was one of motive and of degree: whether the acquisition by employees was incidental to that by other shareholders, or contrariwise. Again, if the vast majority of the shares in a company were owned by two or three major shareholders, with perhaps 5% in the hands of employees, and a rights issue were offered, on the understanding that the major shareholders would decline to take up their rights, leaving all the new shares in the hands of employees, it would have been difficult to argue that they were acquired by the individuals otherwise than 'as employees'.

2.189 For further discussion of the criteria involved in determining whether shares are acquired by reason of employment or office, and examination of the circumstances which are within the terms of the legislation, see 2.36 to 2.49, in the context of the new charges under FA 1988, ss 77 to 89.

THE 'OLD' GROWTH IN VALUE CHARGE: ICTA 1988 s 138(1)(a) (formerly FA 1972, s 79(4))

Crystallising the charge

General

2.190 The 'growth in value' charge under s 138(1)(a) is made under Schedule E (see 7.88–7.96) on the increase in market value from the time of acquisition of the shares or interest in shares to the earliest of:

(a) the expiry of seven years (ICTA 1988, s 138(9)(a));
(b) the time at which the employee ceases to have any beneficial interest in the shares, subject to 2.300 (ICTA 1988, s 138(9)(b)); and
(c) in relation to shares which are subject to restrictions of the type set out at 2.201, the time when, by reason of their ceasing to be subject to such restrictions, the conditions for either the 'normal shares' exemption of ICTA 1988, s 138(3)(a)(i) (see 2.252 to 2.260) or the 'employee-controlled companies' exemption of ICTA 1988, s 138(3)(a)(ii) (see 2.261 to 2.272) would be satisfied if they had been acquired at that time. As restrictions within para (c) of 2.201 do not prevent the employee-control test being met, it would appear that a charge may crystallise where these remain, as by reason of the shares ceasing to be subject to (certain) restrictions within 2.201 that test has been met. It would be possible, alternatively, to argue that since some restrictions within 2.201 remain, the shares cannot be said to have ceased to be 'subject to such restrictions' as required to trigger the charge. The requirement, however, is for the employee control test to be met 'by reason of' the cessation of restrictions, and as those within para (c) cannot affect the position it is suggested that they are irrelevant for this purpose. This third 'trigger' for the growth in value charge does not apply where the employee's acquisition was only of an indirect 'interest in shares' (see 2.184) rather than of the shares themselves (ICTA 1988, s 138(9)(c)). Prior to 19 March 1986 a charge was triggered where *all* such restrictions were removed, irrespective of whether the conditions for either the 'normal shares' or 'employee-control' test would then have been satisfied. The change was effected by FA 1986, s 26(4) & (6)(c). For shares acquired before 23 March 1973, the charge was precipitated when the shares ceased to be subject to any restrictions other than those attaching to all shares of the same class. Such restrictions are now only one of the categories mentioned at 2.201. This change was effected by FA 1973, Sch 8, para 4(1)(c).

2.191 An example may serve to illustrate the charge:

> Bates is given the opportunity, as a result of his employment, to purchase 1,000 shares in his employer company Goddard Ltd, at £2 per share, when their market value is £3. The discount of £1 is taxable in the year of assessment in which he

takes up the shares, under the decision in *Weight v Salmon* (see 2.13–2.24). He still holds the shares seven years after their acquisition, at which time their value has risen to £7. An income tax charge arises for the year of assessment in which that seventh anniversary falls, as follows:

Value on seventh anniversary:	
1,000 × £7	£ 7,000
Value on acquisition:	
1,000 × £3	(3,000)
Amount chargeable under ICTA 1988, s 138(1)(a)	£ 4,000

The example could equally well illustrate the charge under (b) or (c) of 2.190 if £7 were taken to be the value on disposal, or on the removal of the relevant restrictions.

Interests in shares, and part disposals

2.192 Where an individual has less than full beneficial ownership of the shares in question (for example, where he owns them jointly), the amount chargeable is 'such part of [the increase in value of the shares] as corresponds to his interest' (ICTA 1988, s 138(1)(a)). For example, an individual with a 50% interest in 1,000 shares is effectively treated as if he owned 500 shares. It would appear (subject to 2.195) that no attempt is to be made to ascertain the growth in value of the interest itself; the charge is merely calculated arithmetically from the values of the underlying shares.

2.193 Where an individual's beneficial interest in shares is reduced, but not extinguished, he is treated for the purposes of para (b) in 2.190 'as ceasing to have an interest in such part of the shares as is proportionate to the reduction' (ICTA 1988, s 138(9)). The most common application of this provision (subject to 2.194) is the sale of part of a holding, so that, for example, a holder of 3,000 shares who disposes of 1,000 of them incurs, as might be expected, a charge of one-third of the liability which would have arisen on a sale of the entire holding; he is not protected from a charge merely by virtue of the fact that his beneficial interest in 'employee shares' is not totally extinguished.

2.194 It might, alternatively, be argued that while the words 'ceases to have any beneficial interest in the shares' in para (b) of 2.190 are clearly apt to cover a sale of shares, and do not apply only to the disposal of 'an interest in' shares, the reference in 2.193 to a 'reduction' in the individual's beneficial interest refers only to the transition from full beneficial ownership to a reduced indirect interest, or to a diminution of such an existing interest. This interpretation would be justified on the ground that the employee still has full (ie 'unreduced') beneficial ownership of his remaining shares. If this be so, then, as a corollary, the statutory references to 'shares' or 'acquisition of shares' must include shares the full ownership of which is acquired as part of a larger transaction or series of transactions. On this interpretation a disposal of part of a holding is, in effect, a disposal of a complete holding which is 'carved out' for the purpose from the total number of 'employee shares'. Whichever view is strictly correct, however, the net effect is exactly the same.

2.195 Whether or not it applies to a disposal of part of a holding, the provision that on a reduction of his beneficial interest the individual be treated 'as ceasing to have an interest in such part of the shares as is proportionate to the reduction' certainly applies where an individual who has, for example, a 50% interest in 6,000 shares through a trust reduces that interest to 33⅓% by consenting to the variation of the trust so as to include an additional beneficiary. In such a case he is treated, in effect, as having sold 1,000 out of 3,000 shares, leaving him with a holding of 2,000. It is not, of course, necessarily the case that a 50% interest in a certain number of shares is worth exactly the same as a full interest in half the number of shares, but, under the statutory wording quoted from s 138(1)(a) & (9) in 2.192 and 2.193, this assumption is effectively made for the purposes of the section. It is arguable that the words 'such part . . . as corresponds to his interest' in 2.192 or 'such part as is proportionate to the reduction [in his beneficial interest]' in 2.193 should be read as meaning 'corresponding' or 'proportionate' to the *value* of that interest or reduction, so that if a 50% interest in a shareholding was worth only 45% of the value of the underlying shares, the growth in value charge on such an interest on its complete disposal, or on the expiry of seven years, would be based on only 45% of the increase in value of the underlying shares; or in the case of a reduction from a 70% interest (worth, for example, 65% of the underlying share value) to a 20% interest (worth, for the purposes of illustration, 10% of the total value of the shares), the charge would be based on a notional disposal of 55% of the shares (65% less 10%), rather than 50% (70% less 20%). Presumably in such cases the appropriate valuations of the interests as a percentage of the underlying shareholding (as opposed to the valuations of the shares themselves) would be those at the date of the charge, rather than at any earlier date. Fortunately, in view of the complexity, and subjectivity, of the calculations which could be necessary, this interpretation of the legislation does not appear to be the most natural reading of the statutory wording. It may be noted that in the case of a part-disposal of a full beneficial interest—if indeed these provisions apply (see 2.194)—it could result in a notional disposal of a different number of shares from that actually disposed of, where the value of shares varied according to the quantity (see example at 2.141). In practice, the point will rarely be of significance, because in the vast majority of cases where the section applies, the individual holds shares directly, rather than an indirect interest, and even where this is not the case, any differences between the value of such an interest and of a direct holding in an equivalent proportion of the underlying shares are likely to be minimal, particularly in the case of the small holdings which are characteristic of share incentive schemes. Indeed, it may be assumed that the inclusion of 'interests in shares' within the ambit of the section, in addition to shares, was intended to pre-empt the more obvious efforts at avoiding the charge, and, as a result, arrangements involving an indirect interest in shares are extremely unusual.

2.196 Because small quantities are usually involved, the value of shareholdings or interests in shares will normally increase directly in proportion to their size. This will not necessarily be so, however, where larger holdings are involved, particularly in the, admittedly exceptional, case where the limits of 25%, 50% or 75% of total share capital are exceeded (see 1.7). In general, the larger holding will have a disproportionately high value, and in this case it may be advantageous to make a disposal in stages, as illustrated in the following example.

> If 800 shares, out of a total share capital of 1,000, have a value of £3 each (total £2,400) and were originally acquired with a value of £1 each, the charge on their

disposal would be based on a growth in value of £1,600 (£2,400 less £800). If, however, a holding below 50% is worth only £2 per share, a disposal in two stages would produce a result as follows (adopting the preferred interpretation of 'proportionate reduction' discussed at 2.195).

Disposal: 301 shares @ £3	£ 903	
Less acquisition value	(301)	
		£ 602
Disposal: 499 shares @ £2	£ 998	
Less acquisition value	(499)	
		499
		£1,101

For the position if the alternative interpretation of 'proportionate reduction', as at 2.195, were adopted, see the example and discussion at 2.141, in the context of the 'new' growth in value charge under FA 1988, s 79. Such a disposal in stages would, of course, be commercially disadvantageous, producing proceeds of only £1,901 (ie £903 plus £998), as opposed to £2,400 in a sale of the complete holding. If, however, the disposal was by way of gift it would be beneficial (although it should be noticed, in passing, that the inheritance tax rules for valuing a transfer by reference to the diminution in the donor's estate would prevent any corresponding advantage being obtained for the purposes of that tax).

2.197 An increased shareholding will not always command a higher price per share. It may be that the placing of a substantial holding on the market at one time will reduce the value, for example where a large holding is sold on The Stock Exchange. If the shares are actually disposed of, on the open market, the sale price will constitute the market value but if the charge under s 138(1)(a) arises on the expiry of seven years, or on the removal of restrictions (see paras (a) and (c) of 2.190) it will not be possible to discount a market value obtained, for example, from The Stock Exchange Daily Official List, to take account of the assumption that all the shares will be placed on the market at the same time (ICTA 1988, s 140(3); CGTA 1979, s 150(2)), and see also 7.56.

The charge

2.198 The charge to income tax is made under Schedule E (ICTA 1988, s 138(1)(a)), the appropriate Case thereof being determined by the residence status of the individual, and the place where the duties of the employment are carried on (see 2.187 and 7.88 to 7.96).

2.199 The amount chargeable is treated as earned income, whether or not it would otherwise fall to be so treated (ICTA 1988, s 138(1)). With the abolition of the investment income surcharge from 6 April 1984, this provision lost much of its effect, but it may still be of importance, for example, where prior to the introduction of independent taxation of husband and wife on 6 April 1990 an election for separate taxation of wife's earnings is made under ICTA 1988, s 287. The number of cases where an amount chargeable to tax under Schedule E would not be 'earned income' in the absence of this provision must, however, be very small. The situation would presumably only arise where the benefit conferred was out of all proportion to the services rendered.

2.200 The charge arises for the year of assessment in which the expiry of seven years, the disposal (or reduction of beneficial interest in the shares), or the removal of restriction occurs. There is therefore some scope for minimising the charge, insofar as the disposal of shares may be made in a year in which other income is low, so that the higher rate of tax is avoided; or in which losses arise, which may eliminate or reduce the amount charged to tax; or in which the 100% deduction for long absences abroad (see 7.92) is available. Depending on the circumstances, and the individual's position within the company, the date on which restrictions are removed may also be within his control, and while the date on which the seven-year limit expires is not susceptible to change, it may still be possible to ensure that it is in that year that losses from other activities fall, that the 100% deduction for long absences abroad is available, or that investment is made in a 'tax shelter' such as the Business Expansion Scheme. The date of disposal will of course be affected also by commercial considerations as to past movements and expected future movements in the share price, which will limit the flexibility in this area for tax planning purposes, but even where that date is effectively fixed as a result of other factors, the same 'tax shelters' may be applied as when the growth in value charge crystallises in the seventh year.

The cessation of restrictions

2.201 In para (c) of 2.190, reference was made to the charge crystallising when the shares in question cease to be subject to certain restrictions. The restrictions in question are any of the following (ICTA 1988, s 138(6) & (9)(c)):

(a) Restrictions not attaching to all shares of the same class: these might include limitations on transferability or voting power, which applied only to those shares issued to employees, although they did not constitute a separate class. It would usually not be desirable to constitute a separate class of shares for employees and directors, for the reasons set out at 2.256. Arguably, a condition which restricted the rights attaching to *all* shares of the same class, but only at such time as they might be held by employees or directors, would not fall within this category, but it would be caught by category (b) below, as such restrictions would be 'liable to cease' at some time after the acquisition of the shares; see also (c) below.

(b) Restrictions ceasing or liable to cease at some time after the acquisition of the shares: such restrictions might include limitations on transferability or voting power which expired after an initial period of three or four years, and were designed to 'tie' the executive to the company for that period, or to ensure that he did not have a voice in its affairs, as shareholder, until he had proved his loyalty by staying with the company for that period. Restrictions which, while not definitely ceasing at a specified time, would be 'liable to cease' would include those removable at the discretion of the directors, or those which would lapse on a change in status of the shareholder, perhaps on his elevation from employee to director.

(c) Restrictions which depend on the shares being or ceasing to be held by directors or employees of any body corporate: for example, such restrictions might remove the right to dispose of the shares, except to a person approved by the directors, if the shareholder ceased to be an employee of the company issuing the shares, or of another group company, except on reaching normal retirement age; but more arcane restrictions are possible, such as a removal of voting rights on the shareholder becoming an employee of a specified rival company. This category, however, specifically excludes restrictions imposed by a company's articles of association which require shares to be disposed of on ceasing to be held by an employee or director of any body corporate. Most commonly, indeed almost exclusively, such restrictions will take the form of a requirement to dispose of the shares in a company on ceasing to hold office in that company or another member of the same group.

2.202 Categories (b) and (c) in 2.201 were added to the legislation by FA 1973, Sch 8, para 4(1)(c) in relation only to acquisitions of shares after 22 March 1973. It should be noted that to crystallise the charge prior to the change made by FA 1986, as detailed in para (c) of 2.190, *all* restrictions of the specified categories had to be lifted. The rules regarding the crystallisation of the charge by the removal of restrictions could formerly be exploited to escape the 'growth in value' charge by the use of artificial arrangements, but there was considerable doubt as to the efficacy of such arrangements following the decisions of the House of Lords in *WT Ramsay Ltd v IRC* and *Furniss v Dawson* (see 7.79 to 7.82 and 2.280). The FA 1986 change removed the possibility.

Summary

2.203 The 'growth in value' charge, then, crystallises, broadly, on disposal of the shares, expiry of seven years, or removal of restrictions. Clearly the time at which the benefit is realised, on sale of the shares, is an appropriate time at which to charge the growth in value if it is to be charged at all, although if the disposal is by way of gift there will in fact be no funds made available to meet the charge, and no opportunity to 'hold over' the liability as may be done with a CGT charge on a gift. A disposal by way of gift is, however, within the control of the shareholder, and need not be undertaken unless he knows that he has funds available from another source to meet the tax liability. The charge after seven years, if the shares are still held, simply reflects the intention of the legislation that the tax liability on the growth in value should not be deferred indefinitely, by retention of the shares. There appears to be no particular reason for the choice of seven years as the appropriate limit, although it may be noted that the same period is used in ICTA 1988, s 135(2) in determining whether a charge to tax arises on the grant (as opposed to the exercise) of a share option (see 3.38). It is, of course, always open to the shareholder to effect a sale, of some or all of his shares, in order to put himself in funds to pay the tax, and to that extent the charge is not inequitable, although a sale may be forced on him at a time which, judged by normal investment criteria, is inauspicious. If the company concerned is not publicly quoted, a sale may not always be easy to effect, but, broadly speaking, the more difficult it is to sell the shares, the lower will be their open market value, and the lower will be the growth in value charge.

2.204 The crystallising of the charge on the removal of restrictions has a double rationale. It may be that shares have been allocated to employees without giving rise to an immediate Schedule E charge, or with only a small charge because, in view of the restrictions attaching to them, their value has been little or nothing in excess of the price, if any, given for them (see 2.22 to 2.24). If the restrictions are subsequently removed, so that the market value of the shares increases, an immediate benefit accrues to the shareholder, which is distinct from the growth in value arising as the result of a general improvement in the fortunes of the company, and it is therefore taxed immediately. The second point is that if 'employee shares' subject to a multitude of restrictions arising from the shareholder's employment have those restrictions lifted, so that the shareholder can deal with them at will, and effectively makes (if only by default) a new investment decision to retain shares which he is now for the first time free to sell, or to sell without financial penalty, then it is right that those shares should no longer be regarded as 'employee shares', and subjected to the growth in value charge in future. It therefore crystallises on the removal of the restrictions, and comes to an end.

'Restrictions'

The extended definition

2.205 A 'restriction' for the purposes of 2.201–2.204 includes, as regards shares or interests in shares acquired after 18 October 1972, any contract, agreement, arrangement, or condition by which a shareholder's freedom to dispose of the shares or of any interest in them, or to exercise any right conferred by them is restricted (ICTA 1988, s 139(7)). This definition is without prejudice to any more general meaning of 'restriction', and is intended to widen the scope of the term which, in relation to acquisitions after 5 April 1972 and before 19 October 1972, merely bore its general meaning. 'Freedom to dispose of the shares or of any interest in them' covers the complete disposal of shares or of any indirect interest in them, the reduction of full beneficial ownership to a more limited interest, or the further reduction of an already limited interest. The wording 'contract, agreement, arrangement or condition' covers not only restrictions imposed by the terms of the share issue; that is, implicit in the 'bundle of rights' acquired on subscription, but also those imposed by a collateral agreement, by any agreement entered into subsequently which was not contemplated at the time of issue of the shares, or by any other arrangement, however informal, which has the effect of imposing restrictions on the shares. Where the imposition of the restriction postdates the issue of the shares, the time at which the 'growth in value' charge arises is unaffected: it remains the date of disposal, expiry of seven years, or lifting of the restrictions, irrespective of when they were imposed.

2.206 The restrictions most commonly met in practice are of two categories: limitations on transferability and on voting. As regards transferability, the shareholder might be prohibited from disposing of his shares at all (except on death); or from making a disposal other than to a specified person or class of person (such as existing shareholders, or controlling shareholders), or to any person without the agreement of the Board of Directors, or in any way other than sale back to the company itself. He might even be permitted to sell or make a gift of his shares to anyone other than a particular individual or individuals, provided that the same restriction was made a condition of his own gift or contract of sale and, by that gift or contract, of subsequent disposals. A restriction of this nature passing through a succession of contracts or gifts would be extremely difficult to enforce, however, and would be more effectively imposed by a condition attaching to the shares in the provisions of the company's articles of association (although this would be very unusual).

2.207 The second main category of restriction relates to voting rights. Here the shareholder may have no right to vote at all; no right to vote on specified subjects; or a right to vote only on specified issues, such as the variation of class rights or a resolution to wind up the company.

2.208 The statutory wording includes not only votes, but 'any right' conferred by the shares, and this might include rights to a discount on the goods or services provided by the company, rights of access to its premises or to events organised by it, or any of the 'shareholder perks' which are current at the present time. A restriction on dividends, while not limiting the 'exercise' of any right, within the statutory wording, would be within the general meaning of the term.

'Constructive restrictions'

2.209 The term 'restriction' also includes a contract, agreement, arrangement or condition which, while it does not by its terms actually limit the shareholder's freedom to transfer his shares (or interest therein), or to exercise the related rights, has the effect that such a disposal or exercise may result in a disadvantage to him or to a person connected with him (ICTA 1988, s 139(7)). Such a 'constructive restriction' would exist where, for example, under the terms of a share incentive scheme, or of an ancillary agreement, a sale of shares would result in the forfeiture of existing rights to purchase further shares in future. Arguably, the term 'arrangements' is wide enough to encompass a situation where, although there could be no legal contract to that effect, it was made clear to an executive that if he exercised or failed to exercise the votes attaching to his shares in a particular way, his career would suffer.

2.210 The relevant provisions cover not only a disadvantage to the shareholder, but also to a 'connected person', including a company, as defined in 7.22 (ICTA 1988, ss 139(7), 140(2) and 839).

Related loans

2.211 A limitation on the freedom to dispose of, or exercise any right relating to, shares or an interest in shares does not constitute a 'restriction' if it is imposed as a condition of a loan which is not a 'related loan', as defined (ICTA 1988, s 139(7)): for example if, independent of any arrangement with the company, or associated companies, the shareholder takes out a loan from a bank, for which he gives his shares as security, and, because of the bank's legal charge over them, he is not free to dispose of them.

2.212 A loan is a 'related loan' if it is 'made, arranged, guaranteed or in any way facilitated by the body corporate of which [the shareholder] is a director or employee' (ICTA 1988, s 139(8)(a)(i)). The reference to 'the body corporate', rather than to 'a body corporate' makes it clear, in the context, that the company in question is that by virtue of his office with which the individual has been given the opportunity to acquire the shares in question. Thus, the making or guaranteeing of a loan by a completely unconnected company with which he also happened to have a part-time appointment, and the consequent giving of a charge over the shares, limiting his right to dispose of them, would not constitute a 'restriction' for this purpose.

2.213 It is clear enough when a loan has been made or guaranteed by the employing company, but the words 'arranged' and 'facilitated' are less precise. They might cover the situation where a company conducts negotiations with a bank to obtain a loan on behalf of one of its employees; makes a matching deposit with a bank without giving any guarantee or right of set-off; or simply provides the employee with a reference or letter of introduction, thus supporting his application without entering into any formal arrangement with the lender. Similarly, a lender which was not a bank, but a customer or supplier of the employer company, could be induced to make a loan by being afforded preferential terms of trade, or by the prospect of having less advantageous terms imposed. It should be borne in mind that while a company has a legal personality distinct from that of its officers, it can only act through its employees and directors, so that the possibility of 'the company' taking such action in support of a request for a loan by one of its executives is not as remote as might perhaps be supposed.

2.214 The provisions of 2.212 and 2.213 defining a 'related loan' as one made, arranged, guaranteed or in any way facilitated by the employer company extend also to the case where the relevant action leading to the obtaining of the loan is made by an associated company, as defined in 7.10 or, if the employer company or an associated company is a close company, by any person having a material interest in that close company (ICTA 1988, ss 139(8)(a)(ii) & (iii) and (11), and 416). A close company, broadly, is one controlled by its directors or by five or fewer participators (see 7.12 to 7.21) and a 'material interest', broadly, is one, together with 'associates' (see 7.6) of more than 5% in the company: see 7.65 to 7.71 (ICTA 1988, ss 139(12), 168(11), 414, 415 and 417(3)). In addition, a loan made to a person (including a company) who is 'connected' with an individual (see 7.22) is a 'related' loan if it would have been so had it been made to that individual (ICTA 1988, s 139(8)(b)).

2.215 A loan made by an employer company, associated company or person with a material interest in a close company, as described in 2.211 to 2.214 is not, however, 'related' if the company or individual making the loan carries on a business of making personal loans, and the loan is made in the ordinary course of that business (ICTA 1988, s 139(8)). Thus, if an individual receives a loan from a bank or finance company which is, or is associated with, his employer, and gives his 'employee shares' as security for the loan, thus limiting his right to deal in them, that limitation will not be a 'restriction' for the present purposes provided the loan was made in the ordinary course of business.

Directors: the Model Code

2.216 The references in 2.205 and 2.209 to a 'contract, agreement, arrangement or condition' do not include such part of any contract etc as contains provisions similar in purpose and effect to any of the provisions of the Model Rules set out in the Model Code for Securities Transactions by Directors of Listed Companies issued by The Stock Exchange in November 1984. Prior to amendment by FA 1986, s 23(4)(a), with effect from 25 July

1986, the reference was to the Model Code issued in April 1981 (ICTA 1988, s 139(10)). The effect is to exclude situations where the restrictions imposed on directors are simply such as to prevent 'insider dealing' or other improper conduct. Although this provision was not introduced until 1982, it was designed to fill an obvious lacuna in the legislation, and applies, like the extended definition of 'restriction', in respect of any shares acquired after 18 October 1972. Although the Model Code itself (set out in Appendix 4) was not in effect at that time, many directors were nevertheless restricted in their dealings by provisions of similar purposes and effect. For shares acquired on or after 6 April 1972 (the commencement date for what is now ICTA 1988, s 138) and before 19 October 1972, the term 'restriction', as explained at 2.205, was not statutorily defined, but took its general meaning, which, strictly speaking, may have included limitations on dealing within the spirit of the Model Code.

2.217 The definition of 'restriction' in 2.205 to 2.216 applies not only for the purposes of determining whether a restriction has been removed, so as to crystallise a 'growth in value' charge but also in establishing whether the issue comes within the 'normal shares' or 'employee-controlled company' exemptions discussed at 2.252 to 2.260 and 2.261 to 2.272, and for the purposes of any valuation to be made for the purposes of ICTA 1988, s 138 (whether for the 'growth in value' charge under s 138(1)(a) or the 'special benefits' charge under s 138(1)(b); see 2.287 to 2.294 (ICTA 1988, s 139(7)). For the valuation of shares subject to restrictions, see 2.22 to 2.24.

As to the Inland Revenue's view of what may constitute a restriction, see further at 5.82, 5.84, 6.65, 6.66 and Appendix 9, regarding directors' discretionary vetos on share transfers, and pre-emption rights under which a company may compel an employee who leaves his employment to sell his shares to another shareholder.

Agreed adjustments to purchase or sale price

2.218 Where a 'growth in value' charge arises under s 138(1)(a) and, under the terms on which the shares or interest in shares were originally acquired, the acquisition consideration is subsequently increased, the growth in value on which income tax is chargeable is reduced by the amount of that increase (ICTA 1988, s 138(8)(a)). Such a circumstance would arise where the purchase price included an amount to be ascertained according to a formula set out in the purchase agreement. Most commonly, this would be a 'performance related' element, depending on the profitability of the company, or, less frequently, on the movement in the price of the shares on the open market. It could, however, be linked to an indicator which had no direct connection with the shares, such as the retail prices index, or a general stock market index.

2.219 The application of this provision is illustrated by the example given at 2.118 in connection with the 'new' growth in value charge under FA 1988, s 79.

2.220 Where shares are, or an interest in shares is, disposed of at a price below market value, but that disposal takes place in accordance with the terms on which the acquisition was made, the actual proceeds are substituted for market value in the calculation of the 'growth in value' charge (ICTA 1988, s 138(8)(b)). Such a situation would arise, for example, where it was a condition of a share incentive scheme that, if sold within a specified period, the shares could only pass into the ownership of other existing shareholders, or be repurchased by the company, and the price at which the transfer should take place was predetermined, either in absolute terms, or according to a formula. This provision is illustrated by the example at 2.121, dealing with the corresponding provisions for the 'new' growth in value charge under FA 1988, s 79.

2.221 In both the cases discussed at 2.218 and 2.220 above, the legislation provides that such assessments, alterations of assessments, or repayments of tax shall be made as may be necessary to give effect to the reduction (ICTA 1988, s 138(8)). It is thus made clear that the payment of additional consideration, or disposal at less than market value, after the occasion of charge under ICTA 1988, s 138(1)(a) may give rise to relief under these provisions, subject to the normal time limit for making a claim, of six years from the end of the year of assessment to which it relates; i e, the year of the charge (TMA 1970, s 43).

Bonus and rights issues

2.222 Prior to 19 March 1986, the growth in value charge could in certain cases be reduced or eliminated by using bonus and rights issues to 'dilute' the value of the original holding or to secure qualification for the 'normal shares' exemption (see further at 2.281 to 2.285 and 2.257). Detailed rules now apply to bonus and right issues, specifically where (ICTA 1988, s 138(10)):

(a) a person has acquired shares or an interest in shares (the 'original shares'), as an employee or director within the terms of ICTA 1988, s 138(1) (see 2.184 to 2.189);
(b) the circumstances of that acquisition are such that the application of the growth in value charge under s 138(1)(a) is not excluded by any of the provisions discussed in 2.228 to 2.275; and
(c) by virtue of his holding of the original shares or the interest in them he acquires after 18 March 1986 (whether or not for consideration) additional shares or an interest in additional shares.

2.223 In a case within 2.222 above the additional shares are, or the interest in them is, treated in the same way as the original shares or interest, as having been acquired by the shareholder 'as a director or employee' within s 138(1), and in circumstances such that none of the exemptions from the charge under s 138(1)(a) discussed in 2.228 to 2.275 is available (ICTA 1988, s 138(11)(a)). In determining whether the seven year time limit for crystallising the charge under s 138(9)(a) (see 2.190) has expired, they are deemed to have been acquired at the same time as the original shares (ICTA 1988, s 138(11)(a)). For the purpose of calculating the charge under s 138(1)(a), (see 2.191), and of any adjustments under s 138(8) for subsequent increases in consideration, or disposals at less than market value, in accordance with the terms of acquisition (see 2.218 to 2.221) the original shares and the additional shares are treated as one holding of shares, and their market value is determined accordingly (the market value of the original shares at the time of acquisition being attributed proportionately to all the shares in the combined holding (ICTA 1988, s 138(11)(b)). Any consideration given for the acquisition of the additional shares or the interest in them is treated as an increase in the consideration for the original acquisition, given under the terms of that acquisition, within s 138(8)(a) (see 2.218), with the effect that the growth in value charge on a subsequent disposal is reduced accordingly (ICTA 1988, s 138(11)(c)).

Share for share exchanges

2.224 Prior to 19 March 1986, a 'share for share' exchange could crystallise a growth in value charge under what is now ICTA 1988, s 138(1)(a), because it entailed a disposal of the employee's shares in the first company. Detailed provisions apply where, on or after that date, a person, on ceasing to have a beneficial interest in any shares, acquires other shares, or an interest in other shares, and the circumstances are such that for the purposes of CGTA 1979, ss 78 to 81, dealing with company reorganisations, the shares which he disposes of constitute 'original shares' and the shares which he acquires constitute a 'new holding' (ICTA 1988, s 139(13)). For further details of CGTA 1979, ss 78 to 81, see 4.42 to 4.45, and also 2.155, which deals with the corresponding provisions for the new growth in value and special benefits charges under FA 1988, ss 77 to 89. It should be noted that arrangements involving the exchange of shares for debentures, which come within the capital gains tax provisions, are not within the terms of the present legislation. Any debentures given or received in addition to shares will constitute 'additional consideration' within 2.226 and 2.227 below.

2.225 Under the provisions referred to in 2.224, CGTA 1979, s 78 applies for the purposes of ICTA 1988, s 138, with the effect that the reorganisation is not treated as involving any disposal of the original shares or any acquisition of the new holding, but the two are treated as the same asset, acquired as the original shares were acquired (ICTA 1988, s 139(13)(a)). Accordingly, no growth in value charge crystallises on the exchange, and any future charge is calculated by reference to the market value of the original shares on acquisition. Similarly, the seven year period on the expiry of which the charge crystallises in the absence of an earlier disposal (or lifting of restrictions) runs from the time of the original acquisition.

2.226 If, on the exchange, any consideration is given for the new holding, in addition to the old shares, it is treated as an increase in the consideration for the original shares, made under the terms of their acquisition, within ICTA 1988, s 138(8)(a) (see 2.218), with the result that it reduces a subsequent growth in value charge (ICTA 1988, s 139(13)(b)).

2.227 If, on the exchange, any consideration other than the new shares is received for the disposal of the old shares, it is apportioned among the shares comprised in the new holding, and the market value of any of those shares at any future time is taken to be increased by the amount of the consideration apportioned to them, thus in turn increasing any growth in value charge (ICTA 1988, s 139(13)(c)).

Exemptions from the growth in value charge

General

2.228 Various exemptions are provided from the 'growth in value' charge even where the acquisition of the shares in question is 'in pursuance of a right conferred on . . . or opportunity offered [to the individual] as director or employee' of the company concerned, or of any other company 'and not in pursuance of an offer to the public' within the terms of s 138(1) (see 2.184 to 2.189).

Employee shares issued in conjunction with a public offer

2.229 Where a director or employee acquires shares in his employer company or another company (in practice, normally the employer's parent company), in pursuance of an opportunity which is offered to directors and employees in their capacity as such (referred to in the legislation as a 'discount offer'), he is treated, provided certain conditions are satisfied, as acquiring the shares in pursuance of an offer to the public, so that the acquisition is not within the terms of s 138(1) (see 2.184 to 2.189) and no 'growth in value' charge or 'special benefit' charge (see 2.287 to 2.294) can arise (ICTA 1988, s 139(1)). It should be noted that the offer must be made to 'directors and employees'—not necessarily to all directors and employees, but certainly not just to one individual. It would also appear that an offer to directors but not to employees, or to employees but not to directors, would fail to qualify under these provisions. Prudence would therefore dictate the inclusion of a token director or token employee within an arrangement designed primarily for the other category. The relevant provisions were introduced by FA 1984, s 41(1) with effect from 26 July 1984.

2.230 The relevant conditions are that:

(a) The discount offer must be made in conjunction with an offer to the public (the 'main offer') under which shares of the same class may be acquired on the same terms, except that a discount in price is offered to directors and employees (ICTA 1988, s 139(1)(b)). As the offer must be on the same terms (except as to price), it will not be possible to impose any additional restrictions on employee's shares, as it might otherwise be desired to do for commercial reasons.
(b) The director or employee seeking to take advantage of the exemption must be chargeable to tax under Schedule E on the amount of the discount allowed to him (see 2.13 to 2.24). It is not necessary that *all* directors and employees covered by the discount offer should be so chargeable; some may be resident outside the UK and carry out their duties abroad, so that they are not within the scope of Schedule E (ICTA 1988, s 139(1)(c)). Only the particular individual whose position is being considered need be taxable on the discount.
(c) At least 75% of the aggregate number of shares of the class in question which are acquired in pursuance of the discount offer and main offer taken together must be acquired under the main offer (ICTA 1988, s 139(1)(d)). This allows for generous treatment of staff, who may receive up to a quarter of the shares in any issue.

2.231 The provisions in 2.229 and 2.230 apply mutatis mutandis to the acquisition by an employee or director of an interest in shares less than full beneficial ownership (ICTA 1988, s 139(2)).

'Old' (FA 1973) profit-sharing schemes

2.232 The 'growth in value' charge does not apply where the shares acquired by the director or employee in his capacity as such are received under arrangements whereby *employees* receive as part of their emoluments shares, or interests in shares, of their employer company (or of a company which controls it) to an extent determined in advance by reference to the profits of either body (ICTA 1988, s 138(2)(a)). The word 'extent', it is considered, covers either number or value, so that an arrangement might come within this exemption if it provided for a monetary salary to be augmented by (for example) one share for each £15,000 of profit achieved by the parent company; or, alternatively, shares with a market value of £5 for each £100,000 of profit. 'Control' of one company by another is determined in accordance with ICTA 1988, s 840: see 7.23 to 7.24 (ICTA 1988, s 139(11)). The wording of s 138(2)(a) refers only to arrangements where individuals receive shares as 'part' of their emoluments, and a scheme under which remuneration was totally in the form of shares, and included no monetary element would therefore not qualify for exemption (although it would be an easy matter to include a merely nominal amount of remuneration within the package).

2.233 It is considered that, although the reference in ICTA 1988, s 138(2)(a) is only to arrangements involving employees, directors may still be exempt from the charge if the arrangements in question encompass both directors and employees, as the directors still receive their shares by virtue of 'arrangements under which employees . . . receive . . . shares'. Indeed, it is not certain that, as far as executive directors are concerned, the two categories are mutually exclusive. It would, however, be possible to argue alternatively that the expression 'arrangements under which employees . . . receive . . .' relates only to that part of a scheme which deals with employees, even if exactly the same arrangements extend to directors.

2.234 The conditions set out in 2.232 are the only ones that need to be complied with, whenever the shares are actually acquired, if the arrangements were made on or before 22 March 1973, and have not been modified since that date. Where the arrangements were made or modified after that date, however, further conditions must be fulfilled as set out in 2.235 to 2.240 (ICTA 1988, s 138(2)(b)).

2.235 The arrangements must allow every full-time employee of the company concerned who:

(a) has been a full-time employee of that company for a continuous period of at least five years, and
(b) is chargeable to tax in respect of his employment under Schedule E Case I (ie broadly, is resident and ordinarily resident in the UK—see 7.89), and
(c) is not less than 25 years old,

to acquire shares or interests in shares of the same class on similar terms (ICTA 1988, s 138(4)(b)). 'Full-time' in relation to a director or employee means required to devote substantially the whole of his time to service in that office (ICTA 1988, s 139(11)—and see further at 7.46 to 7.50 for the definition of 'full-time' in other contexts). An individual who has served for five years or more with different companies in the same group under separate contracts of service will not, in strictness, qualify under (a) above. Schemes of this nature are not common, and are not subject to formal Inland Revenue approval (see 2.241), so it is not known whether in practice any concessionary treatment would be applied. The problem could be avoided, if foreseen, by establishing an employment with one company, and seconding the employee to other group companies who require his services.

2.236 Under para (a) in 2.235, the scheme must cover every full-time employee of the company operating the scheme. If the shares used are those of the parent company, however, and other group companies have similar schemes, it is not necessary that these schemes should extend to every employee of the group. It may therefore be possible to segregate into one company those executives to whom it is desired to give the benefit of such a scheme. It will be noted also, that it is not necessary that the scheme should extend to all directors of the requisite age and length of service, as well as employees, although, equally, there is nothing to prevent it doing so.

2.237 The restriction under para (b) of 2.235 to employees taxable under Schedule E Case I avoids the necessity to include, for example, overseas employees who might be in tax jurisdictions where the receipt of shares would be treated disadvantageously.

2.238 While the scheme must extend to all employees with the requisite qualifications, it may of course include others with less than five years' service; under the age of 25; and not taxable under Schedule E Case I.

2.239 For a scheme to qualify for exemption under s 138(1)(b), the shares in question must also:

(a) not be subject to such restrictions as will or may result in the person acquiring them, or an interest in them, obtaining benefit through an increase, subsequent to the acquisition, of the value, or the value to him, of the shares or interest; and
(b) not be exchangeable for, or convertible into, shares which are subject to such restrictions (whether by one transaction or a series of transactions) (ICTA 1988, s 138(4)(a)(i) & (ii)).

Restrictions are defined for this purpose as in 2.205 to 2.217 (ICTA 1988, s 139(7)). Few, if any, restrictions would, of themselves, result in an increase in the value of shares, or in their value to a particular individual, but their existence would give rise to the possibility of an increase in value on their subsequent removal. Not all restrictions would have such an effect, however (hence the possibility of crystallising an occasion of charge to precipitate an appeal, as mentioned in 2.241). For example, a requirement that shares could only be sold to existing shareholders would have no depressing effect on the share price where there was a large number of such shareholders, including many willing buyers creating a ready market, and the removal of the restriction would thus not increase their value. Similarly, where control of the company rested with two or three major shareholders, so that minority holders of voting shares had, effectively, no voice in its management, the absence of votes on the scheme shares would not depress their value, nor increase it on their removal. If, however, they were held by one of the two or three major shareholders, the acquisition of just a few extra votes, on the removal of the restriction, might tip the balance of power in his direction, and significantly increase their value 'to him'.

2.240 Further, the shares must be of a class quoted on a recognised stock exchange, or be shares in a company which is not under the control of another company (ICTA 1988, s 138(4)(a)(iii)). A 'recognised stock exchange' is as defined in 7.83 to 7.86 (ICTA 1988, s 841), and 'control' as in 7.23 and 7.24 (ICTA 1988, ss 139(11) and 840). The intention is to exclude the use of subsidiary companies (other than in the comparatively rare case where they are themselves publicly quoted), because their values can too easily be manipulated (either with the deliberate intention of giving or withholding an advantage under the share scheme, or as a result of other considerations, but with the same effect). The making or waiving of management charges, interest charges or group relief payments, and the determination of intra-group pricing policies may all be used in this way. It will be noted, also, that a company which is under the control of another is not eligible to have its shares used in a scheme simply by virtue of being a quoted company. The particular class of shares in use must itself be quoted, again avoiding the situation where the value of unquoted deferred or preference shares might be manipulated without being subject to the controls which obtain in the case of quoted securities.

2.241 There is no procedure for formal Inland Revenue approval of an 'old' (FA 1973) profit-sharing scheme, as in the case of the 'profit-sharing' schemes introduced by FA 1978 (see chapter 4), savings-related share option schemes (see chapter 5), or selective share option schemes, although it would normally be possible to obtain an informal Inland Revenue view on any particular point of difficulty. The only way to obtain a formal ruling against which an appeal may be made is to await the assessment on the growth in value charge which will arise if the necessary conditions are not considered to be fulfilled, and then to appeal against it to either the General or Special Commissioners, and subsequently to the courts if necessary (see 7.1 to 7.5). It may, of course, be seven years before a charge under s 138(1)(a) arises, and it will then be rather late in the day to discover that the requirements for an 'old' profit-sharing scheme are not met. An earlier charge may be crystallised, to provide a 'test case' by a sale of shares (which need only be minimal in amount). Prior to 19 March 1986 the same effect could be achieved by the removal of small restrictions originally placed on the shares solely for the purpose of their subsequent removal (see further at 2.280). Such restrictions, unless carefully formulated, may, however, themselves prevent the profit-sharing scheme meeting all the necessary conditions (see 2.239).

Unit trust schemes

2.242 A further exemption from the 'growth in value' charge of s 138(1)(a) is given where the acquisition by the employee or director is of an interest in shares, rather than shares themselves, and that interest takes the form of shares, or 'units', in an authorised unit trust, and the following conditions are satisfied:

(a) Prior to the acquisition, the unit trust was approved by the Board of Inland Revenue for the purposes of s 138 (as distinct from being approved by the

Department of Trade and Industry as an authorised unit trust—see 7.11—which is also a prerequisite of the exemption), and at the time of the acquisition in question the trust continued to be so approved (ICTA 1988, s 138(3)(b)(i)). The exemption is not affected by the subsequent loss of approval, or of authorised status, before the sale or other event which would otherwise crystallise the charge takes place.

(b) Investments in the company employment with which, or directorship of which, gave rise to the right or opportunity to acquire the units, and in any associated company (as defined in 7.10: ICTA 1988, ss 139(11) and 416) do not make up more than 10% of the value of the trust's investments for any continuous period of one month or more throughout which any director or employee of that company either has a right or opportunity to acquire units which was conferred on him qua director or employee and not in pursuance of an offer to the public (see 2.184 to 2.189), or retains any beneficial interest in units which he so acquired (ICTA 1988, s 138(3)(b)(ii) & (7)). A 'month' in this context is a calendar month (Interpretation Act 1978, Sch 1), as opposed to the more usual period in the Taxes Acts of 30 days. Breach of this condition at any time, whether before or after the acquisition, will result in the loss of the exemption, for any future potential occasion of charge under s 138(1)(a), but will not itself crystallise a charge.

2.243 It should be remembered that a holding in the employer company (or associated companies) which does not represent more than 10% by value of the trust's investments when it is acquired may exceed this limit without any action on the part of the fund managers, as a result of increases in the relevant share prices. The managers will therefore normally keep these prices under review, but the limit may also be exceeded as a result of the fall in value or sale of other unconnected shares. It is possible to argue that the words 'value of the investments' in s 138(7) (para (b) in 2.242) refer to the value of investments made; that is, that the necessary calculations should be based on acquisition cost, not present value, so that the limit could only be exceeded by some positive action, in the form of a purchase or sale by the managers, and not by movements in market prices. This interpretation does not, however, commend itself as the most natural reading of the statutory language and, while it has the advantage of making lesser demands on the vigilance of the managers, its effect, in terms of the level of investment which it would permit in the employer and associated companies, would be entirely arbitrary, increasing the level in some cases and diminishing it in others.

2.244 An 'authorised unit trust' for this purpose is defined in 7.11 (ICTA 1988, ss 468(6) and 832(1)). 'Units', in relation to an authorised unit trust, means an entitlement to a share in the investments subject to that trust (ICTA 1988, s 139(11)).

2.245 The Board of Inland Revenue may, by written notice, require the managers or trustees of any authorised unit trust approved for the purposes of these provisions to provide, within a stipulated time of not less than 30 days, such information as the Board thinks necessary to enable it to determine whether or not the 10% investment limit described in para (b) of 2.242 is, or has at any time been, exceeded, and to determine the tax liability of any unit holder who acquired his shares as described in s 138(1) (see 2.184 to 2.189); that is 'as director or employee' (ICTA 1988, s 139(6)). Failure to comply with such a notice may give rise to penalties, as set out at 7.75 to 7.77. 'Unit holder' is defined in 7.100 (ICTA 1988, s 468(6)). As to the requirement being for such information 'as the Board think(s) necessary', there is no means of appeal against an unreasonable request for information, except perhaps by way of an application for judicial review (see 7.51).

2.246 The provisions described in 2.242 to 2.245 as regards unit trusts were inserted in the legislation by FA 1984, s 40, with effect for acquisitions of units on or after 6 April 1984, to deal with a particular type of savings scheme which it had not previously been appreciated might fall within the compass of the 'growth in value' charge. Typically, such a scheme might involve the purchase of units on behalf of employees by the employer company, which would then reimburse itself by deductions from salary in the same way as it might, with the agreement of the individual concerned, deduct and pay over contributions to a building society or National Savings scheme, or to a staff welfare fund or trade union. The benefit to the employee was normally merely an administrative one, although slightly preferential terms might be negotiated with the managers of a unit trust. The acquisition of the interest in shares represented by the units, however, was made in pursuance of an opportunity offered to the individual concerned 'as an employee' of the company operating the arrangements, and thus fell within the letter, though evidently not the spirit, of the legislation as it then stood.

2.247 Where units are acquired and the exemption is not available, either because the trust is not approved as described at para (a) of 2.242 (or, indeed, is not an 'authorised' unit trust within ICTA 1988, s 468: see 2.244) or because the 10% investment limit described in para (b) of 2.242 is exceeded, so that a 'growth in value' charge under s 138(1)(a) does arise, any reference to 'shares' in relevant provisions of the legislation is construed as a reference to units, and any reference to an 'interest in shares' is ignored (ICTA 1988, s 139(14)). The relevant provisions are s 138(1)(a) & (9) (the calculation of the charge: see 2.190 to 2.204); s 138(8)(a) (additional consideration given after acquisition: see 2.218 and 2.219); s 138(8)(b) (disposal at less than market value under terms of acquisition agreement: see 2.220); CGTA 1979, s 32A(4) (addition of amount chargeable under s 138 to allowable costs for CGT: see 2.295) and ICTA 1988, s 139(4) (disposal not at arm's length, or to connected person, not treated as cessation of beneficial ownership: see 2.300). This provision avoids the agonising over the values of underlying shares and of interests in shares illustrated in 2.195, and the necessity to calculate the growth in value of each underlying shareholding of the trust not only when units are disposed of or held for seven years, but when any shareholding in the trust is disposed of by the managers (and thus an interest in the shares is disposed of by the unit holders).

2.248 While Inland Revenue approval is required for unit trusts to which the exemption applies, no criteria are laid down in the legislation by which the Board of Inland Revenue is to determine whether or not to grant that approval. Although the purpose of the exemption is not specifically mentioned in the legislation, it is clearly designed to remove the 'growth in value' charge in cases where there is a pure 'savings scheme', and no relationship exists between the efforts of the scheme members as employees and the performance of the trust. There is, however, no means of appeal to the Commissioners (see 7.1 to 7.5) against an adverse decision, not even by waiting for an assessment under s 138(1)(a) (or precipitating one, as described in connection with 'old' (FA 1973) profit-sharing schemes at 2.241), as it will be beyond doubt in such an appeal that the unit trust is not approved, irrespective of whether or not it ought to be. An application could perhaps be made for judicial review of the Board's decision, as described at 7.51, if it were felt that the decision was totally unreasonable, or that the Board had misdirected itself in arriving at its determination, but in practice few companies will feel sufficiently strongly to contest the point. The unit trust itself may consider the point more important, particularly if it has grounds to believe that, were approval granted, its units would be widely used in such schemes. The mention of the different attitudes likely to be adopted by the trust and the company highlights the fact that the legislation does not specify who should seek approval, nor any particular procedure, so that presumably it is open to any interested party, even a representative employee, to approach the Inland Revenue.

2.249 Normally, it will not be possible to establish any element of 'incentive' in a unit trust scheme, as there will be no correlation between unit performance and individuals' efforts. One set of circumstances where such a correlation may exist, however, is where directors and employees of a unit trust management company are given the opportunity, by virtue of their employment, to subscribe for units in a fund under the company's control. It is not known what attitude the Inland Revenue might take in such a case, but it is possible that approval might be refused or withdrawn from the trust, with the effect that a scheme of this type could prejudice the availability of the unit trust for use in schemes operated by other, unconnected, companies.

2.250 As stated at 2.246, the exemption for unit trust schemes applies only in the case of acquisitions on or after 6 April 1984, and participants in the schemes which were in existence before that time, and which highlighted the need for corrective legislation to be introduced, are therefore potentially liable to 'growth in value' charges, calculated according to the complex rules mentioned at 2.247 for interests in shares. In practice, however, it is thought that the Inland Revenue has not taken this point.

Previous exemption for shares not subject to special restrictions

2.251 For acquisitions of shares (rather than interests in shares) prior to 23 March 1973, there was an exemption from the 'growth in value' charge if the shares were not subject to any restrictions which did not attach to all shares of the same class, and the majority of shares of that class were acquired otherwise than as mentioned in s 138(1) (ie in pursuance of a right or opportunity conferred on, or offered to, the acquirer as a director or employee of that or any other company, and not in pursuance of an offer to the public: see 2.184 to 2.189). FA 1973, s 19 and Sch 8, para 4(1)(a)(b) limited this relief by substituting two more rigorously drawn exemptions; for 'normal shares' (see 2.252 to 2.260); and for 'employee-controlled companies' (see 2.261 to 2.272), although the latter took effect retrospectively from 6 April 1972.

'Normal shares' exemption

2.252 Exemption from the charge under s 138(1)(a) is provided where the acquisition takes place after 22 March 1973 and is of shares (rather than units in a unit trust or any other interest in shares) which are 'normal shares' (see 2.256) not subject to, or exchangeable for shares subject to (ICTA 1988, s 138(3)(a)(i) & (6)):

(a) restrictions not attaching to all shares of the same class;
(b) restrictions ceasing or liable to cease at some time after the acquisition; or
(c) restrictions depending on the shares being or ceasing to be held by directors or employees of any company (other than restrictions imposed by a company's articles of association which require shares to be disposed of on ceasing to be so held).

Shares are exchangeable for other shares, for this purpose, if they can be exchanged for or converted into the other shares, whether by one transaction or a series of transactions (ICTA 1988, s 138(5)(b)).

2.253 These restrictions are the same as those which crystallise a charge on their removal, as discussed at 2.201 to 2.204, and the same extended definition of 'restriction' set out in 2.205 to 2.217 applies. There is one respect, however, in which the two sets of provisions differ. Shares are not, for the purpose of this exemption, regarded as subject to any restriction by reason only of any 'contract, agreement, arrangement, or condition' providing for the disposal of the shares by an individual when he ceases to hold the office or employment by virtue of which he obtained the right, or was given the opportunity to acquire the shares. This exception applies, however, only where the disposal is to a person nominated in accordance with the contract, agreement, arrangement or condition in question, and the individual is required to dispose of them at a price not exceeding their market value (ICTA 1988, s 139(9)). These provisions cover the case where, for legitimate commercial reasons, a company does not wish an employee or director to retain shares on leaving the company, but the condition that he must sell the shares is not incorporated in the articles of association (see para (c) of 2.252), perhaps because it is not felt necessary or desirable to impose it on all employee/director shareholders. The sale price, as mentioned, must not be above market value. Thus the 'normal shares' exemption is not available where there is a requirement for sale which effectively confers an artificial benefit on the shareholder. In such circumstances, there would also be an income tax charge on a director or higher paid employee under ICTA 1988, s 162(6) (see 2.327 and 2.328).

2.254 It should be noted that, prior to 19 March 1986, the effect of ICTA 1988, s 139(9), as discussed in 2.253, was to create a category of restriction which was not classed as such for the purpose of determining whether the 'normal shares' exemption applied, but which remained a restriction for the purposes of determining whether all restrictions had been lifted so as to crystallise a 'growth in value' charge under s 138(1)(a). Normally the two questions did not have to be considered in conjunction as, if the exemption was available, the question of when the charge was crystallised did not arise. The point could be significant, however, when shares were held by individuals within the charge under s 138(1)(a), and the relevant class of shares was cleared of restrictions with the intention of providing a 'normal shares' exemption for future employee shareholders, and crystallising the charge for existing holders. If a restriction of the kind stipulated in s 139(9) were left attaching to the shares, this would provide an exemption for new holders, but the charge on existing holders would continue to accrue. This point no longer arises, subject to the discussion at 2.190.

2.255 For shares acquired before 26 April 1974, FA 1973, Sch 8, para 7(a) (repealed by FA 1974, s 20(1)(c)) contained a further class of restriction which was not classified as such for the purposes of establishing whether the 'normal shares' exemption applied, but remained a restriction for other purposes. This was (in a case where the shares were acquired at market value: see 7.56 to 7.64) any 'contract, agreement, arrangement or condition' providing for the deposit of the shares with trustees as security for a loan repayable not later than seven years after their acquisition, nor later than the time when the shareholder ceased to hold the office or employment by virtue of which he obtained the right or was given the opportunity to acquire the shares. A deposit as security for a 'non-related' loan would not, in any case, have given rise to a restriction for any purpose (see 2.211 to 2.215), so that this exception in practice applied only to 'related' loans.

2.256 For the 'normal shares' exemption to apply, the shares must, in addition to the absence of restrictions, as discussed in 2.252 to 2.255, meet the test that the majority of the 'available' shares of the same class was acquired otherwise than as mentioned in s 138(1) (ICTA 1988, s 138(3)(a)(i)); that is, otherwise than by virtue of an opportunity offered to the shareholder as employee or director, and not in pursuance of an offer to the public (see 2.184 to 2.189). 'Available' shares for this purpose are those which are not held either by, or for the benefit of, an associated company of the company issuing the shares (ICTA 1988, s 138(5)(a)). For the definition of 'associated company', see 7.10 (ICTA 1988, ss 139(11) and 416). The effect is that, in general, minority holdings of normal shares are not caught by the provisions of s 138(1)(a). If a majority of the shares of any class are held as employee shares, or are held by employees and associated companies (whose voting rights are exercised in practice by directors or senior employees), then the scope for manipulation of share prices is increased, and the exemption is not available.

2.257 Prior to 19 March 1986, bonus or rights issues of shares could be used to ensure that the 'majority test' in 2.256 was satisfied, as such shares were acquired otherwise than as mentioned in s 138(1). Following the amendments made to the legislation in 1986 to prevent 'dilution' of the charge under s 138(1)(a) (see 2.222 to 2.223), bonus or rights issue shares acquired on or after that date are treated as acquired within s 138(1) if the original shares were so acquired, and this avenue of avoidance is therefore blocked (ICTA 1988, s 138(10) & (11)).

2.258 One particular case where the 'normal shares' exemption provides no assistance is where employees or directors obtain shares in an otherwise wholly owned subsidiary company for which they work. They then own *all* the 'available' shares (however small their proportion of the total share capital), and presumably it is considered that the scope for artificial manipulation of the share price is, again, too great. This does, however, prevent what is, in commercial terms, an attractive practice of giving the directors of a subsidiary company the opportunity to acquire shares in the company for which they actually work, and whose results they can affect, rather than shares in a larger and more remote parent company on whose performance their efforts have only an indirect result. The existence of one or more substantial unassociated minority shareholders may make this possible, however, as the directors will then hold a majority of the 'available' shares (even though the available shares may represent a very small proportion of the total share capital).

2.259 The conditions for the 'normal shares' exemption must be satisfied 'immediately after' the acquisition in question (ICTA 1988, s 138(3)(a)). Thus, the imposition of restrictions subsequently will not affect its availability as, far from conferring a benefit on the employee shareholder, this would act to his disadvantage. Similarly, the requirement that the majority of available shares 'was acquired' otherwise than qua employee refers to the acquisitions giving rise to the holdings existing at the time of the relevant acquisition (including that acquisition itself). So, for example, if 'available' shares constituted 40% of the total capital of the class in question (the remaining 60% being held by associated companies), and 25% of the class (5/8 of the available shares) were held by an unrelated party, the remaining 15% of the shares in the class, if acquired by employees, would qualify as normal shares. If the shares of that unconnected party were subsequently made available to employees, by virtue of their employment, then once 5% (or, strictly, 5% less one share) had been sold, on the sale of one more share, 20% of the class (50% of the available shares) would be held as a result of employee opportunities; the majority holding by 'non-employees' would no longer be present, and the sale of that one share, together with any further acquisition by employees of the remaining 20% would be within the scope of the charge under s 138(1)(a). This would not, however, affect the position of the holders of the original 15% of employee shares, or the purchasers of the first 5% of the unconnected party's shares, as the necessary conditions would have been satisfied at the time of their acquisitions. If, by contrast, the legislation provided that exemption was to be withdrawn once the majority of 'non-employee' shareholders was lost, the initially exempt holder would be at constant risk of a change in his position through no action of his own.

2.260 It will be noted that the majority 'non-employee' requirement refers to shares of a particular class. In the majority of cases either a company will have only one class of ordinary shares, or, even if there are other classes, such as fixed dividend preference shares, it will be the ordinary shares with which employees are concerned. Nevertheless, the reference is to the particular class of shares, in order to prevent the creation or adoption of a special class for use in employee schemes, which could be susceptible to manipulation of its value. The corollary is, however, that a class of shares could be created, which would satisfy the majority 'non-employee' test, although it was not met for the share capital as a whole. In such a case, nevertheless, a special benefit could not be given to employees by manipulation of the share value without at the same time giving a greater benefit to independent parties.

'Employee-controlled companies'

2.261 A further major exemption from the 'growth in value' charge is available (with effect from the commencement date of the legislation on 6 April 1972, although not introduced until the following year: FA 1973, Sch 8, para 4(2)) for shares in 'employee-controlled companies' (see 2.262 to 2.271), where, immediately after the acquisition, the shares were not subject to, or exchangeable (as defined in 2.252) for shares subject to the following restrictions (ICTA 1988, s 138(3)(a)(ii) and (6)(a) & (b)):

(a) restrictions not attaching to all shares of the same class; or
(b) restrictions ceasing or liable to cease at some time after the acquisition.

These restrictions are two of the three categories applying in the case of the 'normal shares' exemption (see 2.252). The third category of restriction, that relating to shares being, or ceasing to be, held by directors or employees, is inappropriate in the context of an exemption specifically designed for companies controlled by employees (see 2.262), and which would wish to retain the ability to keep their shares in the hands of employees. It may be noted that, even in the case of the 'normal shares' exemption, this third category of restriction is significantly qualified by the exclusion of certain restrictions appearing in the articles of association (see para (c) of 2.252), and by the provisions of ICTA 1988, s 139(9), discussed at 2.253 and 2.254.

2.262 In addition to the absence of restrictions, to qualify for the 'employee-controlled company' exemption it must be the case that, immediately after the acquisition in question, 'the majority of the available shares (see 2.256) of the same class was acquired by persons who were or had been employees or directors of, or of a body controlled by, [the body in which they were shares], and who were together able as holders of the shares to control that body' (ICTA 1988, s 138(3)(a)(ii)). As with the 'normal shares' exemption, the condition only requires to be satisfied immediately after the acquisition, presumably for the same reasons as discussed at 2.259; that is, that employee shareholders should not be penalised by post-acquisition events over which they have no control. Again, as for the 'normal shares' exemption, the reference is not to a majority of the total share capital, or ordinary share capital, but to a majority of the shares of the relevant class. There will, however, in most cases be only one class of shares, or only one class with significant voting power. The possibility of creating a separate class of shares to meet the 'employee control' test is countered by the fact that the holders of the relevant shares must be able to control not just the class meeting, but the company itself.

2.263 The 'employee shareholders' must be persons who (at the time of the acquisition) 'were or had been' employees or directors. Thus the retirement or resignation of employee shareholders does not disqualify a company from this exemption, although the subsequent sale of the shares, or disposal to non-employees on death, will eventually do so, thus preventing further acquisitions qualifying for relief under these provisions. As a practical matter, therefore, if it is desired to maintain the company as 'employee-controlled' to allow continued employee share acquisitions, it may be advisable to place restrictions on the shares so that they can only be transferred with the approval of the company, perhaps only to existing employees. As mentioned at 2.261, such limitations on transferability would not constitute a proscribed restriction for the purposes of this exemption, although it would be necessary for them to extend to all shares of the same class and not to cease or be liable to cease after the acquisition.

2.264 The term 'employee-controlled' has been adopted here, but this is not a term utilised in the legislation, and has no direct connection with the definition of an 'employee-controlled company' contained in ICTA 1988, s 361(5) for the purpose of regulating the availability of relief for interest paid on a loan taken out to invest in such a company. Inevitably, however, many companies will qualify under both sets of provisions.

2.265 As stated at 2.262, the exemption extends to companies controlled by employees and ex-employees not only of the company itself, but also of any company controlled by it. The requirement is thus, effectively, for control by group employees (or ex-employees), but does not extend to employees of parent or fellow subsidiary companies, as opposed to the company's own subsidiaries, as if the company had either a parent or a fellow subsidiary (which presupposes a common parent), it would in any case be impossible in general for the employees and ex-employees to control it (subject to the matters discussed at 2.267).

2.266 'Control' for the purposes of both the control of the company by the employees, and the control by that company of other companies whose employees may be taken into consideration, is as defined in 7.23 and 7.24 (ICTA 1988, ss 139(11) and 840).

2.267 The legislation refers to 'persons', not 'individuals', who were or had been 'employees or directors' of the relevant company or one controlled by it. Although the intention is generally accepted as being to provide an exemption for companies controlled by individual employees, a company is a legal 'person' and may be a director of another company, for example of its subsidiary; and a company controlled by a corporate director, or by a corporate director together with other individual directors or employees, would apparently be within the scope of this exemption (see *Re Bulawayo Market and Offices Co Ltd* [1907] 2 Ch 458, 76 LJ Ch 673 and CA 1985, s 289(1)(b)). Apart from this somewhat anomalous exception, however, a subsidiary company will, in the normal case, be unable to take advantage of the 'employee-controlled company' exemption, as if it is under the control of another company it cannot also be under the control of its workforce. However, the relevant definition of 'control' (see 7.23 and 7.24) is such that a subsidiary of a parent company controlled by the subsidiary's workforce *could* qualify, as the subsidiary would be controlled indirectly 'by means of the holding of shares or the possession of voting power in or in relation to that *or any other* body corporate'; ie, in this case, the parent (ICTA 1988, s 840(a)). It should be noted, however, that in such a case the shareholders controlling the parent would have to be employees or directors of the subsidiary in which they also had their direct holding of 'employee shares' (or employees or directors of companies controlled by it); to be employees or directors of the parent company would not be sufficient. These circumstances will be rare, and, as for the 'normal shares' exemption, subsidiary companies are, in general, not eligible for relief, because of the ease with which their share prices can be manipulated, or distorted unintentionally, by such means as the payment or withholding of management charges, interest on loans, group relief payments, and intra-group dividends, or by transfer pricing policies for goods or services.

2.268 The requirement that, immediately after the acquisition in question, the majority of the available shares of the same class 'was acquired by persons who were or had been employees or directors' (see 2.262) is strangely worded. At first sight, the phrase 'was held' would seem a more natural expression than 'was acquired'. This would only demand, however, that the majority shareholders were or had at some time been employees, and not that they had acquired their shares at a time when they were employees. There would therefore be a possibility of abuse by simply giving a majority of shareholders a temporary, and brief, part-time employment with the company after they acquired their shares, in order to come within the exception. While it is not absolutely certain that the existing wording excludes this possibility, the most natural reading imposes a requirement that the majority of the available shares 'was acquired by persons who [at the time of their acquisitions, rather than of the acquisition for which the exemption is sought, or at any other time] were or had been employees or directors'. The phrase 'was acquired' directs attention to the situation obtaining at the time of the earlier acquisitions, whereas 'was held' would direct it to the situation at the time of the present acquisition.

2.269 A further question as to timing arises in relation to the requirement that the employee shareholders 'were together' able as holders of the shares to control the company (see 2.262), which could refer to the time of the present acquisition, the times of all previous acquisitions by employee shareholders, or indeed to any time in the past. It is submitted that the first alternative (the time of the present acquisition) represents the most natural reading in the context of the sub-para (ie ICTA 1988, s 138(3)(a)(ii)) as a whole, although the second would have the merit of consistency in that 'were' would refer to the same time as in its previous use in the phrase 'were or had been employees' (assuming the correctness of the analysis at 2.268). The force of this latter argument is, however, diminished by the intervention between these two occurrences of the word of a third, in the phrase 'the body in which they *were* shares' (which appeared in FA 1972, s 79(2)(c)(ii), but became 'that body' on consolidation into ICTA 1988), which is without particular temporal significance; and also by the sheer practical difficulty of meeting the test, and of ascertaining whether or not it had been met, if this interpretation were correct, except in the case where all previous employee shareholdings had been acquired simultaneously.

2.270 Employee shareholders are 'together able' to control the company where, by acting in concert, they could do so. It is not necessary that they should in fact act together according to pre-determined alliances; indeed, they may not even be aware of one another's identities. Nor would the fact that one or more shareholders could be dispensed with without loss of control affect the position. Even the ability of one single 51% employee shareholder to exercise control would not alter the fact that a larger number of employees were 'together able' to do so. A single employee shareholder with a majority of votes, where no other employee shareholders existed, would also appear to meet the requirements for acquisition and control by 'persons' together able to control the company, as the Interpretation Act 1978, s 6 lays down that 'in any Act, unless the contrary intention appears . . . words in the plural include the singular'.

2.271 Control must be exercised by the individuals concerned 'as holders of the shares'; that is, as a result of their shareholding. Control exercised in any other capacity (as trustee for debenture holders on a breach of the conditions of the trust deed, as receiver, or as 'tie breaker' under provisions included in the articles of association) and not as a result of the shareholding, would not be adequate for this purpose. Indeed, the existence of such control would normally preclude employee control within the terms of the exemption.

2.272 It should be noted that both for the 'employee control' exemption and the 'normal shares' exemption discussed in 2.252 to 2.260 the relevant conditions must be satisfied 'immediately after the acquisition', so that the effects of the acquisition itself must be taken into account in determining whether the relevant tests are met. In the case of 'normal shares' an 'employee acquisition' within the terms of s 138(1) is likely, if anything, to prejudice the relief, as it will reduce or eliminate the majority of 'non-employee' shares. In the case of the 'employee-controlled company' exemption, by contrast, it may increase or create the necessary majority of employee shares.

Interaction of the 'normal shares' and 'employee-controlled company' exemptions

2.273 It might seem anomalous that the two major exemptions from the 'growth in value' charge insist on either the absence of a majority employee shareholding (the 'normal shares' exemption), or on its presence (the 'employee-controlled company' exemption), and it would appear, prima facie, that it must, in the nature of the case, be possible to come within one or the other. Indeed, this is true in the great majority of cases. The rationale of the 'normal shares' exemption is that it gives scope for an employee incentive where the existence of the non-employee majority of shareholders provides a safeguard against manipulation. In the alternative case, where the majority of shareholders are also employees, they are (taken together) in a position analogous to that of the company founder, the 'owner-director', who is outside the scope of ICTA 1988, s 138(1) (see 2.45) and who might legitimately expect, like any other trader building up a business, to see the return on his investment, aided by his labours, in the form of a long-term capital gain, rather than as a 'perk' taxable as an emolument of employment.

2.274 In this respect, the 'employee-controlled company' exemption provides, effectively, an extension of the relief for founders of companies which is given implicitly, by the terms of s 138(1) (see 2.45). Using the exemption, founders may take further individuals into 'quasi-partnership', often by the subscription for shares at full value, without the new shareholders being subject to the penalty of income tax on gains (realised or unrealised) which would be subject to CGT in the hands of the original subscribers only on a disposal. In effect, therefore, the founders' shares 'exemption' may be available on an influx of additional capital for a 'fresh start' or a programme of expansion by the company, notwithstanding the fact that the individual concerned was not involved in the company from its foundation.

2.275 Despite the fairly comprehensive coverage of the 'normal shares' and 'employee-controlled company' exemptions taken in conjunction, one category of company in which the issue of shares is normally prevented from obtaining any relief is the otherwise wholly-owned subsidiary, for the reasons given at 2.258 and 2.267. While the use of subsidiaries may be severely restricted, however, many other categories of company subject to considerable restraints in other tax contexts are able to take advantage of these two main exemptions, such as non-UK resident companies, companies incorporated overseas, investment and other non-trading companies, and close companies (see 7.12 to 7.21). In the nature of the case, neither the 'growth in value' charge nor the exemptions can have any relevance to a company limited by guarantee (unless it also has a share capital), but the charge may apply equally to limited and unlimited companies. Similarly, no distinction is drawn between shares quoted on a stock exchange in the UK or overseas, and unquoted shares.

Avoiding the 'growth in value' charge

General

2.276 As stated at 2.273, the 'normal shares' and 'employee-controlled company' exemptions will cover most cases where shares are made available to employees, and the majority of problems arise with subsidiaries, for example, where it is desired to give a director a stake in such a company. Other problems in coming within either of the two major exemptions may arise from the placing of restrictions on the shares which are within the categories discussed at 2.252 to 2.254 and 2.261, but which are considered desirable or indispensable for commercial or personal reasons. In practice, however, restrictions which cause the exemptions to be unavailable were often imposed in ignorance of their tax effects, and could well have been dispensed with had their full impact been appreciated.

The service company

2.277 In some cases, both the 'growth in value' charge under s 138(1)(a) and the 'special benefits' charge under s 138(1)(b) could be avoided by the incorporation of a new company, to supply services to the 'employer' company, and to hold 'employee shares' in it. If that company was used simply as a conduit, receiving fees from the 'employer' company and paying them out as remuneration, its shares would grow in value only to the extent of the increase in the value of the 'employer' company shares which it held. The shareholder/directors of the service company would not be within the charge to tax under s 138 in respect of their shares in that company, which they held as founders (see 2.45). They could not, however, remain as employees or directors of the 'employer' company, or the arrangement would be caught by the provisions discussed at 2.296 to 2.299 governing the issue of shares to a person (i e, in this case, the service company) connected with an employee. It is not thought that those provisions would catch the issue of shares in the 'employer' company to a person (the service company) connected with employees of another body corporate (again, the service company), because such an issue would not be 'by reason of' that employment, but rather by reason of the contractual arrangements between the service company and the 'employer' company. The point is not totally free from doubt, however. The 'service company route', even if successfully followed, leaves the employees open to a potential double charge on capital gains; first, on the sale of 'employer' company shares by the service company, and subsequently on their own sale of service company shares.

2.278 If the individuals themselves were issued with shares in the 'employer' company, directly rather than through the medium of a service company, then even though they are not employees of the first company, they would normally be within the scope of s 138(1), having received those shares as directors or employees of that 'or any other' body corporate (in this case as employees of the service company).

2.279 Almost any tax avoidance device must now be considered in the light of the 'emerging (anti-avoidance) principle' of *WT Ramsay Ltd v IRC* and *Furniss v Dawson*, discussed at 7.79 to 7.82. Although the service company route is by no means self-evidently within the purlieu of these decisions, the Inland Revenue is known to have argued in negotiation that in certain circumstances, involving 'one-man' service companies, PAYE procedures should be employed, as if fees paid to the company had in fact been paid to the proprietor as an individual, the payments to and from the service company being ignored as steps introduced into the transactions with no commercial purpose. While this argument has not reached the courts, or even, so far as is known, the Appeal Commissioners (and may well never do so), the possibility of its use to 'pierce the corporate veil' in any attempt to circumvent the charge under s 138 should not be overlooked. (See also comments of Lord Denning MR in *Wallersteiner v Moir* [1974] 3 All ER 217, [1974] WLR 991 at 1013.)

Artificial restrictions

2.280 A further route to avoid the 'growth in value' charge (though not the 'special benefits' charge) was available prior to 19 March 1986. This involved imposing trivial restrictions on employee shares, which either did not extend to all the shares of the same class (see para (a) of 2.201), or which ceased, or were liable to cease, after the lapse of a short period of time (see para (b) of 2.201). An example might be the inability (not extending to all shares of the same class) to vote on certain issues where the votes of a few shareholders were in any case unlikely to affect the outcome, such as the approval of the accounts or the reappointment of the auditors; or an inability to vote or to transfer shares for a short period such as a month. The removal of these restrictions, by expiry of a set time limit, or by action of the company, would crystallise a charge under s 138(1)(a) & (9)(c) ('removal of restrictions': see para (c) of 2.190) at a time when the growth in value was negligible. As the charge arises at the expiry of a 'period ending at the *earliest* of' seven years, disposal or removal of restrictions (ICTA 1988, s 138(9)) no further charge could arise on sale or on the expiry of seven years, and the tax cost, if any, was minimal. Again, there was a risk that this might be seen as a 'predetermined series of transactions' within the *Ramsay* doctrine, so that the imposition and removal of the restrictions would be ignored, and the charge would crystallise only on the earlier of sale or the expiry of seven years. It is suggested that the risk of the invocation of the *Ramsay* principle here was greater than in the case of an interposed service company, as discussed at 2.277 to 2.279. If the manoeuvre was attempted (and there was normally nothing to lose by so doing if the shares were to be acquired in any case) it was important to ensure that *all* restrictions were lifted, so that the shares ceased altogether to be subject to restrictions within the relevant categories. It achieved nothing to impose and remove trivial restrictions if other relevant restrictions remained. This device ceased to be effective from 19 March 1986 when, as explained at 2.190, it became necessary not only to lift the restrictions, but also to meet the 'normal shares' or the 'employee control' test which, if met initially, would have meant that the shares were outside the ambit of the growth in value charge.

Bonus shares

2.281 A further means of reducing both the 'growth in value' and the 'special benefits' charges, prior to 19 March 1986, was to 'flood' the existing shareholding with a bonus issue; the total holding would remain at the same value, but the value of the original shares was reduced. The bonus shares had been acquired by the individual concerned as a result of his status as an existing shareholder, rather than as an employee, and the additional shares were outside the scope of s 138(1), and would thus escape the charges under s 138(1)(a) and s 138(1)(b). It was, of course, necessary for the company to have sufficient reserves to make the bonus issue, but unless its reserves were so small as to make the use of the procedure an unwarranted administrative expense, they would always enable the charge to be reduced to some extent. If there were no reserves, there was unlikely to be any growth in value. This manoeuvre could never in theory eliminate the charge entirely, but in practice it could reduce it to the level where it would be disregarded on de minimis grounds, as illustrated below.

> Cole Ltd issues 100 £1 shares each to certain of its employees in 1978 as a result of their employment, at their then market (and par) value of £1 per share. In 1985, shortly before the expiry of the seven-year period at the end of which a 'growth in value' charge will arise on those employees still retaining their shares, their value has risen to £8, and the company's reserves amount to £9 per share. In the absence of a bonus issue, a 'growth in value' charge of £7 per share (ie £8–£1) will arise, giving a total amount chargeable of £700 on a holding of 100 shares. If all the reserves are capitalised, the shareholders will receive nine £1 shares for each one held. The value of each share held subsequent to this issue will be £0.80 (£8 ÷ 10). Where 100 shares were held originally, 1,000 will now be held. The 'growth in value' charge will, however, only apply to 100 of these, at an adjusted cost of £0.10. The charge will therefore be:

Market value after seven years:	
100 × £0.80	£ 80
Market value on acquisition (as adjusted):	
100 × £0.10	(10)
Amount chargeable under FA 1972, s 79(4) (now ICTA 1988, s 138(1)(a))	£ 70

> ie, 1/10 of the charge in the absence of the bonus issue.

2.282 The legislation made no specific provisions for the apportionment of the cost between the original and the bonus shares in these circumstances, such as is contained, for CGT purposes, in CGTA 1979, Pt IV, Ch II. It is considered, however, that this follows from general principles, in that the shareholder's rights in the company are neither disposed of nor added to by the bonus issue, but simply recategorised, and that there can be no dispute as to how the original cost is to be allocated between the original and new shares, as these all rank pari passu.

2.283 If there were insufficient reserves to finance a bonus issue, a similar, but more limited, dilution of the charge could be achieved by means of a rights issue.

2.284 The Inland Revenue could have argued that the new shares were acquired 'as employee', being derived, albeit indirectly, from the opportunity originally offered to the employee to purchase shares in that capacity. The longer the interval between the original acquisition and the bonus issue the less persuasive this argument became. The effluxion of time also enabled more reserves to be built up, to dilute the original holding as much as possible. In addition, against the contention that the bonus shares were acquired 'as employee' it could be argued that other, non-employee, shareholders were also receiving the same benefit (or having their holding subjected to the same reorganisation), and it could not be that this happened to some shareholders for one reason and to the remainder for other reasons. For bonus and rights issues occuring after 18 March 1986, however, see 2.222.

2.285 Again, this manoeuvre could have been open to attack under *Ramsay*, and much would have turned in that case on whether the bonus or rights issue was undertaken for purely fiscal reasons, or whether there was also an underlying commercial motive. Such a motive would have been easier to establish in the case of a rights issue, where the main reason for which it was undertaken would normally have been the acquisition of additional capital for the company, and would have been more difficult to establish for a bonus issue, where the company's financial position was unaffected, and any 'commercial' changes were merely cosmetic, or undertaken for reasons of administrative convenience, to encourage dealings in smaller numbers of shares.

Management buy-outs

2.286 Section 138, and in particular the growth in value charge, could give rise to problems in the context of management buy-outs, where shares in the 'target company' were acquired by the buy-out team as part of new financing arrangements, but the offer was only made to them because of their special position as employees, bringing them firmly within s 138(1) ('acquisition as employee': see 2.184 to 2.189). The solution was often to form a new holding company, of which they were founders, to acquire the shares in the target company. If required, the trade could then be transferred to the holding company with the benefit of any losses brought forward, and the holding company could take over the existing company's capital allowance position, under ICTA 1988, s 343 ('company reconstructions without change of ownership').

THE 'OLD' SPECIAL BENEFITS CHARGE: ICTA 1988, s 138(1)(b) (formerly FA 1972, s 79(7))

Persons chargeable

2.287 The 'special benefits' charge under ICTA 1988, s 138(1)(b), like the 'growth in value' charge under s 138(1)(a) (see 2.190 to 2.286) applies where a person, on or after 6 April 1972, acquires shares or an interest in shares (see 2.184) in a body corporate, in pursuance of a right conferred on him or opportunity offered to him (see 2.184 to 2.189) as a director or employee (or prospective director or employee: see 2.184) of that or any other body corporate (for example, as employee of a subsidiary) and not in pursuance of an offer to the public: see *Cheatle v IRC* at 2.46 (ICTA 1988, s 138(1)). Shares acquired under a bonus or rights issue, or on a takeover or other reorganisation of share capital, are treated as acquired by virtue of a directorship or employment if the original shares were so acquired, under the rules discussed at 2.222 to 2.227.

2.288 The charge arises where a person who has acquired shares or an interest in shares as set out in 2.287 receives, by virtue of his ownership of or interest in the shares, any benefit not received by the majority of persons (individuals or others) who hold shares forming part of the ordinary share capital of the same company, and who have acquired the shares otherwise than as set out in s 138(1), ie otherwise than by virtue of employment and not in pursuance of an offer to the public (ICTA 1988, s 138(1)(b)). 'Ordinary share capital' is defined in 7.72 (ICTA 1988, ss 831(2) and 832(1)) and, as will be seen there, may include certain shares with restricted rights, by whatever name they are called. It will be noted that, unlike the provisions relating to the 'growth in value' charge discussed at 2.256 and 2.262, the reference here is not to the particular class of shares but to the whole of the ordinary share capital. Where this includes, for example, non-voting participating preference shares, it is quite possible for holders of these shares to form a majority of the holders of 'ordinary share capital' (excluding employee shareholders), outnumbering those with normal ordinary shares, so that *any* benefit received by a normal ordinary shareholder who acquired that holding by virtue of his employment will be within the charge, even though it is made available to all shareholders of the same class. The reference is to the majority of *persons*, not of shares, so that a charge will still arise if a majority of 'non-employee' shares qualifies for the benefit, but not a majority of non-employee shareholders. Thus, any attempt to exclude the charge by giving the benefit, for example, to employee shareholders and to the parent company would not have the desired effect because, even though holding 51% or more of the shares, the parent would count as only one shareholder. It should be noted also that the employee shareholders themselves are not taken into the calculation; the majority must be found among the remaining members of the company, so that the calculation is not distorted by the multiplicity of small employee holdings.

Benefits chargeable

2.289 Benefits within s 138(1)(b) might include 'gifts' of the company's products, or any other goods or services which as 'shareholder perks' would not normally be taxable. The intention is to prevent the provision to individuals, as shareholders, of benefits which would be taxable as emoluments if they were received by them as employees. To a large extent, however, the legislation has been overtaken by the benefits in kind provisions of ICTA 1988, ss 153 to 168, introduced in 1976, which apply to directors and 'higher paid employees' (see 7.41 to 7.44: broadly, those earning £8,500 pa or more), and which lay down that any benefit provided to such an individual by a corporate employer is deemed to be paid by reason of the employment (ICTA 1988, s 168(3)), irrespective of the actual motive or the manner in which it is given, and is taxable accordingly.

2.290 Section 138(1)(b) applies only where the benefit is not otherwise chargeable to tax, for example as a dividend or other distribution, or under the benefits in kind provisions of ICTA 1988, ss 153 to 168, as discussed at 2.289. The charge is made under the appropriate case of Schedule E (see 7.88 to 7.96) for the year in which the benefit is received, and on an amount equal to the 'value of the benefit'. This wording suggests that it is the value to the recipient rather than the cost to the company which must be considered. The amount so charged is treated as earned income whether or not it would otherwise fall to be treated as such (for the significance of which, see 2.199).

Exclusions

2.291 The charge is excluded if the shares in respect of which the benefit arose were acquired under a profit-sharing scheme by virtue of which employees received shares or an interest in shares as part of their emoluments to an extent determined in advance by reference to profits (ICTA 1988, s 138(2) & (4)). Such schemes are discussed in greater detail in the context of the 'growth in value' charge at 2.232 to 2.241, and the commencement date for the application of the more stringent rules of ICTA 1988, s 138(4), as mentioned at 2.234, applies equally to the 'special benefits' charge.

2.292 As discussed at 2.229 to 2.231, an exemption from the 'growth in value' charge for employee 'discount offers' made in conjunction with an offer to the public is contained in ICTA 1988, s 139(1). This takes the form of an exclusion from s 138(1) ('acquisition as employee etc': see 2.184 to 2.189) by treating the shares as acquired under a public offer, rather than of a specific exemption from the 'growth in value' charge under s 138(1)(a), with the result that it applies equally to the 'special benefits' charge under s 138(1)(b).

2.293 Various means of avoiding the 'growth in value' charge are discussed at 2.276 to 2.286, and two of these had the same effect as regards the 'special benefits' charge, although it was rarely worthwhile to undertake the necessary arrangements for that reason alone. The relevant manoeuvres were the interposition of a service company between the employee and the 'employer' company (see 2.277 to 2.279) and the 'flooding' of the existing shares with a bonus or rights issue (see 2.281 to 2.286).

2.294 It should be noted that the 'special benefits' charge does not come to an end with the expiry of seven years or the lifting of restrictions on the shares, even though these may crystallise a 'growth in value' charge (see 2.190). The liability to the charge expires only with the disposal of the shares.

THE 'OLD' GROWTH IN VALUE AND SPECIAL BENEFITS CHARGES: SUPPLEMENTARY PROVISIONS

Capital gains tax considerations

2.295 Any amount chargeable under the 'growth in value' or 'special benefits' provisions of ICTA 1988, s 138(1)(a) & (b) (see 2.190 to 2.286 and 2.287 to 2.294) is treated, on the first disposal thereafter, as if it had formed part of the consideration given by the person making the disposal for his acquisition of the shares, thus reducing the gain chargeable to CGT (or increasing any loss). It is therefore eligible for indexation allowance calculated from the time of acquisition, or from March 1982, if later (CGTA 1979, s 32A(1) & (4)). Where, however, the charge is on an individual who owns, not shares, but an interest in shares, no allowance is made for any charges under s 138 in calculating the gain on a disposal of that interest (for example the sale of an interest in a trust). The allowance is given only on the disposal of the shares themselves, but is given even where the person subject to the s 138 charge (because of his interest in the shares, or under the provisions relating to connected persons discussed at 2.296 to 2.300) is not the same as the person (for example, the trustee) actually making the eventual disposal.

Acquisitions by persons connected with employees or directors

2.296 Where a person (either an individual or a company) acquires shares or an interest in shares in a company in pursuance of a right conferred on him, or opportunity offered to him, as a person 'connected' with a director or employee of that or any other company, the shares are deemed to be acquired by the director or employee concerned (ICTA 1988, s 139(3)), with the effect that any 'growth in value' or 'special benefits' charge (see 2.190 to 2.286 and 2.287 to 2.294) is made on the director or employee, despite the fact that the advantage being taxed has accrued in the hands of, or been received by, the connected person.

2.297 'Connected person' is defined in 7.22 (ICTA 1988, ss 140(2) and 839). The effect of this provision is to prevent the s 138 charges being circumvented by the issue of shares, for example, to the spouses of employees, or to companies owned by them, rather than to the employees themselves.

2.298 The anomalies which may arise when one person is taxed on a benefit accruing to another are self-evident, but in practice if that other person is acting independently of the employee or director, and is retaining the benefit without his consent, there may be a strong argument that the acquisition was not made by virtue of the latter's employment. This will not cover all 'hard cases', however, particularly where personal relationships change, for example on marital breakdown. In the case of divorce, an ex-spouse will no longer be a 'connected person'. The legislation, however, only addresses itself to whether there is a connection at the time of the acquisition and whether that is the motive for the acquisition, so that any growth in value arising on shares owned by the spouse, after the date of divorce and up to the time when the charge crystallises, will still be taxable on the employee. Problems are rare in practice, however, as, precisely because of the existence of s 139(3), it is only rarely that shares provided by virtue of the employment are made available to a connected person rather than to the employee himself.

2.299 The CGT provisions set out at 2.295 apply in such cases, so as to permit the deduction of any amount charged to tax under s 138 in the calculation of the CGT liability (of the connected person) on a disposal of the shares (ICTA 1988, s 139(3)).

Disposals to connected persons

2.300 A disposal of shares or an interest in shares which is made to a connected person (see 7.22: ICTA 1988, ss 140(2) and 839), irrespective of whether it is at arm's length, or a non-arm's length disposal to any other person, will result in the original owner being deemed not to cease to have a beneficial interest in the shares (ICTA 1988, s 139(4)). The result is that, as with shares originally acquired by a connected person (see 2.296 to 2.299), any 'growth in value' or 'special benefits' charge under ICTA 1988, s 138 will still arise on the employee, and such a 'disposal' cannot be utilised to crystallise a 'growth in value' charge while still, for example, retaining the shares in the family. This provision does not, however, prevent a disposal arising for CGT purposes (although if it is an inter-spouse transfer, no gain or loss will arise: CGTA 1979, s 44) and any charge under s 138 which has arisen before such a disposal of shares will still add to the allowable acquisition costs for capital gains purposes (see 2.295).

Information provisions

2.301 Where an acquisition of shares or of an interest in shares is made which is within s 138(1) ('acquisition by virtue of employment': see 2.184 to 2.189), the company from which the shares are, or interest is, acquired (which may or may not be the employing company) must deliver to the Inspector of Taxes within 30 days of the end of the year of assessment written particulars of the shares and of the acquisition (ICTA 1988, s 139(5)) with penalties being incurred for any failure (TMA 1970, s 98: see 7.75 to 7.77). Particulars must still be delivered even if no charge actually arises due to the exemption for 'discount offers' in conjunction with public offers provided by ICTA 1988, s 139(1) & (2): see 2.229 to 2.231 (ICTA 1988, s 139(5)). Where the shares are provided by an individual, such as a majority shareholder, rather than by a company, it would appear that the requirements for the furnishing of information do not apply.

Exclusions of ICTA 1988, s 138(1)(a) charge for approved schemes

2.302 No 'growth in value' charge under s 138(1)(a) arises in respect of shares the beneficial interest in which is acquired under an Inland Revenue approved 'profit-sharing' scheme (ICTA 1988, s 186(2)(b): see 4.7); an approved savings-related option scheme; or an approved selective share option scheme (provided certain additional conditions beyond the mere approval of the scheme are satisfied) (ICTA 1988, s 185(3)(a): see 5.9 and 6.11). Shares acquired under any such scheme may, however, still give rise to a 'special benefits' charge under s 138(1)(b).

THE 'NOTIONAL LOAN' CHARGE: ICTA 1988, s 162

General

Persons within the charge

2.303 The 'notional loan' provisions of ICTA 1988, s 162 apply where after 5 April 1976 a person employed or about to be employed in director's or higher paid employment, or a person connected with him, acquires shares in a company (whether the employing company or not), and the shares are acquired at an undervalue in pursuance of a right or opportunity available by reason of the employment (ICTA 1988, s 162(1)). The inclusion of persons 'about to be employed' prevents avoidance of the section by persons entering into the relevant arrangements either before employment is taken up, or during a temporary, and perhaps artificially contrived, interruption in employment. A 'director' is specifically defined for the purposes of these provisions (ICTA 1988, s 168(8): see 7.31 to 7.37), but the term 'director's or higher paid employment' is also separately defined (ICTA 1988, s 167: see 7.41 to 7.44) so as to exclude certain directors with no 'material interest' in the company (ICTA 1988, s 168(11): see 7.65 to 7.71) who are either 'full-time working directors' (ICTA 1988, s 168(10): see 7.47) or directors of a non-profit making or charitable concerns.

2.304 The provisions extend also to acquisitions by persons connected with such directors or employees (ICTA 1988, ss 162(1)(a) & (11) and 839: see 7.22), which may include a company. The section applies whether the shares in question are in the employing company or in another company. Most often, such another company will be the parent of the employer, or another company in the same group, but this need not necessarily be so; for example, the employer company may sell off to employees on advantageous terms a holding which it has built up in a completely separate company, and no longer requires. 'Shares' are defined to include stock and securities within 7.97 (ICTA 1988, ss 163(10)(a) and 254(1)) and the provisions of the section apply mutatis mutandis to an interest in shares, other than a share option (ICTA 1988, s 162(9): see 2.330).

'At an undervalue'

2.305 The acquisition of shares 'at an undervalue' means that they are acquired either without payment for them *at the time of acquisition*, or for an amount then paid which is less than the market value of fully paid-up shares of that class (in either case whether with or without obligation to make payment or further payment at some later time) (ICTA 1988, s 162(2)). 'Market value' is defined in 7.56 to 7.64 (ICTA 1988, s 162(10)(d); CGTA 1979, s 150). This wording covers both an acquisition at a permanent discount, and the issue of shares part paid, but at the full value. The undertaking and acknowledgement of indebtedness, or the promise to pay in the future, evidenced for example by a promissory note, does not amount to payment for this purpose (see *Income Tax Commissioner for Bihar and Orissa v Maharajadhiraja of Dharbanga* (1933) 60 IA 146). 'Acquisition', in relation to shares, includes receipt by way of allotment or assignment, 'or otherwise howsoever' (ICTA 1988, s 162(10)(d)) and any reference in the section to payment for shares includes giving any consideration in money or 'money's worth' (as to which see *Weight v Salmon* and *Tennant v Smith* at 2.13 to 2.24), or making any subscription, whether in pursuance of a legal liability or not (ICTA 1988, s 162(10)(c)).

'By reason of employment'

2.306 For s 162 to apply, the acquisition must be made 'in pursuance of a right or opportunity available by reason of [the individual's] employment'. In contrast to the similar tests under ICTA 1988, s 138(1) and FA 1988, s 77, however, (see 2.184 to 2.189 and 2.36 to 2.49) there is no exclusion where, as a matter of fact, the motive underlying the transaction is unrelated to the employment. All provision made for an employee, or for members of his family or household, by his employer is deemed, where that employer is a company, to be made by reason of the employment (ICTA 1988, s 168(3)). This 'deemed motive' does not extend automatically to any provision made to connected persons other than the employee's family or household, although in many cases the provision will, as a matter of fact, still be made by reason of the employment, and thus come within the scope of the section. 'Employment' is defined for these purposes as an office or employment whose emoluments fall to be assessed under Schedule E (see 7.88 to 7.96) (ICTA 1988, s 168(2)), and a person's family or household includes his spouse, his children and their spouses, his parents, and his dependants and guests (ICTA 1988, s 168(4)). These last two categories may of course include more remote relatives.

2.307 Where there is an acquisition of shares at an undervalue in the circumstances detailed above, the employee is treated as having the benefit of a notional interest-free loan obtained by reason of his employment (ICTA 1988, s 162(1)). As in the case of a benefit to a connected person under ICTA 1988, s 138 (see 2.296 to 2.299), where the acquisition is by a connected person it is still the employee himself who is treated as having the benefit (in this case the notional loan, which gives rise to a charge to tax on the notional interest saved under the beneficial loan provisions of ICTA 1988, ss 160 and 161 and Sch 7: see 2.317 to 2.326).

The amount of the notional loan

2.308 The amount of the notional loan initially treated as outstanding is the undervalue at which the shares are acquired (see 2.305), after deducting any part chargeable as an emolument under other provisions (ICTA 1988, s 162(3)). As the issue of shares at a permanent discount gives rise to an emolument taxable as 'money's worth' under ICTA 1988, s 19 (see *Weight v Salmon* at 2.13 to 2.24), or to a charge under ICTA 1988, s 135 where the issue is in pursuance of an option (see Chapter 3) the effect is that, in general, s 162 catches only the issue of shares part paid, or on deferred payment terms. There may perhaps be rare cases, for example where shares are made available by a major shareholder rather than by the company itself, where the acquisition is 'in pursuance of a right or opportunity available by reason of [the] employment' within s 162(1), but the benefit does not proceed from the employment with sufficient directness to constitute an 'emolument therefrom' within the terms of ICTA 1988, s 19. In addition, the section applies where shares are issued under an option granted to an indvidual not within Schedule E Case I at the time of the grant, and thus not within the charge under ICTA 1988, s 135 on its exercise (see 3.12).

2.309 Any payments or further payments for the shares made after the initial acquisition reduce the amount of the notional loan outstanding (ICTA 1988, s 162(3)(b)). This covers the discharge of outstanding instalments in accordance with a predetermined schedule; ad hoc payments where, for example, the agreement with the company is merely to pay off the balance on or before a certain date; and even completely voluntary payments, although in this last case there may be some difficulty in establishing that the payment is indeed made 'for the shares', and not motivated by some other consideration.

The termination of the loan

2.310 The notional loan terminates:

(a) when the whole amount outstanding is made good by payments or further payments as described in 2.309 (ICTA 1988, s 162(3)(a) and (4)(a)); or
(b) in a case where the shares were not fully paid up on acquisition, when any outstanding or contingent obligation to pay for them is released,

transferred, or adjusted so as no longer to bind the employee or any person connected with him (ICTA 1988, s 162(3)(a) and (4)(b)). A contingent obligation might involve, for example, a requirement to pay the balance outstanding on the shares only if the individual left the employment of the company concerned, or if he did so within a specified period. In the latter case the notional loan would terminate automatically with the end of that period, without any further action by the company or the individual. A transfer of the obligation to pay is unlikely, except in the context of a disposal of the shares (as to which see (c) below), but it might arise, for example, where the company wished to release the obligation and make the shares fully paid up, but had insufficient reserves to do so, so that the obligation was transferred, by consent, to its parent company. 'Adjustment' of the amount outstanding, so as to eliminate it, might arise where the amount to be paid by instalments after acquisition was determined by a formula related to the company's results and this formula was modified in the light of events. In such a case, of course, practical difficulties would arise initially in quantifying the amount of the notional loan. The release, transfer or adjustment must be such as no longer to bind the employee or any person connected with him. The effect is that the notional loan cannot be brought to an end by a transfer of the obligation to a connected person, or (if the original acquisition was by a connected person as discussed at 2.304) by its transfer to the employee or to any other person connected with him. If the initial acquisition was by a connected person, the loan will, however, be brought to an end by a transfer to a person connected with the original acquirer, unless that person is also connected with the employee. While the charge to tax on the benefit of the notional interest foregone by the company on the loan comes to an end with the cessation of the loan, a further charge arises on the write-off of the loan itself (see 2.311 to 2.316); or

(c) on the disposal of the shares 'by surrender or otherwise' (for example by sale, gift, or forfeiture on bankruptcy) so that neither the employee nor any person connected with him retains any beneficial interest in them (ICTA 1988, s 162(3)(a) and (4)(c)). The same considerations as to disposals to connected persons apply as in para (b) above and, again, a charge will arise on the notional write-off of the loan (see 2.311 to 2.316); or

(d) on the death of the employee (ICTA 1988, s 162(3)(a) and (4)(d)). It should be noted that where the acquisition was by a connected person as discussed at 2.304 and 2.307, the death of that person does not of itself bring the notional loan to an end, provided the employee survives, although the death may have the effect of transferring beneficial ownership to an unconnected person within para (c) above. *Per contra*, the death of the employee brings the loan to an end even though the shares may have been acquired by, and continue to be owned by, a connected person.

The charge on the write-off of the notional loan

The charge

2.311 As noted in paras (b) and (c) of 2.310, the termination of the loan by release, transfer, or adjustment of the obligation to pay the amount outstanding, or by sale or other disposal of the shares (that is, its termination in any way other than by full payment or on death) gives rise to an income tax charge under the appropriate case of Schedule E (see 7.88 to 7.96) for the year in which the termination occurs, on the amount then outstanding, and written off or deemed to be written off (ICTA 1988, ss 162(5) and 160(2)). This charge does not apply where the amount so written off is already chargeable to income tax under other provisions (ICTA 1988, s 161(5)): the waiver of an amount due to the employer company will normally constitute 'money's worth' chargeable to tax as an emolument in any case, but this will not be so on a disposal of the shares or (necessarily) on a transfer of the obligation, hence the necessity for special provisions. In addition, the charging provisions of ICTA 1988, ss 162(5) and 160(2) are not excluded where the prior charge to tax arises only by virtue of ICTA 1988, s 148 (which taxes lump sum payments in money or money's worth on retirement or removal from employment) or under ICTA 1988, s 677 (which deals, broadly, with capital sums paid to a settlor by a settlement, out of income, and includes payments made via related companies: see 7.98 to 7.99 (ICTA 1988, s 161(5)).

Transactions to be avoided

2.312 The equity of the write-off charge where the obligation to pay the amount outstanding on the shares is released is obvious. Similarly, where the obligation is tranferred, there is an obvious benefit to the employee (although no loss to the company), and such arrangements, as mentioned at para (b) of 2.310, will often involve situations where the cost of the benefit is borne by the employing group, though not by the particular company concerned. A transfer may, however, involve a payment by the employee to an independent party in consideration of his undertaking the obligation, and no allowance will be given for such a payment in calculating the 'write-off' charge, so that it will normally be unwise to enter into arrangements of this nature. The consideration must be paid directly to the company if any relief is to be available (by means of a reduction or elimination of the notional loan without a 'write-off' charge, as described in para (a) of 2.310). The company may, however, be unwilling to accept payment in advance of scheduled instalment dates, depending on the particular circumstances of the case.

2.313 A sale of shares part paid (and at a price which takes into account that fact), or a surrender of the shares for no consideration, may also produce a totally inequitable charge, as illustrated by the following example.

> Fairfax acquires 100 shares in his employer company, Wingfield Ltd, as a result of his employment, for their full market value of £6 each, but under terms whereby he will pay £1 per year for six years. After the initial payment of £100, a charge to tax on the notional interest saved arises on the outstanding 'loan' of £500 (100 × £5), and a reduced charge after the second instalment is paid and the 'loan' decreases to £400. After the payment of the second instalment Fairfax sells the shares, part paid, for £2.20, a price which takes into account the fact that further instalments are due, but not for some time. His profit on the sale of the shares (disregarding the cost of the notional interest charge) is:

Sale proceeds:	
100 × £2.20	£ 220
Cost:	
100 × £2	(200)
	£ 20

He is, however, charged to income tax on a write-off of the amount outstanding at the time of sale, viz £400 (100 × £4).

2.314 A manoeuvre such as that illustrated in 2.313, or a surrender of shares for no consideration (perhaps because the employee cannot afford the further instalments, or no longer regards the shares as representing a good investment) should be avoided wherever possible, for example by the taking out of an independent loan to finance the outstanding instalments. However the various factors involved, such as the size of the potential tax charge, the cost of the loan and the eventual value of the shares will have to be carefully weighed.

Capital gains tax considerations

2.315 When a charge arises on the write-off of the notional loan, under ICTA 1988, s 162(5), as a result of a disposal of the shares or interest in shares (as distinct from a release or transfer of the obligation to make further payments), the amount chargeable to tax is treated for CGT purposes as additional expenditure given for the acquisition of the shares or interest in shares (CGTA 1979, s 32A(1) and (2)(a)), and (as it is treated as part of the original acquisition cost, rather than as enhancement expenditure), indexation allowance thereon is calculated from the time of acquisition (or March 1982), whichever is earlier, rather than from the time of the Schedule E charge—which in practice would mean that no indexation allowance was available.

2.316 If the write-off charge arises otherwise than on a disposal, for example on a release of the remaining calls, the amount charged under Schedule E is added to the cost for CGT purposes on the first subsequent disposal (CGTA 1979, s 32A(1) and (2)(b)). Again, the indexation runs from first acquisition (if after March 1982) and, in both cases, if the acquisition was made by a connected person, that person obtains the benefit of the capital gains tax allowance, notwithstanding the Schedule E charge was suffered by the employee.

The interest charge on the beneficial loan

General

2.317 Where there is a loan from the employer to the employee, and either:

(a) no interest is paid on the loan in respect of the year of assessment during which (or part of which) it is outstanding; or
(b) the amount of interest paid on it for the year is less than interest at the 'official rate' (see 2.318),

then the 'cash equivalent' of the benefit thereby conferred is treated as an emolument of the employment chargeable to tax under Schedule E (ICTA 1988, s 160(1)). A notional loan under ICTA 1988, s 162 in respect of the acquisition of shares, or an interest in shares, at an undervalue is always treated as interest-free for this purpose, even if interest is in fact paid on the amount outstanding (ICTA 1988, s 162(1)). If payment of interest on the outstanding balance of the purchase price is contemplated, therefore, it may be advisable for the employee to take out a separate 'real' loan from the employer, the tax charge on which will be reduced or eliminated by the payment of interest, and to use the funds borrowed to purchase the shares on immediate payment terms.

The official rate

2.318 The 'official rate' is prescribed from time to time by the Treasury under statutory instrument (ICTA 1988, s 160(5)(d)). Although the interest charge under s 160(1) applies to any acquisition of shares at an undervalue after 6 April 1976, that charge itself did not take effect until the year of assessment 1978/79. For the period from 6 April 1978 to 5 May 1980, the official rate was set at 9% by the Income Tax (Official Rate of Interest on Beneficial Loans) Order 1978 (SI 1978/28); from 6 May 1980 to 5 October 1982 at 15% by the Income Tax (Official Rate of Interest on Beneficial Loans) Order 1980 (SI 1980/439); from 6 October 1982 to 5 April 1987 at 12% by the Income Tax (Official Rate of Interest on Beneficial Loans) Order 1982 (SI 1982/1273); from 6 April 1987 to 5 June 1987 at 11.5% by the Income Tax (Official Rate of Interest on Beneficial Loans) Order 1987 (SI 1987/512); from 6 June 1987 to 5 September 1987 at 10.5% by the Income Tax (Official Rate of Interest on Beneficial Loans) (No 2) Order 1987 (SI 1987/886); from 6 September 1987 to 5 December 1987 at 9% by the Income Tax (Official Rate of Interest on Beneficial Loans) (No 3) Order 1987 (SI 1987/1492); from 6 December 1987 to 5 May 1988 at 10.5% by the Income Tax (Official Rate of Interest on Beneficial Loans) (No 4) Order 1987 (SI 1987/1989); from 6 May 1988 to 5 August 1988 at 9.5% by the Income Tax (Official Rate of Interest on Beneficial Loans) Order 1988 (SI 1988/757); from 6 August 1988 to 5 October 1988 at 12% by the Income Tax (Official Rate of Interest on Beneficial Loans) (No 2) Order 1988 (SI 1988/1279); and from 6 October 1988 onwards at 13.5% by the Income Tax (Official Rate of Interest on Beneficial Loans) (No 3) Order 1988 SI 1988/1622.

The de minimis limit

2.319 There is no charge to tax if the cash equivalent (see 2.320 and 2.321) does not exceed £200 or, in a year in which there are two or more loans (or notional loans) outstanding, the total of all the cash equivalents does not exceed that amount (ICTA 1988, s 161(1)). This figure was increased to £200 from £50 with effect for 1980/81 onwards by FA 1980, s 50(1). As a transitional measure following the introduction of the legislation, the cash equivalent for 1978/79 and 1979/80 was reduced by half (FA 1976, s 66(11)(a)), so that the de minimis limit was, in effect, £100 rather than £50. Where the limit is exceeded, the charge is on the whole of the benefit received, not merely on the excess over £200, so that in marginal cases it may be advantageous for the employer to make a small interest charge to bring the benefit within the exemption, although this will be of no assistance in the case of a notional loan.

The cash equivalent

2.320 The 'cash equivalent' is the amount of interest on the loan or notional loan, calculated at the official rate, less the amount of interest, if any, (and in the case of a notional loan there will always be deemed to be none: see 2.317) actually paid on that loan for (but not necessarily *in*) the relevant year of assessment (ICTA 1988, Sch 7, para 3(1)). All loans and notional loans subsisting between the same lender and borrower which are outstanding to any extent in the same year of assessment are treated for this purpose as a single loan (ICTA 1988, Sch 7, para 3(3)).

2.321 The legislation provides for a 'normal' and an 'alternative', more precise, means of calculating the interest payable at the official rate. The alternative basis applies at the option of the Inspector of Taxes or the taxpayer, either of whom must give the other notice in writing of his exercise of that option (ICTA 1988, Sch 7, para 5(1)). In the case of the taxpayer, this must be done within six years after the end of the relevant year of assessment, or, if an assessment has already been made on the normal basis, within the time limit allowed for appealing against that assessment, or such further time as the Inspector may allow (ICTA 1988, Sch 7, para 5(2)). No time limit is laid down for the exercise of the option by the Inspector, but this would not be done after the determination of the assessment unless he made a 'discovery' within TMA, s 29(3), and in practice it is unlikely to be done once an assessment has been issued on the 'normal' basis.

The normal method of calculating interest at the official rate

2.322 The 'normal' method of calculation is to take the average (ie half the aggregate) of the amount of the loan or notional loan outstanding on 5 April preceding the year of assessment and the amount outstanding on 5 April within the year of assessment, and to multiply the resulting figure by the official rate. If the amount outstanding varied at different times of day on either of the two dates of 5 April (due to a repayment or to a further loan or share acquisition made at that time), the maximum amount due at any time in the day is taken into the calculation. If the loan was taken out or shares acquired, or if the amount outstanding was discharged or treated as written off (see 2.311 to 2.314), part way between those two dates, then the commencement date of the loan or notional loan is substituted for the first date of 5 April, and/or the date of discharge or write-off for the second date (ICTA 1988, Sch 7, para 4(a)). Where the loan or notional loan is outstanding for less than the full 12 month period, the resulting average balance is divided by 12 and multiplied by the number of whole months (beginning on the sixth day of the calendar month) for which it was outstanding, before multiplying by the official rate of interest (ICTA 1988, Sch 7, para 4(b)). If the official rate changes during the year, or during the lesser period for which the loan is outstanding, an average rate is applied, ascertained by reference to the number of days in the period for which each rate was in force (ICTA 1988, Sch 7, para 4(c)).

The alternative method of calculating interest at the official rate

2.323 The 'alternative' method (ICTA 1988, Sch 7, para 5(3)) is to:

(a) take each period in the relevant year of assessment during which the official rate of interest remained the same;
(b) for each such period take the maximum amount outstanding on the loan or notional loan on each day, and add those amounts together;
(c) multiply each such aggregate by the official rate of interest, divided by 365; and
(d) add together the resulting figures for each period in the relevant year.

Comparison of the normal and alternative methods

2.324 The two methods of calculating interest at the official rate are compared in the following example:

Graham purchased shares from his employing company at an undervalue in 1985. On 5 April 1986, the notional loan outstanding was £62,000. He made further payments for the shares on the first day of each month, so that on 5 April 1987 the balance outstanding was £50,000. The official rate of interest through the year was 12%.

The cash equivalent under the normal basis of calculation is:

Balance at 5 April 1986	£ 62,000
Balance at 5 April 1987	50,000
	£112,000
Half thereof	£ 56,000
12% × £56,000	£ 6,270

The cash equivalent under the alternative basis of calculation is:

		£000
26 days at £62,000	(6. 4.86–1. 5.86)	1,612
31 days at £61,000	(2. 5.86–1. 6.86)	1,891
30 days at £60,000	(2. 6.86–1. 7.86)	1,800
31 days at £59,000	(2. 7.86–1. 8.86)	1,829
31 days at £58,000	(2. 8.86–1. 9.86)	1,798
30 days at £57,000	(2. 9.86–1.10.86)	1,710
31 days at £56,000	(2.10.86–1.11.86)	1,736
30 days at £55,000	(2.11.86–1.12.86)	1,650
31 days at £54,000	(2.12.86–1. 1.87)	1,674
31 days at £53,000	(2. 1.87–1. 2.87)	1,643
28 days at £52,000	(2. 2.87–1. 3.87)	1,456
31 days at £51,000	(2. 3.87–1. 4.87)	1,581
4 days at £50,000	(2. 4.87–5. 4.87)	200
365		20,580
£20,580,000 × 12% ÷ 365	=	£ 6,766

It will be seen that with a loan reducing at an even rate, the difference between the figures resulting from the two calculations is small (hence the prescription of the simpler calculation for normal use).

2.325 There may be cases, however, where there is a significant difference, as illustrated in the following example, where extreme figures are taken in order to illustrate the point.

Braithwaite has a notional loan of £500 from his employer at 5 April 1986, arising from a purchase of shares at an undervalue. This balance remains unchanged until 5 April 1987, when he receives an actual loan of £1m on which he pays no interest.

The cash equivalent under the normal basis is:

Balance at 5 April 1986	£ 500
Balance at 5 April 1987	1,000,000
	£1,000,500
Half thereof	£ 500,250
12% × £500,250	£ 60,030
Actual interest paid	nil
Cash equivalent	£ 60,030

Under the alternative basis the cash equivalent is:

364 days at £500		£ 182,000
1 day at £1,000,000		1,000,000
		£1,182,000
£1,182,000 × 12% ÷ 365	=	£ 389
Actual interest paid		nil
Cash equivalent		£ 389

Obviously, in this case the taxpayer will elect for the alternative basis, which gives a significantly different result only where there have been large and/or irregular movements in the amount outstanding.

2.326 It should be noted that while the treatment of a notional loan follows that of an actual loan, in the latter case other legislative provisions are also of relevance, which are not dealt with here. See also 7.111.

Disposal of shares at a price in excess of market value: ICTA 1988, s 162(6)

2.327 Where shares are acquired as set out in ICTA 1988, s 162(1) (ie where an individual employed or about to be employed in director's or higher paid employment, or a person connected with him, acquires shares in a company in pursuance of a right or opportunity available by reason of the employment: see 2.303 to 2.307), after 6 April 1976, whether or not at an undervalue, and the shares are subsequently disposed of, by surrender or otherwise, so that neither the employee nor any person connected with him any longer has a beneficial interest in them, and the consideration for the disposal exceeds the then market value of the shares, the excess over market value is treated as an emolument of the individual's employment, and accordingly as chargeable to income tax under Schedule E for the year in which the disposal is effected (ICTA 1988, s 162(6)). As with the 'write-off' and interest charges on a notional loan (see 2.311 to 2.316 and 2.317 to 2.325), where the sale is made by a connected person, it is the employee who suffers the income tax charge, although the connected person may incur a liability to CGT. This provision is designed to catch 'guaranteed buy-back' or 'stop loss' arrangements, whereby, in order to remove an element of risk, or ensure a minimum level of growth, the company undertakes to repurchase the shares at a given price, or a price determined in accordance with a given formula. However, it also catches the case where the obtaining of a price in excess of market value is completely fortuitous.

2.328 Any amount charged to income tax under this provision is excluded from the disposal consideration for CGT purposes (CGTA 1979, s 31(1)). The result is that a capital loss on the shares may be matched by an income tax charge, or that a 'growth in value' charge under ICTA 1988, s 138(1)(a) (see 2.190 to 2.286) or FA 1988, s 79 (for shares in a dependent subsidiary: see 2.84 to 2.121), which is based on the value of the shares on disposal, as opposed to the actual disposal proceeds, may effectively be 'topped up' to charge the whole gain to income tax. The charge under s 162(6) may also arise in cases which are outside the scope of the growth in value charges, for example because of the various exemptions available. While the matching of a capital loss with a charge to income tax may at first sight seem anomalous, it is in effect only treating as an emolument an amount given to the employee which happens to be ascertained by reference to the loss he has incurred in an unfortunate investment, but which is no less an emolument of the employment than an amount determined by any other formula. The right of the employee to sell the shares for more than their market value under arrangements such as those described in 2.327 will normally take the form of, or amount to, a 'put option', and it would seem that it may be possible to avoid a charge under these provisions by making a payment to the employee in consideration of his relinquishing his rights under the option, equal to the excess of the agreed price over market value, and subsequently making the purchase at the latter figure. Again, consideration must be given to whether the *Ramsay* principle (see 7.79 to 7.82) would be applied to treat the two transactions taken together as amounting to the sale of the shares at the guaranteed price, so that s 162(6) would still apply. There would normally be nothing to be lost by attempting the manoeuvre, however. The payment for relinquishing the 'put option' would be chargeable to CGT, but subject to the annual exemption.

Cessation of employment: effect on charges under ICTA 1988, s 162

2.329 The loan 'write-off' charge under ICTA 1988, ss 162(5) and 160(2) (see 2.311 to 2.316), and the charge on a disposal in excess of market value under ICTA 1988, s 162(6) (see 2.327 to 2.328) still arise even if the employee who made the acquisition (or a person connected with whom made the acquisition) has, by the time the charge crystallises, ceased to hold the employment in question, although the interest charge on the notional loan (see 2.317 to 2.325) comes to an end with the cessation of the employment (ICTA 1988, s 162(7)). No charge on a disposal at a price in excess of market value arises however by reference to any disposal made after the death of the employee, whether by his personal representatives or any other person, such as a connected person who has held the shares throughout (ICTA 1988, s 162(8)).

Extension of ICTA 1988, s 162 to interests in shares

2.330 The provisions of ICTA 1988, s 162, giving rise to a tax charge on the notional interest saved (ICTA 1988, ss 162(1) and 160(1): see 2.317 to 2.325); on the 'write-off' of the notional loan (ICTA 1988, ss 162(5) and 160(2): see 2.311 to 2.316); and on a sale at a price in excess of market value (ICTA 1988, s 162(6): see 2.327 and 2.328) all apply in relation to the acquisition of an interest in shares less than full beneficial ownership as they apply in relation to the acquisition and disposal of shares themselves (as defined in 2.304). An 'interest in shares' for this purpose includes an interest in the proceeds of sale of part of the shares, but not a share option, to which separate provisions apply (see Chapter 3) (ICTA 1988, s 162(9)). In applying the provisions of s 162 to such an interest:

(a) for references to the shares acquired there are substituted references to the interest acquired (ICTA 1988, s 162(9)(a));
(b) for references to the market value of shares acquired (see 2.305 and 2.327) there are substituted references to such proportion of the market value of the shares in which the interest subsists as corresponds to the size of the

interest. Prima facie, this means that a 50% interest in the shares is treated as having half the market value of a 100% interest, even if it in fact has a lesser value due to its lack of marketability. This point is discussed further at 2.195 in the context of the 'growth in value' charge under ICTA 1988, s 138(1)(a) (ICTA 1988, s 162(9)(b));

(c) for the reference to shares of the same class as those acquired (see 2.305) there is substituted a reference to shares of the same class as those in which the interest subsists (ICTA 1988, s 162(9)(c)); and

(d) for references to the market value of fully paid-up shares of the relevant class (see 2.305) there is substituted a reference to the proportion of that value corresponding to the size of the interest (ICTA 1988, s 162(9)(d)). The same questions of interpretation arise as in (b) above.

ICTA 1988, s 162: the prevention of a double charge

2.331 ICTA 1988, s 162 only operates in respect of any shares or interest in shares to include an amount in emoluments so far as any amount corresponding to it, and representing the same benefit, does not otherwise fall to be so included under the Tax Acts (ICTA 1988, s 162(11)). As far as the notional loan 'write-off' charge is concerned, such a double charge is already excluded by interaction with the provisions of ICTA 1988, ss 160(2) and 161(5) (see 2.311). The two exceptions mentioned there (terminal payments under ICTA 1988, s 148 and sums paid to a settlor which are taxable under ICTA 1988, s 677) are not overruled by s 162(11), as that provision only prevents a double charge 'by inclusion in emoluments'.

2.332 The charge under s 162(6) on the excess of sale proceeds over market value (see 2.327 and 2.328) is designed, as stated in 2.327, to catch 'guaranteed buy-back' or 'stop loss' arrangements. It would also, however, apply in a situation where a company voluntarily purchased shares back from an employee at an inflated value without prior arrangement. In such a case it is considered that the excess would in any case normally be chargeable as an emolument under ICTA 1988, s 19, being a payment to the employee for no consideration other than his services. In such circumstances, s 162(11) prevents a double charge.

2.333 A double charge could also arise in respect of the charge on notional interest if, instead of being issued part paid with provisions for later calls, shares were issued 'fully paid', with a part payment being made on acquisition, and the balance left on loan account with the company (subject to company law restrictions on a company's giving assistance in the purchase of its own shares). From the company's point of view the difference is simply one of bookkeeping, as it is in the case where an actual loan is taken out from the company and used to pay for the shares, in order to obtain relief for interest actually paid (see 2.317). However, if the balance outstanding is left on loan account, rather than on an account for unpaid calls, a charge would arise both on the actual loan, under ICTA 1988, s 160, and on a notional loan determined by reference to the 'undervalue' (ie the shortfall in the payment made at the time of the acquisition: see 2.305). This double charge is prevented by s 162(11), any charge under s 160 taking priority.

Information provisions

2.334 An employer may be required by notice from the Inspector of Taxes to provide a return of benefits made available to past or present employees (TMA 1970, s 15(1)), and the benefits stipulated by the Inspector may include any amount chargeable to tax under ICTA 1988, ss 160 or 162 in respect of a beneficial loan, or of a notional loan on the acquisition of shares at an undervalue. The notice may simply ask whether such benefits have been provided in respect of the employees in question (TMA 1970, s 15(7)(a)), or may ask for such further particulars as the Inspector requires (TMA 1970, s 15(7)(b)). The return must be delivered within the time limit specified in the notice (TMA 1970, s 15(1)) although, exceptionally, no minimum time is laid down in the legislation. Any unreasonable exercise of this Inland Revenue power would, however, be subject to judicial review (see 7.51). An employer may not be required to include in his return information relating to a year of assessment begining more than six years before the year of assessment in which the notice is given (TMA 1970, s 15(2)).

2.335 A notice under TMA 1970 s 15(1) must specify the employees for whom a return is to be made. This requirement may be met by requesting details for all employees; for all employees in director's or higher paid employment; for named individuals; or for a class of employees identified in some other way (for example, all employees working at a particular location, or earning more than a specified figure (TMA 1970, s 15(3)(a)). 'Employee', for this purpose, means an office holder or employee whose emoluments fall to be assessed under Schedule E (see 7.88 to 7.96), and thus includes a director (TMA 1970, s 15(11)(a)). 'Director's or higher paid employment' is defined in 7.41 to 7.44 (TMA 1970, s 15(11)(b); ICTA 1988, s 167). A notice must also specify the years of assessment or other periods (such as the accounting periods of the company) in respect of which the information is to be provided (TMA 1970, s 15(3)(b)), and may require the return to state the name and place of residence (ie the address, as opposed to the country of residence) of each employee in respect of whom details are given (TMA 1970, s 15(4)).

2.336 Where the employer is a company, the Secretary, or other person (by whatever name called) who performs the duties of the Secretary is treated as the employer, and thus is obliged to comply with the information requirements, but both the company and the relevant official are liable to penalties in respect of a failure in this respect. As to penalties, see 7.75 to 7.77 (TMA 1970, s 98).

2.337 Where a person performs duties of an office or employment in the UK for a continuous period of not less than 30 days and:

(a) the office or employment is under or with a person resident outside (and not resident in) the UK; but
(b) the duties are performed for the benefit of a person resident or carrying on a trade, profession or vocation in the UK,

the information requirements of TMA 1970, s 15 apply as if the person for whose benefit the duties are performed were the employer, but only to the extent of requiring him to make a return of the name and place of residence of the person performing the duties (FA 1974, s 24).

Circumstances in which ICTA 1988, s 162 does not apply

2.338 Where shares are appropriated to an employee at an undervalue under an Inland Revenue approved 'profit-sharing' scheme no interest charge or write-off charge under ICTA 1988, s 162 arises (ICTA 1988, s 186(2)(b): see 4.7). Neither, it seems, can the charge on a sale at a price in excess of market value under s 162(6) apply to such shares (see discussion at 4.8).

2.339 In addition, no interest or write-off charge arises in respect of shares acquired at an undervalue by virtue of options under an approved savings-related share option scheme, or an approved selective share option scheme, provided certain conditions are fulfilled. In neither case is ICTA 1988, s 162 specifically mentioned in the legislation, but it is provided that 'tax shall not be chargeable under any provision of the Tax Acts in respect of the exercise' of the option (ie the acquisition at an undervalue) (ICTA 1988, s 185(3)(a): see 5.8 and 6.10). In addition, where the necessary conditions are not fulfilled for a selective scheme which nevertheless remains approved, so that a notional loan does arise under s 162, the amount of that loan is treated as reduced by the amount of any 'discount' taxed on the grant of the option (ICTA 1988, s 185(8)(b)). Normally a charge on the exercise of an option, under ICTA 1988, s 135, will exclude a charge under s 162 (see 2.308), but there may be cases where s 162 applies and s 135 does not (see 3.12 and 3.13).

'STOP LOSS' ARRANGEMENTS: BENEFICIAL LOANS

2.340 The charge to tax on the write-off of an *actual* loan under ICTA 1988, s 160(2) (see 2.311 to 2.316 for the write-off of a notional loan) does not apply to benefits received under arrangements made at any time with a view to protecting the holder of shares acquired before 6 April 1976 from a fall in their market value (ICTA 1988, s 161(7)). Such arrangements, in their simplest form, might involve the writing off of an existing loan (possibly taken out to assist in the purchase of shares) to the extent of any losses incurred by the employee on his shareholding. As the legislation refers merely to protection 'from a fall in market value', it covers unrealised as well as realised losses, and there is no requirement that a benefit given to compensate for an unrealised loss should be 'recaptured' on a subsequent rise in market value.

2.341 In the same way as ICTA 1988, s 162 ('notional loan on employee shareholdings') applies to an employee or 'connected person' (see 2.304), so s 160, dealing with actual loans, refers to the benefit (to the employee) of a loan to him or to a relative of his (as defined in ICTA 1988, s 160(6): see 7.87), and the employee himself is charged to tax under s 160(2) on the benefit of the write off of a loan to a relative. The exception from the charge under s 160(2) given by s 161(7) for 'stop-loss' arrangements therefore applies equally to the write-off of a loan to a relative where the relative is the shareholder.

2.342 There is no interaction between this provision and ICTA 1988, s 162, as the former applies only to shares acquired before 6 April 1976, and the latter only to shares acquired after that date. Although the shares must be acquired prior to 6 April 1976, the 'stop-loss' arrangements may be made at any time, although arguably a reimbursement of the loss long after it was incurred, rather than simultaneously or shortly thereafter, should not be classified as 'protection' so much as 'compensation' (which is not within the terms of the provision). 'Shares' are not widely defined as they are for the purposes of ICTA 1988, s 162 (see 2.304) and the term therefore does not include other securities such as debentures and loan stock. Neither, in contrast to s 162 (see 2.330), is an interest in shares less than the full beneficial ownership included within this provision. The shares in question need not specifically be in the employer or any related company. There must (it is suggested) be some connection with the employment, however, as the write-off of a loan, quantified arbitrarily by reference to *any* shares showing a realised or unrealised loss which the employee had held since before 6 April 1976, or even by reference to shares in the employing company acquired on the open market, and not by virtue of the employment, would normally constitute an emolument taxable as 'money's worth' under ICTA 1988, s 19, quite irrespective of the beneficial loan provisions of ICTA 1988, s 160. The intention of s 161(7) is to prevent a charge arising under those provisions as a result of arrangements which, taken together, leave the employee in a 'break-even' position, and give no benefit under the general rules of Schedule E.

CAPITAL GAINS TAX: GENERAL CONSIDERATIONS

Exclusion of employee shares from 6 April 1965 market value election

2.343 In general, for CGT purposes, quoted securities held on 6 April 1965 are deemed to have been sold and reacquired by the owner on that date at their then market value, which forms their base cost on a subsequent disposal (CGTA 1979, Sch 5, para 1). Actual cost is substituted only if a smaller gain or loss would result, but where the effect would be to convert a gain to a loss or vice versa, the disposal is treated as giving rise to neither a gain nor a loss (CGTA 1979, Sch 5, para 2). The substitution of 6 April 1965 value does not, however, apply in any case to a disposal of shares or securities of a company by a person to whom they were issued as an employee of the company, or as an employee of any other person, on terms which restrict his right to dispose of them (CGTA 1979, Sch 5, para 1(3)). In such a case the normal rules of time apportionment or election for 6 April 1965 value apply, as for other assets including unquoted shares (CGTA 1979, Sch 5, paras 11, 12 and 13). In practice, the shares or securities are effectively unquoted, as the prices at which dealings take place on The Stock Exchange do not reflect the particular restrictions attaching to those shares, and so do not provide an accurate measure of their value.

2.344 The provisions set out in 2.343 are subject to the changes made by FA 1988, effectively rebasing capital gains tax to 31 March 1988. The old rules remains relevant, however, as the use of the 1982 base value is not permitted to increase a gain or loss; where it would otherwise do so, any gain or loss is restricted to that computed on the basis of original cost (or of 6 April 1965 value, if appropriate). If the use of original cost or 1965 value would give a loss, and the March 1982 value would give a gain (or vice versa) the disposal is deemed to take place at neither a gain nor a loss (FA 1988, s 96(1) to (4)). The taxpayer may make a 'global' election to adopt the 31 March 1982 value for the calculation of all gains and losses (FA 1988, s 96(5) & (6)). In such a case there is no equivalent provision to CGTA 1979, Sch 5, para 1(3) excluding employee shares.

Employee shares: pooling

2.345 The pooling rules for share acquisitions on or after 6 April 1982 introduced by FA 1985 apply separately in relation to any securities held by a person to whom they were issued as an employee of the issuing company, or of any other person, on terms which restrict his right to dispose of them, so long as those terms are in force (FA 1985, Sch 19, para 8(2)).

INHERITANCE TAX CONSIDERATIONS: CLOSE COMPANIES

2.346 Inheritance tax (IHT) may become a factor in employee share schemes where the effect of the arrangements is to make a significant transfer of value from a close company or a company which would be close if resident in the UK (see 7.12 to 7.21) to an employee. Any transfer of value by such a company is apportioned among the participators (excluding loan creditors: see 7.52 to 7.55) according to their respective rights and interests in the company immediately before the transfer (including rights and interests in the assets available for distribution among them in the event of a winding up, or in other circumstances: IHTA 1984, s 102(2)) and any amount so apportioned to another close company is further apportioned among the participators in that company (IHTA 1984, s 94(2)). The amounts apportioned to individual participators are then treated for IHT purposes as 'net' transfers of value by them (that is, in each case, as a transfer of value of such an amount as after deduction of IHT, if any, would be equal to the amount so apportioned), although this amount is reduced to the extent that the value of the participator's estate (excluding his interest in the close company) is increased by the transfer concerned (as, for example, if he himself benefits as an employee from a transfer of shares under an employee share scheme) (IHTA 1984, s 94(1)).

2.347 Any transfer which is brought into account for income tax purposes in the hands of the recipient (such as a straightforward transfer of shares at an undervalue: see 2.13 to 2.24) is, however, disregarded in determining the amount to be apportioned (IHTA 1984, s 94(2)(a)). Where the amount apportioned to an individual is 5% or less of the value transferred by the company, while it remains chargeable to IHT, it is not taken into account in determining his cumulative total of transfers for the purpose of ascertaining the appropriate rate of IHT on a subsequent occasion of charge (IHTA 1984, s 94(4)). Preference shares (see 7.78) in the company making the transfer, or in a participator (or sub-participator) company are ignored in the apportionment, if the transfer of value has only a small effect on the value of those shares (IHTA 1984, s 96).

2.348 The cases where these provisions apply will be limited, as most benefits conferred on employees, and not taxed as income, will be made for commercial motives, and not intended to transfer a gratuitous benefit, and thus will not constitute transfers of value (IHTA 1984, s 10). Where there is a transfer of value, however, as in arrangements involving family members, or otherwise undertaken for personal rather than business motives, the £3,000 annual exemption (IHTA 1984, s 19), and the exemption for normal expenditure out of income (IHTA 1984, s 21) will still be available, as will the benefit of the nil rate band (£110,000 at the time of writing: IHTA 1984, Sch 1), coupled with the falling out of account of transfers made more than seven years previously (IHTA 1984, s 7(1)). A transfer of value apportioned to an individual under IHTA 1984, s 94 cannot qualify as a 'potentially exempt transfer', which would be exempt if the donor survived for seven years after it was made (IHTA 1984, s 3A(6)).

PHANTOM SHARE SCHEMES

2.349 Employee benefits may be provided by means of a 'phantom share scheme'; ie essentially, a cash bonus (subject to tax under Schedule E in the same way as basic salary), the amount of which is calculated by reference to movements in the share price. Such schemes may be of varying levels of sophistication, ranging from a simple £x of bonus for each percentage point by which the share price rises, to the granting of 'notional options' which the employee may choose to 'exercise' at given times within the rules of the scheme in order to realise a gain on the 'sale' of his notional shares, the amount of which will then be paid to him by the company in cash form. The valuation of quoted shares for this purpose will pose no problem, but an unquoted company will not normally wish to undertake the expense of a professional valuation at frequent intervals, and may therefore establish within the rules of the scheme a formula for valuation to have effect for this purpose alone; for example, by applying the average price/earnings ratio of the shares in the FT 30 index (perhaps suitably modified) to the company's profits for the most recent year in respect of which audited accounts are available.

2.350 The primary advantage of such a scheme to the employee is that he receives cash, not shares, and is therefore put in funds to meet any tax liability arising. The company may be content to make a cash payment, for which a tax deduction is available, in preference to an issue of shares which may alter the balance of control in the company, but this liability may prove an embarrassment if profitability and growth in the share price are not matched by cash flow. Even where cash is available, shareholders may take exception to large payments to employees out of profits, as opposed to an issue of shares, which is perceived as being without cost (except for capital duty, prior to 16 March 1988). Cash payments also have a national insurance cost, which does not attach to a payment in the form of shares. Some of the advantages of the 'real' and the 'phantom' share scheme may be combined by the making of a cash payment related to the share price (and deductible for corporation tax purposes) which, under the terms of the scheme, the employee is obliged to use (after the payment of income tax) in subscription for shares.

MISCELLANEOUS

Long service awards

2.351 Inland Revenue Extrastatutory Concession A22 indicates that tax is not charged on long service awards made to directors and employees which consist of 'tangible articles' or of shares in the employing company or another group company, the cost or value of which does not exceed £20 per year of service. For this concession to apply the individual must have been in the company's service for 20 years or more, and have received no similar award within the previous ten years.

3 Unapproved share option schemes

SUMMARY

3.1 Following its decision in *Weight v Salmon* (see 2.13 to 2.24) that a discount on the issue of shares was taxable under Schedule E, the House of Lords went on to consider in *Abbott v Philbin* [1961] AC 352, 39 TC 82 the position where the grant and the exercise of the right to acquire the shares formed two separate transactions, and determined that the *grant* rather than the *exercise* of the right to purchase the shares gave rise to the Schedule E charge, the quantum of the assessment being the value of the option, less any consideration given for it. It followed that any increase in the value of the shares between the grant and the exercise of the option arose from the employee's rights under the option agreement, rather than from his employment, and was not taxable, even on a subsequent disposal of the shares (CGT not then being in existence).

3.2 This general rule was, however, subsequently displaced by specific statutory provisions now found in ICTA 1988, ss 135 and 136, which impose a Schedule E charge on any gain realised by the exercise, assignment, or release of an option. The amount chargeable on exercise is the market value of the shares at that time, less any consideration given for them in accordance with the terms of the option, or paid originally for its grant. The charge to tax on the *grant* of the option, under the general rules established in *Abbott v Philbin* is specifically excluded by s 135, unless the option is capable of being exercised later than seven years after its grant. Any tax arising under this provision on the grant of an option is deducted from a subsequent charge on exercise under s 135, but not so as to give rise to any repayment.

3.3 Once the option is exercised, and the shares acquired, a subsequent sale may give rise either to a charge to CGT, in which case the amount charged to income tax under s 135 is treated as allowable acquisition expenditure; or to a further charge to income tax under the 'growth in value' provisions of ICTA 1988, s 138 or FA 1988, s 79 (for shares in a dependent subsidiary) as discussed at 2.190 to 2.286 and 2.84 to 2.121.

GENERAL PRINCIPLES

3.4 As discussed at 2.13 to 2.24, the decision of the House of Lords in 1935 in *Weight v Salmon* established that where shares were acquired by employees in pursuance of an opportunity afforded to them by their employer company of purchasing the shares below market value the 'discount' constituted 'money's worth' taxable under the general rules of Schedule E (now contained in ICTA 1988, s 19). A share option arrangement inevitably involves the purchase of shares below market value, as, were the agreed price not advantageous, the holder would not choose to exercise the option. The Inland Revenue accordingly sought to apply this decision to an option arrangement in the case of *Abbott v Philbin* [1961] AC 352, 39 TC 92, HL some 25 years later in 1960.

3.5 In that case, a company secretary acquired a non-transferable option for a consideration of £20 entitling him, subject to certain contingencies, to acquire 2,000 shares in the company at any time in the next 10 years at £3.8s.6d, which was their value at the time of the grant of the option. At the time of the first exercise, 18 months later, in respect of 250 shares, the market value of the shares was £4.2s.0d, and the excess of market value over actual acquisition cost, amounting to 13s 6d per share (a total of £168.15s.0d), less the relevant portion of the cost of the option (£2.50) was assessed by the Inland Revenue under Schedule E. It was held by the House of Lords, however, that the taxable perquisite was the grant of the option itself, in the earlier year, not the acquisition of the shares at an undervalue on the exercise of the option. The latter advantage arose from the rights under the option agreement, not from the employment.

3.6 There are, however, severe problems in valuing an option. In theory, its worth is the benefit expected eventually to be obtained from it (which the Inland Revenue sought to tax in full in *Abbott v Philbin*), discounted in respect of the delay in receiving the benefit, and reduced in respect of the fact that the realisation of that benefit is uncertain. Such a formula requires a professional judgement on future movements in interest rates and in inflation in order to arrive at the appropriate discount rate to apply in respect of the deferral of the benefit, and an even more subjective decision as to the level of risk involved. Even where, by the time the tax liability comes under discussion, the benefit actually obtained on exercise is known, such matters are difficult to determine, but where the individual has not yet exercised his option, so that the degree of deferral and the market value at the exercise date are yet to be ascertained, it is almost impossible to arrive at a realistic figure. Profit forecasts may be of some help, but (even when the exercise has taken place before the valuation) the question arises as to whether the starting point for the discounting calculation should be: the benefit actually achieved by the employee; the maximum which could have been achieved by a more astute (or luckier) investor; or that which would have been achieved by a reasonable man, professionally advised. Assuming the last alternative to be correct, the decision as to what would constitute reasonable professional advice is still far from straightforward. Indeed, there may be a case for maintaining that an option to purchase shares at their current market value at the time of the grant is, in itself, worthless, as current market prices already take account of general expectations as to future performance. Against this, it is clear that such options do have some value, as individuals are, in practice, eager to hold them. Such 'hope value' cannot be quantified, and it is suggested that in the case of *Abbott v Philbin* (see 3.5) it would have been impossible to prove that the option, on its grant, had a value in excess of, or even as great as, the £20 given for it, which in 1954 represented much more than a nominal figure.

3.7 By contrast, an option to purchase at a figure below market value obviously has a value at least equal to that discount, unless it cannot be exercised until after the lapse of a given period, within which the share price is expected to fall, in which case its valuation raises all the same questions as discussed in 3.6. The matter is complicated by the fact that in a 'perfect market' such as The Stock Exchange, prices are never (in theory) *expected* to fall, at least in relation to the rest of the market, as such expectation will lead to an immediate fall.

3.8 The problems raised by *Abbott v Philbin* were, however, displaced by new legislation to deal with share options, introduced by FA 1966, s 25 (now ICTA 1988, ss 135 and 136). The question of valuation of options discussed in 3.6 and 3.7 cannot be completely ignored, however, for the reasons discussed in 3.13 and 3.39.

THE CHARGE ON EXERCISE, ASSIGNMENT OR RELEASE: ICTA 1988, ss 135 and 136

The basic rules

General

3.9 A charge now arises under the appropriate case of Schedule E (see 7.88 to 7.96) on any gain (computed as discussed in 3.16 and 3.19) realised by a person on the exercise, assignment or release of a right to acquire shares in a company (ie an option) obtained by that person as a director or employee of that or any other company (ICTA 1988, s 135(1)), rather than on its grant.

3.10 A 'person' liable to a charge under this provision will normally be an individual, but the legislation may apply to a company where that company itself occupies the office of director (see 2.267). A company cannot, however, be an employee. An assignment or release of the option is brought within the scope of the provision in addition to an exercise, as otherwise the disposal for a consideration of an option 'pregnant with gain' would be excluded from the charge. A 'release' includes agreeing to the restriction of the exercise of the right (ICTA 1988, s 136(5)(a)). Such an agreement might be made, for example, where a company was concerned at the acquisition of a large amount of share capital by employees in a particular year, and paid certain employees to defer the exercise of their rights until a later date. 'Shares' includes stock, and other securities as defined in 7.97 (ICTA 1988, ss 136(5)(d), 140(3) and 254(1)).

3.11 The terms 'director' and 'employee' are defined for the purpose of these provisions (see 7.35 to 7.37 and 7.45), and, in particular, include former or prospective employees or directors (ICTA 1988, s 136(5)(b) and (c)).

3.12 The charge under s 135 covers acquisitions not only of shares in the employing company, but also in any other company. As with the 'growth in value' and 'special benefits' charges under ICTA 1988, s 138 and FA 1988, ss 78 to 80 and the 'notional loan' charges under ICTA 1988, s 162 (see 2.184, 2.40 and 2.304) this covers primarily the acquisition by an employee or director of shares in another group company (most often the parent), but could apply to any shares (for example, those previously held by the employer as an investment) the option to acquire which is obtained 'as director or employee'. These words are defined so as to cover an option granted to a person by reason of an office or employment in respect of which he is chargeable to tax under Case I of Schedule E (see 7.89); i e broadly, an individual who is resident and ordinarily resident in the UK, and extend also to an option assigned to a person who has such a Case I office or employment by some other person to whom it was granted by reason of the assignee's office or employment (ICTA 1988, s 140(1)(a) and (b)). If the office or employment has ceased to be held at the time of the grant (whether that grant is to the person himself or to another person who then assigns the option to him) the relevant question becomes whether the director or employee was taxable under Case I of Schedule E in the last chargeable period in which he held it (ICTA 1988, s 140(1)). The result is that if an employee taxed under Schedule E, Case I, ceases employment with the relevant company altogether, a subsequent grant will be caught, but if he changes his residence status or the place of performance of his duties and becomes taxable under Case II or III he will not be within the terms of the section, either while he remains in the employment, or after leaving it. The grant of the option must be 'by reason of' the employment. There is no presumption, as there is in the case of the 'notional loan' charges under ICTA 1988, s 162 (see 2.306) that any benefit given to an employee by a company employer must be by reason of the employment, rather than for any other, unconnected, reason. An option granted, for example, by a close company as a result of the personal relationships between its directors and the recipient will not be within the scope of the section, any more than it is caught by the 'growth in value' or 'special benefits' charges of ICTA 1988, s 138 or FA 1988, ss 78 to 80 (see 2.185 and 2.41).

3.13 The restriction of the s 135 charge to employees who are taxable under Case I of Schedule E at the time of the grant (though not necessarily at the time of the exercise) means that individuals taxable under Case II (and Case III if it is considered possible to 'remit' an option) remain chargeable under the general provisions discussed at 3.4 to 3.8 on the grant rather than the exercise of an option, hence the continuing need to consider the valuation principles set out at 3.6 and 3.7. The excess of the value of the shares on acquisition over the exercise price will, however, be caught by ICTA 1988, s 162 (see 2.303 to 2.339) as a notional loan.

3.14 The extension of the charge to an assigned option which was originally granted by reason of the assignee's employment counters an obvious avoidance device whereby a third party would be granted the option on the employee's behalf, and pass it on to him, so that it could not be said to have been obtained by reason of his employment. Additional provisions deal with the acquisition and exercise of options by connected parties (see 3.24).

3.15 Where tax may become chargeable under s 135 on the exercise of an option, i e where the option is acquired by the option holder 'as a director or employee' under the definition given at 3.12, then, irrespective of whether in the event such a charge arises, tax is *not* chargeable under any provisions of the Tax Acts in respect of the receipt of the option unless it is capable of being exercised more than seven years after it is obtained (ICTA 1988, s 135(2): see also 3.38 to 3.43). This excludes, except in that special case, the charge which would otherwise arise under ICTA 1988, s 19 following the decision in *Abbott v Philbin* (see 3.5).

The calculation of the charge on exercise

3.16 The gain realised on the exercise of an option is the market value of the shares acquired, less the consideration actually given either for them or for the grant of the option itself (ICTA 1988, s 135(3)(a)). 'Market value' is not defined, except as 'the amount that a person might reasonably expect to obtain from a sale in the open market at that time of the shares acquired', but in practice it would seem that the CGTA 1979 definition (see 7.56 to 7.64) is of application, notwithstanding it is not specifically invoked, as it is for other provisions dealing with employee share schemes.

3.17 A simple example may serve to illustrate the calculations of the charge:

Coxe is granted an option in March 1986 for a nominal consideration of £10, to purchase 1,000 shares in his employer company, Campbell Ltd, at any time in the next seven years, at their March 1986 value of £3. In October 1990 he exercises the option, when the market value of the shares is £7. The taxable gain is:

Market value on exercise:		
1,000 × £7		£ 7,000
Actual consideration for shares:		
1,000 × £3	£(3,000)	
Consideration for option	(10)	
		(3,010)
Amount chargeable under ICTA 1988, s 135		£ 3,990

3.18 It should be noted that the employee will have to fund the tax payment from other sources, as the exercise of the option does not give rise to any cash receipt in his hands. He may, of course, sell the shares as soon as possible after acquisition, and this will give rise to only a minimal capital gain or loss, depending on short term price fluctuations.

The calculation of the charge on assignment or release

3.19 The gain on the assignment or release of an option (including the acceptance of a restriction amounting to a release under the definition of ICTA 1988, s 136(5)(a): see 3.10) is the difference between the amount or value of the consideration for the assignment or release (whether in cash or in kind), and the amount or value of the consideration (again, whether in cash or in kind) given for the grant of the option (ICTA 1988, s 135(3)(b)). Such consideration cannot be deducted more than once (ICTA 1988, s 135(4)), so if it is fully utilised (as it must be, if available) in the calculation of the charge on a 'release' under s 136(5)(a) (i e the acceptance of a restriction), it is not then available for deduction in the calculation on a subsequent exercise of the option. If that consideration exceeds the amount received on such a 'release', however, the balance will remain available on a future exercise, assignment or release.

3.20 The relevant calculations are illustrated by the following example:

Dixon obtains for £100 in June 1986 an option to acquire 2,000 shares in Hawkins Ltd (the parent company of his employer) at £4 (as compared to their then market value of £5), the option to be exercised at any time between June 1988 and June 1991. In June 1987, his option has increased in value, following the movement in the price of the underlying shares, and he wishes to realise a gain, without waiting until 1988, when he will be able to exercise the option. He therefore assigns his option to Ford (an unconnected individual) for £800, realising a gain taxable under Schedule E as follows:

Consideration for assignment	£ 800
Consideration for acquisition of option	(100)
Gain taxable under ICTA 1988, s 135	£ 700

Ford will not be liable to any income tax charge on his exercise of the option; only to CGT on his final disposal of the shares, when both the exercise consideration and the £800 given for the option will form allowable expenditure.

If, rather than assign his option, Dixon had released the company from its obligation, for the same consideration of £800, the calculation would have been identical.

If, however, he had waited until June 1988 and then accepted £500 from the company to defer exercise of his option for another two years, he would have incurred a charge as follows:

Consideration for restriction	£ 500
Consideration for grant	(100)
Gain taxable under ICTA 1988, s 135	£ 400

If, subsequently, after the lapse of the two further years he exercised his option in 1990 when the shares stood at a value of £9, he would incur a charge as follows:

Market value on exercise: 2,000 × £9	£ 18,000
Consideration given: 2,000 × £4	(8,000)
Gain taxable under ICTA 1988, s 135	£ 10,000

The option consideration of £100 cannot be deducted again (see 3.19). In addition, there is no allowance in this calculation for the £400 already charged to tax in 1988, as that amount is additional to the gain 'realised' on exercise, and does not affect it. The acceptance of such a restriction might lessen the gain on exercise, if it prevented exercise at the time when the share price was highest, but that 'loss' would automatically give rise to a lower final tax charge.

Apportionment of consideration

3.21 Where an option is exercised in stages, or is released or assigned in part, the option consideration is apportioned as appropriate, so that, in the last example given, if only 1,000 shares had been acquired in 1990, or a restriction amounting to a release had only been accepted in respect of 1,000 shares in 1988, only £50 of the consideration given for the option would have been taken into account in either calculation. The legislative requirement is for a 'just apportionment' (ICTA 1988, s 135(3)). Where all the shares in respect of which the option subsists are of the same class, this presents no problem, but where a composite amount is given for an option over securities of two different classes, the question will arise as to whether the apportionment should be in accordance with the values of those securities at the time of the grant, or at the time of the event giving rise to the charge. Unless one or the other is clearly inequitable in the particular circumstances, the choice effectively lies with the Inland Revenue, as an assessment based on an apportionment by the Inspector could only be displaced on appeal if it were shown to be unjust (not simply if an alternative apportionment were shown to be equally reasonable). In practice, as in the examples above, the consideration given for the option is usually small, and the point is not therefore of major importance.

3.22 Where a combined consideration is given for the option and for another asset or assets, and the allocation of the payment is not specified in the relevant agreement, a 'just apportionment' must, similarly, be reached in the light of all the circumstances (ICTA 1988, s 135(3)).

Option granted in return for the performance of the duties of the employment

3.23 Neither the consideration for the grant of the option, nor any part of a composite consideration apportioned to it as discussed in 3.22 may be taken to include the performance of any duties in, or in connection with, the office or employment by reason of which the option was granted (ICTA 1988, s 135(4)). This is for practical reasons, because of the difficulty of evaluating such consideration, and because the absence of this provision would virtually give carte blanche to deduct almost any amount in the calculation, so as to eliminate the charge, as, in the absence of any gratuitous motive, it could be argued that the benefit conferred by the option, as part of the remuneration package, must equal the value of the services given in return for it (subject to any amount by which the eventual benefit exceeded the value of the option on its grant: see 3.6).

Options granted by reason of another's employment

3.24 If by reason of one person's office or employment (as to which, see 3.12) an option is granted to a second person, then (irrespective of whether the two are connected persons as mentioned below) the first person is chargeable to tax in respect of any gain realised on exercise, assignment or release of the option by the second person (ICTA 1988, s 135(6)(a)). The same applies in respect of a gain realised by the second person where he acquired the option by assignment (and it was originally granted by reason of the first person's office or employment), if the two persons are connected at the time the gain is realised, or if the assignment was made otherwise than by way of a bargain at arm's length. Where the second person has acquired the option by assignment, however, the gain on which the first person is charged (calculated by reference to the original consideration given for the grant of the option) is treated as reduced by any gain realised by a previous holder (often the first person himself) on that, or any previous, assignment (ICTA 1988, s 135(6)(b)). The provisions are illustrated by the following example:

> An option is granted to Cox by reason of his employment; assigned at arm's length to Larkins, an unconnected person; and then assigned to Hodges, who is not connected with Larkins, but is connected with Cox.
>
> On the realisation of a gain by Hodges, Cox will be chargeable, but there will be deducted both his gain on assignment to Larkins, and Larkins' gain on assignment to Hodges.

The provisions are clearly designed to prevent avoidance, but may give inequitable results. In the above case, Cox may derive neither benefit nor satisfaction from a gain realised by Hodges, a connected person, admittedly, but not one to whom he chose to assign his option. Indeed, Cox would still be chargeable on the gain realised by Hodges even if Hodges were connected with neither Cox nor Larkins, but Larkins had made his assignment to Hodges otherwise than at arm's length—a matter totally outside Cox's control.

3.25 These provisions parallel similar charges on the employee or director in cases where a benefit is gained by a connected person under the 'growth in value' or 'special benefits' charges of ICTA 1988, s 138 or FA 1988, ss 78 to 80, or the 'notional loan' provisions of ICTA 1988, s 162 (see 2.296 to 2.300, 2.162 to 2.172 and 2.304). As in the case of those provisions, a 'connected person' is as defined in 7.22 (ICTA 1988, ss 140(2) and 839).

3.26 Where more than one member of a family works for the same company it may be difficult to determine whether an option has been granted to a person by reason of his employment or by reason of that of another individual, such as a spouse. In practice, the higher the recipient's salary, the more likely it is to be accepted that the option was granted by reason of his own employment. In addition, comparison may be made with the treatment of other employees of the same status who do not have more highly placed family connections.

3.27 An individual is not charged in respect of a gain realised by another person as described at 3.24 if he did not assign his option voluntarily, but was divested of it by operation of law on his bankruptcy or otherwise (for example, by order of the court in a divorce settlement). In such a case, the person actually realising the gain is chargeable to tax thereon, not under Schedule E, but under Schedule D, Case VI (ICTA 1988, s 135(7)). The rationale of this provision is that the original holder of the option should not be penalised by having to pay the tax on a gain he has not himself realised where it is quite clear that it was not his intention to confer on the other party the opportunity to obtain that gain. In addition, as a practical matter, there is little point in imposing a charge on a bankrupt who, in the nature of the case, is less likely to be able to pay it than a person who has actually realised the gain.

Sums received on the lapse of options, or on the granting of further options

3.28 Because the basic charge under ICTA 1988, s 135 arises on the exercise, assignment, or release of an option, a number of devices were formerly used to avoid a tax liability, based on options being allowed to lapse in return for consideration, or on further options being granted by the first option holder. Following changes made to the legislation by FA 1986, s 26(1) and (6)(a), an occasion of charge now arises where (ICTA 1988, s 135(8)):

(a) a person has obtained an option (the first option) as a director or employee of a company, within the terms of ICTA 1988, s 135(1) (see 3.9 to 3.14);
(b) he omits, or undertakes to omit, to exercise his option as regards any of the shares to which it relates; or he grants, or undertakes to grant, to another person an option to acquire any of the shares which are the subject of his own option, or to acquire any interest therein; and
(c) in consideration for, or otherwise in connection with, that omission, grant, or undertaking, he receives any benefit in money or money's worth, after 18 March 1986.

3.29 In the circumstances detailed in 3.28 the holder of the first option is treated as realising a gain by its assignment or release (see 3.19), so far as it relates to the shares in question in para (b) of 3.28, for a consideration equal to the amount or value of the benefit which he receives. Indirect methods of turning an option to account are therefore brought within the charge.

3.30 If the individual subsequently exercises the first option (because, for example, his undertaking not to do so has expired, or he is obliged to acquire the shares in order to satisfy the option which he himself has granted), the gain is taxable in the normal way, on the difference between the market value of the shares at that time, and the consideration given for them (see 3.16). The further deduction normally available for the cost of the option itself is not given, however, to the extent that an allowance has already been made for this sum in computing the earlier charge (ICTA 1988, s 135(9)).

Exchange of options

3.31 'Roll-over' provisions deal with the exchange of options for other options over securities in the same or a different company. Where an option is assigned or released in whole or in part for a consideration which comprises other options over securities in the same or another company, the replacement options are not treated as consideration for the assignment or release, giving rise to a charge under 3.9 to 3.27, but simply take the place of, and are treated as having been acquired for the same consideration as, the original options, so far as that consideration has not been taken into account in calculating the gain on an assignment or release within the extended definition in 3.10, either prior to the exchange, or at the same time, if the consideration on the exchange was partly in cash or in another form other than options (ICTA 1988, s 136(1)). This enables a reorganisation or rationalisation of option arrangements to take place without crystallising a charge, for example where, on a company take-over, it is desired to substitute options over shares in the new parent. Transactions within what is now s 136(1) were the subject of an appeal to the High Court in *Monarch Assurance Co Ltd v Special Comrs* [1986] STC 311, ChD, but the actual point at issue in that case was the Inspector's power to call for documents under TMA 1970, s 20.

3.32 Similar 'roll-over' provisions apply where as a result of two or more transactions a person ceases to hold an option, and he or a connected person (see 7.22) comes to hold another option in the same or a different company (whether or not that second option was acquired from a person to whom the first option was assigned). They apply where any of the transactions was effected under arrangements to which two or more holders of options potentially chargeable under s 135 were parties, and direct that, for the purposes of the 'roll-over' provisions of s 136(1) set out at 3.31, all the transactions shall be treated as one single transaction whereby the first option is assigned for a consideration which consists of the second (ICTA 1988, s 136(2)). The two option holders need not necessarily both be within s 135 (ie, have acquired the options by reason of employment). It is only necessary that the options themselves should be rights in respect of which tax may be chargeable under that section. In view of the discussion at 3.24, this would appear to extend to any option originally granted by reason of a Schedule E Case I employment (see 3.12), as even once it has been assigned it may still give rise to a s 135 charge if it passes into the hands of a person connected with the employee. The position is not affected by whether the assignment of the first option precedes, coincides with, or is subsequent to the acquisition of the second (ICTA 1988, s 136(3)). An example may illustrate the type of transactions in view:

Gilbert holds options in Jeffereys Ltd and assigns them to Partridge for a consideration in cash, on condition that Milman Ltd, which is controlled by Partridge, will grant options for a consideration to Cooper, an employee of Milman Ltd who is Gilbert's brother. The original options in Jeffereys Ltd are not treated as disposed of, but the new options in Milman Ltd are treated as having been acquired for the consideration originally given by Gilbert for the options in Jeffereys Ltd, plus the consideration actually given for the Milman Ltd options by Cooper.

3.33 The series of transactions discussed in 3.32 is treated 'for the purposes of [the straightforward 'roll-over' provisions set out in 3.31] as a single transaction whereby the one right [ie option] is assigned for a consideration which consists of or comprises the other right' (ICTA 1988, s 136(2)). Where the second option is granted to a connected person, it is not specifically stated that it is the holder of the first option who remains liable to the tax charge on a subsequent assignment or exercise. Neither would this automatically follow from the fact that the second option is treated as consideration for the first; that is not to say that it is necessarily to be treated as granted or assigned to the holder of the first option. However, this simple exchange of options is deemed to take place 'for the purposes of subsection (1) above' (ie s 136(1): see 3.31), which only contemplates an acquisition of the second option by the holder of the first. It would appear, therefore, that any subsequent charge arises on the original holder, not on the connected person. This is consistent with analogous charges on the employee rather than the connected person under s 135(6) (see 3.24) and under the corresponding provisions of other employee share legislation referred to there.

Pre-May 1966 options

3.34 Where options were granted before 3 May 1966, any gain realised on their exercise, assignment or release is calculated by substituting for the consideration actually given (ie for the option itself, or for the shares, under the terms of the option) the market value of the shares at 3 May 1966, if greater. Thus, the gain cannot exceed the difference between the market value on that date and on the date of the transaction giving rise to the charge (ICTA 1988, s 136(4)(a)). As a corollary, the charge to tax on the grant of the option, under *Abbott v Philbin* (see 3.5), is unaffected by the subsequent enactment of what is now s 135(2) (see 3.15), which removed that charge (except in the case of options exercisable more than seven years after their grant and granted on or after 11 April 1972; see 3.38 to 3.43), but any amount so chargeable under Schedule E, Case I (see 7.89) is treated on a subsequent exercise, assignment or release of the option as if it formed part of the consideration for its grant, so that it is deducted in arriving at the amount of the gain (ICTA 1988, s 136(4)(b)). If the benefit of the grant was taxable under Case II or III, then the gain on exercise is not, in any case, taxable under s 135 (see 3.12).

3.35 Few options granted before 3 May 1966 now remain in existence, but in a company with a steadily advancing share price, where there is no time limit on the exercise of the option, and the holder has no pressing need for liquid funds, it will be advantageous to retain options rather than shares to 'gear up' the return on the investment, as explained at 1.41.

Information provisions

3.36 Requirements are imposed on companies involved in unapproved share option schemes to deliver written particulars of certain transactions to the Inland Revenue not later than 30 days after the end of the year of assessment in which they take place (ICTA 1988, s 136(6)). The relevant transactions are:

(a) the grant by the company of an option, by reason of employment;
(b) the allotment or transfer by the company of any shares, on the exercise of such an option;
(c) the provision by the company of any benefit in money or money's worth, after 18 March 1986, for the assignment of such an option, or for its release in whole or in part; the provision of such a benefit for, or in connection with, an omission, or undertaking to omit, to exercise such an option; or its provision for, or in connection with, the grant or undertaking to grant an option to acquire shares or an interest in shares to which the first option relates. For transactions prior to 18 March 1986 the requirement extended only to the giving of consideration by the company for the assignment or release in whole or in part of such an option (bearing in mind the extended definition of 'release' in 3.10);
(d) the receipt by the company of written notice of the assignment of such an option (which the grantor company will normally require under the terms of its option arrangement, for its own protection).

It should be noted that the reporting requirement lies on the company which carries out the action specified in (a)–(c), or receives the notice mentioned in (d). If, therefore, options are granted to the employees of a subsidiary company by, and over the shares of, the parent company, which carries out all the administration of the scheme, there will be no reporting requirement on the subsidiary. Non-compliance with these reporting requirements renders the offending company liable to the penalties set out at 7.75 to 7.77.

Capital gains tax considerations

3.37 Where a gain is realised on the exercise of an option, either by the employer himself, or by another person, giving rise to a charge on the employee (see 3.24), the gain so chargeable is treated, in calculating the CGT charge on a subsequent disposal of the shares, as if it had formed part of the consideration given for their acquisition (CGTA 1979, s 32A(1) and (3)). This is in accord with corresponding provisions in relation to the 'growth in value' and 'special benefits' charges under ICTA 1988, s 138 and FA 1988, ss 78 to 80, and the charge on the write-off of a 'notional loan' under ICTA 1988, s 162 (see 2.295, 2.173 and 2.315). Where none of the relevant exemptions is available, any subsequent growth in value of the shares will be within the income tax charge under ICTA 1988, s 138, or FA 1988, s 78 or 79 (as explained at 2.48) and, to that extent, will not be within the capital gains tax charge (see 2.295 and 2.173 to 2.175).

OPTIONS CAPABLE OF EXERCISE MORE THAN SEVEN YEARS AFTER GRANT: ICTA 1988, s 135(2) and (5)

3.38 Where an option is obtained by a person on or after 11 April 1972 as an employee or director (as to which see 3.9 to 3.12), and that option is capable of exercise later than seven years after it is obtained, ICTA 1988, s 135(2), which removes the charge to tax on the grant of an option (see 3.15), does not apply, so that the charge on the value of the option under the general Schedule E provisions of ICTA 1988, s 19, in the light of the decision in *Abbott v Philbin* (see 3.5) still applies. Any tax so charged is deductible from any subsequent charge under s 135 on the exercise, assignment, or release of the option, but not so as to give rise to a repayment (ICTA 1988, s 135(5)(a)).

3.39 It therefore becomes necessary to establish the value of the option itself, as discussed at 3.6 and 3.7. A formula for ascertaining a minimum value is provided by s 135(5)(b), and in practice, in view of the difficulties of valuing such a right, this minimum figure is normally accepted as the true value. It is arrived at by ascertaining the value at the time of the grant of the shares which may be acquired by exercise of the option, or (if higher) of shares for which the shares acquired may be exchanged, and deducting the amount of the consideration for which the shares may be acquired under the option (or the value of that consideration if not in cash). If that consideration is variable, for example where it falls to be ascertained under a formula, the least amount or value which may be so paid is taken, thus giving the highest possible value for the option. In cases where the formula includes no lower limit, for example, where the price is a fraction or multiple of the share price at a given future date, the consideration to be taken into account will therefore be nil or minimal, even though, in the event, the amount actually paid may be substantial. While the calculation will not be adjusted to take account of the actual payment, relief will effectively be provided by offset against the charge on exercise, subject, as mentioned at 3.38, to the proviso that no repayment may be made.

3.40 While this formula provides a ready means of establishing the value of the option, and avoids the difficulties of valuation discussed at 3.6 and 3.7, it is, therefore, liable to produce 'rough justice'. This is particularly so where the option is granted on terms which defer the holder's right to exercise it, as no discount is given to take account of this factor.

3.41 The rationale of the legislation is to ensure that the tax charge on the benefit granted cannot be deferred indefinitely, and also perhaps to discourage the grant of options for terms longer than seven years. In practice, particularly in view of the provisions of s 135(5), few such options are granted, and, if they are, they are now unlikely to contain variable payment or deferred exercise clauses, so that the inequities outlined in 3.39 above rarely arise.

3.42 The provisions of what is now s 135(5) were examined in *Williamson v Dalton* [1981] STC 753, [1981] TR 337 where the taxpayer contended that the grant of an option exercisable more than seven years thereafter was not a perquisite of his employment because it was so hedged about with restrictions on its exercise as to confer no benefit at that time. The Commissioners rejected this argument, and held that it was a taxable emolument, but that in practice it had no assessable value at the time of its grant. In the High Court, the finding that it was a taxable benefit was upheld, but the value ascertained under the formula of s 135(5)(b) was substituted for the nil value put on it by the Commissioners, Vinelott J stating simply (at 757) 'It seems to me the Commissioners must have overlooked [s 135(5)(b)]'.

3.43 'Market value' for the above purposes is as defined in 7.56 to 7.64 (ICTA 1988, s 140(3); CGTA 1979, s 150) and the term 'shares' is as defined in 3.10.

PAYMENT OF LIABILITY UNDER ICTA 1988, s 135 BY INSTALMENTS

Time limits

3.44 An election for payment of tax by instalments is available in respect of certain gains realised on the exercise of a share option and chargeable to tax under what is now ICTA 1988, s 135 for the year of assessment 1982/83 or any subsequent year. It does not apply to gains realised on the assignment or release of an option, being designed to recognise the fact that, as discussed at 3.18, the exercise of an option, unlike an assignment or release, may crystallise a tax charge without making any funds available to satisfy it. In addition, an instalment election may only be made where the option was granted before 6 April 1984 (ICTA 1988, s 137(1)(a)). This removal of the instalment facility, except in respect of existing options, only two years after it was first made available, accompanied the introduction of an altogether more favourable regime for share options under Inland Revenue approved selective schemes (see Chapter 6), which was considered to render the existing relief unnecessary.

The exercise price

3.45 For payment by instalments to be possible, the shares must have been acquired, on the exercise of the option, for a consideration not less than the market value (see 7.56 to 7.64: ICTA 1988, s 137(1)(b); CGTA 1979, s 150) of shares of the same class at the time the option was granted, or, if it was granted before 6 April 1982, not less than 90% of that market value (ICTA 1988, s 137(1)(b)). This latter provision for earlier options prevents the instalment facility being denied by the existence of a small discount to market value made available before the facility could have been in contemplation. Shares acquired for less than the required value solely because of a diminution in the market value of shares of the relevant class which is attributable wholly to a variation in the share capital after the grant of the option are treated as meeting the necessary test (ICTA 1988, s 137(2)), thus allowing for adjustments to the exercise price to compensate for reorganisations such as rights issues or the splitting of share capital into smaller units.

The £250 limit

3.46 Broadly speaking, the instalment facility is only available where more than £250 is payable (ICTA 1988, s 137(1)(c)). The requirement of the legislation is that, following an assessment under Schedule E for the year in which the grant was exercised, an amount of tax on that exercise exceeding £250 is payable to the Collector of Taxes under the PAYE regulations. Thus, if there has been an overpayment due to other factors, such as an erroneous coding, with the result that £250 or less remains payable, then despite a s 135 charge in excess of that amount, it will not be possible to pay in instalments.

The election

3.47 An election for payment in instalments must be made to the Inspector by the taxpayer, in writing, within 60 days of the expiry of the year of assessment in which the exercise was made (ICTA 1988, s 137(1)(d) and (3)).

The timing of instalments

3.48 If a valid election is made, payment is due in five equal instalments (three instalments for exercises in the year 1982/83) (ICTA 1988, s 137(4); FA 1982, s 40(4) as enacted, before amendment by FA 1984, s 39(8)). The first instalment is due and payable within 14 days of application for the tax being made by the Collector of Taxes under the PAYE regulations (normally in the July following the year of assessment in which the exercise was made) (ICTA 1988, s 137(4)(a)). The fifth instalment is due and payable on the last day of the fifth year of assessment following the end of the year in which the exercise took place (or the end of the third year, for exercises in 1982/83) (FA 1982, s 40(4)(b), prior to amendment by FA 1984, s 39(8); ICTA 1988, s 137(4)(b)).

3.49 The second, third and fourth instalments (or the second instalment only, in the case of exercises in 1982/83) are due at such dates as will ensure that, as far as possible, the interval between any two consecutive instalments is the same (FA 1982, s 40(4)(c), prior to amendment by FA 1984, s 39(8); ICTA 1988, s 137(4)(c)).

3.50 Where, for any reason, the initial application for tax by the Collector is delayed until 14 days before the end of the fifth year of assessment following that in which the exercise takes place, (or the third year in the case of an exercise in 1982/83) or is issued thereafter, no payment is due until 14 days after the application, but at that stage all instalments are due at once (FA 1982, s 40(5), prior to amendment by FA 1984, s 39(8); ICTA 1988, s 137(5)).

Example

3.51 The application of these rules is illustrated by the following example:

> Suckling has an option to purchase shares in his employer, Bird Ltd, granted in 1983/84, which he exercises in June 1988, realising a gain of £7,500. He elects to make payment in five instalments, before the 60-day time limit expires on 4 June 1989, and receives a demand for the tax due on 21 July 1989.
>
> The first instalment is due on 4 August 1989, and the fifth on 5 April 1994. Between these dates are 1,705 days, so that the second, third and fourth instalments are due on 5 October 1990, 5 December 1991, and 3 February 1993, each 427 or 426 days after the previous payment.

The background to the provisions

3.52 It may seem surprising that the three-year instalment period should have been replaced by a five-year period with effect for options *exercised* after 5 April 1983, when no system of payment by instalments is available at all for options *granted* after 5 April 1984; and it is even more surprising when it is considered that the withdrawal of the relief and its temporary extension were contained in adjacent subsections of FA 1984 (sub-ss (7) and (8) of s 39). The reason for this apparent inconsistency is that the extension to payment by five instalments was originally put forward in cl 29(6) and (7) of the first Finance Bill of 1983, following Sir Geoffrey Howe's last Budget, but failed to pass into law as a result of the General Election of that year. The Government gave an undertaking at that time to reintroduce the measure the following year, and this was accordingly done, with effect from the original commencement date, notwithstanding the decision of the new Chancellor of the Exchequer, Mr Nigel Lawson, to introduce the favourable tax treatment for selective share option schemes discussed in Chapter 6, and, accordingly, to remove the instalment facility altogether for existing schemes.

Payment of outstanding instalments

3.53 Instalments which have not yet become due may nevertheless be paid at any time if the taxpayer so desires. This will normally only be done as an administrative convenience, where small amounts (though above £250: see 3.46) are involved, and the individual wishes to disencumber himself of outstanding debts, for example, because he is emigrating and severing his links with the UK. If the amounts are significant, and he is concerned that whereas he presently has the wherewithal to pay, he may not have in the future, then he will normally be better advised to purchase certificates of tax deposit, on which interest will accrue (subject to detailed rules) pending their use in settlement of the liability. If the individual becomes bankrupt under the law of any part of the UK, all outstanding instalments become payable immediately (ICTA 1988, s 137(6)). There is no provision to make outstanding instalments payable immediately on death, and therefore, while the point is not explicitly stated, it would appear that personal representatives of a deceased person may continue to make payments by instalments, although, with the agreement of the beneficiaries, they may often prefer to pay off the balance earlier than strictly necessary, in order to be in a position to wind up the estate. There is no right for the personal representatives themselves to make the election for instalment payments.

Determining the tax chargeable

3.54 In determining the amount of tax chargeable on a gain for the purpose of applying the instalment facility, the gain on exercise of the option is treated as forming the highest part of the individual's income for the relevant year of assessment, and thus as being taxable at his marginal rates, but subject to any other provision of the Income Tax Acts requiring any other income to be so treated, such as ICTA 1988, s 550, dealing with gains from life assurance, annuity and capital redemption policies (ICTA 1988, s 137(7)).

CIRCUMSTANCES IN WHICH ICTA 1988, s 135 DOES NOT APPLY

3.55 The charge to tax under ICTA 1988, s 135 on the exercise of an option is removed in the case of options granted under an Inland Revenue approved savings-related share option scheme or selective share option scheme, provided that it remains approved at the time of exercise and that certain specified conditions are satisfied (ICTA 1988, s 185(3) to (5): see 5.8 and 6.10).

3.56 Where a charge under ICTA 1988, s 135 does arise on the exercise of options in a selective scheme, because it is no longer approved at that time, or because the conditions mentioned at 3.55 and set out more fully at 6.7 are not fulfilled, the amount of the gain arising is reduced by that part of any 'discount' on the grant of the option which has previously given rise to a charge to tax under ICTA 1988, s 185(6) (see further at 6.12).

MISCELLANEOUS

Pension provision

3.57 It was formerly understood that, in the view of the Inland Revenue Superannuation Funds Office, any amount taxable under what is now ICTA 1988, s 135 on the exercise of a share option could be taken into account in the calculation of pension entitlement, and of the lump sum commutation payment available on retirement. This result from the application of para 6.12(a) of the SFO booklet IR 12 'Occupational pension schemes: notes on approval under FA 1970 [now ICTA 1988, Part XIV, Ch I]', which stated that 'final remuneration' could be remuneration for any one of the five years preceding normal retirement date, and that this figure included the average over a suitable period (usually three or more years) 'of any fluctuating emoluments such as commission or bonuses'. Following F(No 2)A 1987, Sch 3, para 7 (now ICTA 1988, s 612) 'remuneration' does not include 'anything in respect of which tax is chargeable under Schedule E and which arises from the acquisition or disposal of shares or an interest in shares or from a right to acquire shares'.

4 Inland Revenue approved 'profit-sharing' (share appropriation) schemes

SUMMARY

4.1 The Finance Act 1978 introduced provisions for the establishment of Inland Revenue approved 'profit-sharing' schemes, under which a company may provide trustees with funds for the purchase of shares in that company, to be held on behalf of employees. The provision of such funds is a tax-allowable expense to the employing company. If full advantage is taken of such a scheme, there is no charge to tax on the employee under the general provisions of Schedule E in respect of the acquisition of the beneficial interest in the relevant shares (see 2.13 to 2.28). Neither is there any 'growth in value' charge under ICTA 1988, s 138(1)(a) or FA 1988, ss 78 or 79 (see 2.190 to 2.286 and 2.53 to 2.121) or notional loan charge under ICTA 1988, s 162 (see 2.303 to 2.339), though a 'special benefits' charge under ICTA 1988, s 138(1)(b) or FA 1988, s 80 may still arise (see 2.287 to 2.294 and 2.122 to 2.137). CGT is charged on a realisation of the employee's interest, in the normal way.

4.2 To obtain approval, a scheme must provide that an individual may not dispose of his shares within the first two years of ownership, subject to certain exceptions. After that time an income tax charge will arise on a disposal (in addition to any CGT charge) on a percentage of the original market value (or of the disposal price, if lower), as follows:

First four years	100%
Fifth year	75%
Thereafter	Nil

There is, however, still no charge on any growth in value under ICTA 1988, s 138(1)(a) or FA 1988, ss 79 or 80.

4.3 The maximum value of shares which may be allocated to any individual under a scheme in a year of assessment is the greatest of £1,250 or 10% of his remuneration for the year in question or the previous year (excluding benefits in kind), but subject to an overriding limit of £5,000.

4.4 All full-time employees who are resident and ordinarily resident in the UK must be eligible to join the scheme on similar terms, although it is possible to set a minimum qualifying period of employment, not exceeding five years, and the number of shares appropriated to employees may vary according to remuneration, length of service or similar factors.

4.5 Despite the use of the term 'profit-sharing schemes' in the relevant legislation, there need be no relationship between the company's profits and the shares appropriated to employees, by contrast, for example, with 'old' (FA 1973) profit-sharing schemes (see 2.232 to 2.241).

APPROPRIATED SHARES: TAX EXEMPTIONS

General

4.6 The tax exemptions set out in 4.7 to 4.12 apply where, after 5 April 1979, the trustees of an approved scheme appropriate to an individual who participates in the scheme shares (or stock: ICTA 1988, s 187(2)) which they have previously acquired, and in respect of which the 'conditions as to the shares' set out in ICTA 1988, Sch 9, paras 10 to 12 and 14 (see 4.119 to 4.140) are fulfilled (ICTA 1988, s 186(1)). An 'approved' scheme is one approved by the Board of Inland Revenue under the procedure set out in ICTA 1988, Sch 9, paras 1 to 5: see 4.78 to 4.152 (ICTA 1988, s 187(2)). Approval could be sought at any time after the passing of FA 1978 on 31 July 1978, and funds could be passed to the trustees so as to obtain a tax deduction for the company (see 4.75 to 4.77) at any time from the date of that approval. Funds transferred could be applied immediately by the trustees in the purchase of shares, but the shares so acquired could not be appropriated to employees until the following 6 April (FA 1978, s 53(1), now ICTA 1988, s 186(1)). 'Trustees', in relation to an approved scheme or a participant's shares (see 4.13), means the body of persons for the establishment of which the scheme must provide as mentioned in 4.90 (ICTA 1988, s 187(2)).

The employee

4.7 The value of the shares appropriated to an employee, up to the limit discussed at 4.61, is not chargeable to tax as 'money's worth' representing an emolument under Schedule E: see the discussion of *Weight v Salmon* at 2.13 to 2.24 (ICTA 1988, s 186(2)(a)). Neither are the shares so acquired liable to a 'growth in value' charge under ICTA 1988, s 138(1)(a) or FA 1988, ss 78 or 79 (see 2.190 to 2.286 and 2.53 to 2.121) on subsequent capital appreciation, or to an 'interest' charge or a 'write-off' charge under ICTA 1988, s 162 (see 2.303 to 2.339) in respect of the 'notional loan' which would otherwise be created by their acquisition for no consideration (and thus 'at an undervalue' within the terms of s 162) (ICTA 1988, s 186(2)(b)). Thus, provided the shares are retained for the necessary period (see 4.13 to 4.32), the only charge which can arise in connection with them is to CGT on their eventual disposal (as to the calculation of which, see 4.62 to 4.66). A special benefits charge may still arise, however: see 2.122 to 2.137 and 2.287 to 2.294.

4.8 The legislation provides, in s 186(2)(b), that the employee, 'shall not be chargeable to income tax . . . by virtue of section 162 in any case where the shares are appropriated to him at an undervalue within the meaning of that section' (as they will always be, as no consideration whatever is given for them). It would appear from the reference to an undervalue that the intention is only to exclude the 'notional loan' charges of ICTA 1988, s 162, but it appears that the effect is also to prevent any charge under s 162(6), which applies to a disposal of shares, however acquired, at a price in excess of market value (see 2.327 to 2.328).

The trustees

Income tax

4.9 For the intervening period between acquisition of shares by the trustees and their appropriation to employees, the trustees' liability to basic rate income tax on any dividends received is satisfied by the tax credit attaching to them (ICTA 1988, s 231), but the trust remains liable in principle to the 'additional rate' of tax, currently 10%, on the income of accumulation and discretionary trusts (ICTA 1988, ss 686 and 832(1); FA 1988, s 24(4)). Provided, however, that the 'conditions as to the shares' set out at 4.119 to 4.140 are fulfilled, and the shares are appropriated to employees in accordance with the scheme within 18 months of acquisition by the trustees, the additional rate charge does not apply to income consisting of the dividends on those shares (ICTA 1988, s 186(11)). It still, however, applies to any other income, such as the return from investment of the dividend monies, or of receipts from the company which have not yet been used to purchase shares.

Capital gains tax

4.10 Similarly, any appropriation of shares to a 'participant' (defined by ICTA 1988, s 187(2) as 'an individual to whom the trustees of the scheme have appropriated shares') within 18 months of their acquisition, and in accordance with the scheme, is not treated as giving rise to a gain chargeable to CGT under CGTA 1979, s 54 which provides, in normal circumstances, that where a person becomes absolutely entitled to settled property as against trustees, that property is deemed to have been disposed of and reacquired by the trustees—in the latter case as nominees for the person becoming absolutely entitled—for a consideration equal to its market value, as defined in 7.56 to 7.64 (CGTA 1979, s 144A(2)(d)).

General

4.11 In the case of companies subject to the guidelines of the Investment Committee of the Association of British Insurers (see 1.14), the 18 months allowed by the legislation for the appropriation of shares is not in practice available, as immediate allocation of shares to participants is required (see point (6) at Appendix 1).

4.12 For the purpose of the exemptions from the additional rate charge (see 4.9) and from CGT (see 4.10) the question of whether shares are appropriated to a participant within 18 months is determined by treating shares acquired at an earlier time as appropriated before shares of the same class acquired at a later time (a 'first in—first out' rule) (ICTA 1988, s 186(11)).

THE INCOME TAX CHARGE ON EARLY DISPOSAL

General

4.13 No charge to income tax arises on disposal of a participant's shares after the 'release date'. In the original legislation, the release date was the tenth anniversary of appropriation (FA 1978, ss 54(6) and 61(1), now FA 1988, s 187(2)). For appropriations after 5 April 1979, this became the seventh anniversary (FA 1980, s 46(4)), and from 25 July 1985 (irrespective of the date of appropriation), the fifth anniversary (FA 1985, s 45(2)). A 'participant's shares' are defined, somewhat superfluously, as 'the shares which have been appropriated to [him] by the trustees of an approved scheme' (ICTA 1988, s 187(2); subject to Sch 10, para 5, as to which see 4.42 to 4.53). No specific statutory provision is required to ensure that an income tax charge does not arise on disposal after the release date, as no charge would normally arise on the disposal of shares; rather, provisions are included in the legislation to impose a charge to income tax if the trustees (who hold the appropriated shares on behalf of the participant) dispose of any of his shares before the release date or his earlier death. In such a case the participant (not the trustees) is chargeable to income tax under the appropriate Case of Schedule E (see 7.88 to 7.96) for the year of assessment in which the disposal takes place, on the 'appropriate percentage' (see 4.26 to 4.29) of the 'locked-in value' (see 4.14) of the shares at the time of the disposal (ICTA 1988, s 186(4)).

The 'locked-in value'

4.14 The 'locked-in value' of a participant's shares, subject to particular provisions with regard to company reconstructions and amalgamations (see 4.42 to 4.53) and with regard to shares appropriated to an individual in excess of the limits discussed at 4.61 or at a time when he is ineligible to participate in the scheme (see 4.141 to 4.145), is in most cases their 'initial market value' (ICTA 1988, ss 186(5)(b) and 187(2)), which term is defined at 4.15. If, however, prior to the disposal in question the participant has become liable to income tax on a capital receipt (see 4.33 to 4.41) referable to those shares, the locked-in value is the initial market value less the amount of that capital receipt (or its value if it takes the form of a receipt in specie). If there has been more than one such receipt, their aggregate amount or value is deducted (ICTA 1988, s 186(5)(a)). Thus credit is effectively given for any amount already taxed on an earlier 'part-disposal', limiting the total amount charged to tax on all the transactions taken together to the 'appropriate percentage' of the initial market value which was exempted on the acquisition of the shares (see 4.7). See also 7.107.

Initial market value

4.15 The 'initial market value' of any of a participant's shares is their market value (see 4.17) on the date on which they were appropriated to him or, if the Board of Inland Revenue and the trustees of the scheme so agree in writing, their market value on, or by reference to, such earlier date or dates as may be provided for in the agreement (ICTA 1988, Sch 9, para 30(4) and s 187(2)). The determination of value 'by reference to' rather than 'on' a stipulated date has the effect that the legislation is apt (for example) to cover the situation on reorganisation of a company's share capital: if 'B' ordinary shares are appropriated to participants on 5 May, following a reorganisation which substituted two new 'B' ordinary shares for every 'A' ordinary share in the company on 1 May, but written agreement is reached between the Inland Revenue and the trustees for use of a 30 April initial market value, then this cannot be determined according to the value of 'B' shares 'on' 30 April, at which date they did not exist. It can, however, be ascertained 'by reference to' the 30 April value of the 'A' shares (the value of the 'B' shares being half of that figure).

4.16 The value under such an agreement may be determined as at such earlier 'date *or dates*' as may be specified. In the normal course, one date only will be agreed, but by the inclusion of the plural the wording may cover a formula such as 'the highest (or the lowest) figure at which the shares are quoted on The Stock Exchange between 1 June and 8 June 1988', or 'the quoted price on 31 March or 5 April 1988, whichever shall be the higher', or an average price over a range of dates. See also specimen formula in definitions section of Appendix 5, re quoted shares.

4.17 'Market value' is as defined in 7.56 to 7.64 (ICTA 1988, s 187(2); CGTA 1979, s 150), and, in determining that value, no account is to be taken (in the view of the Inland Revenue) of any restrictions on the participant's ability to deal with the shares imposed by his contract with the company under the terms of the scheme, as discussed at 4.78 to 4.87 (Inland Revenue booklet IR 36 'Approved profit-sharing schemes', para 3.2). Any query on the valuation of shares appropriated under an approved profit-sharing scheme should be addressed to: Inland Revenue, Capital Taxes Office, Shares Valuation Division 2 (Employee Share Schemes) Minford House, Rockley Road, London W14 0DF (telephone (01) 630 4622 ext 498 or 494).

4.18 The facility for agreement of initial market value by reference to an alternative date is included as a matter of administrative convenience. For example, it may be desired to send notices of appropriation to participants which include details of the initial market value of the shares, in order to enable them to assess the effect of any future disposal. This would not be possible in the case of quoted shares which fluctuated in price from day to day, using the value on the date of appropriation, as that would not be known until the following day (and, even then, forms and letters would have to be prepared). The use of a figure based on an earlier date obviates this problem. Similarly, if under the terms of the scheme letters had to be sent to all participants and potential participants advising them of their entitlement and inviting them to 'take up' their shares, which would only be appropriated on receipt of a form of acceptance, then appropriations might be 'staggered' over a period of days, or weeks. In such a case, it would obviously be of advantage to have one 'initial market value' for all shares irrespective of their actual date of appropriation. In addition, an appropriation by reference to an as yet unascertained price on the date of appropriation might result in the monetary limits on allocations to any one employee (see 4.61) being exceeded, and the use of an earlier date avoids this problem also.

4.19 In practice, the Inland Revenue will agree the use of an 'earlier price' if the purpose is merely to avoid the complexity introduced by short-term market fluctuations, and where the financial effect is minimal, and could work to the benefit or detriment of the taxpayer. If it is clear that the price of the shares is likely to rise, so that a financial benefit to participants from such an agreement between the Inland Revenue and the trustees is virtually guaranteed, it is unlikely to be forthcoming. The legislation does not, strictly, demand a *prior* agreement, and in certain cases, where the motive was simply administrative convenience, the Inland Revenue might perhaps enter into an agreement after the event. Clearly, however, a prior approach should always be made by the trustees where possible, as the Board cannot be expected to enter into an agreement which is, in the event, prejudicial to the Revenue, even if that effect could not have been foreseen, and its terms are such that had it been proposed beforehand it would almost certainly have been accepted. In general, the Inland Revenue will only agree to determine the initial market value by reference to an earlier date or dates if the same basis is used consistently for all future appropriations (IR 36, para 3.3). If it is expected that a series of appropriations of unquoted shares will be made on different dates, Shares Valuation Division is prepared to negotiate with the company a single initial market value, to apply to all appropriations within a prescribed period, of up to one year. Such an agreement will only be made on the understanding that the valuation may have to be renegotiated if, during that period, there is a major change in the trading or financial position of the company or in the general level of share prices. The Inland Revenue has indicated that it considers the most suitable time for agreeing such a value to be immediately after the publication of the company's statutory accounts. An agreement of this nature is without prejudice to the valuation of the shares for any other tax purposes (IR 36, para 3.5).

Substitution of proceeds for market value

4.20 If, on an occasion of charge as described at 4.13, where shares are disposed of before the five-year release date (or earlier death of the participant) the proceeds are less than the 'locked-in value' (see 4.14) of the shares, then the Schedule E charge arises on the 'appropriate percentage' of the proceeds, rather than of the locked-in value (ICTA 1988, s 186(6)). If, therefore, the charge on disposal is regarded as, effectively, a substitute for the charge which was not made on acquisition (see 4.7), this means that the participant is protected against any fall in value over the period, being taxed on only the 'appropriate percentage' of the amount actually received, not of the value at an earlier date at which he was prohibited (see 4.79 to 4.81) from realising the shares.

Adjustment for rights issues

4.21 For the purpose of applying the rule in 4.20, which substitutes proceeds for locked-in value if the former is smaller, an adjustment is made for any amount paid to the trustees by the participant to enable them to take up shares on his behalf under rights issues. Where a rights issue is made by the company, it is unlikely that in the normal course of events the trustees will have funds on hand to take it up on behalf of all shareholders, unless the company specifically provides them with a contribution for this purpose. Participants may therefore provide the necessary funds themselves, and the rights of those who do not do so will be sold (and the proceeds dealt with as set out at 4.33 to 4.41). Where such a payment has been made to the trustees to take up rights issues, the proceeds of disposal (for the purposes of determining whether they are less than the initial market value; and, if so, of determining the Schedule E charge based on proceeds) are reduced by a proportion of the payment (or of the aggregate of the payments, if there has been more than one). The appropriate proportion is that which, immediately before the disposal, the market value of the shares disposed of bore to the value of all the participant's shares held by the trustees at that time (ICTA 1988, s 186(7)). It appears that this calculation may be affected by whether shares which have passed the five-year release date have been left in the hands of the trustees or transferred to the legal ownership of the participant, although such shares, if they remain in the hands of the trustees, will in any case be treated as forming the first tranche of any disposal (see 4.30), and the Schedule E charge will not apply to that part of the disposal. It will, therefore, be advisable to transfer such 'free' shares to the participant before making the disposal from the 'pre-release' shares, unless it is clear that the proceeds, even when reduced to the maximum extent in respect of rights issue payments, will be greater than the locked-in value, so that the charge will be based on the latter figure. The calculation is illustrated in the following example:

> The trustees of the Bragge Ltd profit-sharing scheme hold 2,500 shares on behalf of Otway, none of which have yet reached the release date. Their initial market value, which, as there have been no capital receipts, is also their locked-in value, is £3,000. This figure takes account of an adjustment in respect of two rights issues, each giving rise to a further holding of 500 shares. To enable the first to be taken up, Otway provided the trustees with £400, and, in respect of the second, with £600.
>
> Before the release date, Otway instructs the trustees to sell 1,000 shares, with a locked-in value of £1,200 (ie £3,000 × 1,000/2,500), and receives proceeds of £1,300.
>
> To determine the figure on the appropriate percentage of which the charge arises, the proceeds must be reduced by:
>
> $$(\pounds 400 + \pounds 600) \times \frac{1{,}300}{3{,}250} = \pounds 400$$
>
> The charge is therefore based on £900 (the proceeds of £1,300 as reduced by rights issue consideration of £400), rather than on the locked-in value of £1,200.

4.22 It should be noted that the formula illustrated in 4.21 will not give a totally equitable result where there have been further appropriations after the rights issue, as it effectively assumes that the rights issue consideration relates equally to all shares held by the trustees for the participant at the time of the disposal. Nevertheless, any calculation which took account of such points would be extremely complex, and the amounts involved can, in the nature of the case, never be very large.

4.23 In assessing the size of any 'payment to the trustees to enable them to exercise rights' within 4.21, no account is taken of any payment if, or to the extent that, it consists of the proceeds of disposal of rights arising under a rights issue (ICTA 1988, s 186(8)(a)). A 'payment to the trustees', in this context, will involve leaving in their hands the sums realised on the disposal of rights to which they have the legal title (but not the beneficial ownership). Although not explicitly stated, it is thought that the legislation cannot be referring to the sale of rights attaching to shares no longer held within the scheme, having been transferred to the participant after the release date (or to rights attaching to completely unrelated shares) as, quite apart from the illogicality of such a provision, there would be insoluble problems of identifying funds with their particular source. If shares remain with the trustees past the release date, however, any proceeds from the sale of rights will be within this provision, and this may provide an additional reason (cf 4.21) for transferring such shares to the legal ownership of the participant.

4.24 To the extent that any payment to the trustees has already been taken into account in determining disposal proceeds on a previous occasion (whether or not the proceeds as so reduced were, in the result, lower than the locked-in value, so as to be substituted for that value in calculating the Schedule E charge), such payment is not deducted from the proceeds (or taken into the aggregate amount deducted from proceeds, as the case may be) on a subsequent disposal (ICTA 1988, s 186(8)(b)).

4.25 'Rights arising under a rights issue' are defined as rights conferred in respect of a participant's shares, being rights to be allotted, on payment, other shares or securities or rights of any description in the same company (ICTA 1988, s 186(8)), so that, for example, the right to subscribe for debenture stock, or to subscribe for options to purchase shares at a later date, would be included within the term 'rights arising under a rights issue'.

The 'appropriate percentage'

General

4.26 As stated at 4.13, the sale of shares by the trustees on behalf of the participant before the five-year release date or the participant's earlier death gives rise to a Schedule E charge on the 'appropriate percentage' of the 'locked-in value' (see 4.14) or of the disposal proceeds if lower (see 4.20). The 'appropriate percentage', subject to special provisions as to excess or unauthorised shares (see 4.54 to 4.61), is as follows (ICTA 1988, Sch 10, para 3 and s 187(2).

Before fourth anniversary of appropriation	100%
On or after fourth anniversary and before fifth anniversary	75%

Where the participant ceases to be an employee or director of the company which has established the scheme or, in the case of a group scheme (see 4.92), a participating company, by reason of injury or disability or on account of his being dismissed by reason of redundancy, within the meaning of the Redundancy Payments Act 1965 or the Contracts of Employment and Redundancy Payments Act (Northern Ireland) 1965; or where he reaches pensionable age, as defined in the Social Security Act 1975, Sch 20 (ie 60 for women and 65 for men), the appropriate percentage is 50% (ICTA 1988, Sch 10 paras 2(a) and 3(c), and s 187(2)).

'Appropriate percentages' under previous legislation

4.27 The percentages set out in 4.26 were introduced, irrespective of the date of appropriation of the shares, for disposals on or after 25 July 1985 (FA 1985, s 43). The original percentages, for shares appropriated before 6 April 1979 (FA 1978, s 54(7)) were:

On or before fifth anniversary of appropriation	100%
After fifth anniversary and before seventh anniversary	50%
On or after seventh and before tenth anniversary	25%

For individuals ceasing employment due to injury, disability or any of the other reasons mentioned in 4.26, a 50% figure applied until its reduction to 25% on the seventh anniversary.

4.28 For shares appropriated after 5 April 1979, FA 1980, s 46(5) altered the appropriate percentages to:

Before fourth anniversary of appropriation	100%
On or after fourth and before fifth anniversary	75%
On or after fifth and before sixth anniversary	50%
On or after sixth and before seventh anniversary	25%

For individuals ceasing employment due to injury, disability, or any of the other reasons set out in 4.26, the 50% percentage mentioned there applied, until its reduction to 25% on the sixth anniversary.

Injury, disability, redundancy or retirement

4.29 In the case of injury, disability or redundancy, the motive for the more generous provision mentioned at 4.26, 4.27 and 4.28 is obvious, in that a sale may be forced on the individual concerned by unforeseen circumstances, but it should be noted that it applies also to those individuals reaching normal retirement age, despite the fact that this eventuality could clearly be foreseen when the shares were appropriated to them, and also that, like CGT 'retirement relief' under FA 1985, ss 69 and 70, and Sch 20, it is in no way dependent on actual retirement.

Identification of shares disposed of

4.30 Where a disposal is made from a holding of shares which were appropriated to a participant at different times, then in determining the initial market value (see 4.15) and the 'locked-in value' where different (see 4.14), and also in determining the appropriate percentage in relation to each share disposed of, shares appropriated earlier are treated as being disposed of before shares appropriated later (i e a 'first in—first out' basis) (ICTA 1988, s 187(8)). This rule holds despite any instruction the participant may give the trustees designating particular shares as those to be disposed of, by reference, for example, to serial numbers of share certificates or to the date of their appropriation (ICTA 1988, s 187(9)). This may mean that different shares are treated as being disposed of (and retained) for the purpose of the Schedule E charge and of the CGT identification rules contained in FA 1985, Sch 19, para 8(2).

Deemed disposals of shares by the trustees

4.31 If at any time a participant disposes of his beneficial interest in shares, without the trustees disposing of the legal interest in them, for example by assigning his rights under the trust, that event is treated as a disposal of the shares by the trustees (with the consequent Schedule E charge on the participant), for a consideration equal to that which the participant obtained for the beneficial interest. No disposal is, however, treated as taking place where in England and Wales or Northern Ireland the beneficial interest becomes vested in any other person on the insolvency of the participant or otherwise by operation of law (for example, by order of the court on a divorce settlement). Similarly, no disposal is treated as occurring if, in Scotland, the beneficial interest concerned becomes vested in a judicial factor, in a trustee on the participant's sequestrated estate, or in a trustee for the benefit of his creditors (ICTA 1988, s 186(9)). There appears to be a lacuna in the legislation here, in that any divestment of the participant's interest by operation of law in Scotland, such as on divorce, will still constitute a disposal unless it is in favour of one of the persons specifically mentioned (ie broadly, unless it takes place on the participant's insolvency). In addition, it should be noted that the loss of the beneficial rights under the trust by the operation of the bankruptcy laws of any territory outside the UK will still constitute a disposal, although it may be difficult to say what is the appropriate consideration to be taken into account.

The substitution of market value for proceeds

4.32 If the transfer of a participant's beneficial ownership of the shares takes place within the 'retention period' (broadly, within two years of appropriation, but see 4.79), the market value (see 7.56 to 7.64) of the shares at that time is substituted for the disposal proceeds (ICTA 1988, s 186(10)(c)). Market value is also substituted for the disposal proceeds, if any, if the Board of Inland Revenue considers that the disposal in question is not at arm's length, and so directs (ICTA 1988, s 186(10)(b)), or if a disposal by the trustees before the five-year release date takes the form of the transfer of the legal ownership to the participant himself (ICTA 1988, s 186(10)(a) and Sch 9, para 2(2)(c)). There is no formal means of challenging the Board's decision that a disposal is not at arm's length, but an appeal to the General or Special Commissioners may be made against any resulting Schedule E assessment (see 7.1 to 7.5).

CAPITAL RECEIPTS

General

4.33 If, before the five-year release date, the trustees become, or the participant becomes, entitled to receive any money (or money's worth in specie) in respect of, or by reference to, the participant's shares, the participant is chargeable to income tax for the year of assessment in which the entitlement arises under the appropriate case of Schedule E (see 7.88 to 7.96) on that 'capital receipt'. The charge is on the 'appropriate percentage' (see 4.26 to 4.29), determined according to the date when the entitlement arises, of so much of the amount of the receipt (or of its value if it is received in kind) as exceeds the 'appropriate allowance' for the year (as defined at 4.34) (ICTA 1988, s 186(3)). Examples of such receipts might include a capital distribution by the company, or, most commonly, a receipt on the sale of rights not exercised in a rights issue.

The 'appropriate allowance'

4.34 The 'appropriate allowance' is £20 plus a further £20 for each year of assessment within the five years immediately preceding the year of the receipt in which shares were appropriated to the participant under the scheme, subject to a maximum of £100 (ICTA 1988, s 186(12)). Prior to 6 April 1986 the appropriate allowance was £20 for each year within the preceding seven in which shares were appropriated to the participant, with a maximum of £140.

The change was effected (in line with the change in the release date, see 4.13) by FA 1985, s 45(4) and (5).

4.35 The appropriate allowance was introduced in its present form for receipts on or after 31 July 1982 (FA 1982, s 42(1) and (5)). Prior to that date, from 6 April 1980 onwards, there was a simple exemption where the value of the receipt (or, if smaller, the locked-in value of the shares from which it derived) was £10 or less. This did not extend to the first £10 of any larger receipt (FA 1980, s 46(6) & (14)). Before 6 April 1980, there was no relief for small capital receipts.

4.36 If in any year before the release date the trustees become, or the participant becomes, entitled to more than one capital receipt, they are set off against the appropriate allowance for that year in the order in which they are received (ICTA 1988, s 186(12)). It should be noted, however, that the 'appropriate allowance' is not reduced to take account of any reduction in the amount chargeable made, by virtue of the allowance, in any previous year. The operation of the allowance is illustrated in the following example:

> Shares in an approved profit-sharing scheme are appropriated to Bickerton in 1984, 1986 and 1987. In 1988, the trustees receive an amount of £600 in respect of the sale of rights attaching to his shares. The charge to income tax is on the 'appropriate percentage' (which will vary for that part of the receipt derived from each tranche of shares) of £520 (i e £600 reduced by £20 and by a further £20 for each of the three years in which appropriations were made). While the point is not specifically covered in the legislation, it seems that this remaining amount must be allocated to different years of appropriation on a pro rata basis before applying the 'appropriate percentage'.

4.37 In practice, the major effect of the 'appropriate allowance' is to exclude altogether a charge on small receipts from the sale of rights, so that the problem of apportioning the receipts to shares appropriated in different years, and applying different 'appropriate percentages' accordingly, is avoided.

Items not constituting capital receipts

4.38 Money or money's worth is not a 'capital receipt' for these purposes to the extent that it constitutes income in the hands of the recipient for the purposes of income tax (as, for example, where it forms a distribution within ICTA 1988, s 209 (ICTA 1988, Sch 10, para 4(1)(a); s 187(2)); or consists of the proceeds of a disposal, already chargeable as described at 4.13 to 4.32 (ICTA 1988, Sch 10, para 4(1)(b)); or consists of 'new shares' as defined within the context of the rules for company reconstructions and amalgamations discussed at 4.42 to 4.53 (ICTA 1988, Sch 10, para 4(1)(c)).

Disposal of rights for reinvestment

4.39 Where, on instructions given by or on behalf of the participant, or by any person in whom the beneficial interest in the participant's shares is for the time being vested (following a disposal as described at 4.32) the trustees dispose of some of the rights under a rights issue (as defined at 4.25), and use the proceeds to exercise other such rights, the money or money's worth which forms the proceeds of that disposal does not constitute a chargeable 'capital receipt' within 4.33 (ICTA 1988, Sch 10, para 4(2)). The rationale for this provision is clear: the participant is gaining no immediate access to funds and the 'disposal' is only undertaken to enable him to 'plough back' the value of his rights into shares at a time when he is unable or unwilling to introduce new consideration to take up all the rights as discussed at 4.21.

Restriction of charge to 'locked-in value'

4.40 If the amount of a capital receipt exceeds the figure which, immediately before the entitlement to the receipt arose, was the 'locked-in value' (see 4.14) of the shares to which the receipt is referable (ie the initial market value less any previous capital receipts) the receipt is treated as if it were of the amount of the locked-in value (ICTA 1988, Sch 10, para 4(3)). In this way, the total Schedule E charge on capital sums arising from the shares is limited to the value of the shares which was exempt from tax on their appropriation (reduced by the amount of the 'appropriate allowance').

Capital receipts arising after death

4.41 If the entitlement to the capital receipt arises after the death of the participant to whose shares it is referable, no income tax charge arises (ICTA 1988, Sch 10, para 4(4)). This is consistent with the restriction of the Schedule E charge on a disposal to events occurring before the release date or the participant's earlier death (see 4.13).

COMPANY RECONSTRUCTIONS AND AMALGAMATIONS

Application of capital gains tax rules

Bonus and rights issues, and alteration of class rights

4.42 Detailed provisions apply where there occurs in relation to a participant's shares (the 'original holding') a company reconstruction or similar transaction which results, for CGT purposes, in a new holding being equated with the original holding (ICTA 1988, Sch 10, para 5(1)). The relevant circumstances include a reorganisation or reduction of a company's share capital (CGTA 1979 s 77(1)), including:

(a) a case where persons are, whether for payment or not, allotted shares in, or debentures of, the company in respect of and in proportion to (or as nearly as may be in proportion to) their existing holdings of shares in, or of any class of shares in, the company: ie bonus or rights issues (CGTA 1979, s 77(2)(a)); or
(b) a case where there is more than one class of share and the rights attaching to any class are altered (CGTA 1979, s 77(2)(b)).

The circumstances in question do not include the reduction of capital by the paying-off of redeemable share capital, or the redemption of other share capital except by the issue of shares or debentures (with or without other consideration: see 4.53).

Conversion of securities

4.43 Other relevant circumstances are the conversion of securities (CGTA 1979, s 82(1)); that is, inter alia, a conversion of securities in a company into shares in that company (CGTA 1979, s 82(3)(a)(i)), including a conversion at the option of the holder of the securities as an alternative to their redemption for cash (CGTA 1979, s 82(3)(a)(ii)) and any exchange of securities in pursuance of an Act of Parliament which provides for compulsory acquisition of any shares or securities and the issue of other securities instead (CGTA 1979, s 82(3)(a)(iii)). 'Security' in the context of such conversions is defined in 7.97.

4.44 The CGT reconstruction provisions also apply where shares or debentures in a second company are issued to a person in exchange for shares or debentures of the original company and the second company holds, or in consequence of the exchange will hold, more than a quarter of the ordinary share capital (see 7.72) of the original company (CGTA 1979, s 85(1)(a)), or the second company issues its shares or debentures in exchange for shares in the original company as the result of a general offer which is made to members of the first company or to any class of them (with or without exceptions for persons connected with the second company), and which is made in the first instance on a condition such that if it were satisfied the second company would have control of the first (even if, in the event, it does not succeed in obtaining such control) (CGTA 1979, s 85(1)(b)). Also treated as an exchange of securities in one company for another is an arrangement between a company and the persons holding shares in, or debentures of, the company, or any class of such shares or debentures, which is entered into for the purposes of, or in connection with, a scheme of reconstruction or amalgamation and under which another company issues shares or debentures to those persons in respect of and in proportion to (or as nearly as may be in proportion to) their holdings of shares of, or debentures in, the first company, but the shares in or debentures of that first company are either retained by those persons or cancelled. In such a case, the original shares or debentures are treated as exchanged for those held in consequence of the arrangements, any shares or debentures retained being regarded for this purpose as cancelled and replaced by a new issue (CGTA 1979, s 86(1)). A 'scheme of reconstruction or amalgamation' in this context means a scheme for the reconstruction of any company or companies, or the amalgamation of any two or more companies, and the reference to shares or debentures being retained includes their being retained with altered rights or in an altered form, whether as the result of reduction, consolidation, division or otherwise (CGTA 1979, s 86(2)).

Tax avoidance arrangements

4.45 An exchange or 'quasi-exchange' ostensibly within 4.42 to 4.44 does not result in the new holding being equated with the old holding for CGT purposes (and thus is not within the reconstruction provisions of ICTA 1988, Sch 10, para 5 dealing with profit-sharing schemes) if the exchange, reconstruction or amalgamation in question is not effected for bona fide commercial reasons, or forms part of a scheme or arrangements of which the main purpose, or one of the main purposes, is avoidance of liability to CGT or corporation tax (CGTA 1979, s 87(1)). A procedure for obtaining Inland Revenue clearance in advance on this point is contained in CGTA 1979, s 88. Even where the transaction fails this test, however, the new and old holdings are still equated if the person to whom the shares or debentures are issued, together with connected persons (see 7.22) does not hold (again with connected persons) more than 5% of, or of any class of, the shares in or debentures of the original company (CGTA 1979, s 87(2) and (3)). As the reference is to the 'person to whom the shares are issued', rather than to beneficial ownership, it is considered that, in the context of an approved profit-sharing scheme, the trustees, rather than the individual participants, must meet this 5% test (thus providing a further reason—see 4.21 and 4.23—for trustees not to retain shares after the five-year release period, but to transfer them into the legal ownership of the participants).

'Roll-over' of scheme shares

General

4.46 Where a reconstruction as described in 4.42 to 4.45 takes place, the legislation governing approved profit sharing schemes is construed, after the reconstruction, as if references to a participant's shares were, or (where some of the original shares have been retained) as if they included, references to the new shares (ICTA 1988, Sch 10, para 5(4)). 'New shares', for this purpose, are shares comprised in the 'new holding' for CGT purposes (see 4.47) which were issued in respect of, or otherwise represent, shares comprised in the original holding (ICTA 1988, Sch 10, para 5(3)), and 'shares' include securities and rights of any description which form part of the 'new holding' for CGT purposes (ICTA 1988, Sch 10, para 5(7)).

4.47 The definition of 'new shares' in 4.46 broadly duplicates the definition of a 'new holding' in the CGT legislation, for the purposes of a reorganisation as described at 4.42 to 4.45, as being 'the shares in and debentures of the company which as a result of the reorganisation represent the original shares (including such, if any, of the original shares as remain)' (CGTA 1979, s 77(1)(b)). It should be borne in mind, however, in considering what follows, that the term 'new holding' includes any of the original shares which are retained, whereas the term 'new shares' does not.

No disposal

4.48 A reconstruction as described in 4.42 to 4.45 is treated for the purposes of the approved profit-sharing schemes rules as not involving a disposal of the shares comprised in the original holding (ICTA 1988, Sch 10, para 5(4)(a)), and thus no income tax charge as described at 4.13 to 4.32 arises as a result of such a transaction taking place before the five-year release date. As the reference to the participant's shares comprised in the original holding is extended to include 'new shares' (see 4.46), the effect is that a holding may pass through any number of reconstructions without crystallising a disposal charge.

Date of appropriation

4.49 The date on which new shares are treated as having been appropriated to the participant is that on which the 'corresponding shares' were appropriated (ICTA 1988, Sch 10, para 5(4)(b)). 'Corresponding shares' are those in respect of which the new shares were issued, or which they otherwise represent (ICTA 1988, Sch 10, para 5(3)). 'Shares', in the context of 'corresponding shares', bears the wide meaning discussed at 4.46, if there has been a previous reorganisation. If there has not, the corresponding shares will always meet the much narrower criteria set out in 4.119 to 4.140. The effect of treating the new shares as appropriated to the participant when the corresponding shares were actually so appropriated (or were treated under this provision as so appropriated) is that the time limits on disposal of the shares (see 4.78 to 4.87) and for determining the 'appropriate percentage' to be brought into charge to tax on a disposal (see 4.26 to 4.29) continue to run from the original acquisition of the beneficial ownership of shares by the participant and are unaffected by the reorganisation.

Conditions for scheme shares

4.50 The conditions as to the shares discussed at 4.119 to 4.140 are treated as fulfilled for any new shares if they were (or were, following a previous reorganisation, treated as) fulfilled with respect to the corresponding shares (ICTA 1988, Sch 10, para 5(4)(c)).

Excluded securities

4.51 On the issue of certain shares or securities in a reconstruction an income tax charge may arise under other provisions, and where this is so the relevant securities are not treated, for the purposes of the provisions described at 4.46 to 4.50, as part of the new holding. The relevant securities are (ICTA 1988, Sch 10, para 5(2)):

(a) any redeemable share capital or any other security (as opposed to share) issued by a company in respect of its shares or other securities otherwise than wholly for new consideration; or such part of any redeemable share capital or other security so issued as is not properly referable to new consideration, and which accordingly constitutes a distribution under ICTA 1988, s 209(2)(c);
(b) shares issued as paid-up otherwise than by the receipt of new consideration (ie bonus or scrip shares), following, after however long an interval, any repayment of share capital which took place after 6 April 1965. The amount so paid up is treated as a distribution made in respect of the shares on which it is paid up (after deducting any amount previously so treated), up to the amount of share capital repaid (ICTA 1988, s 210(1)). This treatment does not apply where the share capital repaid consists of fully paid preference shares (see 7.78) which were issued and fully paid on 6 April 1965 and continued to be fully paid preference shares throughout the period until their repayment, nor if the shares were issued after that date as fully paid preference shares wholly for new consideration not derived from ordinary shares and continued to be fully paid preference shares throughout the period from their issue until repayment (ICTA 1988, s 210(2)); and
(c) shares taxed as stock dividends under ICTA 1988, s 249.

'Locked-in value'

4.52 The 'locked-in value' of shares in a 'new holding' on which a charge arises on disposal (subject to the application of the 'appropriate percentage'—see 4.26

to 4.29—and the substitution of disposal proceeds if smaller—see 4.20) is determined as set out in 4.14, but substituting for the initial market value of the shares their 'locked-in value' immediately after the reconstruction. That, in turn, is found by ascertaining each tranche of shares in the original holding within which the shares have the same locked-in value as each other (normally because they were appropriated to the participant at the same time), and distributing that value pro rata between such of those shares as remain in the new holding and the new shares issued in respect of them (ie the shares in relation to which those in the tranche as ascertained are the 'corresponding shares' (see 4.49). The pro rata apportionment is made according to the market value (see 7.56 to 7.64) of the relevant shares immediately after the reconstruction, and only capital receipts (see 4.33 to 4.41) after that time are deducted in arriving at the locked-in value of shares in a new holding (receipts before that time having been deducted from initial market value in arriving at the pre-reconstruction locked-in value) (ICTA 1988, Sch 10, para 5(5)). This procedure applies equally where the pre-reconstruction holding itself arises as the result of a previous reconstruction. See also 7.107.

4.53 Where the trustees become entitled to a capital receipt (see 4.33 to 4.41) as part of a company reconstruction, their entitlement thereto is treated as arising before the new holding comes into being and thus, for the purposes of ascertaining the locked-in value of shares in the new holding, as described at 4.52, reduces the pre-reconstruction locked-in value of the shares in the original holding, as described at 4.14 (ICTA 1988, Sch 10, para 5(6)).

EXCESS OR UNAUTHORISED SHARES

Excess shares

4.54 If the total of the initial market value (see 4.15) of all the shares appropriated to an individual in any one year of assessment exceeds the 'relevant amount' (see 4.61), the 'appropriate percentage' (see 4.26 to 4.29) on which tax is charged on a disposal of such excess shares is 100% (ICTA 1988, Sch 10, para 6(1)(a) and (4)(a)). An 'excess share' is one which causes that limit to be exceeded, or which is appropriated when the limit has already been exceeded (ICTA 1988, Sch 10, para 6(2)). In the former case, it is not necessary to ascertain which shares in a particular appropriation took the amount up to the limit and which took it beyond it, as any disposal is treated as being of 'non-excess' shares before 'excess' shares (ICTA 1988, Sch 10, para 6(4)(b)), irrespective of any instructions the participant may give relating to specific shares (ICTA 1988, s 187(9)), but without prejudice to the FIFO rule of ICTA 1988, s 187(8) (see 4.30). These provisions apply equally to appropriations under two or more schemes as they apply to a single scheme (ICTA 1988, Sch 10, para 6(1)(a)). If shares are appropriated to an individual at the same time under several schemes, then the unused part of the 'relevant amount' (see 4.61) is treated as taken up by shares of each scheme in proportion to the totals appropriated or, in the words of the legislation, 'the same proportion of the shares appropriated at that time under each scheme shall be regarded as being appropriated before the relevant amount is exceeded' (ICTA 1988, Sch 10, para 6(3)). See also 4.91 and 4.110 re withdrawal of approval.

4.55 Excess shares which are still held by the trustees for the participant at the five-year release date, or, if earlier, the time of his death, are treated as disposed of by the trustees immediately before that date for their market value (see 7.56 to 7.64), so that a Schedule E charge on the participant crystallises, if it has not done so on a prior disposal, at the time when the potential for a charge on scheme shares would otherwise expire (ICTA 1988, Sch 10, para 6(5)).

The 'locked-in value' of excess shares

4.56 The 'locked-in value' of excess shares at any time, on which the Schedule E charge is based, is their market value at that time; see 7.56 to 7.64 (ICTA 1988, Sch 10, para 6(6)). In the result, where there has been an increase in the value of the shares, the whole of their original market value, together with that increase in value, is charged to tax at the 'appropriate percentage' of 100%, whereas, 'non-excess' shares, even if disposed of before the fourth anniversary of appropriation, would give rise to a charge based only on 100% of their initial market value (less any subsequent capital receipts: see 4.14) without any adjustment for the increase in value since appropriation.

Unauthorised shares

4.57 If shares are appropriated to an individual under an approved scheme at a time when he is not eligible to participate, in accordance with the conditions set out at 4.141 to 4.145 (whether by accident or design), this does not of itself result in the withdrawal of approval from the scheme (although it may have that result: see 4.111), but the shares so appropriated ('unauthorised shares') are treated in all respects as excess shares (ICTA 1988, Sch 10, para 6(1)(b) and (2)).

4.58 There is therefore (subject to 4.59) no advantage to be gained by the deliberate appropriation of unauthorised or excess shares, as this will give rise to an effective 'growth in value' charge similar to that under ICTA 1988, s 138(1)(a) or FA 1988, s 79 (see 2.190 to 2.286 and 2.53 to 2.121), but without the many exemptions available under that section. There will, however, be no additional 'interest' or 'write-off' charges under ICTA 1988, s 162 (see 2.303 to 2.339) on the notional loan arising from the acquisition of the beneficial ownership of the shares at an undervalue (indeed, a nil value), as the exemption from those charges, referred to at 4.7, applies whenever an appropriation is made to a participant under an approved scheme and the shares meet the criteria set out at 4.119 to 4.140. A 'participant' is any individual to whom the trustees have appropriated shares (ICTA 1988, ss 186(1) and 187(2)), irrespective of whether they are entitled so to do. This is consistent with the general exclusion of the charges under s 162 where this would create a double liability to income tax, and the same effect would be achieved even if the exemption from s 162 conferred by ICTA 1988, s 186(2)(b) were removed for excess or unauthorised shares, as a result of ICTA 1988, s 162(11) (see 2.331 to 2.333).

4.59 Because any benefit from the issue of excess or unauthorised shares is fully taxed, such an action by the trustees will not automatically result in the withdrawal of Inland Revenue approval from the scheme, as the removal of such approval is not necessary in order to bring about the Schedule E charge. It will, however, result in a breach of the scheme rules which would provide grounds for the withdrawal of approval if the Inland Revenue so wished (see 4.110). Deliberate abuse of the scheme by the appropriation of unauthorised or excess shares could produce a benefit in terms of the deferral of a Schedule E charge which would otherwise arise on acquisition of the beneficial ownership of the shares, and any such systematic abuse could be expected to result in the withdrawal of approval.

Company reorganisations

4.60 Where there has been a company reorganisation as discussed at 4.42 to 4.53, a 'new share', as defined in 4.46, is treated as an excess or unauthorised share if the 'corresponding share' (ie the share in respect of which the new share was issued: see 4.49) or, if there was more than one corresponding share, *each* of them, was an excess or authorised share (ICTA 1988, Sch 10, para 6(7)). It appears, therefore, that where shares of two different classes have been appropriated under the scheme and (for example) under a reconstruction one new 'C' share is issued in exchange for one 'A' share and one 'B' share, and some or all of the 'A' shares are excess or unauthorised, but none of the 'B' shares is, then none of the 'C' shares will be treated as excess or unauthorised, despite the fact that they derive in part from 'A' shares which are so treated, there being no machinery for apportionment if the corresponding shares relating to a new share are partly 'excess or unauthorised' and partly not. In practice, however, the appropriation of more than one class of shares under a scheme will be unusual, and it is extremely unlikely that such shares will be held (by all members of the company, not just scheme participants) in such proportions as to enable a reorganisation of the type outlined.

The 'relevant amount'

4.61 The 'relevant amount', which the initial market value of shares appropriated in any year may not exceed (see 4.54) is 10% of the participant's salary for the relevant year of assessment or the preceding year, whichever is the greater, but subject to a lower limit of £1,250 and an upper limit of £5,000 (ICTA 1988, s 187(2)). 'Salary' for this purpose means such of the emoluments of the office or employment by virtue of which he is entitled to participate in the schemes as are liable to be paid in that year under the PAYE procedure of ICTA 1970, s 203 (and regulations made under that section), after deducting any expense allowances or other amounts taxable under PAYE as a result of the directors' and higher paid employees' benefits in kind provisions of ICTA 1988, ss 153 to 168 (ICTA 1988, s 187(5)). The implications of this definition are discussed further at 6.43 and 6.44 in the context of the analogous definition of 'relevant emoluments' for the purposes of Inland Revenue approved share option schemes. Under the original legislation, the 'relevant amount' (though not called by that name) was £500 (FA 1978, s 58(1)); from 6 April 1980 to 5 April 1982, it was £1,000 (FA 1980, s 46(7)); and from 6 April 1982 to 5 April 1983, £1,250 (FA 1982, s 42(4)). The present figure was introduced by FA 1983, s 25(1).

CAPITAL GAINS TAX

Participants treated as beneficially entitled to shares

4.62 For CGT purposes, notwithstanding any limitation on the participant's dealings with his shares imposed by the statutory rules (see, in particular, the discussion of the 'period of retention' at 4.79), by the rules of the particular scheme or by the trust deed (see 4.146 to 4.152), he is treated as absolutely entitled to his shares as against the trustees (CGTA 1979, s 144A(1)), so that the CGT rules apply as if the shares were vested in the participant, and the trustees' acts in relation to the shares were his acts, disposals by them to him being disregarded accordingly (CGTA 1979, s 46(1)).

Income tax charges

4.63 For the purposes of the CGT calculation on a disposal, no deduction is made from the disposal proceeds in respect of any income tax charge arising: on the disposal under 4.13 to 4.32; on any previous capital receipt (see 4.33 to 4.41); or which has arisen on the release date (or on death) for excess or unauthorised shares: see 4.54 to 4.61 (CTGA 1979, s 144A(2)(a)).

Capital receipts

4.64 Any charge to income tax on a capital receipt as discussed at 4.33 to 4.41 is disregarded in determining whether that amount is a capital distribution for capital gains purposes, on which a charge arises (or which, if small, may be deducted from the base cost of the shares) (CGTA 1979, ss 72(1) & (2) and 144A(2)(b)). Such a provision is necessary as a 'capital distribution' is otherwise defined as 'a distribution . . . except a distribution which in the hands of the recipient constitutes income for the purposes of income tax' (CGTA 1979, s 72(5)(b)), and the charge under the s 186 provisions would therefore, in the absence of a rule to the contrary, remove the relevant receipt from the CGT definition.

The capital gains tax charge

4.65 In the result, the same receipt (whether on a disposal or a capital distribution) may give rise to both a CGT charge and an income tax charge, without any relief for the one against the other. This is equitable, however, as the income tax charge is in effect imposed on the benefit of the initial 'gift' of the shares, and has no relation (except in the case of excess or unauthorised shares) to the gain accruing over the period of ownership. Where an actual disposal of shares takes place (as opposed to the receipt of a capital distribution), the base cost for CGT purposes is the market value (see 7.56 to 7.64) at the time of the appropriation of the shares to the participant. This follows either from CGTA 1979, s 29A(1)(a), which substitutes market value for acquisition cost in the case of a bargain made otherwise than at arm's length, including a gift; or (if the appropriation of shares is regarded not as a gratuitous transfer, but as part of the participant's remuneration package) from s 29A(1)(b), which introduces market value as the base cost where an acquisition is made wholly or partly for consideration that cannot be valued, or 'in consideration of [the acquirer's] or another's services or past services in any office or employment'.

Share identification rules

4.66 The rules as regards the identification of shares or securities disposed of for the purpose of any charge on disposal (see 4.30), and the provisions treating excess or unauthorised shares as disposed of after other shares acquired at the same time (see 4.54) have no effect on the identification of shares disposed of for capital gains purposes, so that it is quite possible for the same disposal to be treated as relating to different shares for income and CGT purposes (and, equally, for different shares to be treated as retained) (ICTA 1979, s 144A(2)(c)).

DEDUCTION OF TAX UNDER PAYE

Disposals and capital receipts

4.67 Where the trustees of an approved scheme receive any amount which constitutes, or forms a part of, the proceeds of a disposal subject to income tax, as described at 4.13 to 4.32, or a chargeable capital receipt, as described at 4.33 to 4.41, they must pass on to the appropriate company (as discussed at 4.69) the sum on which income tax is payable, and the company must then pay that amount over to the participant, subject to deduction of tax under PAYE as if it were additional remuneration (ICTA 1988, Sch 10, para 7(1)). Where the 'appropriate percentage' (see 4.26 to 4.29) is less than 100%, this will mean that part of the sum received by the trustees may be passed directly to the participant, without deduction of tax, or, if all three parties agree, and it is administratively simpler, the full amount may be paid via the company, but only the 'appropriate percentage' subjected to the PAYE procedure. The amounts liable to PAYE under these provisions are not liable to Class 1 National Insurance contributions, and should not therefore be included in gross pay for National Insurance purposes.

Disposals to the trustees

4.68 Where the participant disposes of his beneficial interest in any of his shares to the trustees (who will take them back, initially, into their pool of unappropriated shares), so that under ICTA 1988, s 186(9) (as discussed at 4.32) the trustees are deemed to have disposed of the shares in question, the provisions as regards the application of PAYE set out at 4.67 apply equally to the consideration payable by the trustees to the participant (ICTA 1988, Sch 10, para 7(2), introduced as FA 1978, s 59(1A) with effect from 6 April 1980 by FA 1980, s 46(8) to fill a lacuna in the original legislation). Where the beneficial interest is disposed of as described at 4.32, otherwise than to the trustees, the proceeds do not pass through the hands of the trustees or the appropriate company, so it is not possible to apply PAYE; instead, they are received directly by the participant, and the income tax due can only be recovered by a Schedule E assessment.

The appropriate company

4.69 The 'appropriate company' referred to in 4.67 (though the term is not found in the legislation) is that of which the participant is an employee or director at the time the trustees receive the proceeds in question (ICTA 1988, Sch 10, para 7(3)(a)), and whose employees are at that time eligible (subject to the terms of the scheme and the conditions set out at 4.141 to 4.145) to be participants in the scheme (ICTA 1988, Sch 10, para 7(3)(b)). If there is more than one company which meets those conditions; for example, where an individual is employed by more than one company in a group scheme (see 4.92), then the 'appropriate company' is that one which the Board of Inland Revenue directs (ICTA 1988, Sch 10, para 7(3)). There is no appeal against such an administrative decision, except by way of an application for judicial review (see 7.51), and such an application is extremely unlikely to succeed (in that it would be most difficult to show that the selection of any particular group company was unreasonable, even if the selection of a different company would have been equally, or more, reasonable). Equally, a perverse decision by the Inland Revenue is unlikely to cause more than a minor inconvenience, and, while there is no statutory procedure to enable application to be made to nominate one company rather than another, in practice suggestions may be made to the Inland Revenue as to what would be most convenient for all parties (see IR 36, para 9.3).

4.70 Where a sum of money is received by the trustees as described at 4.67, to which PAYE should apply, but either there is no company which meets the tests described at 4.69, or else the Board of Inland Revenue considers that it is impractical for that company (or any of those companies, if more than one) to apply PAYE procedures, and so directs, then the trustees must apply PAYE on the appropriate percentage of the receipt as if the participant were a former employee of theirs, which means, broadly, that income tax must be deducted at the basic rate (ICTA 1988, Sch 10, para 7(4)). The situation where there is no such company may arise where the participant has left the company's employment, and the second case, where the Inland Revenue considers the application of PAYE impractical, might arise if the company had become non-resident. Again, a decision of the Board on this point would only be susceptible to challenge by way of judicial review (see 7.51).

4.71 Any other company, for example, a subsequent employer, may be used as a conduit for the funds in question, by direction of the Board of Inland Revenue, with the agreement of the trustees, the nominated company and the company or companies, if any, which would (or one of which would) normally be used to make the payment, as described at 4.69. In such a case the nominated company makes the PAYE deduction in the normal way, unless the participant is not its employee, in which case he is treated as a former employee (see 4.70) (ICTA 1988, Sch 10, para 7(5)).

4.72 The PAYE regulations made under ICTA 1988, s 203 apply to any payment made to the participant by a company or by the trustees, as discussed in 4.67 to 4.71, in the same way as to any other remuneration taxable under Schedule E (ICTA 1988, Sch 10, para 7(6)).

Transfers of legal ownership to participants

4.73 If the participant directs the trustees to transfer shares, of which he already has the beneficial ownership, into his legal ownership at any time before the five-year release date, and thus pays to the trustees a sum equal to basic rate income tax on the 'appropriate percentage' (see 4.26 to 4.29) of the 'locked-in value' (see 4.14) of the shares at that time, as required by the provisions discussed at 4.82, that sum is treated as if it were a PAYE deduction made by the trustees as discussed at 4.70, in respect of a disposal by them as discussed at 4.67 (ICTA 1988, Sch 10, para 7(7)), and must thus be remitted to the Inland Revenue. Any adjustment necessary in respect of an underpayment (where the participant is liable at the higher rate) or an overpayment (where he has losses or allowances to set against the amount charged under Schedule E) is then a matter for settlement between the participant and the Inland Revenue, without involving the trustees.

Excess or unauthorised shares

4.74 In general, unless the Board of Inland Revenue directs to the contrary, where money which constitutes or forms part of disposal proceeds or of a capital receipt (see 4.33 to 4.41) is received by the trustees in respect of excess or unauthorised shares (see 4.54 to 4.61), the amount to be paid over to the appropriate company, as described at 4.69, and treated as additional remuneration for PAYE purposes, or, where there is no appropriate company through which to channel the payment, the amount of the PAYE deduction to be made by the trustees themselves, as described at 4.70, is determined as if the shares were not excess or unauthorised (ICTA 1988, Sch 10, para 7(8)). The effect is that tax may be suffered initially based on a lower 'appropriate percentage' (the percentage applicable to excess or unauthorised shares always being 100%: see 4.54), and a lower 'locked-in value' (as the locked-in value of such shares, unlike others, may rise with increases in their market value after appropriation; see 4.56). This provision makes for administrative simplicity, as it does not become necessary for the trustees to enquire minutely into the circumstances of the appropriation, to ensure that they are not dealing with excess or unauthorised shares; and neither need they attempt to ascertain the present market value of the shares, as opposed to the locked-in value of 'non-excess' shares, which will be readily available. Any balance of tax underpaid as a result will normally be recovered by the issue of a Schedule E assessment, but the Board of Inland Revenue does have the power to direct that the 100% appropriate percentage and the full locked-in value be used to determine the amount of the relevant payment or PAYE deduction if it considers that a loss of tax may otherwise result, or considers it appropriate for other reasons. Such a direction could apply to all payments in respect of excess or unauthorised shares by the trustees of a particular scheme, or to specified payments only; for example, where it has reason to believe that a particular individual will not meet any liability directly assessed. It does not affect the position of the appropriate company, which, whether or not a direction is made on the trustees, simply applies the PAYE system to the amount received.

TAX DEDUCTIBILITY OF PAYMENTS TO TRUSTEES BY THE COMPANY

4.75 Any sum expended by the 'grantor' (ie a company which has established an approved scheme: ICTA 1988, Sch 9, para 1(1) and s 187(2)) or, in the case of a group scheme (see 4.92), expended by any participating company, in making a payment to the trustees which meets one of the relevant conditions (see 4.76) is deductible as a trading expense in the computation of the company's Schedule D, Case I profit or loss, or in the case of an investment company or life assurance company, as a management expense in arriving at its profits subject to corporation tax (ICTA 1988, ss 85(1), 75 and 76).

4.76 The relevant conditions, one of which must be fulfilled if the payment is to be deductible, are that:

(a) the sum is necessary to meet the trustees' reasonable expenses in administering the scheme (ICTA 1988, s 85(2)(b)); or
(b) before the expiry of a period of nine months beginning on the day following the end of the period of account in which the sum is charged as an expense of the company, or within such longer period as the Board of Inland Revenue may allow by written notice to the company, the sum in question is applied by the trustees in the acquisition of shares for appropriation to individuals who are eligible to participate in the scheme by virtue of their being or having been employees or directors of the company making the payment (ICTA 1988, s 85(2)(a) and (3)).

Trustees are taken for these purposes to apply sums paid to them in the order in which they are received (a 'first in—first out' basis) (ICTA 1988, s 85(4)). In the representations of the Consultative Committee of Accountancy Bodies (CCAB) on the 1978 Finance Bill (TR 289), it sought the Inland Revenue's view as to whether a deduction would be available under what is now ICTA 1988, s 85 for sums paid to the trustees by the company beyond those required to meet administrative expenses and the cost of share purchases; for example, to meet a CGT liability (see 4.10). The Inland Revenue confirmed at a subsequent meeting (notes of which were published as TR 308) that a deduction would be available for such payments.

4.77 It will be noted that, even in a group scheme, a company cannot obtain a deduction for a sum which is applied in providing shares for the employees of other group companies. The appropriation of the shares to individuals, as opposed to their acquisition by the trustees, need not take place within any particular time limit in order for relief to be available to the company but, as discussed at 4.9 and 4.10, it must take place within 18 months of the acquisition if the additional rate of income tax on discretionary and accumulation trusts, and CGT on appropriation, are to be avoided by the trustees. In practice, for those companies subject to them, the guidelines of the Investment Committee of the Association of British Insurers (see 1.14) require that funds made available to trustees by the company shall be applied 'as far as practicable forthwith' in the purchase of shares, and that those shares be 'immediately' appropriated to participants (see point (6) at Appendix 1). Under ICTA 1988, s 418(2), where a close company (see 7.12 to 7.21) incurs expense in connection with the provision to a participator (see 7.73 and 7.74) of 'benefits or facilities of whatever nature', the amount so expended is treated as a 'distribution' for tax purposes, with the result that advance corporation tax must be paid by the company, and higher rate income tax, where applicable, by the recipient. The Inland Revenue confirmed to the CCAB in June 1978 that sums provided to trustees by the company under what is now ICTA 1988, s 85 would not be treated as distributions for this purpose.

CONDITIONS FOR APPROVAL OF SCHEMES

Period of retention and release date

General

4.78 A scheme may not be approved unless the Board of Inland Revenue is satisfied that every participant is bound by contract with the employing company in certain particulars. These conditions, as set out in 4.79 to 4.87, may form part of the terms of the scheme, by which the employee agrees to be bound, or be imposed in some other way, by a separate contract, or as part of the general contract of employment (ICTA 1988, Sch 9, para 2(2)).

The period of retention

4.79 The participant must be bound to permit his shares to remain in the hands of the trustees throughout the 'period of retention' (ICTA 1988, Sch 9, para 2(2)(a)). That period, in relation to any of a participant's shares, begins on the date of appropriation, and ends on the earliest of (ICTA 1988, s 187(2)):

(a) the second anniversary of that date (ICTA 1988, Sch 10, para 2, previously FA 1978, s 54(4) as amended by FA 1980, s 46(3) in relation to shares appropriated on or after 6 April 1979; formerly the fifth anniversary); or
(b) the date when the participant ceases to be an employee or director of the grantor by reason of injury or disability (ICTA 1988, Sch 10, para 2(a)); or
(c) the date of dismissal by the grantor on the grounds of redundancy within the meaning of the Employment Protection (Consolidation) Act 1978 or the Contracts of Employment and Redundancy Payments Act (Northern Ireland) 1965 (ICTA 1988, Sch 10, para 2(a)); or
(d) the date on which the participant reaches pensionable age, as defined in Social Security Act 1975, Sch 20 (60 for women, and 65 for men) (ICTA 1988, s 187(2) and Sch 10, para 2(b)); or
(e) the date of his death (ICTA 1988, Sch 10, para 2(c)); or
(f) where the participant's shares are redeemable shares in a workers' co-operative (see 4.133), the date on which he ceases to be employed by, or by a subsidiary (see 4.134) of the co-operative (ICTA 1988, Sch 9, para 2(d)). This last provision was added to the legislation by FA 1986, s 24(3)(b), with effect from 25 July 1986.

The effect, broadly, is that the participant must be obliged to leave his shares in the hands of the trustees for two years, or until he leaves the company otherwise than of his own volition or through his own fault. If he is dismissed for misconduct or leaves of his own accord he must be obliged to leave them with the trustees until the second anniversary of appropriation, or his earlier death or attainment of pensionable age. It is not necessary for approval of the scheme that the participant actually be obliged to retire on reaching pensionable age, so he may be permitted to instruct the trustees to dispose of his shares at that time, even though he continues in his employment, and in such a case the 'appropriate percentage' of the locked-in value, on which a Schedule E charge arises, will be 50% (see 4.26). When the legislation was first introduced, the Inland Revenue interpreted the time limits set out in (a)–(e) as imposing fixed, rather than minimum periods, and would not give approval to schemes which incorporated longer retention periods. Following representations by The Law Society's Standing Committee on Revenue Law in May 1980, the official view changed, and the 1981 edition of IR 36, 'Approved profit-sharing schemes' clearly refers to the statutory provisions regarding the period of retention as imposing a '*minimum* period during which a participant's shares must remain with the trustees of the scheme' (para 1.4).

Group schemes

4.80 The references to employment (or dismissal) by the 'grantor' in paras (b) and (c) of 4.79 extend to any participating company in a group scheme (see 4.92), and a participant is not treated as leaving his employment or being redundant until he is no longer an employee or director of *any* of the participating companies (ICTA 1988, Sch 10, para 2). This prevents manipulation of the rules where, for example, an individual is 'invalided out' of one job, but immediately takes up another employment within the group, so that if the organisation had taken the form of one company operating in divisions, no question of an early end to the retention period or of a 50% 'appropriate percentage' would arise.

Disposals of beneficial interests

4.81 The participant must be bound not to assign, charge or otherwise dispose of his beneficial interest in the shares during the retention period, as defined in 4.79 (ICTA 1988, Sch 9, para 2(2)(b)). Thus the shares could not be used, for example, as security for a loan. If a participant does assign, charge, or otherwise dispose of the beneficial interest in any of his shares (an action which is outside the control of the trustee), then he is treated as if at the time those shares were appropriated to him he was ineligible to participate in the scheme, so that they become 'unauthorised shares', dealt with as discussed at 4.54 to 4.61 (ICTA 1988, Sch 10, para 1(3)).

Transfer of legal ownership to participant

4.82 The participant must be bound, if he directs the trustees to transfer the legal ownership of his shares to him (in addition to his beneficial ownership) at any time before the five-year release date (which he could not in any case do before the end of the retention period: see 4.79) to pay to the trustees, before the transfer takes place, a sum equal to income tax at the basic rate on the appropriate percentage (see 4.26 to 4.29) of the locked-in value of the shares (see 4.14) at the time that he gives that direction (ICTA 1988, Sch 9, para 2(2)(c)). As to the treatment of this sum by the trustees, see 4.73. Such an obligation does not, however, bind the participant's personal representatives to pay any sum to the trustees (ICTA 1988, Sch 10, para 1(2), introduced as FA 1978, s 54(1A) by FA 1980, s 46(2), for the avoidance of doubt, with effect from 6 April 1980).

Disposal for 'best consideration in money'

4.83 The participant must be bound not to direct the trustees to dispose of his shares at any time before the five year release date in any way other than by sale for the best consideration in money that can reasonably be obtained at the time of the sale or, since 25 July 1986, in the case of redeemable shares in a workers' co-operative (see 4.133), by redemption (ICTA 1988, Sch 9, para 2(2)(d), as amended for shares in a workers' co-operative by FA 1986, s 24(3)(a)). This provision prevents any sale for less than full value; for example, to a connected party with gratuitous intent, or as one step in a larger transaction which, as a whole, benefited the participant. Such a sale would result in a lower Schedule E charge on the disposal (as described at 4.20). If the consideration was in money's worth, rather than money, problems of valuation would be posed, and these are avoided by the insistence on monetary consideration. Disputes may of course arise on a matter as subjective as whether a disposal actually took place for the best obtainable consideration, and while failure to include this obligation as a requirement of the scheme (whether through the scheme rules or under some other contractual arrangement) will result in its failure to obtain Inland Revenue approval, and a breach of the obligation by a participant may result in the withdrawal of approval (see 4.107), a more immediate remedy, where the transaction is not at arm's length, lies in the substitution of market value for actual consideration under ICTA 1988, s 186(10), as discussed at 4.32.

Takeovers, general offers, and schemes of arrangement

4.84 The obligations imposed as detailed in 4.78 to 4.83, restricting the participant's ability to deal freely with his shares before the end of the retention period and, to a lesser extent, before the release date, do not prevent him from taking the necessary action in the case of take-over bids and similar circumstances, as set out in 4.42 to 4.53. He may direct the trustees to accept an offer for any of his shares on a take-over, reconstruction or amalgamation which will result in a new holding being equated with the original shares for CGT purposes (ICTA 1988, Sch 10, para 1(1)(a) and s 187(2); CGTA 1979, ss 77–87: see 4.42 to 4.45). This effectively provides a derogation from the requirement to leave the shares in the trustees' hands throughout the retention period (see 4.79), and from the requirement to make a disposal only for the 'best consideration in money' possible (see 4.83).

4.85 The participant may also direct the trustees to agree to a transaction affecting his shares, or such of them as are of a particular class, if the transaction would be entered into pursuant to a compromise, arrangement, or scheme applicable to or affecting all the ordinary share capital (see 7.72) of the company in question; or all the shares of the class in question; or all the shares, or shares of the class in question, held by a particular class of shareholders, identified otherwise than by reference to their employment or their participation in an approved scheme (ICTA 1988, Sch 10, para 1(1)(b)). Thus, a scheme or arrangement offering replacement securities to all employee shareholders or all participants in the particular profit sharing scheme, but not to other shareholders, could not be accepted (or, strictly, the trustees could not be directed to accept it), but an arrangement which offered particular terms to UK shareholders but not overseas residents, or to individual but not corporate shareholders, would be acceptable. As with the reconstruction arrangements sanctioned under 4.42 to 4.55, this permits derogations from the restrictions discussed in 4.79 to 4.83.

4.86 The participant may also direct the trustees to accept an offer of cash, with or without other assets, for his shares if the offer forms part of a general offer which is made to all holders of shares of the same class as those which he holds, or to all shareholders in the company, and which is made in the first instance on a condition such that if it is satisfied the person making the offer will have control of the company, as defined in 7.25 to 7.30 (ICTA 1988, Sch 10, para 1(1)(c) and s 416). Again, the effect is a derogation from the requirements of 4.79 to 4.83, in the case of the requirements in 4.83 both by permitting disposal for non-cash consideration, and also in allowing acceptance of a cash-only offer without enquiry as to whether it represents the best possible terms.

Disposal of beneficial interest to trustees

4.87 The participant may also agree, after the expiry of the period of retention, to sell the beneficial interest in his shares to the trustees (who already own the legal interest) for the best consideration in money (as opposed to money's worth) that could reasonably be expected to be obtained at that time on a sale of the shares themselves (ICTA 1988, Sch 10, para 1(1)(d)). It is not clear that any of the obligations in 4.79 to 4.83 would in fact prevent such a manoeuvre, but the point is put beyond doubt by this provision, thus preventing a situation where the participant is willing to sell shares, and the trustees to buy, but both have to go to the open market, and possibly incur additional costs, in order to find third parties to complete the desired transactions.

General conditions for approval

4.88 The Board of Inland Revenue is obliged to approve a profit-sharing scheme on application by the company which has established it (the 'grantor', in the terms of the legislation), if it meets the conditions set out in 4.89 to 4.103.

Restrictions on participants' dealings in shares

4.89 The scheme must comply with the conditions set out at 4.78 to 4.87 restricting the participant's ability to deal with his shares within the period of retention and before the release date. As discussed at 4.78, however, such restrictions, while they must be a matter of contract between the participant and the company concerned, need not actually be incorporated in the rules of the scheme or the trust deed (ICTA 1988, Sch 9, paras 1(1) and 2(2); Sch 10, para 1(1) and (2)).

The trustees

4.90 The scheme must provide for the establishment of a body of persons resident in the United Kingdom ('the trustees') who:

(a) out of monies paid to them by the grantor or, in the case of a group scheme (see 4.92) by a participating company, are required by the terms of the scheme to acquire shares which meet the conditions set out in 4.119 to 4.140 (ICTA 1988, Sch 9, para 30(1)(a). See also 7.106.);
(b) are under a duty to appropriate such shares to individuals who participate in the scheme, and who are eligible to do so in accordance with the conditions set out at 4.141 to 4.145 (ICTA 1988, Sch 9, para 30(1)(b)); and

(c) whose functions with respect to the shares held by them are regulated by a trust constituted under the law of England and Wales, or of Scotland, or of Northern Ireland, and the terms of which are embodied in a trust instrument which complies with the conditions set out at 4.146 to 4.152 (ICTA 1988, s 187(2) and Sch 9, para 30(1)(c)).

Limits on shares appropriated

4.91 The scheme must provide that the total of the initial market value (see 4.15) of the shares appropriated to any one participant in a year of assessment will not exceed the 'relevant amount' as defined at 4.61 (broadly, 10% of current or previous year's salary subject to a maximum of £5,000 and a minimum of £1,250) (ICTA 1988, Sch 9, para 30(3)). Lower limits previously applied as set out at 4.61.

Group schemes

4.92 Where the grantor controls another company or companies (within the definition of 'control' set out at 7.23 and 7.24: ICTA 1988, ss 187(2) and 840) the scheme may extend to all or any of the companies of which it has control. Such a scheme covering more than one company is referred to as a 'group scheme', although it need not extend to all companies grouped together for tax or company law purposes. The term 'participating company', used in relation to a group scheme, means the company which has established the scheme or any company for the time being controlled by it and to which the scheme is expressed to extend (ICTA 1988, s 187(2) and Sch 9, para 1(3) and (4)). While the establishing company (the 'grantor') need not be the ultimate controlling company of those participating, it must be the most 'senior' of those involved. A group scheme may thus include a subsidiary and its sub-subsidiaries, without the parent, but may not be set up by a subsidiary to include its parent (although the parent's shares may be used in the scheme: see 4.119). If the parent wishes to be included it must set up the scheme itself. As to jointly controlled companies, see Appendix 11 'Inland Revenue Extrastatutory Concession B27: Approved employee share schemes—jointly owned companies'.

Employees who must be eligible to participate

4.93 The Board of Inland Revenue must be satisfied that at any time all full-time employees or directors of the company concerned (or, in the case of a group scheme, all full-time employees or directors of participating companies) who have been such throughout the last five years (or such shorter qualifying period, if any, as is imposed by the scheme rules) will be eligible to participate in the scheme on similar terms. This requirement extends only to those who are chargeable to tax in respect of their office or employment under Case I of Schedule E (see 7.89), and is subject to the exclusions set out at 4.141 to 4.145. The Board must also be satisfied that those who do participate in the scheme actually do so on similar terms (ICTA 1988, Sch 9, paras 1(1) and 36(1)). A 'full-time' director or employee is not defined in the legislation (but see 7.46 to 7.50). See also 7.105.

4.94 It is not obligatory that participants should have worked for the company for a five-year period, but companies will normally wish to impose some qualifying period, and the legislation stipulates a five-year maximum. Any longer period might in practice effectively restrict the scheme to senior employees, particularly where there was rapid staff turnover at lower levels, thus countering the objective of the legislation to promote wide share ownership amongst the workforce. Where there is a qualifying period, it should be noted that it relates to continuous service, so that an aggregate of eight years' employment with the company, broken into two periods of four years each would not automatically qualify an individual to participate.

4.95 It is not, of course, necessary for an employee to meet all the conditions in 4.93 before he can participate in the scheme. The minimum qualifications are dealt with at 4.141 to 4.145. The conditions in 4.93 are those which, if met, *must* permit the employee to participate.

4.96 The requirement that employees meeting the conditions in 4.93 must be *eligible* to participate in the scheme on similar terms was extended by FA 1983, s 25(4), with effect from 13 May 1983, for both new and existing schemes, to include the stipulation that those who participate must actually *do so* on similar terms, thus preventing a situation where, although theoretically eligible for equal treatment, certain employees might be put under pressure, or given to understand that they are expected, not to take their full entitlement under the scheme.

4.97 Participants are not regarded as ineligible to participate on similar terms or, since 13 May 1983 (FA 1983, s 25(4)), as not actually participating on similar terms, merely by virtue of the fact that the number of shares appropriated to them varies by reference to their level of remuneration (for which, indeed, specific provision is made in the definition of the relevant amount: see 4.61), or by reference to the length of their service or similar factors (ICTA 1988, Sch 9, para 36(2)). It is not clear what might constitute a 'similar factor', but perhaps a staff grading not specifically related to remuneration might be within this term. What the legislation is aiming at is not absolute equality of treatment, but a situation where there is no element of selectivity governing who obtains the benefit of the scheme; if a staff grading was used to single out individuals for special treatment this would not be acceptable.

4.98 The Board of Inland Revenue must be satisfied that there are no features of the scheme which have, or would have, the effect of discouraging any description of employees or former employees who fulfil the conditions set out in 4.93 from actually participating in the scheme, subject to the criteria for elegibility of participants discussed at 4.141 to 4.145 (ICTA 1988, Sch 9, para 2(3)(a)). This condition, like that discussed at 4.96, was introduced with effect from 13 May 1983 by FA 1983, s 25(5) for both new and existing schemes, to fill a lacuna whereby theoretical eligibility to participate was taken into consideration in the legislation but the practicalities were not. Features which would discourage participation might include, for example, the publication of the names of those involved, where a political group to which many employees belonged had adopted it as policy not to give any encouragement to the scheme; or the forfeiting of other benefits by participators. The reference to a 'former employee' meeting the conditions at 4.93, which refer specifically to the eligibility of current employees, is at first puzzling, but the intention appears to be to prevent a situation whereby current employees who qualify as participants in the light of those conditions leave the company's employment and are required under the terms of the scheme to dispose of their shares before the release date, thus ceasing to participate in the scheme.

4.99 Where the grantor (ie the company establishing the scheme) is a member of a group of companies (whether or not the scheme is a group scheme as described at 4.92), the Board of Inland Revenue must be satisfied that the scheme does not and would not have the effect of conferring benefits wholly or mainly on directors of group companies, or on those group employees who are in receipt of the higher or highest levels of remuneration (ICTA 1988, Sch 9, para 2(3)(b), formerly FA 1978, Sch 9, para 2(3)(b), as introduced, again, with effect from 13 May 1983 by FA 1983, s 25(5) for both new and existing schemes). This could otherwise be done, for example, by segregating the highest paid employees into one company, which alone established a scheme, and which carried out management services for other group companies. Directors, similarly, could be employees of such a company while remaining directors of other group companies. A 'group' for this purpose means a company and any other companies of which it has control as defined in 7.23 and 7.24 (ICTA 1988, Sch 9, para 2(4); ss 187(2) and 840).

4.100 The conditions set out at 4.96 and 4.98 to 4.99, introduced with effect for both existing and new schemes by FA 1983, s 25, had the effect that existing schemes which did not meet the new requirements were liable to have their approval withdrawn. However, the Inland Revenue confirmed to the Consultative Committee of Accountancy Bodies (CCAB) in July 1983 that companies likely to be affected would be given a 'substantial' period of notice to enable them to make the necessary amendments. The CCAB had previously suggested a 12 month period, which was merely 'noted' by the Inland Revenue, thus suggesting that, in some cases, at least, the 'substantial' period would be shorter than this (See CCAB Technical Release 511, 'Notes of a meeting with the Board of Inland Revenue in July 1983', paras 21–23).

Extraneous features

4.101 If the conditions in 4.89 to 4.100 are satisfied, the Inland Revenue must approve the scheme unless it appears to the Board that there are features of the scheme which are neither essential nor reasonably incidental to the purpose of providing for employees and directors benefits in the nature of interests in shares (ICTA 1988, Sch 9, para 2(1)). A feature which, while not essential, might be considered reasonably incidental to the main purpose might be a requirement to belong to an employee-shareholders association, at meetings of which matters affecting the scheme could be discussed. A feature which would be neither essential nor reasonably incidental to the purposes of the scheme might be a requirement for participants to belong to, or abstain from belonging to, a particular trade union or political party.

Procedure for obtaining approval

4.102 An application for the approval of a scheme must be in writing, and contain such particulars and be supported by such evidence as the Board of

Inland Revenue may require (ICTA 1988, Sch 9, para 1(2)). The detailed procedure is set out in the Inland Revenue booklet IR 36 'Approved profit-sharing schemes' at para 2.2. No special form of application is necessary, but two copies of each of the following items (except where the contrary is indicated) should be sent with the application to: Inland Revenue, Technical Division (Employee Share Schemes), Somerset House, London WC2R 1LB. (Telephone enquiries should be made to (01) 438 7708 or (01) 438 7803.)

(a) A statement giving the name and the address of the registered office of the company which has established the scheme, together with details of the Inspector of Taxes' office which deals with its corporation tax affairs, and its reference number in that office. The same information is required in respect of the company whose shares are to be appropriated under the scheme (see 4.119), if that is not the company which has established the scheme. In the case of a group scheme (see 4.92), the same details are required in respect of each company to which the scheme is expressed to extend. In all cases a statement is required either confirming that the scheme extends to all companies in the group, or explaining how the condition set out in 4.99 is met (i e how the Inland Revenue may be satisfied that the scheme would not have the effect of conferring benefits wholly or mainly on directors of group companies, or on those group employees in receipt of the higher or highest levels of remuneration).
(b) The memorandum and articles of association of the company whose shares are to be appropriated, with any relevant amendments (one copy only).
(c) The trust instrument (see 4.146 to 4.152) (three copies).
(d) The rules of the scheme (three copies).
(e) A copy of the proposed contract which is required to be entered into between the company which has established the scheme and each participant. As explained at 4.78, this may simply take the form of an agreement to be bound by the rules of the scheme; or the relevant conditions, described at 4.79 to 4.87, may be embodied in a separate contract or incorporated in the general contract of employment.
(f) A declaration by the company which has established the scheme that the shares which are to be acquired by the trustees and appropriated to participants under the scheme will satisfy the conditions set out in 4.119 to 4.140 (one copy only).
(g) If the shares which are to be acquired and appropriated under the scheme are not shares in the company which has established the scheme, a further declaration specifying which of the conditions as to the companies whose shares may be used in the scheme (set out at 4.119 to 4.121) is met, and how the necessary relationship with the company which has established the scheme exists (one copy only).
(h) Any other documents which will be issued to participants and/or shareholders in connection with the scheme, for example, the announcement of the scheme to shareholders and employees, and the statements which will be provided to participants following an appropriation of shares (one copy only).

4.103 The Technical Division of the Inland Revenue will comment informally on draft documentation, in advance of the establishment of a scheme and the making of a formal application for approval, and, similarly, will give an informal opinion on any proposed alteration to an approved scheme or to the terms of the trusts on which the shares are held (see 4.146 to 4.152).

Withdrawal of approval

General

4.104 The Board may withdraw its approval of a scheme in any of the circumstances set out in 4.105 to 4.116. This may take effect from the date of the default giving rise to the withdrawal, or from such later time as the Board may specify (ICTA 1988, Sch 9, para 3(2)). In cases of flagrant abuse, the earliest possible date may be expected to apply, but where retrospective action would disadvantage innocent participants, the Inland Revenue may be expected to make the withdrawal of approval effective only from the date of their notice, so that appropriations of shares made before that date are not prejudiced. In cases of genuine dispute where the Inland Revenue finally decides to withdraw approval, it might even do so from a future date to enable the trustees to make any necessary arrangements. The Board is empowered, but not obliged, to withdraw approval in the circumstances laid down, and may therefore permit temporary or technical derogations, although this should not be relied upon. Approval is a condition only for the exemptions on the appropriation of the shares (see 4.7 to 4.8) and the reliefs given to the company and the trustees (see 4.75 to 4.77 and 4.9 to 4.12). Its withdrawal does not precipitate a charge on existing participants or the recapture of relief already given to the company or the trustees. Nor does it alter the income tax charge applying on a disposal before the release date, or oblige the trustees to dispose of any shares, or the participants to dispose of their beneficial ownership therein.

Breach of participants' contractual obligations

4.105 Approval may be withdrawn if any participant is in breach of his obligation (see 4.79) to permit his shares to remain in the hands of the trustees throughout the period of retention (ICTA 1988, Sch 9, paras 2(2)(a) and 3(2)(a)).

4.106 Approval may also be withdrawn if any participant breaches his obligation (see 4.82) to pay to the trustees an amount equal to basic rate tax on the appropriate percentage (see 4.26 to 4.29) of the locked-in value (see 4.14) of any shares which he directs them to transfer to him before the five-year release date (ICTA 1988, Sch 9, paras 2(2)(c) and 3(2)(a)).

4.107 Approval may also be withdrawn if any participant breaches his obligation (see 4.83) not to direct the trustees to dispose of shares at any time before the release date except by sale for the best consideration in money that can reasonably be obtained at the time of the sale or, since 25 July 1986, in the case of redeemable shares in a workers' co-operative, by redemption (ICTA 1988, Sch 9, paras 2(2)(d) and 3(2)(a)). The provision covering shares in a workers' co-operative (defined at 4.133) was introduced in ICTA 1988, Sch 9, para 2(2)(d) (then FA 1978, s 54(1)(d)) by FA 1986, s 24(3)(a).

4.108 While a breach of his contractual obligations by a single participant in any of the three cases set out at 4.105 to 4.107 could result in a withdrawal of approval from the entire scheme, in practice any such breach could be frustrated by a refusal of the trustees to co-operate, justified at law by the terms of the trust deed (if properly drafted), although they could not rely on the contract between the participant and the company (see 4.78) to which they were not party. The continued approval of the scheme is not, therefore, as precarious as might at first sight appear. It is assumed that a direction by the participant within 4.107 would not be treated as such if it were not in fact acted upon.

4.109 At 4.79 to 4.83, details are given of four contractual obligations which must be met by the participant before approval can be granted. Only three of those obligations however, if breached, give rise to a withdrawal of approval as described at 4.105 to 4.107. The remaining obligation (see 4.81) is that placed on the participant not to assign, charge or otherwise dispose of his beneficial interest in his shares during the period of retention (ICTA 1988, Sch 9, para 2(2)(b)). A breach of this condition, (which is wholly outside the control of the trustees) cannot result in the withdrawal of approval from the scheme, but as explained at 4.31 will give rise to an immediate tax charge on the participant himself. A breach of his obligation by the participant must be distinguished from a removal of the obligation by the company, which *would* give grounds for the withdrawal of approval (see 4.111).

Contravention of scheme rules or trust deed

4.110 Approval may also be withdrawn if there is, with respect to the operation of the scheme, any contravention of its rules or of the provisions of the trust deed (ICTA 1988, Sch 9, para 3(2)(b)). Various conditions which must be met by the scheme are set out at 4.88 to 4.103, and various statutory provisions as to the terms of the trust instrument are discussed at 4.146 to 4.152. Approval may, however, also be withdrawn for contravention of other provisions included in the scheme rules or the trust instrument at the volition of the company and without statutory obligation. While this is unlikely in practice, in respect of administrative or non-essential features, the Inland Revenue might act in respect of such a contravention when its effect was unfairly to favour one group of employees as against another (see also 4.93 and 4.99), or it otherwise represents an abuse of the scheme.

Contravention of statutory provisions

4.111 Approval may also be withdrawn if there is a contravention 'with respect to' the operation of the scheme of any of the relevant statutory provisions (ICTA 1988, Sch 9, para 3(2)(b)). Such a contravention could arise, for example, in respect of a failure to apply the PAYE provisions set out at 4.67 to 4.74, or a cessation of the four contractual obligations of the participant to the company referred to at 4.79 to 4.87 and 4.105 to 4.109 (ie shares to remain with trustees throughout retention period; participant to retain beneficial ownership throughout that period; tax payment to trustees on transfer of beneficial ownership to participant before release date; trustees not to be directed to sell for less than best price in money: ICTA 1988, Sch 9, para 2(2)). It could perhaps be argued that a change in the participants' obligations in any of these respects affected the constitution, not the operation, of the scheme, but it is considered that a change in the constitution is nevertheless a change 'with respect to' the operation of the scheme under the constitution. If the contractual obligation forms part of the terms of the scheme itself, its removal will in any case give grounds for the withdrawal of approval as discussed at 4.110, or will constitute an alteration to the scheme which will require (but will not obtain) Inland Revenue consent as discussed at 4.117, thus automatically removing approval. However, as discussed at 4.78, these obligations may also be satisfied by a contract outside the terms of the scheme, in which case withdrawal of approval will have to be based on the present provision.

Different treatment of shares of the same class

4.112 Approval may also be withdrawn if any shares of a class which has been used in the scheme receive different treatment in any respect from the other shares of that class; in particular, but not exclusively, where they receive different treatment in respect of:

(a) the dividend payable;
(b) repayment of share capital;
(c) the restrictions attaching to the shares; or
(d) any offer of substituted or additional shares, securities or rights of any description in respect of the shares (ICTA 1988, Sch 9, para 3(2)(c)).

The intention, as with the conditions regarding the shares set out at 4.119 to 4.140, is to ensure that employee shareholders participate in the benefits available to shareholders generally, and are neither advantaged nor disadvantaged by comparison with them. Other shareholders of the same class will always exist, as will be seen at 4.136, because it is not possible to issue one class of shares solely for use in the scheme: any attempt to do so would not gain approval initially (see 4.90); or would constitute an unapproved alteration to the scheme resulting in the loss of the existing approval as described at 4.117; or would render the scheme liable to withdrawal of approval for the contravention of its rules as described at 4.110.

4.113 As regards the withdrawal of approval, where there is different treatment of shares of the same class in respect of dividends payable, it does not consitute such a ground if newly issued shares receive, in respect of dividends payable with respect to a period beginning before the date of issue of the shares, treatment which is less favourable than that accorded to shares issued earlier (ICTA 1988, Sch 9, para 3(3)). It is, of course, common practice for newly issued shares not to rank for subsequent dividends made out of profits accruing before their issue, and this provision merely takes account of normal commercial procedure. It does, however, open the way for shares to be issued under an employee share scheme which do not rank for a dividend which is paid in respect of other shares issued only days or weeks before.

Restrictions on employees' eligibility to participate

4.114 Approval may also be withdrawn if the Board of Inland Revenue ceases to be satisfied as described at 4.93 and 4.96; that is, broadly, that all full-time employees meeting certain conditions are eligible to participate in the scheme on similar terms, and that those who do participate actually do so on similar terms (ICTA 1988, Sch 9, paras 3(2)(d) and 36). As with other events giving rise to a withdrawal of approval, mentioned at 4.111 and 4.112, if this alteration in circumstances were brought about by a change in the rules of the scheme (as opposed to a change in practice as to actual participation on similar terms), it would also constitute an amendment to the scheme requiring specific Inland Revenue consent if the existing approval were not to lapse.

4.115 Approval may also be withdrawn if the Board ceases to be satisfied as described in 4.98 and 4.99; that is, broadly, that there are no features of the scheme which discourage eligible employees from taking part, or which confer benefits wholly or mainly on directors and highly paid employees in a group (ICTA 1988, Sch 9, paras 2(3) and 3(2)(d)).

Failure to provide information

4.116 Approval may also be withdrawn if the body of trustees, the company establishing the scheme or, in the case of a group scheme (see 4.92) any other company which is or has been a participating company, fails to provide any information which it is required to provide to the Inland Revenue under the provisions set out at 4.153 and 4.154 (ICTA 1988, Sch 9, para 3(2)(e)). This provision (formerly FA 1978, Sch 9, para 3(1)(e)) was introduced with effect from 13 May 1983 by FA 1983, s 25(6), although it would appear to have been covered already by the provision discussed at 4.111 regarding contravention of any relevant statutory provision, which includes the powers to obtain information contained in ICTA 1988, Sch 9, para 6. As discussed there, it is considered that the words 'with respect to' the operation of the scheme in ICTA 1988, Sch 9, para 3(2)(b) have a wider meaning than merely 'in the operation of the scheme', and are apt to cover the requirements to deliver information in connection with the operation of the scheme. However that may be, the addition made by FA 1983 puts the matter beyond a doubt.

Alterations to schemes

4.117 If at any time after the Board of Inland Revenue has approved a scheme, an alteration is made to it or to the terms of the trust under which the shares are held, approval lapses from that time unless the alteration is approved by the Board (ICTA 1988, Sch 9, paras 4 and 30(2)). Under the wording of the legislation, it would appear that such approval could be retrospective, conferring the available reliefs and exemptions on transactions which had taken place in the interim period, but, clearly, it is always advisable to seek approval for any change in advance. If the alteration is made and the approval is not forthcoming, the situation cannot be totally redeemed simply by reversing the alteration. Formal approval for the scheme, as restored, will need to be sought again, and transactions in the interim period will not have the benefit of the exemptions and reliefs.

Appeals

4.118 If the company establishing the scheme is aggrieved by the failure of the Board of Inland Revenue to approve it, or to approve an alteration as described at 4.117, or by the withdrawal of approval, it may by written notice to the Board within 30 days of being notified of that decision require the matter to be considered by the Special Commissioners, who will hear the case and determine the point in dispute in the same way as in an appeal against an assessment (ICTA 1988, Sch 9, para 5(a) and (c): see 7.1 to 7.5). Another participating company, in the case of a group scheme, cannot initiate an appeal.

Conditions as to the shares

Relevant companies

4.119 The shares used in the scheme must form part of the ordinary share capital (see 7.72) of:

(a) the 'grantor'; ie the company establishing the scheme (ICTA 1988, Sch 9, para 10(a)); or
(b) a company which has control of the grantor, within the definition of control in 7.23 to 7.24 (ICTA 1988, Sch 9, para 10(b) and ss 187(2) and 840); or
(c) a company which either is or controls (see 7.23 and 7.24) a member company of a consortium which owns the grantor, or owns a company which controls that company (ICTA 1988, Sch 9, para 10(c)(i) and ss 187(2) and 840). The consortium member company must beneficially own 15% or more of the grantor, or of the company which controls it, as the case may be (ICTA 1988, Sch 9, para 10(c)(ii)). For this purpose a company is a member of a consortium owning another company if it is one of a number of companies which between them beneficially own at least 75% of that other company's ordinary share capital (see 7.72), and each of which beneficially owns at least 5% (ICTA 1988, s 187(7)). Prior to amendment by FA 1986, s 23(5)(a), with effect from 25 July 1986, a consortium for this purpose consisted of not more than five companies (FA 1978, Sch 9, para 17).

4.120 The broad effect of the provisions set out in 4.119 is that the shares utilised may be those of the grantor or a company higher up the chain of ownership within a group or a consortium context. More specifically, the effect of the legislation is that shares in the following may qualify:

(a) the grantor;
(b) a company which controls the grantor;
(c) a company which is a 15% member of a consortium which owns the grantor;
(d) a company which controls a company which is a 15% member of a consortium which owns the grantor;
(e) a company which is a 15% member of a consortium which owns a company which controls the grantor; or
(f) a company which controls a company which is a 15% member of a consortium which owns a company which controls the grantor.

4.121 The possibilities in 4.120 may be illustrated diagrammatically as follows, where G is the grantor; E indicates any other company whose shares may be used in the scheme; a solid line indicates control; and a dotted line an interest in a consortium company. For this purpose all the consortia are assumed to consist of five companies, each with a 20% interest.

(a)

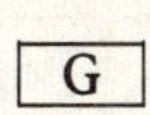

(b)

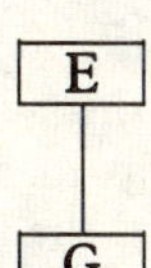

(c)

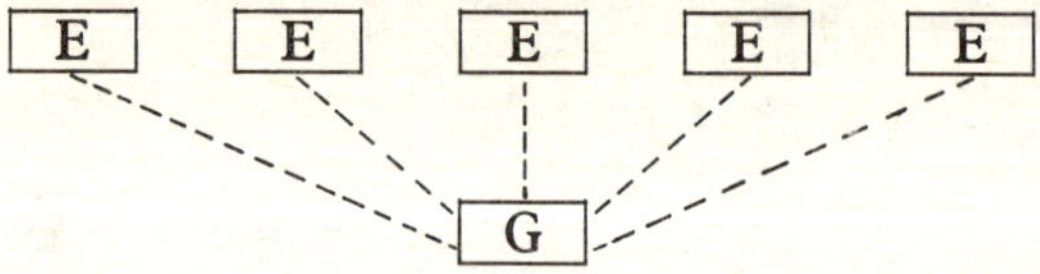

(d)

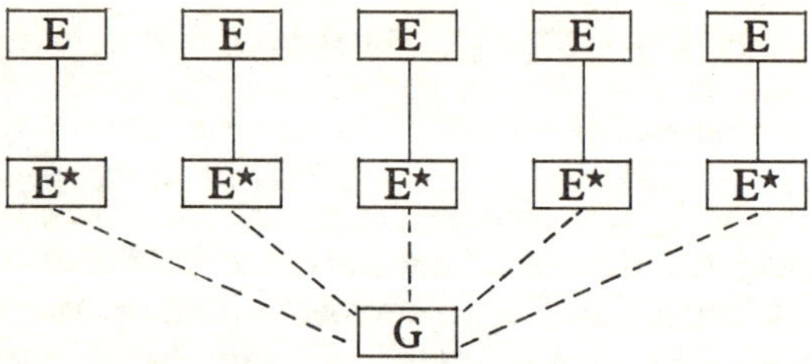

*Subject to 4.122, excluding a company under the control of another company, unless other conditions are met.

The control indicated by the solid lines may be direct or indirect, so that other eligible companies may intervene between the top tier and the second (subject to the conditions set out at 4.122).

(e)

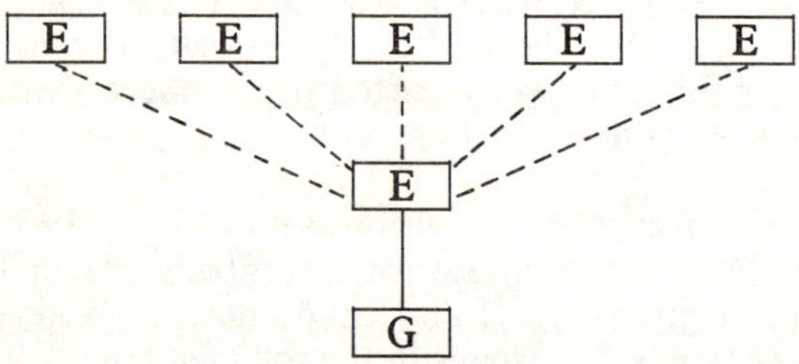

Again, the control indicated by the solid line may be direct or indirect, so that (subject to 4.122) other companies may intervene between the second and the bottom tier. The restrictions at 4.122 do not affect the company in the second tier as, while it is owned by a consortium, it is not controlled by any other company.

(f)

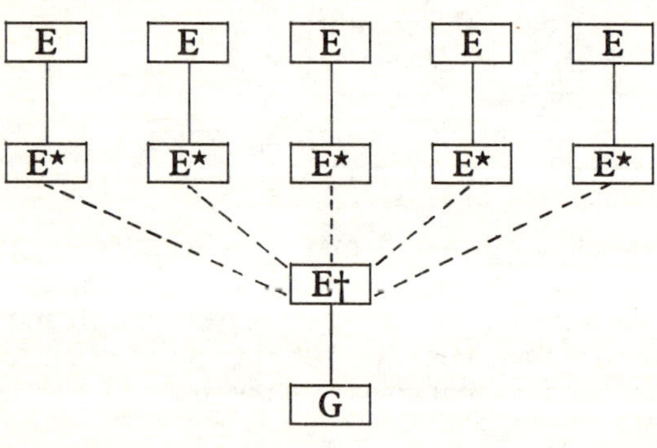

*Subject to 4.122.
†Unaffected by 4.122, as not under the control of any one other company.

Again, the control indicated by the solid line may be direct or indirect, so that (subject to 4.122) other companies may intervene between the top tier and the second tier; and between the third tier and the bottom tier.

Other requirements

4.122 The shares used in the scheme, in addition to being shares in an appropriate company within 4.119 to 4.121, must be:

(a) shares of a class quoted on a recognised stock exchange (ICTA 1988, Sch 9, para 11(a) and s 841: see 7.83 to 7.86); or
(b) shares in a company not under the control of another company (ICTA 1988, Sch 11(b) and ss 187(2) and 840: see 7.23 and 7.24); or
(c) shares in a company which is under the control (ICTA 1988, ss 187(2) and 840: see 7.23 and 7.24) of a second company whose shares are quoted on a recognised stock exchange (ICTA 1988, s 841: 7.83 to 7.86), except where that second company is a close company (ICTA 1988, ss 414 and 415: 7.12 to 7.21) or would be a close company if resident in the United Kingdom (ICTA 1988, Sch 9, para 11(c)). This third category was introduced by FA 1980, s 46(10), as FA 1978, Sch 9, para 6(c), with effect from 6 April 1980.

Stock Exchange quotation

4.123 In the case of para (a) in 4.122 it should be noted that not only must the company be quoted, but the particular class of shares used in the scheme must be. In the case of para (c) it would appear that a quotation for any class of shares of the controlling company is sufficient, although it is possible to argue that the words 'whose shares are quoted' indicate that all shares of whatever class must be quoted, so that the existence of a small number of unquoted preference shares in a controlling company whose ordinary shares were all quoted would prevent the use in the scheme of shares in the controlled company. Common sense would perhaps demand that the ordinary shares at least, but not necessarily any others, should be quoted, but such an interpretation is difficult to justify from the legislation.

4.124 A quotation on the Unlisted Securities Market is not treated as one on a 'recognised stock exchange' for this purpose (see Inland Revenue Statement of Practice SP 18/80 of 23 December 1980 'Securities dealt in on The Stock Exchange Unlisted Securities Market: status and valuation for tax purposes', reproduced at Appendix 8—and also a statement by Mr John Moore, the Financial Secretary to the Treasury, in connection with Inland Revenue approved selective share option schemes, during the Committee stage debates on the 1984 Finance Bill: HC Official Report, SC A, 24 May 1984, col 682).

4.125 The intention of the conditions set out in 4.119 to 4.124 is, broadly, to ensure that if the shares involved are in a company which is controlled by another, then it, or the group of which it forms a part, is, by virtue of its quotation, subject to some measure of public and institutional scrutiny and extrastatutory regulation, thus inhibiting the manipulation of the share price, whether to the advantage or disadvantage of employee shareholders. The general effect is to discourage the use of shares in subsidiary companies, just as their use in unapproved share schemes is particularly affected by the growth in value charges of ICTA 1988, s 138(1)(a) and FA 1988, s 79 (see 2.275 and 2.84 to 2.121), and is discouraged in the provisions for profit-sharing schemes under FA 1973 (see 2.240).

Restrictions; partly paid shares; redeemable shares

4.126 In addition, the shares must be fully paid up, not redeemable (except in the case of shares in a workers' co-operative), and not subject to any restrictions which do not attach to all shares of the same class other than (since 25 July 1986) restrictions within 4.127 below (ICTA 1988, Sch 9, para 12(1)). The term 'restrictions' is very widely defined for the purposes of the 'growth in value' charge under ICTA 1988, s 138(1)(a) (see 2.205 to 2.217). Similarly, parallel provisions to those discussed in this paragraph, which apply in the case of Inland Revenue approved SAYE share option schemes and selective share option schemes also include within the term certain 'constructive restrictions' whereby the shareholder is disadvantaged if he takes a particular course of action (see 5.79 and 6.51). In the present context, however, the word bears its narrower general meaning of a condition attaching to the shares under their terms of issue, or in accordance with the company's articles of association, which limits the shareholder's freedom of action in relation to the shares. Arguably, however, it does not include a restriction imposed on the shareholder, as opposed to the share, by an independent contract between the shareholder and any other party (including, possibly, the company itself). This view is borne out by the Inland Revenue's booklet IR 36 (1981) 'Approved profit-sharing schemes', which states (at para 2.18) that 'restrictions' for this purpose 'do not include personal restrictions imposed on a particular shareholder (eg the contractual restrictions imposed on all participants by [ICTA 1988, Sch 9, para 2(2)])': see 4.78. Certainly, the definition is narrow enough that it is not felt necessary to include within the legislation the saving provision found in ICTA 1988, Sch 9, para 13(2) in relation to approved share option schemes and in ICTA 1988, s 139(10) in relation to the charge under ICTA 1988, s 138(1)(a) excluding from the definition of a restriction any provision similar in purpose and effect to any part of the Model Rules set out in the 'Model Code for Securities Transactions by Directors of Listed Companies' issued by The Stock Exchange in November 1984 (see 2.216 and Appendix 4).

4.127 The restrictions which have been permitted, since 25 July 1986, as indicated at 4.126 above, even though they may not attach to all shares of the same class, are those which meet all the following conditions:

(a) they are imposed by the company's articles of association (ICTA 1988, Sch 9, para 12(2));
(b) they require all shares held by directors and employees of the company, or of any other company of which it has control (see 7.23) to be disposed of on ceasing to be so held (ie, when the office or employment terminates, or when the shares pass by operation of law, as on death, to any other person) (ICTA 1988, Sch 9, para 12(2)(a));
(c) they require all shares acquired, in pursuance of rights or interests obtained by such directors or employees, by persons who are not (or have ceased to be) such directors or employees to be disposed of when they are acquired (ICTA 1988, Sch 12, para 12(2)(b)). This would cover, for example, shares obtained by an ex-employee, or his executor, under an option granted when he was an employee;
(d) they require the disposal to be by way of sale (not gift), and for a consideration in money (rather than money's worth) on terms laid down in the articles (ICTA 1988, Sch 9, para 12(3)(a));

(e) the articles also contain general provisions under which any person disposing of shares of the same class (whether or not held by directors or employees of the company or of any other company of which it has control—see 7.23—or acquired in pursuance of rights or interests obtained by such employees) may (but need not necessarily) be required to sell them on terms which are the same as those mentioned in para (d) (ICTA 1988, Sch 9, para 12(3)(b)); and

(f) except in the case of redeemable shares in a workers' co-operative (see 4.133) the restrictions do not have the effect of obliging a participant, before the release date (see 4.13), to dispose of his beneficial interest in shares the ownership of which has not been transferred to him (ICTA 1988, Sch 9, para 12(4)).

4.128 The legislation permitting the limited restrictions set out in 4.127 was introduced by FA 1986, s 22(1), (4) and (5), prior to which a company which wished to retain control over the distribution of its shares by requiring employees to dispose of their shares on the termination of employment was prevented from introducing an approved scheme. Although under para (b) of 4.127 above all shares held by directors and employees must be required actually to be disposed of, the Financial Secretary to the Treasury indicated during the parliamentary debates on the 1986 Finance Bill that, in practice, a requirement that such individuals should simply offer their shares for sale would be treated as meeting this condition. It would, clearly, be impractical to oblige a departing employee to sell shares to the remaining shareholders in the company, who might be unwilling, or unable, to purchase them.

4.129 Even prior to the changes made in 1986, the Inland Revenue did not regard as a restriction for the purpose of 4.126 a provision in a company's articles of association requiring an employee who had ceased to work for the company to transfer his shares, provided he was not required to do so until after their legal ownership had passed to him from the trustees; i e either at his specific and voluntary direction before the release date (see 4.82), or after the five-year period to that date had expired (see Inland Revenue Press Release of 11 June 1985, 'Approved employee share option schemes: Revenue revise practice on some share restrictions', reproduced at Appendix 9).

4.130 The exclusion of shares subject to restrictions which do not attach to all shares of the same class (other than those indicated) reflects the intention behind the legislation of involving employees on equal terms with other shareholders, and parallels the prohibition on creating a special class of shares purely for use in the profit-sharing scheme (see 4.136).

4.131 The prohibition on the use of partly-paid shares (see 4.126) prevents the 'gearing-up' of the number of shares appropriated to a participant by giving him a larger number of shares while still coming within the 'relevant amount' discussed at 4.61. It also prevents a situation whereby the employee is faced with the alternatives of adding to the value of his holding out of his own resources or forfeiting the shares, and avoids administrative complexity and the possibility, or appearance, of manipulation.

4.132 The use of redeemable shares (other than those in a workers' co-operative) is excluded as it would be a means of passing to the employee a guaranteed sum, payable at a future date, and would reflect a departure from the principle of involving employees in both the rewards and risks of equity investment in the company for which they work.

4.133 The exclusion from the prohibition on redeemable shares of shares in a workers' co-operative was introduced by FA 1986, s 24(1) and (2), with effect from 25 July 1986. A workers' co-operative for this purpose means a registered industrial and provident society within the meaning of ICTA 1988, s 486 which is a co-operative society, and the rules of which include provisions which secure (ICTA 1988, s 187(10)):

(a) that the only persons who may be members of it are those who are employed by, or by a subsidiary of, the society and those who are the trustees of its profit sharing scheme; and
(b) subject to any provision as to qualifications for membership which may from time to time be made by the members of the society by reference to age, length of service, or other factors of any description, all such employees or trustees may be members of the society. The exception for 'other factors of any description', while very broad, would nevertheless appear to exclude rules which allow the inclusion or exclusion of individual employees on an arbitrary basis.

4.134 'Co-operative society' within 4.133 above is defined by ICTA 1988, s 187(10) by reference to the Industrial and Provident Societies Act 1965, s 1 or the Industrial and Provident Societies Act (Northern Ireland) 1969, s 1. The meaning of 'registered industrial and provident society' is extended by ICTA 1988, s 486 to include any co-operative association established and resident in the United Kingdom, and which has as its object or primary object the assisting of its members in the carrying on of agricultural or horticultural businesses on land occupied by them in the United Kingdom, or in the carrying on of businesses consisting in the catching or taking of fish or shellfish. 'Subsidiary' within para (a) of 4.133 above is not defined. The term has no general meaning in the Taxes Acts, except in the context of '51% subsidiary', '75% subsidiary' and '90% subsidiary' (ICTA 1988, s 838) and it is therefore assumed that it has here its meaning for company law purposes, by which one body corporate is a subsidiary of another if that other body holds more than half in nominal value of its equity share capital, or is a member of the first body and controls the composition of its board of directors (or if the first company is a subsidiary of another subsidiary of that other company (CA 1985, s 736(1)).

4.135 Where, for the purpose of securing and maintaining approval of its profit sharing scheme, the rules of a society which is a workers' co-operative, or which is seeking to be registered under the industrial and provident societies legislation as a workers' co-operative, contain provision for membership of the society by the scheme trustees, then provisions denying voting rights to those trustees, or other provisions which appear to the Registrar to be reasonably necessary for that purpose, those provisions, which would otherwise conflict with the requirements of the legislation, are disregarded in determining whether the society should be, or continue to be, registered under that legislation as a bona-fide co-operative society (FA 1986, s 24(4) and (5)).

Distribution of the shares

4.136 Various conditions as regards the distribution of the shares used in the scheme must be fulfilled. These apply except where the shares are in a company whose ordinary share capital (see 7.72), at the time of the acquisition of the shares by the trustees, consists of one class only. Where there is more than one class of share capital, the majority of the issued shares of the same class either must be employee-control shares (see 4.138), or must be held by persons other than:

(a) persons who acquired their shares in pursuance of a right conferred to them or an opportunity afforded to them as a director or employee of the grantor or of any other company (usually, in practice, another company within the same group) and not in pursuance of an offer to the public (ICTA 1988, Sch 9, para 14(1)(a)); and
(b) trustees holding shares on behalf of persons who acquired their beneficial interests in the shares as in (a) above (ICTA 1988, Sch 9, para 14(1)(b)); and
(c) persons within 4.137.

4.137 Where the shares are not of a class quoted on a recognised stock exchange (although other shares in the company may be), but the company is under the control of another company whose shares are so quoted (other than a close company or a company which would be close but for not being resident in the UK)—i e a company within para (c) but not within para (a) of 4.122—the category of persons who must not, together, hold more than a minority interest in the shares of that class is extended to include companies which have control (see 7.23 and 7.24: ICTA 1988, ss 187(2) and 840) of the company whose shares are in question, or of which that company is an associated company within ICTA 1988, ss 187(2) and 416: see 7.10 (ICTA 1988, Sch 9, para 14(1)(c), introduced as FA 1978, Sch 9, para 8(c) by FA 1980, s 47(11) with effect from 6 April 1980).

4.138 Shares in a company are 'employee-control' shares within 4.136 above if (ICTA 1988, Sch 9, para 14(3)):

(a) the persons holding the shares are, by virtue of their holding, together able to control (see 7.23) the company (not just to control the class of shares); and
(b) those persons are or have been employees or directors of the company, or of another company which is under the control (see 7.23) of the company.

The provisions permitting the majority of the shares to be employee-control shares was introduced by FA 1986, s 23(1) to (3), with effect from 25 July 1986.

4.139 The basic intention of the provisions regarding the distribution of the shares, discussed in 4.136 to 4.138, is to prevent the use of a class of shares solely held by, or controlled by, employee shareholders, the value of which, or the benefits attaching to which, could be manipulated to their advantage or detriment. What is in contemplation is primarily a class of shares relating particularly to the profit-sharing scheme in question, but the category of employee shareholders in para (a) of 4.136 will include not only participants in profit-sharing schemes, but those who have acquired shares under unapproved share incentive and share option schemes (see Chapters 2 and 3), profit-sharing schemes under FA 1973, Sch 8 (see 2.232 to 2.241), Inland Revenue approved savings-related share option schemes (see Chapter 5), and approved selective share option schemes (see Chapter 6). The inclusion of trustees for such employees within the 'minority only' category of shareholders (see para (b) of 4.136) prevents an obvious device for avoidance by transferring shares to nominees or other trustees, as well as taking account of the fact that initially scheme shares under the present provisions will be held by trustees. The further inclusion of controlling or associated companies within 4.137 extends the same principles, recognising that a majority holding by employees and connected companies (over which those employees might also have influence) could open the way for manipulation or abuse. Where, as under the provisions described in 4.138, the employee shares give control of the company as a whole, this risk of manipulation is significantly reduced as, broadly, the interests of the individuals concerned qua shareholder and qua employee are balanced.

4.140 The rules as to the nature and distribution of the shares set out at 4.119 to 4.139 must be incorporated in the scheme before it can obtain approval (see 4.90). Any change in the rules will result in the lapsing of approval (see 4.117), and any breach of them in the withdrawal of approval at the discretion of the Board of Inland Revenue (see 4.110). The conditions must therefore continue to be fulfilled throughout the life of the scheme, not simply when it is set up, and particular attention must be paid to the requirement that a majority of the shares of the relevant class be employee-control shares or be held by 'ordinary' or 'normal' shareholders. Unlike the other conditions, this could be breached by the cumulative effect of a number of small transactions.

Individuals ineligible to participate

Non-employees

4.141 To obtain approval, the scheme must not permit the appropriation of shares to ineligible persons (see 4.90). An individual is not eligible to have shares appropriated to him at any time unless he is, or was within the previous 18 months, a director or employee of the 'grantor' (ie the company establishing the scheme) or, in the case of a group scheme (see 4.92), a director or employee of a participating company (ICTA 1988, Sch 9, para 35(1)). An individual prevented by this provision from obtaining a beneficial interest in any further shares is not, however, obliged to divest himself of his existing holdings, nor does he suffer any income tax penalty on a disposal after the five-year release date, or any increase in the 'appropriate percentage' on which tax is charged on a disposal before that date (see 4.26). In practice most companies will not wish to make shares available to employees who have chosen to leave and take up alternative positions, but the 18 month 'tolerance' does allow scope to make shares available to those who have recently retired, or left on the grounds of disability or redundancy. In particular, it allows shares to be appropriated in the situation where the amount of the company's 'donation' to the trustees is determined by reference to the profits of the preceding accounting period. The determination of the 'relevant amount', or maximum value of shares which may be appropriated to a participant by reference to his emoluments for the current *or preceding* year (see 4.61) also takes account of the possibility that the participant may no longer be employed in the current year.

Participants in other schemes

4.142 An individual is not eligible to have shares appropriated to him under a scheme in any year of assessment in which shares have been appropriated to him under another approved profit sharing scheme established by (ICTA 1988, Sch 9, para 35(2)):

(a) the grantor (ie the employer company);
(b) a company which controls the grantor;
(c) a company which is controlled by the grantor;
(d) a company which is controlled by a company which also controls the grantor;
(e) a company which is a member of a consortium which owns the grantor;
(f) a company which is owned in part by the grantor as a member of a consortium (ie 75% or more of the ordinary share capital of which is owned by a consortium of which the company concerned is a member).

'Control' for the purposes of (b) to (c) above is as defined in 7.23 to 7.24, and thus includes indirect control via another company (ICTA 1988, ss 187(2) and 840). A 'consortium' for the purposes of (e) and (f) is as defined in para (c) of 4.119 (ICTA 1988, s 187(7)).

4.143 This provision prevents the proliferation of benefits by creating multiple employments with a number of companies in a group (or within a looser association of companies involving a consortium), each with their own scheme. This would otherwise be possible, as an individual need only be an employee, not necessarily a full time employee, in order to be eligible to participate within 4.141. It also prevents the rather more obvious device of having more than one scheme set up by the same company to run concurrently.

Individuals with a 'material interest'

4.144 An individual is not eligible to have shares appropriated to him at any time when he has, or has had within the previous 12 months, a 'material interest' in a close company which is (ICTA 1988, Sch 9, para 8):

(a) the company whose shares are to be appropriated under the scheme; or
(b) a company which has control of that company; or
(c) a company which is a member of a consortium which owns that company.

For these purposes 'control' is as defined in 7.23 and 7.24 (ICTA 1988, ss 187(2) and 840), and 'consortium', 'ownership' of a company by a consortium, and 'membership' of a consortium have the meanings set out at para (c) of 4.119. 'Close company' is as defined in 7.12 to 7.21 (ICTA 1988, Sch 9, para 8 and ss 414 and 415) but also includes companies which would be close but for the exclusion from the general definition of companies not resident in the UK (ICTA 1988, Sch 9, para 8 and s 414(1)(a)), and of certain quoted companies in which 35% or more of the voting power is held by the public (ICTA 1988, Sch 9, para 8 and s 415). A 'material interest' in a close company for this purpose is, broadly, an interest, with associates, of more than 25% in the ordinary share capital or distributable income of the company (or such an interest held by associates even where the individual himself has no interest at all). The normal definition of 'material interest', formerly contained in ICTA 1970, s 285(6) and now appearing, with adaptations, in ICTA 1988, s 168(11) (see 7.65 to 7.71) is, broadly, an interest of 5% or more. The 25% figure used in the context of approved profit-sharing schemes is substituted for the usual 5% by ICTA 1988, s 187(3). 'Associate' is defined in ICTA 1988, s 417(3) and (4), and the details are set out at 7.6. Broadly, the term includes a business partner, a husband, wife, parent, remoter ancestor, child or remoter descendant, brother or sister; the trustees of any settlement made by the individual or by such a relative; and the trustees or the personal representatives of the deceased in the case of any trust or estate which includes among its assets shares in the company in question, and of which the individual in question is a beneficiary. Prior to 6 April 1986 the term did not include this last category of trustees or personal representatives, but included any other person with an interest in such a settlement or estate, except in the case of certain employee trusts where the individual was not, and could not by the operation of the trust become (with or without relatives), the beneficial owner of more than 5% of the company. For the purposes of defining 'associate' so as to determine whether an individual had a 'material interest' under the approved profit-sharing scheme legislation, this figure of 5% was increased to 25% (FA 1978, Sch 9, para 11(3)(c)(ii)), and in the definition of an employee trust, the reference to employees and directors of the company was read in the case of a group scheme (see 4.92) as a reference to employees and directors of any participating company (FA 1978, Sch 9, para 11(3)(c)(i)). These two, lapsed, modifications to the definition of 'associate' were introduced by FA 1980, s 46(12) with effect from 6 April 1980, but the substitution of 25% for 5% in the basic definition of 'material interest' formed part of the original legislation. The most recent changes, taking effect from 6 April 1986, were made by FA 1987, s 37 and Sch 16, Pt V. See further at 7.65 to 7.71.

4.145 The rationale underlying the provisions of ICTA 1988, Sch 9, para 8, as set out in 4.144, is that an individual should not be eligible to participate in a scheme if he has a holding in the company issuing the shares, or in a company higher up the chain of control (or consortium ownership), so great that he could exercise a significant degree of influence over the value of the shares (for example, through decisions as to the pricing of intra-group transactions or the level of dividends), or over the level of company 'donations' to the trustees. Any director might, of course, be in a position to exercise such influence, but subject to the supervision of the company in general meeting. As discussed at 1.7, a holding greater than 25% would automatically give the power to block special or extraordinary resolutions, and in practice might confer much greater power through the obtaining of other shareholders' votes in return for co-operation in passing such resolutions on other matters, or simply by virtue of the fact that, while only a minority holding, it represented the largest number of shares in single, or related, ownership.

The trust instrument

General

4.146 The trust instrument under which the trustees of the scheme hold the shares must include certain specified provisions, without which the scheme will not gain initial Inland Revenue approval (see 4.90); any formal alteration in which will result in the automatic loss of approval (unless itself approved) (see 4.117); and any breach of which will give the Board of Inland Revenue power to withdraw approval at its discretion (see 4.110).

Notice of appropriation

4.147 The trust instrument must provide that, as soon as practicable after any shares have been appropriated to a participant, the trustees will give him written notice of the appropriation, specifying the number and description of the shares so appropriated, and stating their 'initial market value': see 4.15 (ICTA 1988, Sch 9, para 31). The requirement to commit these details to writing individually in respect of each participant (rather than, for example, simply displaying a notice to the effect that each employee has been allocated fifty shares) ensures that both the trustees and the employees concerned have the information necessary to calculate any future tax liability, and also, so far as possible, that employees who may be financially unsophisticated are left in no doubt as to the benefits which have accrued to them under the scheme. This is particularly important in view of the fact that, by the nature of the arrangements, legal ownership of the shares is divorced from beneficial ownership, so that the participant has no share certificate, and the company no record in its share register of the fact that the appropriation has taken place.

Limitations on share disposals

4.148 The trust instrument must prohibit the trustees from disposing of any shares during the 'period of retention' (ie the two years following appropriation, or the period until earlier retirement age or cessation of employment due to injury, disability or redundancy: see 4.79), whether by transfer to the participant or otherwise. There are exceptions for the circumstances set out at 4.84 to 4.86; ie broadly, on a take-over or a scheme of arrangement affecting the shares (ICTA 1988, Sch 9, para 32(1) and Sch 10, para 1(1)(a), (b) and (c)). The exemption for a take-over, reconstruction or amalgamation as set out in 4.84 was included in the original legislation, but those for a compromise or arrangement, as set out in 4.85, and for the acceptance of a general offer, as set out in 4.86, presumably omitted in error, were introduced by FA 1980, s 46(12), into what was then FA 1978, Sch 9, para 13(1), with effect from 6 April 1980.

4.149 The trust instrument must prohibit the trustees disposing of any shares after the end of the period of retention (see 4.79) and before the five-year 'release date' except pursuant to a direction given by or on behalf of the participant or any person in whom the beneficial interest in his shares is for the time being vested, and by a transfer which would not involve a breach of the participant's obligations set out in 4.82 and 4.83 (ICTA 1988, Sch 9, paras 2(2)(c) & (d) and 32(2)). Broadly, this provision permits a disposal of the legal ownership to the participant himself (after the expiry of the retention period) provided he pays to the trustees a sum equal to basic rate income tax on the 'appropriate percentage' (see 4.26 to 4.29) of the 'locked-in value' of the shares (see 4.14) at that time; or (again, after the expiry of the retention period) a sale to a third party for the best monetary consideration that can reasonably be obtained at that time, or in the case of redeemable shares in a workers' co-operative, their redemption. It prevents the trustees taking any action by way of disposal of the shares before the release date without the permission of the participant (the reference to a direction 'on behalf of' the participant being taken to refer to someone with legal authority to act on his behalf, such as a trustee in bankruptcy, a trustee of a mentally incapacitated person acting under the authority of the Court of Protection or the holder of a power of attorney. Paragraph 32(2), (then FA 1978, Sch 9, para 13(2)), was amended by FA 1980, s 46(13), with effect from 6 April 1980, to make it clear that these restrictions on the trustees after the expiry of the period of retention did not extend beyond the release date.

Obligation to pay disposal proceeds etc to participants

4.150 The trust instrument must also contain a provision requiring the trustees to pay over to the participant any money or money's worth received by them in respect of, or by reference to, any of his shares, other than money's worth consisting of new shares obtained on a reconstruction or take-over within ICTA 1988, Sch 10, para 5 (see 4.42 to 4.53). This requirement is subject to the trustees' obligations either to pay over all or part of the proceeds to a company, in order that tax may be deducted under PAYE, or to operate PAYE themselves (see 4.67 to 4.74: ICTA 1988, Sch 10, para 7). An exception is also made for the case where the sum received arises from the disposal of rights under a rights issue and, in accordance with a direction given by or on behalf of the participant or other person in whom the beneficial interest in the participant's shares has come to vest, the proceeds of the disposal are used to exercise other rights under that rights issue (see 4.39: ICTA 1988, Sch 10, para 4(2)). This provision (ICTA 1988, Sch 9, para 33(a)) is clearly aimed at protecting the rights of participants, as against a body of trustees appointed by the company, where there might be possibilities for abuse, with tax relief being gained for 'donations' to the trustees by the company but the proceeds of sale ultimately being withheld from the employees. To legislate as to the provisions of the trust deed does not, of course, ensure compliance, but any breach of the deed would empower the Board of Inland Revenue to withdraw approval, thus removing relief for the company's donations, and the breach of trust would give the participants grounds for an action at law to recover the amounts misappropriated. The wholesale making off with the participants' funds by the trustees is, perhaps, an unlikely event, but the provision also has the effect of preventing any deduction from amounts due to the participants in respect of administrative expenses or 'penalties' for early sale (beyond those tax penalties prescribed by law). Any administrative costs must be borne by the trustees out of the company's 'donations' to the trustees; out of investment income arising in the period of up to nine months (see 4.76) before shares are acquired; or out of dividends arising from the shares in the period of up to 18 months (see 4.9 and 4.10) before shares are appropriated to employees. In practice, such costs will normally be borne by the company and 'lost' in its own administrative expenses, although strictly it may be argued that their allowability for tax purposes in fact relies on ICTA 1988, s 85 ('Schedule D deduction of payments to trustees': see 4.75 to 4.77) and that they would otherwise be excluded from deduction by ICTA 1988, s 74(a) as 'money not wholly and exclusively laid out or expended for the purposes of the trade, profession, or vocation'.

Exercising of rights

4.151 The trust instrument must also contain a provision as regards any right arising in respect of a participant's shares to be allotted other shares, securities, or rights of any description, requiring them to deal with such rights only pursuant to a direction given by or on behalf of (see 4.149) the participant or any other person in whom the beneficial ownership of the shares then vests (ICTA 1988, Sch 9, para 33(b)). This prevents the trustees taking arbitrary decisions as to how to deal with rights issues, options to take stock dividends in preference to cash, or the grant of other benefits, such as vouchers for concessional purchases. In the absence of such a provision in the legislation, the company might well decide to set up a scheme on the basis that the decision on such matters lay with the trustees, rather than the participant. This would avoid considerable administrative complexity by enabling a uniform approach to be adopted on a rights issue, either selling the rights, or selling sufficient rights to obtain the funds necessary to take up the remainder. As it is, trustees may find themselves pursuing each of these courses in relation to different participants' holdings, and taking up rights in full in respect of others, with additional funds provided by the participants for the purpose (see 4.21). Participants may thus deal with the shares in which they have beneficial ownership as nearly as possible in the same way as if they had full legal ownership, subject only to the restrictions which are the essence of the scheme, or are necessarily for the protection of the Revenue.

Maintaining records

4.152 The trustees must also be obliged under the terms of the trust instrument to maintain the necessary records to enable them to carry out their obligations as regards deduction of PAYE, or payment of appropriate sums to a company for the deduction of PAYE, as set out at 4.67 to 4.74 (ICTA 1988, Sch 9, para 34(a)). Where a participant becomes liable to a Schedule E charge, on a disposal (see 4.13 to 4.32) or a capital receipt (see 4.33 to 4.41) before the five-year 'release date', the trustees must also be obliged, under the terms of the trust instrument, to inform the participants of any facts relevant to determining that liability, such as the 'appropriate percentage' (see 4.26 to 4.29), the 'locked-in value' (see 4.14), any previous capital receipts, the sale proceeds which may be substituted for the locked-in value (see 4.20), and the effects of any take-over or share reorganisation: see 4.42 to 4.53 (ICTA 1988, Sch 9, para 34(b)). They cannot of course notify him of his tax liability itself, which will be affected by extraneous factors, such as his marginal rate and residence status. The legislation thus, again, recognises the possibility that a large number of participants may be financially unsophisticated, and transfers the burden of compliance, in large measure, to the trustees. The obligation is not dependent upon a request by the participant, who may not realise his need of such information, but must be required under the terms of the trust instrument to be fulfilled in all cases.

INFORMATION POWERS

4.153 The Board of Inland Revenue may serve written notice on any person requiring him to furnish, within such time as the Board may direct (but with a minimum time limit of 30 days), such information as it thinks necessary to enable it to perform its functions in connection with approved schemes (ICTA 1988, Sch 9, para 6). In particular, this includes the information necessary to determine whether to approve a scheme or withdraw approval already given (ICTA 1988, Sch 9, para 6(a)); and that necessary to determine the income tax or CGT liability of a participant in an approved scheme (ICTA 1988, Sch 9, para 6(b)). Other information not specifically detailed in the legislation, but which might be sought under the general power of para 6, is that required in order to determine whether contributions by the employer company had been utilised by the trustees in the acquisition of shares within the time limit necessary in order to obtain a tax deduction (see 4.76) or whether shares had been appropriated to participants by the trustees within the time limits necessary to avoid the imposition of CGT and the additional rate of income tax on discretionary trusts (see 4.9 and 4.10). On consolidation into ICTA 1988 the legislation was effectively amended to specify also, in particular, 'information in relation to the administration of a scheme and any alteration of the terms of a scheme', a form of words which had previously appeared only in the FA 1984 legislation governing approved selective share option schemes. This was presumably considered not to represent a substantive change in the law, as it was covered by the general power of para 6 (then FA 1978, s 53(7)). The consolidation also had the effect of restricting the information which could be required to that which the person to whom the notice was addressed has or can reasonably obtain. This limitation already applied in the case of both savings-related and selective share option schemes. There is no appeal against a request for information, except by means of an application for judicial review (see 7.51) on the grounds that in the circumstances of the case it is unreasonable to require that person (who may be neither employee, employer or trustee) to provide the information; that the information is not necessary to enable the Board to perform their functions; or that the time allowed is too short.

4.154 Details of the penalties for the failure to comply with a request for information as detailed in 4.153 are given at 7.75 to 7.77. In practice, trustees are required by Technical Division (Employee Share Schemes) to complete a return annually (by reference to years of assessment rather than to the company's accounting period) covering matters such as appropriations, capital receipts and company reconstructions. The participant may also be required, under general legislation, to include in his own tax return any share acquisitions and (subject to de minimis limits) any capital gain arising from the disposal of shares, although tax return forms no longer routinely request details of assets acquired.

5 Inland Revenue approved savings-related share option schemes

SUMMARY

5.1 The Finance Act 1980 introduced a favourable tax regime for savings-related share option schemes. Under such a scheme, which must be approved by the Inland Revenue, there is no charge to income tax under general Schedule E rules on receipt of the option, or on its exercise under ICTA 1988, s 135 (see Chapter 3), nor on the growth in value of the shares once acquired, under ICTA 1988, s 138(1)(a) or FA 1988, ss 78 and 79 (see 2.35 to 2.302). An occasion of charge to CGT arises in the normal way on the eventual disposal of the shares, at which time the actual consideration given for them forms the base cost, rather than the market value at the time of acquisition (as would otherwise be the case in a transaction carried out on a non-arm's length basis).

5.2 Detailed conditions must be satisfied before a scheme can obtain Inland Revenue approval. In particular, it must be linked to a contractual savings ('SAYE') scheme run by the Department for National Savings or by a building society, and the shares in respect of which the options are granted must only be capable of acquisition out of repayments or interest from that SAYE contract. Contributions under the scheme may not exceed £100 per month (£50 prior to 1 September 1984) and must be such that the repayments made (with interest) match as nearly as possible the cost of the shares to be acquired. That cost must not normally be 'manifestly less' than 90% of the market value of shares of the same class at the time the option is granted. The option must not, in general, be capable of exercise before the date of repayment of the SAYE investment, which is either five or seven years from the first monthly payment, although this condition is relaxed in certain limited circumstances. All full-time employees who are resident and ordinarily resident in the UK must be eligible to join the scheme on similar terms, although it is possible to set a minimum qualifying period of employment, not exceeding five years, and differing rights may be allocated according to level of remuneration, length of service or other similar factors without violating this condition.

THE TAX EXEMPTIONS

General

5.3 Various income tax exemptions are available where, on or after 15 November 1980, an individual obtains a right to acquire shares in a company or other body corporate (hereafter referred to simply as an 'option') by reason of his office or employment as a director or employee of that company, and in accordance with a savings-related share option scheme approved by the Inland Revenue (ICTA 1988, s 185(1)(a)). The original legislation of FA 1980 provided that the relevant exemptions should apply to acquisitions of options on or after the 'appointed day', which was defined as such day as the Treasury by order made by statutory instrument should appoint for the coming into force of the relevant provisions of the Act (FA 1980, s 47(3)), and the date of 15 November 1980 was actually so appointed by the Finance Act 1980 (Savings-Related Share Option Schemes) Commencement Order 1980 (SI 1980/1546).

5.4 For a general discussion as to the circumstances in which an option, or any other benefit, is conferred 'by reason of' an office or employment, see 2.36 to 2.49, although the specific statutory provisions discussed there do not apply to approved share option schemes.

5.5 Similar exemptions apply (ICTA 1988, s 185(1)) where the option is granted as result of a directorship of, or employment with, any other company; for example, where the individual is employed by a subsidiary and shares in the parent company are issued to him under a group scheme (see 5.19).

The grant of the option

5.6 No tax charge arises on the receipt of an option under an approved SAYE-linked scheme (ICTA 1988, s 185(2)), subject to the point discussed at 5.11 (exercise within three years of grant). This provision prevents a charge on the value of the option as 'money's worth' under the general Schedule E provisions of ICTA 1988, s 19, in accordance with the decision in *Abbott v Philbin* (see 3.5). Such a charge would not otherwise be excluded by ICTA 1988, s 135(2), as is normally the case for the receipt of an option under an unapproved scheme (see 3.15), as that subsection only displaces the general rule in circumstances where tax will become chargeable under ICTA 1988, s 135(1) on the *exercise* of the option, and that charge, too, is eliminated for SAYE-linked schemes (see 5.8). Furthermore, in the absence of the exemption conferred by s 185(2), a charge on the grant of the option could still arise under general rules where the employee was not resident and ordinarily resident in the UK (see 3.12 and 3.13).

5.7 In addition, no income tax charge on the grant can arise under the exception to the general rule of s 135(2), which applies where the option is capable of being exercised more than seven years after its grant (see 3.38 to 3.43). This provision might otherwise apply, as, while the shares must be purchased out of the proceeds of a SAYE contract with a maximum life of seven years (see 5.32), the option itself may be capable of exercise up to six months after the maturity of that contract (see 5.31).

The exercise of the option

5.8 If the individual exercises the option in accordance with the provisions of the scheme at a time when it continues to be approved, tax is not charged on the exercise under any provision of the Tax Acts (ICTA 1988, s 185(3)(a)), subject to the point discussed at 5.11 (exercise within three years of grant). The effect is that:

(a) there is no liability under ICTA 1988, s 135, the general provision which, for an unapproved scheme, transfers the income tax charge from the grant of the option to the gain 'realised' on its exercise (see 3.9 to 3.37);

(b) there is no charge under ICTA 1988, s 162 on the benefit of the notional loan arising by reason of the issue of shares at a discount to their then current market value. As discussed at 2.308, such a charge would normally be eliminated by the prior liability under ICTA 1988, s 135, but where that earlier charge is removed, as here, the ICTA 1988, s 162 charge would revive in the absence of a provision to the contrary. Hence the 'blanket' exemption from any tax charge, rather than simply an exclusion of the charge under ICTA 1988, s 135. In addition, where the employee was not taxable under Case I of Schedule E at the time of the grant of the option, he would not be liable under s 186 on its exercise (see 3.12 and 3.13) and a charge under ICTA 1988, s 162 might then arise, in the absence of the present exemption.

5.9 Similarly, provided the option is exercised in accordance with the provisions of the scheme at a time when it is still approved, no charge arises under ICTA 1988, s 138(1)(a) or FA 1988, ss 78 or 79 (see 2.190 to 2.286 and 2.53 to 2.121) in respect of the growth in value of the shares after their acquisition, even if by the time the charge would otherwise crystallise (on disposal; changes in rights or restrictions attaching to the shares; or expiry of seven years) the scheme is no longer approved, or no longer in existence (ICTA 1988, s 185(3)(a)). The scope for restrictions on the shares in an approved scheme is in fact limited (see 5.79 to 5.84), but there are some categories which are permitted, and the removal of which could crystallise a charge under ICTA 1988, s 138(1)(a) or FA 1988, s 78. A 'special benefits' charge under ICTA 1988, s 138(1)(b) or FA 1988, s 80 (see 2.287 to 2.294 and 2.122 to 2.137) may still arise in respect of the shares.

CAPITAL GAINS TAX CONSIDERATIONS

5.10 In certain circumstances, under the CGT legislation, the market value of an asset on a disposal is substituted for the actual consideration given in the calculation of any capital gain or loss arising, either on that disposal or on a subsequent disposal by the transferee. The most common case where this rule applies is on a gift, where no consideration is given, but it applies also where an asset is acquired by an individual 'in consideration for or recognition of his . . . services or past services in any office or employment' (CGTA 1979, s 29A(1)(b)). Subject to the point discussed at 5.11 (exercise within three years of grant), where shares are acquired by the exercise of an option granted under an approved savings-related scheme, at a time when the scheme continues to be approved (and thus the income tax exemptions discussed at 5.8 and 5.9 are available) this 'market value rule' is overridden (ICTA 1988, s 185(3)(b)), so that the actual consideration given (both for the grant of the option and for the acquisition of the shares themselves: CGTA 1979, s 137(3)) is taken into account in calculating any gain or loss arising on a subsequent disposal of the shares. Acquisitions will, in practice, always take place at a price below market value (as the holder would not otherwise choose to exercise the option) so the effect of this provision is to prevent an artificial restriction on the CGT charge or an artificial increase in the amount of any allowable loss. The application of the 'market value rule' is excluded not only as regards the acquisition of shares by the employee, but also as regards any corresponding disposal of them to him. This extension of the legislation to disposals was effected by FA 1984, s 39(1) and (9), amending FA 1980, s 47(1)(b)(ii) with effect from the commencement date of the original legislation on 15 November 1980. In the normal case, where new shares are issued by the company, there will be no such disposal, but where, for example, an option scheme is set up under which the shares will be provided, not by the company, but by a majority shareholder out of his existing holding, then this provision will come into effect and prevent a charge on the transfer of the shares based on an artificially inflated gain. Prior to 10 March 1981, similar provisions applied to the application of the 'market value' rule contained in CGTA 1979, s 19(3), for which s 29A was substituted by FA 1981, s 90, which also substituted a reference to the new legislation in the present context.

EXERCISE WITHIN THREE YEARS OF GRANT

5.11 Where the option is exercised within three years of its grant as described at 5.41 to 5.45, the income tax exemptions described at 5.6 to 5.9 and the suspension of the 'market value rule' for CGT as described at 5.10 do not apply, even though the exercise is within the terms of the scheme (ICTA 1988, s 185(4)). Paragraphs 5.41 to 5.45 describe provisions which permit options under an approved savings-related scheme to be exercised before the maturity of the related SAYE contract in the case of: a takeover of the company; a compromise with its creditors, by leave of the courts; the acquisition of minority dissenting shareholders' interests under provisions of the Companies Acts; or the passing by the company of a resolution for its voluntary winding up. Such an early exercise, or the inclusion in the scheme of provision for such early exercise, does not affect the approved status of the scheme for those employees who choose to wait until maturity of their SAYE contracts (in the limited number of the cases described where this is possible) but simply has the effect of withdrawing, for such early exercise, the special treatment otherwise available. In practice, the removal of the income tax exemption on the grant of the option will normally have no effect, except where it is capable of exercise more than seven years after its grant (see 3.38 to 3.43) or the option holder was not within Schedule E, Case I at the time of the grant, and the major effect will be to crystallise a charge on exercise under ICTA 1988, s 135.

5.12 Where an early exercise takes place more than three years after the grant in the circumstances described at 5.41 to 5.45, all the exemptions set out at 5.6 to 5.9 are available (together with the consequent CGT treatment set out in 5.10), notwithstanding that the relevant SAYE contract has not matured. As explained at 5.41 to 5.45, the scheme may provide for the exercise of options within six months of the event in question, or within a longer or shorter period in the case of the acquisition of the shares of dissentient shareholders, so that it may be possible, by making use of that period, to ensure that the exercise falls outside the three year period even though the event precipitating it does not.

APPROVAL OF SCHEMES

General

The application

5.13 On application by a company which has established a savings-related share option scheme (referred to in the legislation as the 'grantor')

(ICTA 1988, s 187(2) and Sch 9, para 1(1)) the Board of Inland Revenue is obliged to grant it approval if it meets the conditions set out in 5.26 to 5.99. Such an application must be made in writing and contain such particulars, and be supported by such evidence, as the Board may require (ICTA 1988, Sch 9, para 1(2)). The procedure to be followed, and information required in practice, are set out in the Inland Revenue booklet IR 39 'Approved savings-related share option schemes', at paras 2.1 and 2.2.

5.14 No special form of application is necessary, but the request for approval should be sent to:

Inland Revenue
Technical Division (Employee Share Schemes)
Somerset House
London
WC2R 1LB
(Telephone: 01–438 7803 or 7801)

and accompanied by two copies (except where indicated to the contrary) of each of the following documents:

(a) A statement giving the name and registered office of the grantor, and details of the tax district which deals with its corporation tax affairs, with the relevant reference number. If the company whose shares are to be used in the scheme is different (see 5.72), the same information is required for that company, and in the case of a group scheme (see 5.19) it is also required for each company to which the scheme is expressed to extend.
(b) The memorandum and articles of association of the company whose shares are to be used, and any relevant amendments (one copy only).
(c) The scheme rules.
(d) The form of contract under which the option is to be granted.
(e) A declaration by the company concerned that the shares to be used will satisfy the conditions in ICTA 1988, Sch 9, paras 10 to 14, discussed in 5.71 to 5.89 (one copy only).
(f) If the shares over which the option is to be granted are not shares in the grantor, or are in a company which is under the control of another company, a further declaration indicating precisely how the conditions in 5.71 to 5.89 are met (one copy only).
(g) Any other documents which will be issued to participants and/or shareholders in connection with the scheme.

5.15 An informal opinion may be obtained in advance of a formal application for approval. The Inland Revenue is prepared to comment on draft documentation and, if necessary, to hold discussions on particular points of difficulty (IR 39, para 2.3).

Inclusion of all eligible employees

5.16 The Board of Inland Revenue must be satisfied that the scheme meets the conditions for approval set out in 5.26 to 5.99 (ICTA 1988, Sch 9, paras 1(1) and 7 to 26) and also that there are no features of the scheme, other than those which are included in order to fulfil the statutory requirements, which would have, or, where continued approval is under consideration, already have the effect of discouraging any eligible employee within 5.90 to 5.99 from actually participating in the scheme (ICTA 1988, Sch 9, para 2(3)(a)). This second requirement was introduced as FA 1980, Sch 10, para 1(1)(aa) by FA 1984, s 39(2) and (9) with effect from 26 July 1984, in relation to all schemes whenever approved. As to examples of such conditions, see the discussion of the parallel provisions in the approved 'profit-sharing' schemes legislation at 4.98.

5.17 Where the company concerned is a member of a group of companies (whether or not the scheme is a group scheme as described at 5.19), the Board must be satisfied that the scheme would not (or, where continuing approval is under consideration, does not) have the effect of conferring benefits wholly or mainly on directors of group companies, or on those group employees who are in receipt of the higher, or highest level of remuneration (ICTA 1988, Sch 9, para 2(3)(b), introduced as FA 1980, Sch 10, para 1(ab), again with effect from 26 July 1984, and with respect to all schemes whenever approved, by FA 1984, s 39(2) and (9)). A 'group' for this purpose means a company and any other companies of which it has control, as defined in 7.23 and 7.24 (ICTA 1988, Sch 9, para 2(4), introduced as FA 1980, Sch 10, para 1(1A), by FA 1984, s 39(3) and (9); ICTA 1988, s 840). As to the measures which this provision is designed to circumvent, see the commentary on the parallel provisions in the approved 'profit-sharing' schemes legislation, at 4.99.

Extraneous features

5.18 The Board is obliged to approve a scheme meeting all the necessary conditions unless it appears that there are features of the scheme which are neither essential nor reasonably incidental to the purpose of providing options for employees and directors (ICTA 1988, Sch 9, para 2(1)). For a discussion of the parallel provision in the approved 'profit-sharing' schemes legislation, see 4.101.

Group schemes

5.19 As with 'profit-sharing' schemes, where the grantor controls another company or companies (within the definition set out at 7.23 and 7.24: ICTA 1988, ss 187(2) and 840) the scheme may extend to all or any of the companies of which it has control. Such a scheme covering more than one company is referred to as a 'group scheme', although it need not extend to all companies grouped together for tax or company law purposes (ICTA 1988, s 187(2) and Sch 9, para 1(3)). The term 'participating company', used in relation to a group scheme, means the company which has established the scheme or any company controlled by it and to which the scheme is expressed to extend (ICTA 1988, s 187(2) and Sch 9, para 1(4)). While the establishing company (the 'grantor') need not be the ultimate parent company of those participating, it must be the most 'senior' of those involved: a group scheme may thus include a subsidiary and its sub-subsidiaries, without the parent, but may not be set up by a subsidiary to include its parent (although the parent's shares may be used in the scheme: see 5.72). If the parent wishes to be included it must set up the scheme itself. As to jointly controlled companies, see Appendix 11 'Inland Revenue Extrastatutory Concession B27 Approved employee share schemes—jointly owned companies'.

Conditional approval

5.20 Prior to 25 July 1986, it was possible to obtain conditional approval of a scheme. If, at the time the application was pending, the Board had no evidence that the condition as to the exercise price set out at 5.67 to 5.70 (broadly, that it was not manifestly less than 90% of market value at the time of the grant) was satisfied, then, if all the other requirements were satisfied, it could give approval subject to that condition being met. If, in the event, it was not met, then the approval would not take effect (FA 1980, Sch 10, para 2). This provision recognised that where the share price was subject to fluctuation, it would not be possible to determine an exercise price which met this condition far in advance of the grant of the option, unless a formula related to market price was used, which is normally only appropriate in the case of quoted shares. It also recognised that there might well be subsequent grants of options under the same scheme, and enabled a different exercise price to be used without any application for Inland Revenue approval in advance. Care had to be exercised on this point, however, as it appears that, strictly, if this condition was not fulfilled on a subsequent grant, then approval of the scheme was to be withdrawn ab initio, even in respect of earlier grants for which the condition was fulfilled. In practice, the problem could be avoided by including in the scheme rules, instead of a fixed exercise price, either a formula, as mentioned above, or a provision in similar terms to the legislative requirement itself, leaving the actual price to be fixed in compliance with this on each occasion. This was made easier by the fact that the legislation also includes provision for the agreement of a price, in advance, between the company and the Inland Revenue, as discussed at 5.67. These provisions governing conditional approval were repealed with effect from 25 July 1986, by FA 1986, s 25(2).

Withdrawal of approval

5.21 If, at any time after the Board of Inland Revenue has given its approval to a scheme, it ceases to be satisfied that the conditions mentioned in 5.16 to 5.20 (including meeting the detailed conditions in 5.26 to 5.99) are fulfilled, or the company concerned fails to provide information requested by the Inland Revenue under the provisions set out at 5.105 and 5.106, approval may be withdrawn (at the discretion of the Board) with effect from that time or such later time as the Board may specify (ICTA 1988, Sch 9, para 3(1)). By contrast with the corresponding provisions in the legislation governing approved 'profit-sharing' schemes, the failure to provide information can only result in the withdrawal of approval if it is perpetrated by the 'grantor' (i e the company setting up the scheme), despite the fact that the information requirements, and penalties, extend to 'any person' (see 5.105). In the case of the 'profit-sharing' schemes legislation, a failure by another participating company is specifically made grounds for withdrawal of approval (see 4.116). In practice, the distinction makes little difference, as information regarding other participating companies can be requested from the parent, which, by virtue of its control of the other companies, can 'reasonably obtain' such information, within the terms of the legislation (see 5.106).

5.22 Where options are obtained under a scheme before approval is withdrawn, and are exercised afterwards, the exemptions from income tax set out at 5.8 and 5.9 (i e from a charge under ICTA 1988, s 135 on the gain 'realised' by the exercise; and from a charge under ICTA 1988, s 138(1)(a) or

FA 1988, ss 78 or 79 on any subsequent growth in value) still apply, as does the suspension of the 'market value rule' for CGT purposes, as described at 5.10 (ICTA 1980, s 185(3) and Sch 9, para 3(1)). The effect is that any employee who has accepted options and entered into a SAYE contract in good faith is not prejudiced by any subsequent failure on the part of the company.

Alterations to a scheme

5.23 If any alteration is made in the terms of the scheme after it has received Inland Revenue approval, that approval lapses from the time of the alteration, unless the alteration itself has been approved by the Board (ICTA 1988, Sch 9, para 4). Inland Revenue Technical Division will give an informal opinion on any proposed changes.

Appeals

5.24 The company which has set up the scheme may appeal against (ICTA 1988, Sch 9, para 5):

(a) the failure of the Board to approve the scheme;
(b) the Board's failure to decide that a condition subject to which the approval has been given is satisfied (see 5.20);
(c) a failure to approve an alteration in the scheme; or
(d) the withdrawal of approval.

5.25 An appeal must be made by written notice to the Board, within 30 days of the company being notified of its decision, and is heard and determined by the Special Commissioners in the same way as an appeal against an assessment (ICTA 1988, Sch 9, para 5: see 7.1 to 7.5). Another participating company, in the case of a group scheme, cannot initiate an appeal.

Detailed conditions for approval

General

5.26 Various conditions as regards the rules of the scheme are set out by the legislation, which must be met before approval of a scheme can be obtained (as explained at 5.16), and which, if they cease to be met, will result in the withdrawal of approval, as explained at 5.21. By contrast with the legislation on approved 'profit-sharing' schemes (see 4.110), no specific provision is made for the withdrawal of approval where, while the rules of the scheme continue to meet the necessary conditions, they are breached in practice. It is considered, however, that this would be treated by the Inland Revenue as a de facto change in the rules, leading to withdrawal of approval. In addition, the provisions discussed at 5.27 to 5.70, together with conditions as to the shares dealt with in 5.71 to 5.89 and the conditions as to eligibility of individuals in 5.90 to 5.99, all state that 'the scheme' must have certain features, rather than that the 'rules of the scheme' must have those features, and it is therefore arguable that consideration must be given to what actually happens as much as to what it is laid down should happen.

The shares

5.27 The scheme must provide for the grant to directors and employees of options to acquire shares ('scheme shares') which meet the conditions set out at 5.71 to 5.89 (ICTA 1988, Sch 9, para 9(1)).

The SAYE contract and exercise date

5.28 The scheme must also provide for the scheme shares to be paid for with monies not exceeding the amount of any repayments, and interest, under a certified contractual savings scheme, as defined in ICTA 1988, s 326, which has been approved by the Board of Inland Revenue for use in conjunction with a share option scheme (ICTA 1988, Sch 16(1) and s 187(2)). It should be noted that certification by the Treasury under ICTA 1988, s 326(2)(c) or (3)(b) does not, of itself, enable a savings arrangement to be used in conjunction with a share option scheme, although it is a prerequisite to it being considered for approval by the Inland Revenue. See also 7.108, and rule 9.7 in Appendix 6.

5.29 A 'contractual savings scheme' is a scheme governed by regulations made under the National Debt Act 1958, s 12 or FA 1969, s 52 in respect of money raised under the National Loans Act 1968, s 12 (ie a National Savings scheme) which provides for periodical contributions by individuals for a specified period, and for repayment in accordance with those regulations of contributions together with any additional sum by way of bonus or interest (ICTA 1988, s 326(2)(a) and (b)), and a 'certified' contractual savings scheme is one certified by the Treasury as qualifying for tax exemption as described below (ICTA 1988, ss 326(2)(c) and 187(2)). A scheme providing for periodical contributions by individuals, for a specified period, to a share account with a building society (within the meaning of the Building Societies Act 1986 (ICTA 1988, s 832(1)) may also be certified by the Treasury as corresponding to a National Savings scheme as described above, and as qualifying for the same exemption (ICTA 1988, s 326(3)). The exemption in question takes the form of disregarding any terminal bonus, interest, or other sum payable in respect of a scheme for all purposes of income tax and CGT (ICTA 1988, s 326(1); CGTA 1979, s 149B(4)). The result is that in considering Inland Revenue approved savings-related share option schemes, the position is not complicated by any question as to the tax liability on the SAYE contract itself; the only liability which can arise is in connection with the option arrangement.

5.30 The purchase of shares under the option must be made 'with monies not exceeding' the proceeds of the SAYE contract, rather than 'out of the proceeds', so there is no necessity specifically to identify the funds so obtained and 'earmark' them for the purchase (ICTA 1988, Sch 9, para 16(1)).

5.31 Subject to the points made at 5.34 to 5.50, the options must not be capable of exercise before the 'bonus date'; ie the date on which repayments under the certified contractual savings scheme are due (ICTA 1988, Sch 9, para 17 and s 187(2)). Neither must they be permitted to be exercised more than six months after the bonus date, except where the option holder dies (see 5.34 and 5.35), when that period may be extended to a maximum of 12 months (ICTA 1988, Sch 9, para 22(b)). This gives adequate time for the formalities of exercise to be completed, without liberating the funds from the SAYE repayment to be used for purposes other than the purchase of shares under the scheme.

5.32 Contractual savings schemes approved for this purpose at the time of writing (National Savings Save As You Earn Share Option Issue Series C, and equivalent schemes available from building societies) provide for a bonus equal to 12 monthly payments to be added to the principal after five years, and the total amount may then be withdrawn. Alternatively, this amount may be left with the Department for National Savings, or building society, for a further two years (without making any further contribution), at the end of which time the bonus will be doubled to equal 24 monthly payments. If contributions cease before sixty monthly payments have been made, and repayment is made before the first anniversary of the commencement of the scheme, no interest is added to the repayment. If repayment is made on or after the first anniversary of the starting date, compound interest (with monthly rests) is paid at 5% pa. Where all sixty contributions are paid, and repayment is made between the fifth and seventh anniversaries, the amount received is the repayment (with bonus) due on the fifth anniversary, together with compound interest thereon (with monthly rests) at 5% pa for the period thereafter. Where the participant fails to pay a contribution by the due date, the due dates for the remaining contributions, and the bonus date, may be deferred by up to six months. The terms of such contracts change from time to time, and up-to-date details can be obtained from:

Savings Certificate and SAYE Office, Millburngate House, Durham, DH99 INS. (Telephone: 091–386 4900)

or any local office of a building society which operates approved schemes.

5.33 Either the seven- or the five-year bonus date must be selected as the appropriate date for the purposes of the share option provisions, and this must be determined in advance, at the time the options are granted (ICTA 1988, Sch 9, para 17(c)). A scheme may stipulate either a five- or seven-year date for all participants, or the choice may be left to each participant individually, provided it is made at the time he enters the scheme (but see 5.66). As the current arrangements for SAYE contracts could be changed, the legislation making available the choice between a five and a seven-year bonus date is cast in general terms: accordingly, the 'repayments' out of which the share purchase is made may be taken as including or not including a bonus (ICTA 1988, Sch 9, para 17(a)). This enables the additional bonus which would accrue over the sixth and seventh years to be taken into account or not, as desired, and also covers the situation where no bonus is payable, on early withdrawal (see 5.34 to 5.50). The time when such 'repayments' are due (i e the 'bonus date': see 5.31), is defined, in a case where the maximum bonus is included, as the earliest date on which that bonus is payable (i e currently, the seventh anniversary); and, in any other case, as the earliest occasion on which a bonus is payable under the scheme (i e currently the fifth anniversary) (ICTA 1988, Sch 9, para 17(b)).

Early exercise on death, cessation of employment, etc

5.34 The scheme must provide that if an option holder dies before the bonus date the options must be exercised, if at all, within twelve months after his death (ICTA 1988, Sch 9, para 18). That is to say, the personal representatives or other persons to whom the options pass are not obliged to exercise them at all (since to do so might, depending on the then market price of the shares, be financially disadvantageous), but, if they choose to do so, the maximum period available to them is 12 months. This provision does not overrule the requirement set out in 5.28 for the purchase of shares to be made with monies not exceeding the repayments and interest under a SAYE scheme, and the early repayment on the employee's death will itself, therefore, limit the extent to which the options can be taken up.

5.35 If an option holder dies within six months after the bonus date, without yet having exercised his options (see 5.31) the scheme must provide that they may be exercised within 12 months of the bonus date; that is, within a period varying between 6 and 12 months of the death (ICTA 1988, Sch 9, para 18). Accordingly, if an employee is prevented only by illness and/or death from taking steps to exercise options, a reasonable opportunity to do so is given to his personal representatives or heirs.

5.36 If an option holder ceases to hold the office or employment which qualifies him to participate in the scheme, and that event arises by reason of injury, disability, redundancy (within the meaning of the Employment Protection (Consolidation) Act 1978), retirement on reaching pensionable age within the meaning of the Social Security Act 1975, Sch 20 (65 for men; 60 for women), or retirement at any other age at which he is bound to retire in accordance with the terms of his contract of employment, then the scheme must provide that his options must be exercised, if at all, within six months of the cessation of employment (ICTA 1988, Sch 9, para 19 and s 187(2)). Again, the extent to which shares can be taken up will depend on the amount of the repayments and interest on early withdrawal from the SAYE scheme. It is not possible, within the terms of the legislation, to retain the savings contract and make the exercise by reference to the amount which *would* have been received on early withdrawal. That amount must actually have been received (ICTA 1988, Sch 9, para 16(1)). See also rule (13) in Appendix 1, regarding grants within two years of retirement.

5.37 If an employee or director ceases to hold the relevant office or employment within three years of obtaining options under the scheme, other than for one of the reasons set out in 5.36, the scheme must provide that they cannot be exercised at all, except under a provision of the scheme dealing with the situation where a company is transferred out of the group, or a business is transferred to an unconnected party, as set out at 5.46. This exception was added to what was then FA 1980, Sch 10, para 8 with effect from 25 July 1986 by FA 1986, s 25(3). If he ceases to hold the relevant office or employment after three years, the scheme must either provide that the options cannot be exercised, or that they must be exercised within six months of the cessation of the employment (ICTA 1988, Sch 9, para 19). Again, the amount received on surrender of the SAYE contract will determine the extent to which options can be taken up.

5.38 An individual is not treated as ceasing to hold an employment which entitles him to participate in a scheme until he ceases to hold an employment with any of: the company setting up the scheme (the 'grantor'); an 'associated company'; or a company of which the grantor has control within 7.23 (ICTA 1988, Sch 9, para 23). This prevents any artificial manoeuvre by which an individual would leave his employment, enabling him to exercise his options, only to take up a similar post in a related company (which could then second him back to his original employer if desired). The term 'associated company' is defined in 7.10, and, in general, two companies are associated if at a given time one of the two has control of the other, or both are under the control of the same person or persons. In the present context, however, the normal provision that they are also associated if that control has existed at any time within one year previously does not apply, as it could catch perfectly legitimate changes of employment, for example, where an individual made redundant was able to obtain employment by virtue of his connections with the directors of a subsidiary sold out of the group within 12 months previously, and now completely independent (ICTA 1988, ss 187(2) and 416). As to the position where a company leaves a group and consequently ceases to be a participating company in a group scheme, see 5.46. See also 7.109.

5.39 Where an option holder continues in the office or employment which entitled him to participate in the scheme after reaching retirement age within the meaning of the Social Security Act 1975, Sch 20 (currently 65 for men and 60 for women), the scheme must provide that he may exercise the options within six months after reaching that age (ICTA 1988, Sch 9, para 20 and s 187(2)). There is no statutory requirement that he *must* be required to do so, however, and, again, the number of shares taken up would be reduced by early surrender of the SAYE contract, so that he may well prefer to wait until the bonus date.

Early exercise on takeovers and other changes in control

5.40 The scheme may also allow early exercise of options (limited by early withdrawal of the SAYE contract) in various circumstances involving take-over or liquidation of, or compromise with creditors by, the company in which the shares would be held on exercise of the option, as set out in 5.41 to 5.45. It is not, however, obliged to include such provisions.

5.41 If a person obtains control of a company whose shares are used in the scheme ('scheme shares'), as a result of making:

(a) a general offer to acquire the whole of the issued ordinary share capital (see 7.72) of the company, which is made on a condition such that if it is satisfied the person making the offer will have control of the company; or
(b) a general offer to acquire all the shares in the company which are of the same class as the scheme shares;

then the scheme may allow options to be exercised within six months of the time at which the person making the offer has obtained control of the company, and any condition subject to which the offer is made has been satisfied (ICTA 1988, Sch 9, paras 15(1) and 21(1)(a)). 'Control' for this purpose is as defined in 7.23 and 7.24 (ICTA 1988, ss 187(2) and 840), with the additional provision that a person is deemed to have obtained control of a company if he and others acting in concert with him have together obtained control of it (ICTA 1988, Sch 9, para 21(2)). This extended definition applies to 'obtaining control', as in the opening words of this paragraph, but not specifically to 'having control', as used in (a) above to define the relevant category of general offer. It would appear, however, that since a person can only 'have' control by virtue of having previously 'obtained' it, the extended definition applies in both contexts. Its effect is to bring within the terms of the permissible rules a provision of the scheme to allow exercise of options on a 'takeover', for example, by a co-ordinated number of customers of the company not in any group relationship, but acting together to safeguard their source of supply of raw materials. It should be noted that it is not sufficient simply that another person or persons should come to control the company, if this is not by means of a general offer as described in (a) or (b) above, and that, in the case of (b), while the offer need only relate to shares of one class, the result must be to give control of the company as a whole, not simply of that class of shares. The rationale behind the provisions is to provide a 'way out' for option holders (by means of exercise, followed by sale of the shares), not if control of the company merely shifts, but if its future prospects as a whole change because of a full scale takeover. See also 5.51 to 5.61.

5.42 If, under the provisions of the Companies Act 1985, s 425, or the Companies (Northern Ireland) Order 1986, Art 418, which enable a company to reach a compromise with its creditors and members, the court sanctions a compromise or arrangement proposed for the purposes of, or in connection with, a scheme for the reconstruction of a company whose shares are used in the option scheme, or for its amalgamation with any other company or companies, the rules of the share option scheme may permit options to be exercised within six months of the court sanctioning the compromise or arrangement (ICTA 1988, Sch 9, para 21(1)(b)). This enables option holders to acquire full rights as shareholders and to have a voice in the affairs of the reconstructed company, or to extricate themselves by a sale of those shares (or of any shares for which they are exchanged under the arrangement) from a company which has changed its nature or constitution significantly since the option was granted. In practice, in such circumstances, the value of the shares may well have fallen prior to the reconstruction, so that there may in fact be no incentive to obtain shares at the stipulated exercise price.

5.43 Similarly, if a person becomes bound, or entitled, to acquire shares in a company whose shares are scheme shares (whether or not they are shares of the same class) under the Companies Act 1985, ss 428 to 430 or the companies (Northern Ireland) Order 1986, Arts 421 to 423, which give power to acquire the shares of shareholders dissenting from schemes or contracts approved by a majority, the rules of the scheme may provide that options may be exercised at any time when that person remains bound or entitled to acquire dissentient shareholders' interests (ICTA 1988, Sch 9, para 21(1)(c)). Again, the effect is that option holders can, by early exercise, put themselves in a position more effectively to safeguard their rights, as full shareholders.

5.44 Early exercise will, of course, prevent the option holder obtaining maximum benefit from his options (quite apart from the reduced funds available for that purpose, due to early surrender of the SAYE contract), in that he has to invest his money earlier. Any future growth in share value will accrue to him irrespective of the stage at which he exercises the option, but early exercise will expose him to the risk of a fall in the share price which would not have affected him had he waited until the bonus date.

5.45 If a company whose shares are used in a scheme passes a resolution for voluntary winding up, the scheme rules may permit options to be exercised within six months of the passing of the resolution (ICTA 1988, Sch 9, para 21(1)(d)). This enables option holders to participate in any surplus available to ordinary shareholders on winding up, although, as mentioned at 5.42 in connection with a compromise with creditors, the liquidation may well indicate that the share price has fallen below the level at which it will be beneficial to exercise the option.

5.46 If a participant ceases to hold an office or employment by virtue of which he is eligible to participate in the scheme solely because (ICTA 1988, Sch 9, para 21(1)(e)):

(a) his office or employment is in a company of which the grantor ceases to have control (see 7.23); or
(b) that office or employment relates to a business or part of a business which is transferred to a person who is neither an associated company of the grantor (ICTA 1988, s 187(2) and 416: see 7.10), nor a company of which it has control (see 7.23, and the extended definition at 5.41),

the scheme may (but need not) permit options held by that person to be exercised within six months of his office or employment ceasing to be with a relevant company. This provision was introduced as FA 1980, Sch 10, para 10(1)(e), with effect from 25 July 1986, by FA 1986, s 25(4). For the position prior to that date, see Appendix 10.

5.47 Where a scheme approved by the Inland Revenue before 1 August 1986 was altered before 1 August 1988 (subject to the normal rules for Inland Revenue approval, see 5.23) so as to include a provision within 5.46 above, it was permitted to apply that provision to options granted before the date on which the alteration took effect (ICTA 1988, Sch 9, para 21(3)(a), introduced as FA 1986, s 25(8)(a) and (9)).

5.48 If, before the alteration took effect (again, for alterations of pre 1 August 1986 schemes before 1 August 1988), a participant who had held options on 18 March 1986 ceased to hold an office or employment by virtue of which he was eligible to participate in the scheme, as a result solely of circumstances within paras (a) or (b) of 5.46, then the scheme was permitted (but not obliged) to allow him to take advantage of the alteration to the rules as if it had been made immediately before he ceased to hold that office or employment (ICTA 1988, Sch 9, para 21(3)(b), introduced as FA 1986, s 25(8)(b)).

5.49 In a case within 5.47 or 5.48, the application of the new provision to existing (or already lapsed) options, though representing an extension of the benefits available to the participant, was not treated as the acquisition of further rights under the scheme (ICTA 1988, Sch 9, para 21(3)(c), introduced as FA 1986, s 25(8)(c)).

5.50 As explained at 5.11, where an option is exercised before the bonus date, as discussed at 5.41 to 5.49, the exemptions normally available on exercise under a savings-related share option scheme will be denied if less than three years have elapsed since the grant of the option (ICTA 1988, s 185(4)).

Exchange of options on a takeover

5.51 Prior to 15 May 1987, on a company takeover the participants in an approved savings-related share option scheme could find themselves obliged either to exercise their options early, and perhaps forfeit tax relief (see 5.50), or to continue to hold options over shares in a company which had become an unquoted subsidiary of another company (subject to 5.75). With effect from 15 May 1987 the relevant legislation was amended (by FA 1987, s 33(1) and Sch 4, para 1, inserting FA 1980, Sch 10, para 10A) so that the rules of an approved scheme are permitted (but not obliged) to allow that on a takeover a participant may release his options in return for new options over shares in the acquiring company (or in a related company, as explained at 5.72 to 5.74). The acquiring company is not obliged by the legislation to agree to such an exchange, although certain companies may be subject to obligations under the City Code on Takeovers and Mergers.

5.52 Specifically, the scheme may provide that if any company ('the acquiring company') (ICTA 1988, Sch 9, para 15(1)):

(a) obtains control (see 7.23) of a company whose shares are scheme shares, as a result of making a general offer to acquire the whole of the issued ordinary share capital of the company, which is made on a condition such that if it is satisfied the person making the offer will have control of the company (ie, a general offer within para (a) of 5.41 above);
(b) obtains control of such a company as a result of making a general offer to acquire all the shares in the company which are of the same class as the scheme shares (ie, a general offer within para (b) of 5.41 above);
(c) obtains control of such a company in pursuance of a compromise or arrangement sanctioned by the court under the Companies Act 1985, s 425 or the Companies (Northern Ireland) Order 1986, Art 418 (see also 5.42); or
(d) becomes bound or entitled to acquire shares in such a company under the Companies Act 1985, ss 428 to 430 or the Companies (Northern Ireland) Order 1986, Arts 421 to 423 (see 5.43)

any participant in the scheme may at any time within the 'appropriate period' set out in 5.53 below, by agreement with the acquiring company, release his options under the old scheme in consideration of the grant to him of new options relating to shares in a different company (whether the acquiring company itself, or a related company within 5.72). The new options must be 'equivalent' to the old options, as explained in 5.54.

5.53 The 'appropriate period' within which the release of the old options must take place is (ICTA 1988, Sch 9, para 15(2)):

(a) in the case of a general offer within para (a) or (b) of 5.52, the six months beginning with the time when the person making the offer has obtained control of the company and any condition subject to which the offer is made is satisfied;
(b) in the case of a compromise or arrangement within para (c) of 5.52, the period of six months beginning with the time when the court sanctions the compromise or arrangement; and
(c) in the case of an acquisition of dissenting shareholders' interests within para (d) of 5.52, the period during which the acquiring company remains bound or entitled to acquire shares under those provisions.

5.54 New options are 'equivalent' to old options, as required in 5.52 above, if (ICTA 1988, Sch 9, para 15(3)):

(a) they satisfy the conditions for scheme shares set out in 5.71 to 5.89;
(b) they are exercisable in the same manner as the old options, and subject to the provisions of the old scheme as it had effect immediately before the release of the old options;
(c) the total market value, immediately before the release, of the shares which were subject to the participant's old options is equal to the total market value, immediately after the grant of the participant's new options, of the shares to which those new options relate; and
(d) the total amount payable by the participant for the acquisition of shares on the exercise of the new options is equal to the total amount that would have been payable on the exercise of the old options.

5.55 Where replacement options are granted under provisions included in a scheme as set out at 5.51 to 5.54, they are treated for the purpose of the savings-related share option legislation (including any subsequent application of the replacement options provisions) as having been granted at the time when the old options were granted (ICTA 1988, Sch 10, para 15(4)). As the new options are granted under the terms of the scheme, the normal tax exemptions are available, as set out at 5.3 to 5.9. As they are treated as granted at the time when the old options were granted (or the time when the old options are treated as having been granted, under a previous application of these provisions), their exercise under the terms of the scheme within the following three years will not give rise to a charge as set out at 5.11, unless this takes place within three years of the original grant. If such a charge does arise, the rollover provisions of ICTA 1988, s 136(1) (see 3.31) will apply to include in the computation the consideration given for the original options, rather than the consideration given for the new options in the form of the release of the old options. The same provisions will in any case prevent an immediate charge under ICTA 1988, s 135 on the release of the old options.

5.56 Where options are released, and granted, under these provisions, the transaction is not treated for capital gains tax purposes as involving any disposal or acquisition of either asset; the new option is treated as the same asset as the old option, acquired as that old option was acquired, provided the original option (or its predecessor) was acquired by reason of the participant's office or employment as a director or employee of the company whose shares are in question, or any other company (CGTA 1979, s 144A(4)).

5.57 Where a scheme approved before 1 August 1987 is altered before 1 August 1989 so as to include provision for replacement options on a takeover, as described at 5.51 to 5.54, the scheme, as altered, may (but need not) apply that provision to options obtained under the scheme before the date on which the alteration takes effect (ICTA 1988, Sch 9, para 15(5), introduced as FA 1987, Sch 4, para 3(1)). Where the alteration to the scheme takes place on or after 1 August 1989, it can only apply to options granted after the date of the change.

5.58 Where a scheme is amended to include a replacement option provision with effect for options granted before the date of the change, under 5.57 above, and, on or after 17 March 1987 but before the date on which the alteration takes effect, an event (such as a general offer: see 5.52 above) has occurred as a result of which an individual holding options would be able to take advantage of that replacement provision, the scheme may (but need not) permit an individual who held options immediately before that event to take advantage of the replacement provision (ICTA 1988, Sch 9, para 15(6)(a), introduced as FA 1987, Sch 4, para 3(2)(a)). In a case where those options would otherwise have ceased to be exercisable, as a result of the event, the scheme may (but need not) provide that the replacement provision is to apply as if those options were still exerciseable (ICTA 1988, Sch 9, para 15(6)(b), introduced as FA 1987, Sch 4, para 3(2)(b)).

5.59 The application of a replacement provision to existing or recently lapsed options under 5.57 or 5.58 is not itself regarded as the acquisition of additional option rights for the purposes of the savings-related share scheme legislation, even though there is a gratuitous element which is not present on a straightforward application of the provision where the right to the new options is already implicit in the terms of the old options (ICTA 1988, Sch 9, para 15(7), introduced as FA 1987, Sch 4, para 3(3)).

5.60 Both the inclusion of a replacement option provision in an existing scheme, and its 'backdating' as set out in 5.57 or 5.58, are subject to the normal rules regarding Inland Revenue approval for the alteration of a scheme, as discussed at 5.23 (ICTA 1988, Sch 9, para 4 and para 15(8), introduced as FA 1987, Sch 4, para 3(5)).

5.61 As originally enacted, the legislation governing takeovers discussed in 5.51 to 5.60 referred to an 'exchange' of options for options over shares in another company, rather than to their release in consideration of the grant of such new options, and technically, therefore, this was the position between 15 May 1987 and 23 July 1987, when the new wording was inserted by F(No 2)A 1987, s 59. That section also removed (with effect from the enactment of the original legislation on 15 May 1987, rather than from Royal Assent to the F(No 2)A 1987 on 23 July 1987) a provision included in FA 1987, Sch 4, para 1(2) that the general prohibition on the transfer of options (see 5.62) should contain an exclusion for transfers under the takeover provisions, as originally enacted. The retrospective removal of this exclusion effectively delayed the implementation of the takeover 'exchange' provisions until they could take effect in their new form (unless such an exclusion could be implied from the existence of provisions specificaly referring to certain transfers as permissible). The purpose of the change in the legislation was to avoid capital gains and administrative complexities which could arise where the acquiring company was left holding options in its new subsidiary.

Transfer of options

5.62 The scheme rules must not permit options to be transferred, except on death, when they must be exercised, if at all, within a specified period, varying from 6 to 12 months: see 5.34 and 5.35 (ICTA 1988, Sch 9, para 22(a)). This reflects the object of the legislation to encourage employee shareholdings, a design which would be frustrated if the options themselves could be transferred even before exercise.

Limits on contributions

5.63 The rules of the scheme may not impose a minimum contribution under the SAYE contract in excess of £10 per month (ICTA 1988, Sch 9, para 24(2)(b)), nor permit monthly contributions in excess of £100 in aggregate (ICTA 1988, Sch 9, para 24(2)(a)). These limits were introduced for all schemes, whenever approved, by FA 1984, s 39(5) and (9) and the Finance Act 1984 (Savings-Related Share Option Schemes) Commencement Order 1984 (SI 1984/1180), with effect from 1 September 1984. Prior to that date the maximum limit (FA 1980, Sch 10, para 13(1)) was £50, and there was no minimum. Contributions are normally paid, by the employee's authority, by means of a deduction from weekly or monthly wages or salary.

5.64 The limit on the minimum contribution prevents less well-off employees being 'priced out' of the scheme in an effort either to direct benefits principally at higher-paid employees, or to minimise the administrative work involved in maintaining the scheme. The upper limit, similarly, reflects the intention of the legislation to provide a modest benefit widely spread among the workforce, rather than a major addition to the remuneration package such as is provided by approved selective share option schemes (see Chapter 6).

5.65 The Treasury may amend the upper and lower limits by statutory instrument, subject to annulment by resolution of the House of Commons (ICTA 1988, Sch 9, para 24(3)), but, for companies affected by them (see 1.14), the guidelines of the Investment Committee of the Association of British Insurers, of July 1987, impose an upper limit of £150 per month, irrespective of the current statutory maximum (see point (19) of Appendix 1).

5.66 The rules of the scheme must provide for an employee's contributions under the SAYE contract, as well as falling within the limits set out in 5.63, to be of such amounts as to secure, as nearly as may be, repayment (after five or seven years, as chosen) of an amount equal, with bonus, to the total exercise price of his options at the bonus date (ICTA 1988, Sch 9, para 24(1)).

The exercise price

5.67 Under the rules of the scheme, the exercise price of the options (ie the purchase price of the shares obtained in pursuance of the option) must be stated at the time the option is granted, and must not be 'manifestly less' (see 6.63) than 90% of the market value (see 7.56 to 7.64: ICTA 1988, s 187(2); CGTA 1979, s 150) of shares of the same class at the time of the grant, or, if the Board of Inland Revenue and the grantor so agree in writing, at such earlier time or times as may be provided in that agreement (ICTA 1988, Sch 9, para 25) (normally not more than 30 days prior to grant: IR 39, para 2.11). For companies subject to the guidelines of the Investment Committee of the Association of British Insurers (see 1.14), the requirement is for a price not less than 90% of the middle market price (thus excluding the use of the 'quarter up' basis discussed at 7.57, and there is no provision for the value at an earlier date to be substituted for that at the time of the grant (see point (17) at Appendix 1). In practice, a share option scheme will normally be initiated by the company writing to the eligible employees offering the relevant options and stating the price at which they will be exercisable. The employees will usually have to respond within a stated time, and only after that time has elapsed will options actually be granted. Clearly, the market value of the shares may fluctuate between the time of the initial offer letter and the date of grant of an option, particularly in the case of quoted shares, and the procedure for prior agreement of the exercise price caters for this possibility.

5.68 The 90% requirement mentioned in 5.67, it is considered, is not, essentially, designed to allow an additional benefit to employees, but to allow a 'tolerance' in the agreement of the exercise price. This is particularly useful in the case of unquoted shares, the valuation of which is an imprecise science, and an error in which could result in the failure to obtain, or retain, Inland Revenue approval of the scheme. Scope for genuine difference of expert opinion, but not for conceptual or computational errors in the calculation (however innocently made), is also provided by the fact that to forfeit approval the discount to market value must be not only over 10%, but 'manifestly' so. In the result, a larger discount, arising from differences of opinion between Shares Valuation Division of the Inland Revenue and professional valuers on such matters as appropriate yields and price/earnings ratios, need not (in theory) necessarily lead to the loss of approval, even if the view of the former is ultimately adopted. However, if the difference of view becomes apparent before the grant of the option, the discount is much more likely to be considered 'manifest', the company being on notice that their view, even if still genuinely maintained at that stage, is open to challenge.

5.69 Any query concerned solely with the valuation of shares in approved schemes should be addressed to:

Inland Revenue
Capital Taxes Office
Shares Valuation Division 2
(Employee Share Schemes)
Minford House
Rockley Road
London
W14 0DF
(Telephone: 01–603 4622 Ext 459 or 495)

Until a scheme has been approved, however, Shares Valuation Division will normally require prior instructions from Technical Division (see 5.14) before negotiating the value of unquoted shares.

5.70 The scheme may provide for adjustments to the exercise price (and, by necessary implication, to the number of shares: see Appendix 6, rule (8)) to take account of variations in the share capital concerned, such as 'bonus issues', share 'splits' and rights issues, although the calculations as to the change in price necessary to take account of the depressing effect on the share price of a rights issue may, in the case of unquoted shares, be extremely complicated, (ICTA 1988, Sch 9, para 25).

Conditions as to the scheme shares

General

5.71 As explained at 5.27, various conditions as to the shares (or stock: ICTA 1988, s 187(2)) used in the scheme must be met before Inland Revenue approval can be obtained and, if they cease to be met, will result in the withdrawal of approval.

The company whose shares are used

5.72 The shares used in the scheme must form part of the ordinary share capital (see 7.72) of:

(a) the 'grantor'; i e the company establishing the scheme (ICTA 1988, Sch 9, para 10(a)); or
(b) a company which has control of the company concerned, within the definition of control in 7.23 and 7.24 (ICTA 1988, Sch 9, para 10(b) and ss 187(2) & 840); or
(c) a company which either is or controls (see 7.23 and 7.24) a member company of a consortium which owns the grantor, or owns a company which controls that company (ICTA 1988, Sch 9, para 10(c)(i), and ss 187(2) & 840). The consortium member company must beneficially own 15% or more of the company concerned, or the company which controls it, as the case may be (ICTA 1988, Sch 9, para 10(c)(ii)). For this purpose, a company is a member of a consortium owning another company if it is one of a number of companies which between them beneficially own at least 75% of that other company's ordinary share capital (see 7.72), and each of which beneficially owns at least 5% (ICTA 1988, s 187(7)). Prior to amendment by FA 1986, s 23(5)(a), with effect from 25 July 1986, a consortium for this purpose consisted of not more than five companies.

5.73 The broad effect of the provision set out in 5.72 is that the shares utilised may be those of the grantor or a company higher up the chain of ownership within a group or a consortium context. More specifically, the effect of the legislation is that shares in the following may qualify:

(a) the grantor;
(b) a company which controls the grantor;
(c) a company which is a 15% member of a consortium which owns the grantor;
(d) a company which controls a company which is a 15% member of a consortium which owns the grantor;
(e) a company which is a 15% member of a consortium which owns a company which controls the grantor; or
(f) a company which controls a company which is a 15% member of a consortium which owns a company which controls the grantor.

5.74 The situations in 5.73 are illustrated diagrammatically at 4.121 in connection with the parallel legislation governing Inland Revenue approved 'profit sharing' schemes. In paras (d) and (f) of 4.121, reference is made to the further conditions in 4.122. In the present context, references to 4.122 should be taken as references to 5.75, which contains the same conditions, in respect of savings-related share option schemes.

Other conditions

5.75 The shares used in the scheme, in addition to being shares in an appropriate company within 5.71 to 5.74, must be

(a) shares of a class quoted on a recognised stock exchange (ICTA 1988, Sch 9, para 11(a) and s 841: see 7.83 to 7.86); or
(b) shares in a company not under the control of another company (ICTA 1988, Sch 9, para 11(b), and ss 187(2), 840; see 7.23 and 7.24); or
(c) shares in a company which is under the control (ICTA 1988, ss 187(2) and 840) of a second company whose shares are quoted on a recognised stock exchange, except where the second company is a close company (ICTA 1988, ss 414 and 415: 7.12 to 7.21) or would be a close company if resident in the United Kingdom (ICTA 1988, Sch 9, para 11(c)).

5.76 In the case of para (a) in 5.75 it should be noted that not only must the company be quoted, but the particular class of shares used in the scheme must be. In the case of para (c), it would appear that a quotation for any class of shares of the controlling company is sufficient, although it is possible to argue that the words 'whose shares are quoted' indicate that all shares of whatever class must be quoted, so that the existence of a small number of unquoted preference shares in a controlling company whose ordinary shares were all quoted would prevent the use in the scheme of shares in the controlled company. Common sense would perhaps demand that the ordinary shares at least, but not necessarily any others, should be quoted, but such an interpretation is difficult to justify from the legislation.

5.77 A quotation on the Unlisted Securities Market is not treated as one on a 'recognised stock exchange' for this purpose (see Inland Revenue Statement of Practice SP 18/80 of 23 December 1980 'Securities dealt in on The Stock Exchange Unlisted Securities Market: status and valuation for tax purposes', reproduced at Appendix 8—and also a statement by Mr John Moore, the Financial Secretary to the Treasury, in connection with approved selective share option schemes, during the Committee stage debates on the 1984 Finance Bill: HC Official Report, SCA, 24 May 1984, col 682).

5.78 The intention of the conditions set out in 5.75 to 5.77 is, broadly, to ensure that if the shares involved are in a company which is controlled by another, then it, or the group of which it forms a part is, by virtue of its quotation, subject to some measure of public and institutional scrutiny, and extrastatutory regulation, thus inhibiting the manipulation of the share price, whether to the advantage or disadvantage of employee shareholders. The general effect is to discourage the use of shares in subsidiary companies, just as their use in unapproved share schemes is particularly affected by the growth in value charges of ICTA 1988, s 138(1)(a) and FA 1988, s 79 (see 2.275 and 2.84 to 2.121), and is discouraged in the provisions for profit-sharing schemes under FA 1973, Sch 8 (see 2.240) and approved 'profit-sharing' (share appropriation) schemes (see 4.125).

Restrictions on the shares

5.79 In addition, the shares must be fully paid up, not redeemable, and not subject to any restrictions which do not attach to all shares of the same class, other than (from 25 July 1986) restrictions within 5.80 below (ICTA 1988, Sch 9, para 12(1)). For this purpose, a restriction attaching to shares includes any contract, agreement, arrangement or condition which restricts the holder's freedom to dispose of the shares, or of any interest in them, or of the proceeds of their sale, or which limits his freedom to exercise any right conferred by the shares, such as voting rights. It also includes 'constructive restrictions' under which the shareholder's freedom to do these things is, theoretically, not limited, but arrangements are made whereby the disposal or exercise may result in any disadvantages to him or to a 'connected person' (such as the withdrawal of the entitlement to participate in the share option scheme) (ICTA 1988, Sch 9, para 13(1)). As to the definition of 'connected person' see 7.22 (ICTA 1988, ss 187(6) and 839). Any provision similar in purpose and effect to any part of the Model Rules set out in the 'Model Code for Securities Transactions by Directors of Listed Companies' issued by The Stock Exchange in November 1984 and, broadly, intended to prevent 'insider dealing' (see Appendix 4) does not, however, constitute a restriction for these purposes (ICTA 1988, Sch 9, para 13(2)). This last provision, though introduced only by FA 1982, s 41, is deemed always to have had effect. Prior to amendment by FA 1986, s 23(4)(a), with effect from 25 July 1986, the reference was to the Model Code issued in April 1981.

5.80 The restrictions which have been permitted, since 25 July 1986, as indicated at 5.79 above, even though they may not attach to all shares of the same class, are those which meet all the following conditions:

(a) they are imposed by the company's articles of association (ICTA 1988, Sch 9, para 12(2));
(b) they require all shares held by directors and employees of the company, or of any other company of which it has control (see 7.23) to be disposed of on ceasing to be so held (ie, when the office or employment terminates or when the shares pass by operation of law, as on death, to any other person) (ICTA 1988, Sch 9, para 12(2)(a));
(c) they require all shares acquired, in pursuance of rights or interests obtained by such directors or employees, by persons who are not (or have ceased to be) such directors or employees to be disposed of when they are acquired (ICTA 1988, Sch 12, para 12(2)(b)). This would cover, for example, shares obtained by an ex-employee, or his executor, under an option granted when he was an employee;
(d) they require the disposal to be by way of sale (not gift) and for a consideration in money (rather than money's worth), on terms laid down in the articles (ICTA 1988, Sch 9, para 12(3)(a));
(e) the articles also contain general provisions under which any person disposing of shares of the same class (whether or not held by directors or employees of the company or of any other company of which it has control —see 7.23—or acquired in pursuance of rights or interests obtained by such employees) may (but need not necessarily) be required to sell them on terms which are the same as those mentioned in para (d) (ICTA 1988, Sch 9, para 12(3)(b)).

5.81 The legislation permitting the limited restrictions set out in 5.80 was introduced by FA 1986, s 22(2) and (4), prior to which a company which wished to retain control over the distribution of its shares by requiring employees to dispose of their shares on the termination of employment was prevented from introducing an approved scheme. Although under para (b) of 5.80 above all shares held by directors and employees must be required actually to be disposed of, the Financial Secretary to the Treasury indicated during the parliamentary debates on the 1986 Finance Bill that, in practice, a requirement that such individuals should simply offer their shares for sale would be treated as meeting this condition. It would, clearly, be impracticable to oblige a departing employee to sell shares to the remaining shareholders in the company, who might be unwilling, or unable, to purchase them.

5.82 Prior to the legislative changes detailed in 5.80 and 5.81, the Inland Revenue considered pre-emption rights under which a company could compel an employee who left his employment to sell his shares to another shareholder as constituting a restriction, and this continues to be the case where the detailed requirements of 5.80 are not met. The position is referred to in para (3) of the press release reproduced at Appendix 9.

5.83 A general pre-emption right, extending to all shareholders, is acceptable within the terms of ICTA 1988, Sch 9, para 12(1), as referred to at 5.79. This was confirmed by Mr John Moore, Economic Secretary to the Treasury, in the course of the debates on the 1985 Finance Bill, where he said (HC Official Report, SCB, 18 June 1985, col 661):

> The conditions for Revenue approval of an employee profit-sharing or share option scheme include a requirement that any restrictions attaching to shares, used in the company's scheme, must attach to all shares of the same class. Therefore, if a company has in its articles of association a provision that any shareholder wanting to sell must offer first refusal to existing shareholders, there would be no objection.

5.84 Prior to 11 June 1985, the Inland Revenue considered a directors' discretionary veto on share transfers to be a restriction not attaching to all shares of the same class. A press release of that date, 'Approved employee share option schemes: Revenue revise practice on some share restrictions' (see Appendix 9) indicated a change of view, so that it is now acceptable for a company to have in its articles of association a provision authorising the directors to refuse to register a transfer of shares. Since, however, the exercise of such a veto in a discriminatory way could offend the statutory requirement, before giving approval to a scheme the Inland Revenue now asks any company whose articles contain such a provision to complete, and make known to participants, a declaration to the effect that this power will not be exercised so as to discriminate against the transfer of shares acquired under the scheme.

The distribution of the shares

5.85 Various conditions as regards the distribution of the shares used in the scheme must be fulfilled. These apply except where the shares are in a company whose ordinary share capital consists of one class only. Where there is more than one class of share capital the majority of the issued shares of the same class either must be 'employee-control' shares, or must be held by persons other than:

(a) persons who acquired their shares in pursuance of a right conferred on them or an opportunity afforded to them as a director or employee of the grantor or of any other company (usually, in practice, another company

within the same group) and not in pursuance of an offer to the public (ICTA 1988, Sch 9, para 14(1)(a)); and
(b) trustees holding shares on behalf of persons who acquired their beneficial interests in the shares as in (a) above (ICTA 1988, Sch 9, para 14(1)(b)); and
(c) persons within 5.86.

5.86 Where the shares are not of a class quoted on a recognised stock exchange (although other shares in the company may be) but the company is under the control of another company whose shares are so quoted (other than a close company or a company which would be close but for not being resident in the UK)—that is, a company within para (c) but not within para (a) of 5.75—the category of persons who must not, together, hold more than a minority interest in the shares of that class is extended to include companies which have control (see 7.23 and 7.24: ICTA 1988, ss 187(2) and 840) of the company whose shares are in question, or of which that company is an associated company within ICTA 1988, s 416: see 7.10 (ICTA 1988, s 187(2) and Sch 9, para 14(1)(c)).

5.87 Shares in a company are 'employee-control' shares within 5.85 above if (ICTA 1988, Sch 9, para 14(3)):

(a) the persons holding the shares are, by virtue of their holding, together able to control (see 7.23) the company (not just to control the class of shares); and
(b) those persons are or have been employees or directors of the company, or of another company which is under the control (see 7.23) of the company.

The provision permitting the majority of the shares to be employee-control shares was introduced by FA 1986, s 23(1) and (3), amending FA 1980, Sch 10, para 19, with effect from 25 July 1986.

5.88 The basic intention of the provisions regarding the distribution of the shares, discussed in 5.85 and 5.86, is to prevent the use of a class of shares held by, or controlled by, employee shareholders, the value of which, or the benefits attaching to which, could be manipulated by the shareholders as a whole to the advantage or detriment of employee shareholders. Where, as under the provisions described in 5.87, the employee shares give control of the company as a whole, this risk of manipulation is significantly reduced as, broadly, the interests of the individuals concerned *qua* shareholder and *qua* employee are in balance.

5.89 What is in contemplation in 5.85 and 5.86 is primarily a class of shares relating particularly to the share option scheme in question, but the category of employee shareholders included in para (a) of 5.85 will include not only participants in approved savings-related schemes, but those who have acquired shares under 'unapproved' share incentive and share option schemes (see Chapters 2 and 3), approved 'profit-sharing' schemes and those under FA 1973, Sch 8 (see 2.232 to 2.241 and Chapter 4), and approved selective share option schemes (see Chapter 6). The inclusion of trustees for such employees within the 'minority only' category of shareholders prevents an obvious device for avoidance by transferring shares to nominees or other trustees. The further inclusion of controlling or associated companies within 5.86 extends the same principle, recognising that a majority holding by employees and related companies (over which those employees might also have influence), without the moderating effect of 'outside' shareholders, could open the way for manipulation and abuse.

Persons eligible to participate

General

5.90 Various conditions as to the persons eligible to participate in the scheme must be met before Inland Revenue approval can be obtained, and if they cease to be met will result in the withdrawal of approval.

All full-time employees and directors

5.91 The scheme rules must provide that all full-time employees or directors of the company concerned, (or, in the case of a group scheme—see 5.19—all full-time employees or directors of participating companies) who have been such throughout the last five years (or such shorter qualifying period as is imposed by the scheme rules), and who are chargeable to tax in respect of their office or employment under Case I of Schedule E (see 7.89), are eligible (subject to the exclusions set out at 5.95 to 5.99) to participate in the scheme on similar terms (ICTA 1988, Sch 9, para 26(1)). In addition, those who actually do participate must do so on similar terms (a provision added to ICTA 1988, Sch 9, para 26(1), then FA 1980, Sch 10, para 20(1), by FA 1984, s 39(6) and (9) with effect from 26 July 1984 for all schemes, whenever approved). A 'full-time' director or employee is not defined in the legislation (but see 7.46 to 7.50). See also 7.105.

5.92 Where there is a qualifying period of service, it should be noted that the requirement relates to continuous service, so that an aggregate of eight years' employment with the company, broken into two periods of four years each would not automatically qualify an individual to participate.

5.93 Participants are not regarded as ineligible to participate on similar terms or, since the addition made to the legislation by FA 1984, s 39 (see 5.91) as not actually participating on similar terms, merely by virtue of the fact that the number of shares over which options are granted to them varies by reference to their level of remuneration or by reference to the length of their service or similar factors (ICTA 1988, Sch 9, para 26(2)). This provision is the subject of further comment at 4.97 in the context of the parallel legislation governing approved 'profit-sharing' schemes.

5.94 Except as discussed at 5.36, 5.37 and 5.46 above (exercise following injury, redundancy, retirement, sale of the business, etc), an individual must not be eligible, under the rules of the scheme, to participate therein at any time unless he is, at that time, a director or employee of the grantor (i e the company establishing the scheme) or, if the scheme is a group scheme (see 5.19), a director or employee of a participating company (ICTA 1988, Sch 9, para 26(3)). This contrasts with the corresponding rule for approved 'profit-sharing' schemes, which allows participation in the scheme by those who have been employees or directors within the previous 18 months. The difference reflects the fact that in a profit sharing scheme the employee is being given a share in past profits as well as future profits (see 4.141), whereas in an option scheme the participant stands to benefit only from the company's future success.

Participants in other schemes

5.95 Prior to 25 July 1986, a person could not under the scheme rules be eligible to participate in any year of assessment if at any time in that year options had been granted to him under another approved savings-related scheme established by (FA 1980, Sch 10, para 22):

(a) the grantor (ie the employer company);
(b) a company which controlled the grantor;
(c) a company which was controlled by the grantor;
(d) a company which was controlled by a company which also controlled the grantor;
(e) a company which was a member of a consortium which owned the grantor; or
(f) a company which was owned in part by the company concerned as a member of a consortium.

This provision was repealed by FA 1986, s 25(7).

5.96 'Control' for the purposes of paras (b)–(d) in 5.95 was as defined in 7.23 and 7.24, and thus included indirect control via another company (ICTA 1988, s 187(2) and 840). For the purposes of paras (e) and (f), a company was a member of a consortium owning another company if it was one of not more than five companies which between them beneficially owned 75% or more of the other company's ordinary share capital (see 7.72) and each of which beneficially owned 5% or more (FA 1980, Sch 10, para 26(5)). For subsequent changes to the definition of a consortium, see 5.72.

Individuals with a material interest in a relevant company

5.97 An individual is not eligible to participate in the scheme (that is, to obtain and exercise rights under it) at any time when he has, or has had within the previous 12 months, a 'material interest' in a close company which is (ICTA 1988, Sch 9, para 8):

(a) the company whose shares may be acquired by the exercise of an option under the scheme; or
(b) a company which has control of that company; or
(c) a company which is a member of a consortium which owns that company.

5.98 For the purposes of 5.97, 'control' is direct or indirect as defined in 7.23 and 7.24 (ICTA 1988, s 187(2) and 840), and 'consortium', 'ownership' of a company by a consortium, and 'membership' of a consortium have the meanings set out at 5.72. 'Close company' is as defined in 7.12 to 7.21 (ICTA 1988, s 414), but also includes companies which are not close, but would be so but for the exclusion from the general definition of companies not resident in the UK, and of certain quoted companies in which 35% or more of the voting power is held by the public (ICTA 1988, Sch 9, para 8 and ss 414(1)(a) and 415). A 'material interest' in a close company for this purpose is, broadly, an interest, with associates, of more than 25% in the ordinary share capital or distributable income of the company (or such an interest held by associates even where the individual himself has no interest at all). The normal definition of 'material interest', formerly contained in ICTA 1970, s 285(6) and now appearing, with adaptations, in ICTA 1988, s 168(11) (see 7.65 to 7.71) is, broadly, an interest of 5% or more. The 25% figure used in the context of savings-related share option schemes is substituted for the usual 5% by ICTA 1988, s 187(3). 'Associate' is defined in ICTA 1988, s 417(3) and (4) and the details are set out at 7.6. Broadly, the term includes a husband, wife, parent, remoter ancestor, child or remoter descendant, brother or sister; the trustees of any settlement made by the individual or by such a relative; and the trustees or personal representatives of the deceased in the case of any trust or estate which includes among its assets shares in the company in question, and of which the individual in question is a beneficiary. Prior to 6 April 1986 the term did not include this last category of trustees or personal representatives, but included any other person with an interest in such a settlement or estate, except in the case of certain employee trusts where the individual was not, and could not by the operation of the trust become (with or without relatives) the beneficial owner of more than 5% of the company. For the purposes of defining 'associate' so as to determine whether an individual had a 'material interest' under the savings-related share option legislation, this figure of 5% was increased to 25% (FA 1980, Sch 10, para 26(3)(b)), and in the definition of an employee trust, the reference to employees and directors of the company was read, in the case of a group scheme (see 5.19), as a reference to employees and directors of any participating company (FA 1980, Sch 10, para 26(3)(a)). See further at 7.65 to 7.71.

5.99 For a discussion of the rationale underlying the provisions of ICTA 1988, Sch 9, para 8, as set out in 5.97 and 5.98, see 4.145, which considers the conditions as they apply in the context of the approved profit-sharing schemes legislation.

TRANSITIONAL ARRANGEMENTS

5.100 Where a person already held an SAYE contract before the savings-related share options legislation took effect, with the object of exercising share options on its maturity in broadly the way envisaged by the legislation, it is possible to bring those arrangements within the provisions for Inland Revenue approval.

5.101 It is necessary to satisfy the Board of Inland Revenue that (ICTA 1988, Sch 9, para 16(2)):

(a) the person has entered into a contractual savings scheme within the meaning of ICTA 1988, s 326 (see 5.29) before the date appointed for the coming into force of the FA 1980 legislation; ie 15 November 1980 (FA 1980, s 47(3); The Finance Act 1980 (Savings-Related Share Option Schemes) Commencement Order 1980, SI 1980/1546; see now ICTA 1988, Sch 9, para 16(2)(a)); and

(b) he has, whether before or after 15 November 1980, obtained options under a scheme established before that date to acquire shares in a company of which he is an employee or director (or in a company of which that employing company has control—see 7.23 and 7.24; ICTA 1988, ss 187(2) and 840) using repayments made under the certified contractual savings scheme.

Where these conditions are satisfied, the repayments and interest under the SAYE scheme are treated as being received under a scheme approved by the Inland Revenue as described at 5.28 (without the Inland Revenue in fact having any discretion as to its approval), and such sums may be used for the purchase of shares under an approved savings-related share option scheme (ICTA 1988, Sch 9, para 16(2)) subject to 5.102. The 'unapproved' options will accordingly be allowed to lapse, unless, under the terms of their grant, they can also be exercised out of funds provided from other sources, and the employee chooses so to do (subject to the tax regime described in Chapter 3).

5.102 While specific Inland Revenue approval of the SAYE scheme is not required, the repayments and interest which may be used to purchase options as described in 5.101 are limited to the amounts to which the participant would have been entitled if the terms of the SAYE scheme had corresponded to those of a scheme approved as described at 5.28 (ICTA 1988, Sch 9, para 16(3)).

5.103 As explained in para (b) of 5.101, the transitional rules apply not only to options acquired before 15 November 1980, but also to those acquired after that day under a pre-15 November 1980 scheme. This allows advantage to be taken of the rules, for example, by employees who become entitled to such options on the expiry of a minimum period of service after that date. The company over whose shares the options exist must, however, be the employing company or a company over which it has control, as distinct from the much wider range of companies whose shares may be used in an approved scheme (see 5.72). On the other hand, the 'old scheme' need only provide for the issue of 'shares' (or stock: ICTA 1988, s 187(2)) of any sort, not only shares or stock which form part of the company's ordinary share capital (see 5.72). The definition of 'ordinary share capital' (see 7.72) is so wide, however, that very few old schemes are likely to have involved shares, such as non-participating preference shares, which would not have fallen within that category.

5.104 There is no requirement that the old and new schemes be run by the same company, so that if the individual has changed employments, the existing SAYE contract may be linked to an approved scheme run by the new employer, and, similarly, if he holds concurrently posts with two companies, an SAYE contract originally intended for use with an old scheme run by one may be diverted to an approved scheme established by the other. In the nature of the case, the 'bonus date' for the old SAYE contract may well be less than the normal five or seven years from the commencement of the new scheme, and its rules may therefore provide for the early exercise of options in such cases while still coming within the terms of the rules discussed at 5.31.

INFORMATION POWERS

5.105 The Board of Inland Revenue may, by written notice, require any person (see comment at 4.153 in the context of the approved 'profit-sharing' legislation) to furnish, within a specified period of not less than 30 days, such information as is necessary to enable it to perform its functions under the legislation governing savings-related share option schemes, including in particular (ICTA 1988, Sch 10, para 6):

(a) information to enable it to determine whether to approve a scheme or withdraw an approval already given;
(b) information in relation to the administration of a scheme and any alteration in its terms; and
(c) information to enable it to determine the liability to income tax or CGT of any person who has participated in a scheme.

5.106 The provisions of 5.105 are restricted to such information 'as the person to whom the notice is addressed has or can reasonably obtain'. In practice, Technical Division (Employee Share Schemes) requires the completion of an annual return including detailed particulars of options granted, and a summary of the share allotments and transfers on the exercise of options. Details of shares acquired by individual employees are not normally requested. Under general rules, the participant may also be required to record on his tax return any acquisitions of assets (whether options or shares acquired on exercise) and (subject to de minimis limits) any capital gain arising from participation in the scheme. However, tax return forms no longer routinely request details of assets acquired. As to penalties, see 7.75 to 7.77. In practice, it was never necessary to record the grant of an option (IR 39, para 3.1).

6 Inland Revenue approved selective share option schemes

SUMMARY

6.1 Provisions were introduced from 6 April 1984 enabling companies, with Inland Revenue approval, to establish schemes to provide employees and directors with options to acquire shares in the employing company, a company which controls it, or certain companies which have an interest in it through a consortium. In contrast to the treatment of unapproved schemes, and in common with the savings-related schemes introduced by FA 1980, no income tax charge arises on the exercise of the option or on the sale of the shares acquired, the only charge to tax being the normal CGT liability on the disposal of the shares. An income tax charge may, however, arise on the grant of an option to purchase shares at less than their market value (although any 'manifest discount' to market value will, in any case, prevent the scheme obtaining approval). A major feature of the FA 1984 schemes is that they enable companies to grant options to employees and directors on a selective basis, rather than obliging them to offer similar benefits to their entire workforce. Indeed, it is understood that the Inland Revenue will approve a scheme for a single employee or director, provided the rules encompass the possibility of others participating (thus meeting the statutory requirement to make provision for 'directors' and 'employees' to receive options). Furthermore, while there is a limit to the benefits which may be conferred on any particular individual, that limit is considerably higher than those prevailing under approved 'profit-sharing' or SAYE linked share option schemes. An individual may hold options over shares up to the value (at the time of grant) of £100,000 or four times his emoluments for the current or the previous year, whichever is the highest figure. Whereas the earlier schemes were directed towards encouraging 'worker participation', the 1984 provisions enabled significant incentives to be offered to senior management.

6.2 In order to obtain the full benefit of the available exemptions the employee must not exercise options earlier than three years, or later than ten years, after their grant, nor more frequently than once every three years.

THE TAX EXEMPTIONS

General

6.3 Various exemptions from tax apply where, on or after 6 April 1984, an individual obtains an option to acquire shares in a company by reason of his office or employment as a director or employee of that company, in accordance with a scheme approved by the Inland Revenue under ICTA 1988, Sch 9 (see 6.18 to 6.81).

6.4 Similar exemptions may apply where the option is granted as a result of a directorship of, or employment with, any other company; for example, where the individual is employed by a subsidiary and shares in the parent company are issued to him under a group scheme: see 6.29 (ICTA 1988, s 185(1)). Although FA 1984, which introduced selective share option schemes, specified a commencement date of 6 April 1984, no scheme could be formally approved by the Inland Revenue until after the Act received the Royal Assent on 26 July 1984. That approval could, however, be given with retrospective effect (see 6.25).

The grant of the option

6.5 No tax charge arises under any provision of the Tax Acts in respect of the grant of the option except where the combined effects of the grant and its exercise would be to enable shares to be acquired at less than their market value at the time of the grant: see 6.12 and 6.13 (ICTA 1988, s 185(2)). The effect of this 'blanket' exemption is to prevent a charge on the value of the option as 'money's worth' under the general Schedule E provisions of ICTA 1988, s 19 (in accordance with the decision in *Abbott v Philbin*: see 3.5). This charge would not be excluded by ICTA 1988, s 135(2), as it would in the case of an unapproved scheme (see 3.15), as that subsection only displaces the general rule in circumstances where tax will become chargeable under s 135(1) on the *exercise* of the option, and that charge too is eliminated for approved selective share option schemes (see 6.10). Furthermore, in the absence of the exemption conferred by s 185(2), a charge on the grant of the option could still arise under general rules where the employee was not resident and ordinarily resident in the UK (see 3.13).

6.6 In addition, any charge on the grant of the option under ICTA 1988, s 19 as a result of the exception to ICTA 1988, s 135(2), which applies where the option is capable of being exercised more than seven years after it is obtained (see 3.38 to 3.43) is eliminated by s 185(2). This is of particular importance as, while (due to the terms of s 135(2)) most unapproved schemes provide that options must be exercised within seven years, the full tax benefits of an approved selective scheme may be obtained at any time within ten years from the grant (see 6.7). The ten-year limit is not, however, a condition of approval of the scheme, and even if there is a longer time limit, or no restriction whatever is prescribed, and options are not in fact exercised within ten years, still no charge can arise on the grant (although the benefit of the tax exemptions provided on *exercise* of an option under an approved scheme, as discussed at 6.7 to 6.11, will be lost).

The exercise of the option

Conditions to be satisfied

6.7 To obtain the favourable tax treatment applying on the exercise of an option, certain conditions must be satisfied as follows, subject to the exceptions in the case of the option holder's death detailed at 6.61 (ICTA 1988, s 185(3) and (5)):

(a) the period from the grant of the option to its exercise must not be less than three, nor more than ten years (ICTA 1988, s 185(5)(a)); and

(b) the exercise must not take place within three years of the date on which the participant last exercised an option under the scheme in question or under any other approved selective scheme, in circumstances such that the tax exemptions set out in 6.10 and 6.11 applied (ignoring any other exercise taking place on the same day) (ICTA 1988, s 185(3)(b)).

The combined effect of these rules is that, for any one scheme, it is possible to exercise options and obtain the full tax benefits on a maximum of three occasions. This presumably reflects the intention that participants should regard their options as a long-term stake in the company's future, and not as an opportunity to 'play the market', taking advantage of short term fluctuations in the share price, or as a form of 'disguised remuneration'. The restrictions also minimise the administrative work involved, both on the part of the company and of the Inland Revenue. In the course of the Committee Stage debates on the 1984 Finance (No 2) Bill, the Financial Secretary to the Treasury, Mr John Moore, explained that:

> The condition . . . that options may not be exercised more than once in three years, has been inserted because of the risk that options could otherwise be treated as a tax-efficient substitute for, or addition to, normal salary.

He went on to explain that the intention was to prevent 'annualisation', whereby:

> . . . companies could set up schemes designed to give senior executives annual options which would produce annual gains, taxed at significantly below the 30% rate, when a comparable increase in salary could be taxed at up to 60%. Official Report, SCA, 22 May 1984, col 537.

Since the time of that statement the top rate of income tax has been reduced to 40%, and capital gains tax rates aligned with income tax rates, by FA 1988. The implications of these changes are discussed at 1.55 to 1.59.

6.8 The provision that any other exercise on the same day is to be disregarded ensures that an individual who is a participator in a number of schemes is not disadvantaged by comparison with one who is involved in one scheme only. Both can exercise options to any value they wish (within the limits of their entitlement under the scheme or schemes) once every three years. An individual will not normally be eligible to *join* (as opposed to belong to) more than one scheme at any time, as, broadly speaking, it is a condition of a scheme's receiving approval that only full-time employees or directors, or those devoting a substantial proportion of their time to the company, may be eligible to participate (although the definition of a 'qualifying employee' for this purpose is such that there may in fact be cases where an individual is entitled to join two schemes: see further at 6.31). An approved scheme may, however, permit members to retain their rights under the scheme despite having ceased to be employees or directors, and in these circumstances there is nothing to prevent the individual becoming a member of another scheme operated by his new employer, while retaining membership of his old employer's scheme.

6.9 Where an option is exercised in circumstances such that the favourable tax treatment afforded by the legislation (and discussed at 6.10 and 6.11) is not available, for example where the exercise takes place less than three years after the receipt of the option, or less than three years after a previous (favourably treated) exercise, this does not prejudice the availability of relief on a later occasion. Such an event is ignored for the purpose of the 'three-year test'. Were this not so, a 'non-exempt exercise', perhaps forced on the participant by outside circumstances, would incur a double penalty, losing its own tax relief and also depriving the next exercise of relief, or deferring the date on which it could take place. For companies subject to the guidelines of the Investment Committee of the Association of British Insurers (see 1.14), however, the rules of the scheme may not in any case allow options to be granted for more than ten years, nor to be exercised within three years of the date of grant except in the event of the take-over of the company, or the death or cessation of employment of the participant. For further details, see point (13) of Appendix 1.

The tax exemptions

6.10 Provided the conditions set out in paras (a) and (b) of 6.7 are satisfied, and the option is exercised in accordance with the provisions of the scheme at a time when it is approved under ICTA 1988, Sch 9 (see 6.18 to 6.81), tax is not charged in respect of the exercise under any provision of the Tax Acts (ICTA 1988, s 185(3)(a)). The effect is that:

(a) there is no liability under ICTA 1988, s 135 (the general provision transferring the income tax charge on unapproved schemes from the grant of the option to its exercise: see 3.9 to 3.30);
(b) there is no charge under ICTA 1988, s 162 (see 2.303 to 2.339) on the benefit of the notional loan where shares are issued at an undervalue. As discussed at 2.308, such a charge would normally be eliminated by the prior liability under s 135, but where that earlier charge is removed by statute the s 162 charge would revive in the absence of an express rule to the contrary. Hence the 'blanket' exemption from any tax charge afforded by s 185(3)(a), rather than simply an exclusion of the charge under ICTA 1988, s 135. In addition, where the employee was not resident and ordinarily resident in the UK (and thus taxable under Case I of Schedule E) at the time of the grant of the option, he would not be liable under s 135 on its exercise (see 3.13) and a charge under ICTA 1988, s 162 might then arise, in the absence of the present exemption. The fact that ICTA 1988, s 185(3)(a) (then FA 1984, s 38(3)(a)) excludes the possibility of a charge under ICTA 1988, s 162 (then FA 1976, s 67), or indeed under any of the benefits in kind legislation, was specifically confirmed by the Inland Revenue in response to a query by the CCAB (see TR 546 'Finance Bill 1984' and TR 551 'Notes of a meeting with the Board of Inland Revenue in May 1984').

6.11 Similarly, provided the scheme remains approved when the option is exercised, no charge will arise under ICTA 1988, s 138(1)(a) or FA 1988, ss 78 or 79 (see 2.190 to 2.286 and 2.53 to 2.121) in respect of the growth in value of the shares from that time onward (ICTA 1988, s 185(5)(a)), even if by the time when the charge would otherwise crystallise (on disposal; variation or removal of rights or restrictions attaching to the shares; or expiry of seven years) the scheme is no longer approved, or no longer in existence. A 'special benefits' charge may still, however, arise in respect of the shares under ICTA 1988, s 138(1)(b) or FA 1988, s 80 (see 2.287 to 2.294 and 2.122 to 2.137).

OCCASIONS OF CHARGE TO INCOME TAX

The grant of the option

6.12 Despite the exemptions discussed at 6.5 and 6.6, a charge to income tax may arise on the grant even of an approved option, if the terms on which it is granted confer on the employee an immediate benefit. If at the time an option to purchase shares is granted, the aggregate of any consideration given for its grant and the consideration which would be given for the shares on its exercise is less than the market value, at that time, of the same quantity of issued shares of the same class, the difference is taxable under Schedule E in the year of assessment in which the option is granted, and this 'discount' is treated as earned income, whether or not it would otherwise fall to be so treated (ICTA 1988, s 185(6)). With the abolition of the investment income surcharge from 6 April 1984, the provision that the discount is always treated as earned income lost much of its effect, but it may still be of importance where an election for separate taxation of wife's earnings is made under ICTA 1988, s 287 (for periods prior to the introduction of independent taxation of husband and wife on 6 April 1990). The number of cases where an amount chargeable to tax on a full-time employee under Schedule E would not be 'earned income' in the absence of this provision must, however, be very small. The situation would presumably only arise where the benefit conferred was out of all proportion to the services rendered.

6.13 Under the terms on which schemes achieve approved status, the price at which shares may be acquired under an option may not be 'manifestly less' than their market value when the option is granted (ICTA 1988, Sch 9, para 29). Income tax charges under ICTA 1988, s 185(6) will therefore be limited both as to frequency and amount, and the particular circumstances in which they may arise are discussed further at 6.66.

The exercise of the option

6.14 A charge may arise under ICTA 1988, s 135 (general provisions covering the exercise of options in unapproved schemes: see 3.9 to 3.37), or under ICTA 1988, s 162 (interest charge on notional loan; see 2.317 to 2.325) if, when an option granted under an approved scheme is exercised, the conditions for exemption set out at 6.7 are not fulfilled. This could arise because the scheme had ceased to be approved, or because three years had not elapsed since the grant of the option or the last tax exempt exercise. For the reasons explained at 2.308 and 6.10, a charge under s 135 would prevent a charge arising also under s 162. Where, however, the employee was not resident and ordinarily resident in the UK (and thus within Case I of Schedule E) at the time of the grant of the option no charge under s 135 will arise (see 3.12 and 3.13), and thus the notional loan charge under s 162 may still apply.

6.15 In either case, the amount chargeable under ICTA 1988, s 135, or the amount of the notional loan under ICTA 1988, s 162, is reduced by the amount of any discount already charged under ICTA 1988, s 185(6) in respect of the shares in question (ICTA 1988, s 185(8)).

CAPITAL GAINS TAX CONSIDERATIONS

Exclusion of the 'market value' rule

6.16 In certain circumstances, under the CGT legislation, the market value of an asset on a transfer of ownership is substituted for the actual consideration given, in the calculation of any capital gain or loss arising, either on that transfer or on a subsequent disposal by the transferee. In particular, this rule applies where an asset is acquired by an individual 'in consideration for or recognition of his . . . services or past services in any office or employment' (CGTA 1979, s 29A(1)(b)). Where shares are acquired by the exercise of an option granted under an approved selective scheme, in circumstances such that the tax exemptions on exercise set out at 6.7 to 6.11 apply, this rule is overridden (ICTA 1988, s 185(3)(b)), so that the actual consideration given (both for the grant of the option and for the acquisition of the shares themselves) is taken into account in calculating any capital gain or loss arising on disposal of the shares. Acquisitions will, of course, always take place at a price below market value (as the holder would not otherwise choose to exercise the option), so the effect of this provision is to prevent an artificial restriction on the CGT charge or an artificial increase in the amount of any allowable loss.

Allowance for income tax charge on grant

6.17 Where an income tax charge under ICTA 1988, s 185(6) arises on the discount to market value at the time of the grant of the option, as discussed at 6.12 and 6.13, the amount of the discount on which the charge is based is added to the cost of the shares for CGT purposes, as if it were expenditure incurred at the time of acquisition (CGTA 1979, s 32A(1) and (5)). A charge under s 185(6) can only arise in connection with the grant of an option under an approved scheme, but the fact that the subsequent exercise of the option may not be such as to obtain the benefit of the tax exemptions discussed at 6.7 to 6.11, or that the scheme may no longer be approved at that time, does not affect the operation of this provision (ICTA 1988, s 185(7) and CGTA 1979, s 32A(5), which appear to duplicate each other).

CONDITIONS FOR APPROVAL OF SCHEMES

General procedure

General

6.18 A scheme is approved by the Board of Inland Revenue on application by the company concerned ('the grantor') if the Board is satisfied that the conditions for approval set out in ICTA 1988, Sch 9 (see 6.30 to 6.81) are met (ICTA 1988, Sch 9, para 1(1) and s 187(2)). The Board has no discretion to waive any of these requirements. In addition, it may not approve a scheme 'if it appears to [the Board] that there are features of the scheme which are neither essential nor reasonably incidental to the purpose of providing for employees and directors benefits in the nature of rights to acquire shares' (ICTA 1988, Sch 9, para 2(1)). Such features might include, for example, a requirement for the option holder to be a member of a particular social or political organisation, or of a professional body or trade union.

6.19 The relevant statutory provisions refer to an application by a company which 'has established' a share option scheme (ICTA 1988, Sch 9, para 1(1)), and it is therefore necessary, in theory, formally to set up the scheme before it is known whether it will obtain approval. In practice, however, the Inland Revenue's explanatory notes, Approved executive share option schemes', of June 1988, indicate (at para 2.3) that the Technical Division is prepared to comment informally on draft documents, and, if necessary, to hold discussions on particular points of difficulty.

6.20 Schemes already in operation can be submitted for approval, although if they were set up prior to the introduction of the relevant legislation in 1984 they will normally require amendment before they comply with the statutory requirements.

Documentation

6.21 An application for approval must be made in writing and contain such particulars, and be supported by such evidence, as the Board of Inland Revenue may require (ICTA 1988, Sch 9, para 1(2)).

6.22 The detailed arrangements for dealing with applications were set out in an Inland Revenue Press Release of 19 June 1984 and reiterated in the explanatory notes referred to at 6.19. Applications should be made to:

Inland Revenue, Technical Division (Employee Share Schemes), Somerset House, London, WC2R 1LB. Telephone enquiries are dealt with on: 01–438 7801; 01–438 7803 or 01–438 7771.

6.23 No special form of application is required, but two copies of the following documents should accompany the application (except where the contrary is indicated):

(a) A statement giving the name and registered office of the company which has established the scheme, together with the name of the tax office to which it makes its returns and its Inland Revenue reference number. The same information is also required for the company whose shares are to be the subject of the options, if that is not the same company as has established the scheme (see 6.46). In the case of a 'group scheme' (see 6.29) the same information is also required for all the companies to which the scheme is expressed to extend.

(b) The memorandum and articles of association of the company whose shares are to be used, and any amendments (one copy only).

(c) The scheme rules (three copies).
(d) The form of contract under which the option is to be granted (eg, letter of invitation and application form if used; otherwise option certificate alone).
(e) A declaration by the company which has established the scheme that the shares to be used satisfy the conditions for scheme shares set out at 6.46 to 6.59, stating briefly which of the alternative conditions are satisfied (one copy only). A statement signed by the company secretary on company headed notepaper will meet this requirement.
(f) If the shares which are to be the subject of the options are not shares in the company which has established the scheme, or are shares in a company which is under the control of another company, a further declaration indicating precisely how the conditions set out in 6.46 to 6.59 are met (one copy only).
(g) Any other documents which will be issued to participants and/or shareholders in connection with the scheme, including the option certificate and notice of exercise (including, specifically, one copy of any declaration as at 6.56, with confirmation that this will be made known to participants).

The application should state the date on which the scheme was approved or adopted by the company. If it has been amended prior to approval being sought, eg where an existing scheme has been adapted in the light of the introduction of the legislation in 1984, the date on which, and the authority by which, it was altered to its present form should also be stated. A certified copy of the approval of the resolution adopting or amending the scheme should also be forwarded.

Alterations to the scheme

6.24 If any alteration is made to the scheme after Inland Revenue approval has been given, the approval lapses from the date of the alteration, unless the change is itself approved by the Board (ICTA 1988, Sch 9, para 4). The explanatory notes referred to at 6.19 indicate (at para 2.7) that Technical Division (Employee Share Schemes) should be notified immediately, in duplicate, of any alteration or addition to the information supplied as described at 6.23, and that companies contemplating changes in an approved scheme can consult the Inland Revenue informally. They also state, at para 3.5, that a scheme may provide for adjustments to the subscription price and number of shares subject to the option, to take account of variations in share capital, but that such a rule should be expressed to require prior Inland Revenue approval.

Retrospective approval

6.25 There is no general provision for retrospective approval, although where the provisions of a scheme are approved pursuant to an application submitted before 1 January 1985 (and the approval has not been withdrawn) any option granted before 1 July 1985 is treated, as regards the tax position on both its grant and exercise, as if the scheme had been approved during the period beginning with the date of the grant and ending on the date when those provisions were actually approved (ICTA 1988, s 185(9)). As the exemptions set out in 6.3 to 6.11 only took effect for options obtained on or after 6 April 1984, options granted before that time under an established scheme are unable to benefit from the legislation, even if the scheme subsequently obtains approval without any change to its rules. The six-month interval between 1 January and 1 July 1985 was incorporated in the legislation in order to allow time for any such application to pass through the approval process. When the relevant legislation was introduced as an amendment at the committee stage of the 1984 Finance (No 2) Bill, Mr John Moore, the Financial Secretary to the Treasury, made the point that:

> Companies that decide to take advantage of the facility provided by this amendment will appreciate that the options they grant in advance of formal approval must be subject to the terms of the scheme as it is finally approved. Those terms may differ from the terms ruling at the time of the grant. Companies may wish therefore to take the precaution of making any such 'pre-approval' grants expressly subject to the terms of the scheme as it is finally approved.

An application is not regarded as submitted before 1 January 1985 if it has merely been the subject of an informal approach as outlined in 6.19. In the case of pre-1 July 1985 options, Shares Valuation Division was prepared to negotiate a share value even though the scheme had not yet been approved (contrary to the general practice mentioned in 6.64), but production of the scheme rules for valuation purposes before 1 January 1985, again, did not constitute an application for approval.

Withdrawal of approval

6.26 If, after approval has been given, any of the relevant requirements of ICTA 1988, Sch 9 (see 6.30 to 6.81) cease to be satisfied, or the company fails to provide the Inland Revenue with any information which it has requested in accordance with the powers discussed at 6.28, the Board may withdraw approval with effect from that time or from such later time as it may specify (ICTA 1988, Sch 9, para 3(1)). The power to withdraw approval is permissive, not mandatory, and it is therefore possible that in exceptional cases, or in the event of minor or temporary derogations or defaults, a scheme might retain approved status despite a departure from the statutory rules or a failure to furnish information. Clearly, however, it would be unwise to place reliance on the favourable exercise of such Inland Revenue discretion.

Appeals

6.27 If approval of a scheme or of an alteration is refused or, once given, is withdrawn, the company may, within 30 days of the date on which it is notified of the Board's decision, require the matter to be determined by the Special Commissioners, who will hear and decide the case in the same manner as an appeal against an assessment to tax (ICTA 1988, Sch 9, para 5). Appeals on a point of law may then proceed to the courts in the normal way (see 7.1 to 7.5).

Information powers

6.28 The Board of Inland Revenue may, by notice in writing, require any person (not just the 'grantor' company) to provide it with such information as it considers necessary for the performance of its functions under the selective share options legislation, provided the person to whom the notice is addressed has, or can reasonably obtain, that information (ICTA 1988, Sch 9, para 6). Without limiting the generality of that power, the legislation specifies, in particular:

(a) information to enable the Board to determine whether to approve or to withdraw approval from a scheme;
(b) information to enable it to determine the liability to income tax or CGT of any participant, or former participant, in a scheme; and
(c) information in relation to the administration of a scheme, and any alteration in its terms.

Any such request may specify a time limit, of not less than 30 days, for the provision of the information in question. Failure to comply with a request for information under these provisions renders the person concerned liable to penalties as set out at 7.75 to 7.77. In practice companies are required to make an annual return to Technical Division (Employee Share Schemes), including details of all options granted, and of shares allotted or transferred on the exercise of options. The participant may also be required, under general legislation, to include in his own tax return details of assets (including shares or options) acquired, capital gains realised (subject to de minimis limits), and amounts liable to income tax, although in practice tax returns no longer routinely require details of assets acquired.

Group schemes

6.29 Where the company granting options (the 'grantor') has control of another company or companies, the scheme may extend to all or any of such companies (a 'group scheme'), the companies concerned being referred to as 'participating companies' (ICTA 1988, Sch 9, para 1(3) and (4) and s 187(2)). The definition of 'control' applying for this purpose is that set out in 7.23 and 7.24 (ICTA 1988, s 187(2) and 840). As to jointly controlled companies, see Appendix 11 'Inland Revenue Extrastatutory Concession B27: Approved employee share schemes—jointly owned companies'.

Eligible participants

General

6.30 A scheme must not provide for any individual to participate in it (that is, to obtain or exercise options) unless he is a 'full-time director' (see 7.46 to 7.50: broadly, a director working 25 hours per week or more) or 'qualifying employee' of the grantor company; or, in the case of a group scheme, of a participating company. Having once obtained options in such a capacity, however, the scheme may (but need not) permit an individual to exercise those options after the employment or directorship has ceased (ICTA 1988, Sch 9, para 27(1)). See also point (13) of Appendix (1), re employees approaching retirement.

Qualifying employees

6.31 A 'qualifying employee', in relation to a company, is one (other than a director, or a director of a participating company in a group scheme) who is required under the terms of his employment to work for the company for at least 20 hours a week (ICTA 1988, Sch 9, para 27(4)). In theory this might make it possible for an individual with two part-time jobs to participate in two separate schemes, but such circumstances are likely to arise only rarely. The Inland Revenue's explanatory notes, referred to in 6.19, make it clear that, in the Revenue view, those 20 hours exclude meal breaks (para 3.7).

Group employment

6.32 In the provisions providing relief for interest on a loan to invest in a close company (referred to in 7.47), there is a requirement that the individual should have worked for the greater part of his time in the actual management or conduct of the company 'or of an associated company'. There is in the approved selective share option legislation no statutory recognition of the possibility that an individual may meet the 'full-time director' or 'qualifying employee' tests in relation to a group of companies taken as a whole, while not doing so in relation to the one company which has established the approved scheme. Similarly, in the context of a group scheme the test of eligibility must, in strictness, be met in relation to one particular participating company. This does not automatically exclude directors with diverse group responsibilities, as they will normally work for one particular company which has the responsibility of providing services to other group companies and which will then make management charges, designed directly or indirectly to recover the costs involved. The individuals concerned may therefore be said to be working for one company even when involved in group matters, just as a solicitor or accountant is working for his employing firm even though engaged on the affairs of its clients.

6.33 This point was discussed at a meeting held in May 1984 between the Inland Revenue and the CCAB to discuss the latter's submissions on the 1984 Finance (No 2) Bill. The original submission was published as TR 546, 'Finance Bill: Memorandum submitted in May 1984 to the Chancellor of the Exchequer on behalf of the Councils of the constituent members of the Consultative Committee of Accountancy Bodies', and the relevant para (no 45) read as follows:

> We would welcome confirmation that an individual who is a full time director or employee within a group of companies may participate in any company which introduces a scheme without his necessarily being a full-time employee of one particular company.

The Inland Revenue response was recorded in TR 551 'The Finance Bill 1984: Notes of a meeting with the Board of Inland Revenue in May 1984' at para 45, and addressed a somewhat different question:

> The CCAB asked about the position of an employee who worked full-time for a number of companies within a group: commonly, he might be paid by one member of the group and, though he worked full-time for companies in the group which were 'participating companies' in a single 'group scheme', he did not work full-time for any one particular company among them. The Revenue said that they foresaw no difficulty in practice in accepting that such a case met the 25-hour criterion. The CCAB accepted this view.

(Reproduced by kind permission of the Consultative Committee of Accountancy Bodies.)

6.34 It will be seen that the point on which agreement was sought was narrowed in the course of the consultation: the original question referred to directors and employees, while the second statement referred only to employees; the earlier submission dealt with any grantor company which was part of a group, while the later statement was restricted to the situation where all the companies in that group are participating companies in a group scheme (see 6.29); and the original submission was in terms wide enough to encompass an individual with a multiplicity of employments within a group, while the response refers specifically to an employee paid by one member of the group only. There appears therefore to be little element of concession in the approach set out in TR 551. The Inland Revenue's explanatory notes (see 6.19), however, indicated (at para 3.7(c)) that, for the purposes of both the 'full-time director' and 'qualifying employee' tests, a person may aggregate the hours he works for all participating companies in a group scheme. This does not, however, cover the case of multiple employments or directorships with group companies, one or more of which have approved schemes, but where there is no group scheme within 6.29.

Material interest in a close company

6.35 The rules of the scheme must prohibit participation by an individual who has (or has had within the preceding twelve months) a 'material interest' in a close company which is (ICTA 1988, Sch 9, para 8):

(a) the company whose shares may be acquired under the scheme; or
(b) a company which has control of that company; or
(c) a company which is a member of a consortium which owns that company.

For these purposes, 'control' is direct or indirect as defined in 7.23 and 7.24 (ICTA 1988, ss 187(2) and 840). 'Close company' is as defined in 7.12 to 7.21 (ICTA 1988, s 414), but also includes companies which are not close, but would be so but for the exclusion from the general definition of companies not resident in the UK and of certain quoted companies in which 35% or more of the voting power is held by the public (ICTA 1988, Sch 9, para 8 and ss 414(1)(a) and 415). For the purposes of (c), a company is a member of a consortium owning another company if it is one of a number of companies which between them beneficially own 75% or more of that other company's ordinary share capital (see 7.72), and each of which beneficially owns not less than 5% thereof (ICTA 1988, s 187(7)).

6.36 A 'material interest' in a close company for the purpose of 6.35, is, broadly, an interest, with associates, of more than 10% in the ordinary share capital or distributable income of the company (or such an interest held by associates even where the individual himself has no interest at all). The normal definition of 'material interest' previously contained in ICTA 1970, s 285(6), and now appearing, with adaptations, in ICTA 1988, s 168(11) (see 7.65 to 7.71) is, broadly, an interest of 5% or more. The 10% figure used in the context of approved selective share option schemes is substituted for the usual

5% by ICTA 1988, s 187(3). 'Associate' is defined in ICTA 1988, s 417(3) and (4), and the details are set out at 7.6. Broadly, the term includes a husband, wife, parent, remoter ancestor, child or remoter descendant, brother or sister; the trustees of any settlement made by the individual or by such a relative; and the trustees or personal representatives of the deceased in the case of any trust or estate which includes among its assets shares in the company in question, and of which the individual in question is a beneficiary.

6.37 Prior to 6 April 1986 the term 'associate' did not include trustees or personal representatives within the last category mentioned in 6.36, but included any other person with an interest in such a settlement or estate, except in the case of certain employee trusts where the individual was not, and could not by the operation of the trust become (with or without relatives) the beneficial owner of more than 5% of the company. For the purposes of defining 'associate' so as to determine whether an individual had a 'material interest' under the approved selective share option legislation, this figure of 5% was increased to 10% (FA 1984, Sch 10, para 4(4)), and in the definition of an employee trust the reference to employees and directors of the company was read, in the case of a group scheme (see 6.29), as a reference to employees and directors of any participating company (FA 1984, Sch 10, para 15(2)). See further at 7.65 to 7.71.

6.38 For a discussion of the rationale underlying the provisions as to employees with a material interest in a close company, as set out at 6.35 to 6.37, see 4.145, which considers these conditions as they apply in relation to the approved 'profit-sharing' schemes legislation.

Maximum rights obtainable under a scheme

General rules

6.39 The scheme rules must contain provisions to ensure that no individual obtains options which, at the time they are granted, would cause the aggregate 'market value' (ICTA 1988, s 187(2); CGTA 1979, s 150: see 7.56 to 7.64) of the shares which he may acquire to exceed, or further exceed, the 'appropriate limit' (ICTA 1988, Sch 9, para 28(1)), which is the greater of (ICTA 1988, Sch 9, para 28(2)):

(a) £100,000; and
(b) four times his relevant emoluments for the current or preceding year of assessment (whichever of those years gives the greater amount). Where there were no relevant emoluments for the preceding year of assessment, there is taken into account, instead, four times the amount of the relevant emoluments for the period of 12 months beginning with the first day during the current year of assessment in respect of which there are relevant emoluments (ICTA 1988, Sch 9, para 28(2)(c)). The effect is that if the payment of relevant emoluments commenced (usually by virtue of the commencement of the employment, but see further at 6.44) part-way through the preceding year of assessment, the emoluments for the current year will be taken into account unless, exceptionally, they are exceeded by those for the earlier part-year. If the payment of relevant emoluments began on or after 6 April in the current year, then the payments for the

ensuing 12 months will be taken into consideration. It should be borne in mind that, if the current year's or first 12 months' expected emoluments are used in the calculation, and they are not, for any reason, actually achieved, the option will not have been granted in accordance with the provisions of an approved scheme (see 6.3), and none of the tax exemptions set out in 6.5 to 6.11 will be available. There is no question of partial relief, up to the amount of the limit which should have been applied.

6.40 For the purpose of 6.39, the market value of shares over which existing options are held is the value at the time those options were granted, or at such earlier time as may have been agreed with the Inland Revenue under ICTA 1988, Sch 9, para 29(b): see 6.63 (ICTA 1988, Sch 9, para 28(3)). In a scheme taking maximum advantage of the rules (see, again, 6.63) this will also be the exercise price. Subsequent movements in the share price, whether up or down, do not affect this figure. Options which have already been exercised do not count towards the limit, which is concerned only to restrict the potential, rather than the realised, benefit under an approved scheme. For companies affected by the guidelines of the Investment Committee of the Association of British Insurers (see 1.14) more stringent conditions may apply as to the maximum entitlement of any one employee, and the entitlement to exercise the options must be linked to a growth in the company's earnings per share (see point (11) and addendum in Appendix 1).

6.41 Options under any approved selective scheme established by the grantor or an 'associated company' (see 7.10) are considered together in establishing whether the limit is exceeded (ICTA 1988, Sch 9, para 28(1)) but no account is taken of any unapproved scheme or approved SAYE-linked scheme, nor of any approved selective scheme established by an unrelated company.

6.42 It is unclear from the legislation whether, in taking into account associated companies, one must consider whether two companies were associated at the time either's scheme was set up (or approved) or at the time when it comes to be ascertained whether a further grant of options would take an individual's entitlement over the permissible limits (or both). While the latter would seem to be the more relevant consideration, in practice it will normally be found that, if two companies are associated at all, they will be associated at all material times.

Relevant emoluments

6.43 The 'relevant emoluments' taken into account as described at 6.39 in determining the limit on options which may be granted are such part of the emoluments of the employment giving rise to the entitlement to participate in the scheme as are liable to tax under PAYE by virtue of ICTA 1988, s 203, excluding amounts included by virtue of ICTA 1988, ss 153 to 168 (benefits of directors and higher paid employees) (ICTA 1988, Sch 9, para 28(4)). The effect is to exclude employers' or employees' contributions to approved superannuation funds (which by virtue of ICTA 1988, ss 592(7) and 596 respectively, are not liable to tax, or are allowable for tax purposes), and also monetary amounts, such as expense allowances, taxable under the benefits in kind provisions. Additional voluntary contributions (AVCs) to a pension scheme may therefore reduce the availability of share options, and this must be borne in mind in weighing up the advantages of such payments. Other, non-monetary benefits in kind chargeable under the benefits in kind provisions, such as company cars, or scholarships to the employee's children, together with benefits which are also taxable on lower paid employees, such as the provision of living accommodation, are in any case excluded from the computation by the reference to deduction of tax under ICTA 1988, s 203, as while such items may be taken into account in setting a PAYE coding (and may thus increase the deduction of tax from cash emoluments), they are not themselves paid under deduction of tax. See also 7.110.

6.44 Where the employee or director is non-resident, he will not have emoluments liable to deduction of tax under PAYE, and the £100,000 limit will apply automatically with no alternative higher limit, irrespective of the level of his earnings. By contrast, in the case of the 100% deduction under ICTA 1988, s 193(1) and Sch 12 for earnings from work done abroad during a 'long absence' of 365 days or more (allowing for limited return trips to the UK) it is understood to be the practice of the Inland Revenue to treat the gross amount, before the deduction, as constituting the relevant emoluments. (For the 100% deduction, see further at 7.92.)

Calculation of maximum rights

6.45 The calculation of the maximum rights obtainable under a scheme is illustrated by the following example:

In 1988/89, Smallridge is granted options to acquire 1,000 £1 ordinary shares in Wright Ltd. The market value of the shares at the time of the grant is £90,000, and Smallridge's relevant emoluments are £20,000.

In 1993/94, he exercises his options in respect of 300 shares, and in 1995/96, when his relevant emoluments are £50,000, and the value of the shares is £200 each, the company wishes to make him a further grant of options.

The first grant is clearly within the appropriate limit of £100,000 despite exceeding four times the relevant emoluments of £20,000. On the second grant, the appropriate limit is £200,000 (i e four times £50,000) and the market value of Smallridge's existing options is as follows:

Value of shares under 1988/89 grant (at time of grant) (cf value in 1995/96 of £200,000)	£ 90,000
Less exercised 1993/94 (£90,000 × $\frac{300}{1,000}$)	(27,000)
	63,000
Appropriate limit	(200,000)
Maximum value of shares for which options may be granted in 1995/96 (685 shares)	£ 137,000

Scheme shares

Conditions as to the shares

6.46 Under the terms of the scheme, the shares (or stock: ICTA 1988, s 187(2)) over which options are granted must form part of the ordinary share capital (see 7.72) of (ICTA 1988, Sch 9, para 10):

(a) the grantor company; or
(b) a company which has control of the grantor, as the term 'control' is defined in 7.23 and 7.24 (ICTA 1988, ss 187(2) and 840); or
(c) a company which either is, or controls, a company which is a member of a consortium (see 6.35) owning either the grantor or a company which controls the grantor, and which beneficially owns at least 15% of the ordinary share capital of the company so owned.

It should be noted that 'ordinary shares', as defined, may include so-called 'funny shares' such as participating preference shares.

6.47 For companies subject to the guidelines of the Investment Committee of the Association of British Insurers (see 1.14), options may normally be granted only over the share capital of the parent company of a group, or certain quoted or overseas subsidiaries (see point (14) of Appendix 1).

6.48 In addition to meeting the requirements set out in 6.46, the scheme shares must be (ICTA 1988, Sch 9, para 11):

(a) shares of a class quoted on a recognised stock exchange (as defined in ICTA 1988, s 841: see 7.83 to 7.86). A quotation on the Unlisted Securities Market is not treated as one on a 'recognised stock exchange' for this purpose (see Inland Revenue Statement of Practice SP 18/80 of 23 December 1980, 'Securities dealt in on The Stock Exchange Unlisted Securities Market: status and valuation for tax purposes' (Appendix 8), and also a statement by Mr John Moore, the Financial Secretary to the Treasury, during the Committee Stage debates on the Finance (No 2) Bill 1984: HC Official Report, SCA, 24 May 1984, col 682); or
(b) shares of a company which is not under the control (again, as defined in ICTA 1988, s 840: see 7.23 and 7.24) of another company; or
(c) shares in a company which is under the control of a second company whose shares are quoted on a recognised stock exchange, provided the second company is not a close company (see 7.12 to 7.21), and is not prevented from being close merely by virtue of being resident outside the UK.

6.49 For a more extended examination of the provisions as to the scheme shares set out in 6.46 to 6.48, with diagrams, see 4.119 to 4.125, where the corresponding provisions in the approved 'profit-sharing' schemes legislation are discussed.

6.50 Further rules provide that, under the terms of the scheme, shares must be fully paid up, not redeemable, and not subject to any restrictions which do not attach to all shares of the same class, other than (from 25 July 1986) restrictions within 6.53 below (ICTA 1988, Sch 9, para 12(1)).

6.51 A restriction attaching to shares includes any contract, agreement, arrangement or condition which restricts the holder's freedom to dispose of the shares, or of any interest in them, or of the proceeds of their sale, or which limits his freedom to exercise any right conferred by the shares, such as voting rights. It also includes 'constructive restrictions' under which the shareholder's freedom to do these things is, theoretically, not limited, but arrangements are made whereby the disposal or exercise may result in a disadvantage to him or to a person connected with him (such as the withdrawal of the entitlement to participate in the share option scheme) (ICTA 1988, Sch 9, para 13(1)). 'Connected person' for this purpose is defined in ICTA 1988, s 839, as applied by s 187(6) (see 7.22). Any provision similar in purpose and effect to any part of the Model Rules set out in the 'Model Code for Securities Transactions by Directors of Listed Companies' issued by The Stock Exchange in November 1984 (see Appendix 4) does not, however, constitute a restriction for these purposes (ICTA 1984, Sch 9, para 13(2)). Prior to amendment by FA 1986, s 23(4)(b), with effect from 25 July 1986, the reference was to the Model Code issued in April 1981. If the period between the exercise of the option and the allotment of the shares exceeds 30 days, the Inland Revenue regards this as imposing a restriction on the shares (IR explanatory notes, para 3.15).

6.52 The general definition of 'restriction' in 6.51 above does not include any terms of a loan making provision about how it is to be repaid or the security to be given for it (ICTA 1988, Sch 9, para 13(3), inserted by FA 1988, s 69, with effect from the commencement of the legislation in 1984). This enables participants to take out a loan in order to obtain the funds to exercise their options, on the security of the shares which they will thereby acquire, or under an agreement to sell some of the shares in order to finance the repayment of the loan, without prejudicing the approval of the scheme.

6.53 The restrictions which have been permitted since 25 July 1986 as indicated at 6.50 above, even though they may not attach to all shares of the same class, are those which meet all the following conditions:

(a) they are imposed by the company's articles of association (ICTA 1988, Sch 9, para 12(2));
(b) they require all shares held by directors and employees of the company, or of any other company of which it has control (see 7.23) to be disposed of on ceasing to be so held (ie, when the office or employment terminates or when the shares pass by operation of law, as on death, to any other person) (ICTA 1988, Sch 9, para 12(2)(a));
(c) they require all shares acquired, in pursuance of rights or interests obtained by such directors or employees, by persons who are not (or have ceased to be) such directors or employees to be disposed of when they are acquired (ICTA 1988, Sch 9, para 12(2)(b)). This would cover, for example, shares obtained by an ex-employee, or his executor, under an option granted when he was an employee;
(d) they require the disposal to be by way of sale (not gift) and for a consideration in money (rather than money's worth), on terms laid down in the articles (ICTA 1988, Sch 9, para 12(3)(a));
(e) the articles also contain general provisions under which any person disposing of shares of the same class (whether or not held by directors or employees of the company or of any other company of which it has control—see 7.23—or acquired in pursuance of rights or interests obtained

by such employees) may (but need not necessarily) be required to sell them on terms which are the same as those mentioned in para (d) (ICTA 1988, Sch 9, para 12(3)(b)).

6.54 The legislation permitting these limited restrictions was introduced by FA 1986, s 22(3) and (4), prior to which a company which wished to retain control over the distribution of its shares by requiring employees to dispose of their shares on the termination of employment was prevented from introducing an approved scheme. Although under para (b) of 6.53 above all shares held by directors and employees must be required actually to be disposed of, the Financial Secretary to the Treasury indicated during the parliamentary debates on the 1986 Finance Bill that, in practice, a requirement that such individuals should simply offer their shares for sale would be treated as meeting this condition. It would, clearly, be impracticable to oblige a departing employee to sell shares to the remaining shareholders in the company, who might be unwilling, or unable, to purchase them.

6.55 Prior to the changes in legislation detailed at 6.53 and 6.54, the Inland Revenue considered pre-emption rights under which a company could compel an employee who left his employment to sell his shares to another shareholder as constituting a restriction, and this continues to be the case where the detailed requirements of 6.53 and 6.54 are not met. The position is referred to in para (3) of the press release reproduced at Appendix 9. As to general pre-emption rights, extending to all shareholders, see comments at 5.83, in the context of savings-related share-option schemes.

6.56 Prior to 11 June 1984, the Inland Revenue considered a directors' discretionary veto on share transfers to be a restriction not attaching to all shares of the same class. A press release of that date, 'Approved employee share option schemes: Revenue revise practice on some share restrictions' (see Appendix 9) indicated a change of view, so that it is now acceptable for a company to have in its articles of association a provision authorising the directors to refuse to register a transfer of shares. Since, however, the exercise of such a veto in a discriminatory way could offend the statutory requirement, before giving approval to a scheme the Inland Revenue now asks any company whose articles contain such a provision to complete, and make known to participants, a declaration to the effect that this power will not be exercised so as to discriminate against the transfer of shares acquired under the scheme.

Conditions as to the distribution of shareholdings

6.57 Except where the scheme shares are in a company whose ordinary share capital consists of shares of one class only, the majority of the issued shares of the same class as the scheme shares either must be 'employee-control' shares or must be held by persons other than (ICTA 1988, Sch 9, para 14(1)(a) and (b)):

(a) persons who acquired their shares in pursuance of a right conferred on them, or an opportunity offered to them, as a director or employee of the grantor or any other company, and not in pursuance of an offer to the public. This category will include persons who have made acquisitions under approved selective share options schemes, unapproved schemes, approved SAYE-linked schemes and approved 'profit sharing' schemes, as well as other acquisitions by virtue of employment, but the principal intention of the provision would appear to be to prevent the creation of a separate class of share specifically for use in the approved selective scheme; and

(b) trustees holding shares on behalf of persons who acquired their beneficial interests in the shares as described in para (a); and

(c) persons within 6.58.

6.58 Where the scheme shares are not of a class quoted on a recognised stock exchange (although other shares in the company may be) but the company is under the control of a company whose shares are so quoted, other than a close company, or a company which would be close but for not being resident in the UK (ie where the shares are within para (c) but not within para (a) of 6.48) the category of persons who must not, together, hold more than a minority interest in the shares of that class is extended to include companies which have control (ICTA 1988, ss 187(2) and 840: see 7.23 and 7.24) of the company whose shares are in question or of which that company is an associated company, within the definition of ICTA 1988, s 416, as applied by ICTA 1988, s 187(2): see 7.10 (ICTA 1988, Sch 9, para 14(1)(c)).

6.59 Shares in a company are 'employee-control' shares within 6.57 above if (ICTA 1988, Sch 9, para 14(3)):

(a) the persons holding the shares are, by virtue of their holding, together able to control (see 7.23) the company (not just to control the class of shares); and

(b) those persons are or have been employees or directors of the company, or of another company which is under the control (see 7.23) of the company.

The provisions permitting the majority of the shares to be employee-control shares was introduced by FA 1986, s 23(1) to (3), amending FA 1984, Sch 10, para 11, with effect from 25 July 1986.

Transfer of rights

6.60 The rules of an approved scheme must not permit any person to whom options are granted to transfer them. It may, however, permit them to be exercised by his personal representatives within one year after his death (ICTA 1988, Sch 9, para 27(2)).

6.61 Where such a provision is included in the scheme rules, and the personal representatives exercise the options in accordance with that provision, and before the expiry of the period of ten years beginning with the grant of the right, the exemptions from tax on its exercise granted by ICTA 1988, s 185(3) (see 6.10 and 6.11) are available notwithstanding the fact that less than three years may have elapsed since the grant, or since the last 'exempt exercise' under the scheme. Similarly, the actual exercise price is substituted for market value for CGT purposes, as discussed at 6.16 (ICTA 1988, Sch 9, para 27(3)).

6.62 The relevant exemptions are from the charges under ICTA 1988, s 135 (see 3.9 to 3.37), under ICTA 1988, s 162 (see 2.303 to 2.339), ICTA 1988, s 138(1)(a) (see 2.190 to 2.286) and FA 1988, ss 78 and 79 (see 2.53 to 2.121). In fact, it may perhaps be questioned whether this provision is necessary (and thus whether the ten-year time limit it imposes is effective) as these charges only apply to persons who have obtained benefits by virtue of their employment. The personal representatives, by contrast (it may be argued), have acquired the options by devolution on death, and it may therefore be considered that they simply constitute chargeable assets for CGT purposes (within CGTA 1979, s 19(1)(a): 'options, debts and incorporeal property generally') the proceeds on disposal of which are subject only to CGT in their hands.

The share price

6.63 The 'exercise price' (ie the price at which scheme shares may be obtained by the exercise of an option obtained under the scheme) must be stated at the time the option is granted, and must not be 'manifestly less' than the market value of shares of the same class at that time, or, if the Board of Inland Revenue and the grantor company so agree in writing, at such earlier time or times as may be provided in the agreement (ICTA 1988, Sch 9, para 29). As to 'market value', see 7.56 to 7.64. In the case of companies subject to the guidelines of the Investment Committee of the Association of British Insurers (see 1.14), the price must not be less than the middle market price of the shares in question at the time the option is granted, 'or similar formula' and that time must be not before, and within 42 days following, publication of the results of the grantor company. Nor, under the guidelines, may the value at an earlier date be substituted for that at the time of the grant as permitted by the legislation (see point (12) in Appendix 1).

6.64 In practice, a share option scheme will normally be initiated by the company writing to the eligible employees offering the relevant options and stating the price at which they will be exercisable. The employees will usually have to respond within a stated time, and only after that time has elapsed will options actually be granted. Clearly, the market value of the shares may change between the initial offer letter and the date of grant of an option, particularly in the case of quoted shares, and the procedure under ICTA 1988, Sch 9, para 29 as described at 6.63 caters for this possibility. The Inland Revenue will not normally agree to the use of a value more than 30 days before the grant. If the average market value over a period is employed for this purpose (in accordance with the reference in 6.63 to an agreement for the use of a value at an earlier time 'or times'), the Inland Revenue will not agree a figure based on a period commencing more than 30 days before the grant of the option. Valuations of unquoted shares are dealt with by the Shares Valuation Division at the address and telephone number given in 5.69 (on extensions 498 or 456), and, as stated there, until a scheme has been approved Shares Valuation Division will normally require prior instructions from Technical Division before negotiating a value.

6.65 As the legislation stands, there is nothing, in theory, to prevent the Inland Revenue, by agreement, giving ex post facto approval to a scheme established by reference to the market value of shares on a date prior to the grant, but companies may be understandably reluctant to proceed in such circumstances without prior assurances of official blessing.

6.66 If the exercise price, though not 'manifestly' less than current market value at the appropriate time, subsequently proves in fact to be less than the value at the time of the grant, a charge to tax under Schedule E will arise on the 'discount' under ICTA 1988, s 185(6), as discussed at 6.12 and 6.13. This may arise, in theory, in the following situations:

(a) where the exercise price, by agreement with the Inland Revenue under ICTA 1988, Sch 9, para 29, is established by reference to a date prior to the grant and is less than the market value on grant due to fluctuations in the market price in the intervening period. In practice, however, the Inland Revenue will not normally invoke s 185(6) in these circumstances unless the increase in value arises as a result of the company's flotation; and

(b) where revisions are made to the valuation of unquoted shares, perhaps following negotiations with the Inland Revenue's Shares Valuation Division, and the exercise price placed on the shares at the time of grant, while not self-evidently or 'manifestly' less than market value, subsequently proves to have been too low. In such a case the penalty for the 'error' in valuation is the charge under ICTA 1988, s 185(6) (which will not normally be large, in a case where the discount was not 'manifest'), as opposed to the much more Draconian penalty of total withdrawal of Inland Revenue approval from the scheme, which would apply if the exercise price was at a 'manifest' discount to market value. If values are agreed with Shares Valuation Division in advance, such 'errors' will not in practice arise.

6.67 The phrase 'manifestly less' appears also in the legislation for approved SAYE-linked share option schemes (see 5.67), in ICTA 1988, Sch 9, para 25, but there has been no judicial guidance as to its precise meaning. The Inland Revenue's explanatory notes, 'Approved Executive Share Option Schemes' indicate at para 3.4 the Revenue view that:

> If the price at which shares may be acquired on the exercise of an option is at the date of grant known (or should have been known) to be less than their market value on the agreed date, then that price is demonstrably (ie 'manifestly') less than such market value, however small the difference may be.

6.68 The scheme may provide for adjustments to the exercise price (and, by necessary implication, to the number of shares: see Appendix 7, rule (8)) to take account of variations in the share capital concerned, such as bonus issues, share 'splits' and rights issues, although the calculations of the appropriate change in price to take account of a rights issue may, in the case of unquoted shares, be extremely complicated (ICTA 1988, Sch 9, para 29).

6.69 In its representations on the 1984 Finance Bill (TR 546), the CCAB sought confirmation that the exercise price could be increased beyond market value at the time of the grant by reference to a formula based on the company's profitability. The Inland Revenue confirmed that this was acceptable, provided it was not possible for the formula to produce a price below that figure (TR 551: 'Notes of a meeting with the Board of Inland Revenue in May 1984').

Exchange of options on a takeover

6.70 Prior to 15 May 1987, on a company takeover the participants in an approved selective share option scheme could find themselves obliged either to exercise their options early, and perhaps forfeit tax relief (if the exercise was within three years of the grant, or within three years of the last exercise: see 6.7), or to continue to hold options over shares in a company which had become an unquoted subsidiary of another company (subject to 6.48). With effect from 15 May 1987 the relevant legislation was amended (by FA 1987, s 33(1) and Sch 4, para 2), so that the rules of an approved scheme are permitted (but not obliged) to allow that on a takeover a participant may release his options in return for new options over shares in the acquiring company (or in a related company, as explained at 6.46). The acquiring company is not obliged by the legislation to agree to such an exchange, although certain companies may be subject to obligations under the City Code on Takeovers and Mergers.

6.71 Specifically, the scheme may provide that if any company ('the acquiring company') (ICTA 1988, Sch 9, para 15(1)):

(a) obtains control (see 7.23) of a company whose shares are scheme shares, as a result of making a general offer to acquire the whole of the issued ordinary share capital of the company, which is made on a condition such that if it is satisfied the person making the offer will have control of the company;
(b) obtains control of such a company as a result of making a general offer to acquire all the shares in the company which are of the same class as the scheme shares;
(c) obtains control of such a company in pursuance of a compromise or arrangement sanctioned by the court under the Companies Act 1985, s 425 or the Companies (Northern Ireland) Order 1986, Art 418; or
(d) becomes bound or entitled to acquire shares in such a company under the Companies Act 1985, ss 428 to 430 or the Companies (Northern Ireland) Order 1986, Arts 421 to 423,

any participant in the scheme may at any time within the 'appropriate period' set out in 6.73 below, by agreement with the acquiring company, release his options under the old scheme in consideration of the grant to him of new options relating to shares in a different company (whether the acquiring company itself, or a related company within 6.46). The new options must be 'equivalent' to the old options, as explained in 6.74.

6.72 Prior to consolidation into ICTA 1988, the legislation referred to in para (a) of 6.71 above (then FA 1984, Sch 10, para 4A(1)) referred to the 'issued share capital' of the company, rather than to the 'issued *ordinary* share capital'. The change results from combining the otherwise identical rules for exchange of options in savings-related share option schemes with those for selective schemes, in one paragraph of ICTA 1988, Sch 9, which applies to both types of scheme. The difference in the original legislation of FA 1987, Sch 4 which introduced these provisions arose from the fact that the circumstances set out in (paras (a) and (b) of 6.71 were already referred to in the legislation governing savings-related schemes, in the context of early exercise of options, and the new provisions governing exchange of options were expressed by cross reference to those existing provisions (see 5.41 and 5.52).

6.73 The 'appropriate period' within which the release of the old options must take place is (ICTA 1988, Sch 9, para 15(2)):

(a) in the case of a general offer within para (a) or (b) of 6.71, the six months beginning with the time when the person making the offer has obtained control of the company and any condition subject to which the offer is made is satisfied;
(b) in the case of a compromise or arrangement within para (c) of 6.71, the period of six months beginning with the time when the court sanctions the compromise or arrangement; and
(c) in the case of an acquisition of dissenting shareholders' interests within para (d) of 6.71, the period during which the acquiring company remains bound or entitled to acquire shares under those provisions.

6.74 New options are 'equivalent' to old options, as required in 6.71 above, if (ICTA 1988, Sch 9, para 15(3)):

(a) they satisfy the conditions for scheme shares set out in 6.46 to 6.56;
(b) they are exercisable in the same manner as the old options, and subject to the provisions of the old scheme as it had effect immediately before the release of the old options;
(c) the total market value, immediately before the release, of the shares which were subject to the participant's old options is equal to the total market value, immediately after the grant of participant's new options, of the shares to which those new options relate; and
(d) the total amount payable by the participant for the acquisition of shares on the exercise of the new options is equal to the total amount that would have been payable on the exercise of the old options.

6.75 Where replacement options are granted under provisions included in a scheme as set out at 6.70 to 6.74, they are treated for the purpose of the selective share option legislation (including any subsequent application of the replacement options provisions) as having been granted at the time when the old options were granted (ICTA 1988, Sch 9, para 15(4)). As the new options are granted under the terms of the scheme, the normal tax exemptions are available, as set out at 6.3 to 6.11. As they are treated as granted at the time when the old options were granted (or the time when those options are treated as having been granted, under a previous application of these provisions), their exercise under the terms of the scheme within the following three years will not give rise to a charge as set out at 6.14, unless this takes place within three years of the original grant or of a previous exercise under the scheme. If such a charge does arise, the rollover provisions of ICTA 1988, s 136(1) (see 3.31) will apply to include in the computation the consideration given for the original options, rather than the consideration given for the new options in the form of the release of the old options. The same provisions will in any case prevent an immediate charge under ICTA 1988, s 135 on the release of the old options.

6.76 Where options are released, and granted, under these provisions, the transaction is not treated for capital gains tax purposes as involving any disposal or acquisition of either asset; the new option is treated as the same asset as the old option, acquired as that old option was acquired (CGTA 1979, s 144A(4)).

6.77 Where a scheme approved before 1 August 1987 is altered before 1 August 1989 so as to include provision for replacement options on a takeover, as described at 6.70 to 6.76, the scheme, as altered, may (but need not) apply that provision to options obtained under the scheme before the date which the alteration takes effect (ICTA 1988, Sch 9, para 15(5), introduced as FA 1987, Sch 4, para 3(1)). Where the alteration to the scheme takes place on or after 1 August 1989, it can only apply to options granted after the date of the change.

6.78 Where a scheme is amended to include a replacement option provision with effect for options granted before the date of the change, under 6.77 above, and, on or after 17 March 1987 but before the date on which the alteration takes effect, an event (such as a general offer: see 6.71 above) has occurred as a result of which an individual holding options would be able to take advantage of that replacement provision, the scheme may (but need not) permit an individual who held options immediately before that event to take advantage of the replacement provision (ICTA 1988, Sch 9, para 15(6)(a), introduced as FA 1987, Sch 4, para 3(2)(a)). In a case where those options would otherwise have ceased to be exerciseable, as a result of the event, the scheme may (but need not) provide that the replacement provisions are to apply as if those options were still exerciseable (ICTA 1988, Sch 9, para 15(6)(b), introduced as FA 1987, Sch 4, para 3(2)(b)).

6.79 The application of a replacement provision to existing or recently lapsed options under 6.77 or 6.78 is not itself regarded as the acquisition of additional option rights for the purposes of the selective share option scheme legislation, even though there is a gratuitous element which is not present on a straightforward application of the provisions where the right to the new options is already implicit in the terms of the old options (ICTA 1988, Sch 9, para 15(7), introduced as FA 1987, Sch 4, para 3(3)).

6.80 Both the inclusion of a replacement option provision in an existing scheme, and its 'backdating' as set out in 6.77 or 6.78 are subject to the normal rules regarding Inland Revenue approval for the alteration of a scheme, as discussed at 6.24 (ICTA 1988, Sch 9, para 4, and para 15(8), introduced as FA 1987, Sch 4, para 3(5)).

6.81 As originally enacted, the legislation governing takeovers discussed in 6.70 to 6.80 referred to an 'exchange' of options for options over shares in another company, rather than to their release in consideration of the grant of such new options, and technically, therefore, this was the position between 15 May 1987 and 23 July 1987, when the new wording was inserted by F(No 2)A 1987, s 59. That section also removed (with effect from the enactment of the original legislation on 15 May 1987, rather than from Royal Assent to the F(No 2)A 1987 on 23 July 1987) a provision included in FA 1987, Sch 4, para 2(2) that the general prohibition on the transfer of options (see 6.60) should contain an exclusion for transfers under the takeover provisions, as originally enacted. The retrospective removal of this exclusion effectively delayed the implementation of the takeover 'exchange' provisions until they could take effect in their new form (unless such an exclusion could be implied from the existence of provisions specifically referring to certain transfers as permissible). The purpose of the change in the legislation was to avoid capital gains and administrative complexities which could arise where the acquiring company was left holding options in its new subsidiary.

7 Definitions and general information

APPEALS

7.1 An appeal against an assessment to tax, and against certain other decisions of the Board of Inland Revenue, may be made to the General or Special Commissioners (TMA 1970, s 31). The former are lay persons, akin to magistrates, appointed by the Lord Chancellor in England and Wales, and in Scotland by the Secretary of State (TMA 1970, s 2(2) and (3)). The latter are experts in taxation appointed by the Lord Chancellor, in consultation with the Lord Advocate, from barristers, advocates, or solicitors of not less than ten years' standing (TMA 1970, s 4). Certain matters can only be dealt with by the Special Commissioners (TMA 1970, s 31(3)) but the taxpayer may in any case elect for a hearing before that body (TMA 1970, ss 31(4) and 46(1)). The General Commissioners, on application by the Inland Revenue, may direct that such an election be disregarded where the appellant has not satisfied them that he has arguments or evidence to present in pursuit of his appeal (TMA 1970, ss 5A to 5E). The General Commissioners also have power to refer complex cases to the Special Commissioners (TMA 1970, s 44(3A)).

7.2 In Northern Ireland there are no General Commissioners, and all appeals are heard by the Special Commissioners (TMA 1970, s 58(1)) except where, for a matter which may be dealt with by the General Commissioners in Great Britain, the taxpayer elects for a hearing before the County Court (TMA 1970, s 59). With effect from a date yet to be appointed by statutory instrument, these special arrangements will cease to apply to Northern Ireland, and General Commissioners will be appointed, as in the remainder of the United Kingdom (FA 1988, ss 134 and 135).

7.3 The taxpayer or the Inland Revenue may require the Commissioners (or County Court) to state a case for the opinion of the High Court (in England and Wales) (TMA 1970, s 56(1) to (7)), the Court of Session (in Scotland) (TMA 1970, s 56(10)), or the Court of Appeal (in Northern Ireland) (TMA 1970, ss 56(11) and 58(2)), who may consider any question of law involved. While the Commissioners or the County Court are the final arbiters on points of fact, the question as to whether the evidence is such as to justify their findings of fact is a point of law, so that in practice they may be overruled by the courts on matters of fact if their determination is one such as no reasonable body of Commissioners could possibly have reached on the evidence. However, the courts will not disturb a determination of the Commissioners if it was one which they could reasonably make, notwithstanding that the court itself, or another body of Commissioners, might reasonably have reached a different conclusion on the same evidence (*Edwards v Bairstow & Harrison* [1956] AC 14, 36 TC 207).

7.4 An appeal may be made from the High Court in England and Wales to the Court of Appeal, and thence to the House of Lords, subject in the latter case to the grant of leave to appeal, either by the Court of Appeal or by the House of Lords itself (TMA 1970, s 56(8)). From the Court of Session or the Court of Appeal in Northern Ireland, there is an automatic right of appeal to the House of Lords (TMA 1970, ss 56(10) and 58(2)). In England and Wales, an appeal may pass direct from the High Court to the House of Lords under the 'leapfrog' procedure laid down in Pt II of the Administration of Justice Act 1969, if the High Court certifies under s 12 of that Act that a point of law of general public importance is at issue, and the House of Lords grants leave under s 13 (TMA 1970, s 56(8)(b)). In practice, however, this procedure is used only rarely in tax cases. Appeals may also be made directly from the Special Commissioners to the Court of Appeal, if the parties and a single judge of the Court of Appeal consent, and the Commissioners certify that the case involves a point of statutory construction which has been fully argued before them and considered by them (TMA 1970, s 56A; The Revenue Appeals Order 1987, SI 1987/1422).

7.5 As to the alternative means of seeking redress through the courts by way of judicial review, see 7.51.

ASSOCIATE

7.6 The term 'associate', as defined initially for the purposes of the legislation in ICTA 1988, Pt XI dealing with 'close companies' (see 7.12 to 7.21) and adopted for use in many other contexts, covers:

(a) an individual's relative; that is, husband or wife, parent or remoter forebear, child or remoter issue, brother or sister (ICTA 1988, s 417(3)(a) and (4));
(b) a business partner (ICTA 1988, s 417(3)(a));
(c) the trustee or trustees of any settlement of which the individual is, or any relative of his as defined in (a) above, (whether living or dead) is or was a settlor (ICTA 1988, s 417(3)(b)). 'Settlement' includes any disposition, trust, covenant, agreement or arrangement which involves an element of 'bounty' (*Bulmer v IRC* [1967] Ch 145, 44 TC 1; *IRC v Plummer* [1980] AC 896, [1979] STC 793; *IRC v Levy* [1982] STC 442, 126 Sol Jo 413), and 'settlor', in relation to a settlement, means any person by whom the settlement was made, whether directly or indirectly, and, in particular, any person who has provided or undertaken to provide funds, directly or indirectly, for the purpose of the settlement, or has made a reciprocal arrangement with any other person for that other person to make or enter into the settlement (ICTA 1988, ss 417(3)(b) and 681(4)); and
(d) where the individual has an interest in any shares or other obligations of the close company in question which are subject to any trust, or are part of the estate of a deceased person, the trustee or trustees of the settlement concerned or, as the case may be, the personal representatives of the deceased (ICTA 1988, s 417(3)(c)(i)). Prior to 6 April 1986 (or, so far as the definition is relevant to determining eligibility for interest relief on a loan taken out to finance an investment in a close company, under ICTA 1988, ss 353 and 360, for loans made before 14 November 1986) any other person with an interest in the settlement or estate was within the definition of an

associate (but the trustees or personal representatives were not), with the proviso that this did not extend to interests in the trusts of occupational pension schemes approved by the Inland Revenue under what is now ICTA 1988, ss 590 and 591 or to a case where the trust in question was exclusively for the benefit of employees, or employees and directors, of the company or of their dependants (and not wholly or mainly for the benefit of directors and their relatives, as defined in (a) above), and the individual was not (and could not as a result of the operation of the trust become), either on his own or with his relatives, the beneficial owner of more than 5% of the ordinary share capital of the company (ICTA 1970, s 303(3)). The expression 'either on his own or with his relatives' included the situation where the individual himself had no holding or could obtain no holding, but his relatives were, or could become, beneficial owners of over 5% of the share capital (ICTA 1970, s 303(6), now ICTA 1988, s 417(6)). In determining whether the trust was exclusively for the benefit of employees etc, any charitable trust which might arise on the failure or determination of other trusts was disregarded (ICTA 1970, s 303(3), proviso). In a press release of June 1968, the CCAB indicated that the Inland Revenue had confirmed that, in its view, holders of units in a unit trust were not 'associates' merely by reason of their common membership of the trust. The change to ICTA 1970, s 303(3) from 6 April 1986 (or for loans made on or after 14 November 1986) was effected by FA 1987, s 37, and the consequential change to s 303(6) by FA 1987, Sch 16, Pt V. See also 7.103.

7.7 For the purposes of determining whether an individual has a 'material interest' (see 7.65 to 7.71) in a close company (see 7.12 to 7.21), disqualifying him from participation in an Inland Revenue approved 'profit-sharing' scheme, savings-related share option scheme, or selective share option scheme (but not for any other purpose) where:

(a) an individual was one of the objects of a discretionary trust, and
(b) the property subject to the trust at any time consisted of or included any shares or obligations of the close company in question,

if neither the individual nor any associate of his (excluding any person who is an associate only by virtue of para (d) in 7.6: ICTA 1988, Sch 9, para 37(4)) had received any benefit under the trust before 14 November 1986, then, as regards any time before that date, the trustees of the settlement are not regarded, by reason only of the matters referred to in (a) and (b) above, as having been associates of the individual concerned (ICTA 1988, Sch 9, para 37(1) and (2)).

7.8 If, on or after 14 November 1986,

(a) an individual ceases to be eligible to benefit under a discretionary trust which has at any time held shares or obligations in the close company in question, by reason of an irrevocable disclaimer or release executed by him under seal (except in Scotland, where there is no requirement for the document to be under seal: ICTA 1988, Sch 9, para 37(5)), or by reason of the irrevocable exercise by the trustees of a power to exclude him from the objects of the trust;
(b) immediately after he so ceases, no associate of his (again, excluding any person who is an associate only by virtue of para (d) in 7.6: ICTA 1988, Sch 9, para 37(4)) is interested in the shares or obligations of the company which are subject to the trust; and

(c) during the period of twelve months ending with the date on which he so ceases, neither he nor any associate (again, excluding para (d) of 7.6: ICTA 1988, Sch 9, para 37(4)) received any benefit under the trust,

he is not regarded, by reason only of the matters referred to in (a) and (b) of 7.7 above, as having been interested in the shares or obligations of the company within para (d) of 7.6 at any time during that twelve month period (ICTA 1988, Sch 9, para 37(3)).

7.9 The provisions set out in 7.7 and 7.8 were introduced by FA 1987, Sch 4, para 6. See also 7.102.

ASSOCIATED COMPANY

7.10 The term 'associated company' is defined by ICTA 1988, s 416(1), which lays down that two companies are associated at any given time if, at that time or at any time within one year previously, one of the two has control of the other, or both are under the control of the same person or persons. For this purpose 'control' is not defined according to the general criteria of ICTA 1988, s 840, as discussed at 7.23 and 7.24, but according to the rules of ICTA 1988, s 416(2) to (6), the primary application of which is to the close company legislation of ICTA 1988, Pt XI (see 7.25 to 7.30).

AUTHORISED UNIT TRUST

7.11 An 'authorised unit trust' is a unit trust scheme in the case of which an authorising order under the Financial Services Act 1986, s 78 is in force for all or part of the trust's current accounting period (ICTA 1988, ss 468(6) and 832(1)).

CLOSE COMPANY

7.12 A 'close company' is one which is under the control (see 7.25 to 7.30: ICTA 1988, s 416) of five or fewer participators (see 7.73 and 7.74), or of any number of participators who are directors (see 7.38 to 7.40) (ICTA 1988, s 414(1)), with the following exceptions:

(a) a company not resident in the UK (ICTA 1988, s 416(1)(a));
(b) an industrial and provident society registered or deemed to be registered under the Industrial and Provident Societies Act 1965 or the Industrial and Provident Societies Act (Northern Ireland) 1969 (ICTA 1988, ss 416(1)(b) and 486(12));
(c) a building society within the meaning of the Building Societies Act 1986 (ICTA 1988, ss 414(1)(b) and 832(1));
(d) a company controlled by or on behalf of the Crown (and independently of any other person) and which is not otherwise a close company under the control of persons acting independently of the Crown (ICTA 1988, s 414(1)(c) and (4)). A company controlled by the Crown (within the definition of 'control' in ICTA 1988, s 416: see 7.25 to 7.30) may nevertheless be controlled by its directors or by five or fewer other

participators so as to make it a close company, as control by one party does not necessarily exclude control by another (as explained at 7.27 and 7.28).

(e) a company controlled (within the definition of 'control' in ICTA 1988, s 416: see 7.25 to 7.30) by a company which is not a close company (and which would not be close if resident in the UK: see (a) above), or by two or more companies none of which is a close company (nor would be if resident in the UK), and which cannot be treated as close except by taking as one of the required five or fewer participators, (control by which is necessary to establish close company status), a company which is not close (nor would be if UK resident) (ICTA 1988, s 414(1)(d), (5)(a) and (6)). Again, the second arm of this exclusion, as in (d) above, is required because of the possibility of 'dual control' discussed at 7.27 and of 'overlapping control' by groups of persons with members in common (see 7.28);

(f) a company which cannot be treated as close except by virtue of the inclusion in the definition of control under ICTA 1988, s 416 of possession of, or entitlement to acquire, the right to receive the major part of the assets of the company available for distribution among the participators in the event of its winding up or in any other circumstances (see 7.25), and which would not be close if the reference to participators in that context did not include loan creditors (see 7.52 to 7.55) who are companies other than close companies (or companies which would be close if resident in the UK) (ICTA 1988, s 414(1)(d), (5)(b) and (6));

(g) a quoted company in which at least 35% of the voting power is held by the public, and not more than 85% of the voting power is held by 'principal members': see further at 7.15 to 7.21 (ICTA 1988, ss 414(1)(d) and 415).

7.13 For the purposes of paras (e) and (f) in 7.12, if shares in any company ('the first company') are held on trust for an occupational pension scheme approved by the Inland Revenue under ICTA 1988, s 592, then the persons holding the shares are deemed to be the beneficial owners and, in that capacity, to be a non-close company, unless it is established wholly or mainly for the benefit of persons who are, or are dependants of, directors or employees or past directors or employees of (ICTA 1988, s 414(7)):

(a) the first company;
(b) an associated company (see 7.10) of the first company;
(c) a company which is under the control (ICTA 1988, s 416: see 7.25 to 7.30) of any director or associate (see 7.38 to 7.40 and 7.6) of a director of the first company or of two or more persons each of whom is such a director or associate; or
(d) a close company.

7.14 Subject to the 'public control' test at para (g) of 7.12 (and dealt with in more detail at 7.15 to 7.21), a company resident within the UK, but not within para (b) or (c) of 7.12 is also close if, on the assumption that it were so (or that it and any other such companies were so), more than half of any investment income of the company which fell to be apportioned to participants under the rules contained in ICTA 1988, s 423 (including any amount of income apportioned to the company, or which could be apportioned to it on those assumptions) could be apportioned among five or fewer participators, or among participators who were directors (ICTA 1988, s 414(2)). In applying this test in any case where there is an original apportionment and a sub-apportionment, account is taken only of the persons to whom income is finally apportioned as a result of the whole process, but the test of apportionment to five or fewer participators or to participators who are directors is made by reference to participators in, or directors of, any company to which an original or a sub-apportionment could be made, not simply participators in, or directors of, the company subject to the final apportionment (ICTA 1988, s 414(3)). These provisions cover the case where entitlement to income is not in proportion to shareholdings, but the definition of control by reference to entitlement to the greater part of income (ICTA 1988, s 416(2)(b): see 7.25) does not apply due to indirect holdings through other companies.

7.15 A company falls within the exception for quoted companies with a substantial public holding in para (g) of 7.12 if:

(a) shares (or stock: ICTA 1988, s 415(8)) carrying 35% or more of the voting power (and not entitled to a fixed rate of dividend, with or without a further right to participate in profits) have been allotted unconditionally to, or acquired unconditionally by, the public and at the time the company's status falls to be determined continue to be beneficially held by the public: see 7.16 to 7.19 (ICTA 1988, s 415(1)(a)); and
(b) such shares have within the preceding 12 months been the subject of dealings on a recognised stock exchange (see 7.83 to 7.86: ICTA 1988, s 841) and the shares have within those 12 months been quoted in the official list of the same or another recognised stock exchange (ICTA 1988, s 415(1)(b)).

7.16 For the purpose of para (a) in 7.15, shares are beneficially held by the public if:

(a) they do not form part of the holding of a 'principal member': see 7.21 (ICTA 1988, s 415(4)(c)); or
(b) they are held by a non-close UK-resident company, or a non-resident company which would not be close if it were UK-resident (see para (a) in 7.12). Such shares are held by the public even if the company in question is a principal member (ICTA 1988, s 415(4)(a)); or
(c) they are held by an occupational pension scheme approved by the Inland Revenue under ICTA 1988, s 592 (even if that scheme is a principal member) (ICTA 1988, s 415(4)(b)).

7.17 Shares are not held by the public if held:

(a) by any director (see 7.38 to 7.40) or associate (see 7.6) of a director of the company (ICTA 1988, s 415(5)(a)); or
(b) by any company which is under the control (ICTA 1988, s 416: see 7.25 to 7.30) of any such director or associate as mentioned in (a) above, or of two or more persons each of whom is such a director or associate (ICTA 1988, s 415(5)(b)); or
(c) by any associated company of the company: see 7.10 (ICTA 1988, s 415(5)(c)); or
(d) as part of any fund the capital or income of which is applicable or applied wholly or mainly for the benefit of, or of the dependants of, the employees or directors, or past employees or directors, of the company or of any company within (b) or (c) above (ICTA 1988, s 415(5)(d)).

7.18 For the purposes of (a) to (d) in 7.17, references to shares held by any person include shares the rights or powers attached to which are possessed by another person on his behalf or which another person may be required to exercise on his direction or behalf (ICTA 1988, ss 415(5) and 416(5)).

7.19 The criteria set out in 7.16 to 7.18 to determine whether shares are beneficially held by the public apply mutatis mutandis to determine whether they have been allotted unconditionally to, or acquired unconditionally by, the public, in accordance with the requirements set out at 7.15 (ICTA 1988, s 415(3)).

7.20 Despite 35% or more of the voting power being held by the public and the company being quoted, as set out at 7.15, a company is not prevented from being close if the total percentage of voting power possessed by all its 'principal members' (see 7.21) exceeds 85% (ICTA 1988, s 415(2)).

7.21 A person is a 'principal member' of a company if he possess more than 5% of the voting power and, if there are more than five such persons, if he is one of the five who possess the greatest percentages. If, because two or more persons have equal voting power, there are no such five persons, then a person is a principal member if he is one of the six or more persons (including those two or more with equal voting power), who possess the greatest percentages (ICTA 1988, s 415(6)). In calculating the voting power possessed by any person for this purpose, there is attributed to him any such power held by nominees on his behalf (ICTA 1988, ss 415(7) and 416(5)), and any such power held by controlled companies and associates which would be attributed to him for the purpose of establishing control under ICTA 1988, s 416(6) (see 7.30). The attribution of the powers of such companies and associates which is discretionary for the purposes of s 416 (see 7.30) is, however, compulsory in the present context (ICTA 1988, ss 415(7) and 416(6)).

CONNECTED PERSON

7.22 Under ICTA 1988, s 839, an individual is connected with:

(a) his or her spouse (ICTA 1988, s 839(2));
(b) a relative (ie brother, sister, ancestor or lineal descendant: ICTA 1988, s 839(2) and (8));
(c) the spouse of a relative (ICTA 1988, s 839(2));
(d) the spouse of a relative of the individual's husband or wife (ICTA 1988, s 839(2));
(e) the trustee of a settlement (in his capacity as such), where the individual is the settlor, or is connected (within the terms of the section) with the settlor (ICTA 1988, s 839(3)). As to the definition of 'settlement' and 'settlor', see para (c) in the definition of 'associate' at 7.6 (ICTA 1988, s 681(4));
(f) a business partner, or the spouse or relative of such a partner (except in relation to acquisitions or disposals of partnership assets pursuant to bona fide commercial arrangements (ICTA 1988, s 839(4));
(g) a company of which he has control (within the definition in ICTA 1988, s 416: see 7.25 to 7.30) or a company of which he has such control together with other persons who are connected with him within the terms of s 839 (ICTA 1988, s 839(6) and (8));

(h) any other person or persons (not necessarily individuals) with whom he is acting together to secure or exercise control of a company (within ICTA 1988, s 416: see 7.25 to 7.30) and any person acting on the directions of any of them to secure or exercise control of the company. Persons are only connected under this provision in relation to the company over which the control is being exercised (ICTA 1988, s 839(7)).

CONTROL (ICTA 1988, s 840)

7.23 The Taxes Acts contain two definitions of control: a general definition to be found in ICTA 1988, s 840, and a more detailed definition in ICTA 1988, s 416 (see 7.25 to 7.30), the primary application of which is to the close company legislation of ICTA 1988, Pt XI. Under the general definition of s 840, 'control' of a company means the power of a person to secure:

(a) by means of the holding of shares or the possession of voting power in or in relation to that or any other company (ICTA 1988, s 840(a)); or
(b) by virtue of any powers conferred by the articles of association or other document regulating that or any other company (ICTA 1988, s 840(b)),

that the affairs of the company in question are conducted in accordance with his wishes. For the position on a mortgage of shares, see SP 5/80.

7.24 Thus, for example, if Bennet Ltd owns 60% of the issued ordinary share capital of Long Ltd, and Long Ltd owns 60% of the issued ordinary share capital of Morris Ltd then, assuming there are no special voting rights or other exceptional circumstances, Bennet Ltd will have control of Morris Ltd for the purposes of s 840, as it can direct Long Ltd how to exercise its majority vote in the affairs of that company. This is so notwithstanding Bennet Ltd's indirect beneficial interest in Morris Ltd is only 30% (ie 60% × 60%) and thus Morris Ltd would not be a 51% subsidiary of Bennet Ltd within ICTA 1988, s 838.

CONTROL (ICTA 1988, s 416)

7.25 The Taxes Acts contain two definitions of control: a general definition to be found in ICTA 1988, s 840, which is discussed at 7.23 and 7.24, and a more detailed definition in ICTA 1988, s 416, the primary application of which is to the close company legislation of ICTA 1988, Pt XI. (As to close companies, see 7.12 to 7.21.) Under this specialised definition, a person (including a company) has control of a company if he exercises, or is able to exercise, or is entitled to acquire control, whether direct or indirect, over the company's affairs, and in particular (but not exclusively) if he possesses or is entitled to acquire (ICTA 1988, s 416(2)):

(a) the majority of the authorised share capital, issued share capital, or voting power in the company; or
(b) such part of the issued share capital of the company as would, if the whole of the income of the company were distributed among the participators, (without regard to the rights of loan creditors: see 7.52 to 7.55) entitle him to receive the greater part of the amount so distributed. (This provision

takes account of a capital structure where different classes of shares have varying rights to income); or

(c) such rights as would, in the event of a winding up of the company, or in any other circumstances, entitle him to receive the greater part of the assets then available for distribution among the participators.

7.26 The general criterion of exercising, or being able to exercise or entitled to acquire, control may be satisfied without reference to the particular cases detailed in paras (a) to (c) of 7.25 if, for example, the company's articles of association, or an independent agreement between the shareholders, give an individual or company an ultimate veto over the decisions of the company in question; or if such power is reserved to another body or official by Act of Parliament; or if, while having in theory no voice in the company's affairs, an individual or body can in fact control the actions of the company by reason of influence deriving from personal relationships, or from economic power, such as that of a major creditor, or of a supplier or customer who accounts for the bulk of the company's purchase or sales.

7.27 It should be noted that where there is a substantial number of non-voting shares, possession of a majority of the equity as in para (a) of 7.25 may not give a majority of votes, and the holder may not, as a matter of fact, be able to control the company any more than the person entitled to the major part of the income or assets under paras (b) or (c) of 7.25. It might be argued that the wording of the legislation in merely giving three examples 'in particular, but without prejudice to the generality of the preceding words' is not sufficient, without a clear statement of intent, to deem control to exist where it does not actually do so. Against this, of all the five sets of circumstances specified in the three paragraphs the only one which would normally confer actual control is a majority of votes, so that it would appear that the intention must be specifically to extend the definition to certain classes of 'deemed control'. In practice, matters are rarely so finely balanced that a person with 'deemed control' under para (a), (b) or (c) would not have actual control. Further, it would appear that one person can be 'deemed' to have control when another has actual control, so that for these purposes a company can be under the control of two completely unconnected parties, one, for example, with a majority of total issued share capital, and the other with a majority of voting shares.

7.28 Where two or more persons together satisfy conditions (a), (b) or (c) in 7.25, they are taken to have control of the company (ICTA 1988, s 416(3)). This may result in 'overlapping' control by groups of persons with members in common.

7.29 A person is treated as 'entitled to acquire' within 7.25 anything which either he is presently entitled to acquire at a future date, or will at a future date be entitled to acquire (ICTA 1988, s 416(4)). Any rights and powers which a person possesses as nominee on behalf of another person, or which he may be required to exercise on that person's direction or behalf, are attributed for these purposes to that other person (ICTA 1988, s 416(5)).

7.30 At the discretion of the Inland Revenue there may also be attributed to any person under ICTA 1988, s 416(6) the rights and powers of any company or companies of which he, or he and 'associates' of his as defined at 7.6, have control (within 7.25 to 7.30), and also the rights and powers of any associate or associates themselves. For the purposes of such a discretionary attribution, account may be taken of rights and powers which are attributed to a company or associate under ICTA 1988, s 416(5) because they are possessed by a nominee on behalf of (or may be required to be exercised on the direction of) that company or associate, but account may not be taken of rights and powers which can only be attributed to the company or associate by the exercise of the discretion given by s 416(6) itself. Thus associates' rights and powers may be taken into account, but not those of associates of associates. It is provided that 'such attributions shall be made under this subsection as will result in the company being treated as under the control of five or fewer participators if it can be so treated'. This may be taken as indicating that the discretionary attribution, if exercised at all, must be exercised in this way, or, alternatively, that the discretionary attribution becomes compulsory if its effect will be to treat a company as under the control of five or fewer participators. The latter appears to be the more natural reading of the legislation.

DIRECTOR (RECEIVING BENEFITS IN KIND)

7.31 The term 'director' is specifically defined for the purposes of the benefits in kind legislation of ICTA 1988, ss 153 to 168 in somewhat narrower terms than apply in the definition of a director of a close company, as set out at 7.38 to 7.40.

7.32 For this purpose, the term covers (ICTA 1988, s 168(8)):

(a) in relation to a company whose affairs are managed by a board of directors or similar body, any member of that board or similar body;
(b) in relation to a company whose affairs are managed by a single director or similar person, that director or person; and
(c) in relation to a company the affairs of which are managed by the members themselves, a member of the company.

7.33 The definition also includes any person in accordance with whose directions or instructions the directors of the company (as defined in paras (a), (b) or (c) of 7.32) are accustomed to act, unless that advice is given in a professional capacity (ICTA 1988, s 168(8) and (9)).

7.34 This definition, which is incorporated into the definition of the term 'director's or higher paid employment' for the purpose of the benefits in kind legislation (ICTA 1988, s 167: see 7.41 to 7.44) is broadly similar to that which applies for the purposes of the charge on the exercise of a share option, under ICTA 1988, s 135 (see 7.35 to 7.37), except that the latter does not include persons in accordance with whose instructions the directors are accustomed to act, but does include persons who are to be, or have been, directors.

DIRECTOR (re ICTA 1988, s 135)

7.35 The term 'director' for the purposes of the charge on the exercise of share options under ICTA 1988, s 135 means (ICTA 1988, s 136(5)(b)):

(a) in relation to a company the affairs of which are managed by a board of directors or similar body, a member of that board or similar body;
(b) in relation to a company the affairs of which are managed by a single director or similar person, that director or person; and
(c) in relation to a company the affairs of which are managed by the members themselves, a member of the company.

7.36 The definition also includes any person who is to be or has been a director. It is considered that the term 'is to be' covers only the case where the subsequent directorship is intended at the time the individual's status is considered, and does not apply to someone who simply happens to become a director at a much later date, as he could not then be granted options 'by reason of' the directorship.

7.37 This definition is broadly similar to that which applies for the purposes of the benefits in kind legislation of ICTA 1988 ss 153 to 168 (see 7.31 to 7.34), except that the latter does not include individuals who are to be, or have been directors, but does include persons in accordance with whose directions or instructions the directors of the company are accustomed to act. A wider definition of the term applies in relation to the close company legislation (see 7.38 to 7.40).

DIRECTOR (OF A CLOSE COMPANY)

7.38 A 'close company' (as defined in 7.12 to 7.21) includes, subject to certain exceptions, any company which is controlled by 'participators' (see 7.73 and 7.74) who are 'directors'. For this purpose, the term 'director' includes (ICTA 1988, s 417(5)):

(a) any person occupying the position of director by whatever name called;
(b) any person in accordance with whose directions or instructions the directors are accustomed to act; and
(c) any person who is a manager of the company or otherwise concerned in the management of its trade or business, and who is (either on his own or with one or more associates: see 7.6) the beneficial owner of 20% or more of the company's ordinary share capital (see 7.72). This category extends also to a manager or other person in a managerial capacity who, while not the beneficial owner, is able, on his own or with one or more associates, directly or through the medium of other companies or by any other indirect means to control 20% or more of the ordinary share capital of the company. For this purpose 'control' is as defined in ICTA 1988, s 416 (see 7.25 to 7.30), not as defined in ICTA 1988, s 840 (see 7.23 and 7.24).

7.39 For the purposes of para (c) in 7.38 an individual is treated as owning or controlling 20% or more of the share capital of the company with one or more associates if such associate or associates have the necessary interest, even if he does not himself own or control any share capital (ICTA 1988, s 417(6)).

7.40 Separate definitions of 'director', in somewhat narrower terms, apply for the purposes of the benefits in kind legislation of ICTA 1988, ss 153 to 168 (see 7.31 to 7.34) and the charge on the exercise of a share option under ICTA 1988, s 135 (see 7.35 to 7.37).

DIRECTOR'S OR HIGHER PAID EMPLOYMENT

7.41 'Director's or higher paid employment' for the purposes of the legislation of ICTA 1988, ss 153 to 168 relating to benefits in kind means employment as a director of a company (ICTA 1988, s 168(8): see 7.31 to 7.34) or employment with emoluments at the rate of £8,500 per year or more (ICTA 1988, s 167). 'Employment' is, in turn, defined as an office or employment the emoluments of which fall to be assessed under Schedule E (ICTA 1988, s 168(2): see 7.88 to 7.96).

7.42 For this purpose, emoluments are calculated as if they included all amounts taxable on higher paid employees under the benefits in kind legislation of ICTA 1988, ss 153 to 168, together with amounts charged, irrespective of the level of emoluments, under ICTA 1988, s 145 for living accommodation provided for the employee, and under ICTA 1988, ss 141 to 143 for cash or other vouchers. Amounts chargeable under ICTA 1988, s 146 in respect of living accommodation costing or valued at over £75,000 are not, however, included. No deduction is made for necessary expenses, or for fees and subscriptions to professional bodies or learned societies allowable for tax under ICTA 1988, ss 198, 201 or 332(3). Where a charge under other provisions (discharge of employee's liability—ICTA 1988, s 19; vouchers or credit-tokens—ICTA 1988, ss 141 to 144; or expenses payments—ICTA 1988, s 153) is not made in respect of a company car because the scale charge under ICTA 1988, s 157 applies (ICTA 1988, s 157(3)), both the scale charge *and* the other charge which it displaces are taken into account for the purposes of this calculation (ICTA 1988, s 157(2)).

7.43 Where a person is employed in two or more employments by the same company, or by companies under the control of the same individual or company (within the definition of 'control' in ICTA 1988, s 840: see 7.23 and 7.24) and either:

(a) the total of the emoluments from those employments, taken together and calculated as at 7.42, is at the rate of £8,500 per year or more; or
(b) one or more of those employments is a director's or higher paid employment;

then all the employments are treated as 'director's or higher paid' (ICTA 1988, s 167(3) and (4)).

7.44 An employment is not within the 'director's or higher paid' category, unless it is otherwise caught by 7.43, or is remunerated at a rate of £8,500 pa or more, if the individual in question has no material interest in the company (see 7.70 and 7.71) and either his employment is as a full-time working director (ie a director who is required to devote substantially the whole of his time to the service of the company in a managerial or technical capacity: ICTA 1988, s 168(10)) or the company is non profit-making (that is, it neither carries on a trade nor do its functions consist wholly or mainly in the holding of investments or other property; or, alternatively, it is established for charitable purposes only: ICTA 1988, s 167(5)).

EMPLOYEE (re ICTA 1988, s 135)

7.45 The term 'employee', for the purposes of the charge on the exercise of share options under ICTA 1988, s 135, includes any person taking part in the management of the affairs of the company who is not a director, and any person who has been or 'is to be' an employee (ICTA 1988, s 136(5)(c)). For the interpretation of the words 'is to be', see the definition of 'director' in 7.36. It should be noted that this definition is not dependent on a person's classification for the purposes of employment law, or even on whether he is taxable under Schedule E (see 7.88 to 7.96), so that in certain circumstances a consultant or 'freelance' contractor might fall within the definition, if his connection with the company were sufficiently close.

'FULL-TIME' EMPLOYEE OR DIRECTOR

7.46 The expression 'full-time' in relation to employees or directors is used but not defined in the legislation governing Inland Revenue approved 'profit-sharing' schemes, savings-related share option schemes and selective share option schemes. In the last case the term is relevant only to directors, as 'full time' employment is not the relevant test for 'qualifying employees' (see 6.31). A definition was, however, provided in the earlier approved share options rules of FA 1972, which were substantially repealed in 1974 (see 1.50), and still applies to 'old' (FA 1973) profit sharing schemes (see 2.232 to 2.241). Under this definition a 'full-time' director or employee is one 'required to devote substantially the whole of his time to service as a director or employee' (ICTA 1988, s 139(11)).

7.47 Assistance in the interpretation of the term as used for the current Inland Revenue approved schemes is also given by the definition of 'full-time *working* director', in ICTA 1988, s 168(10) (the benefits in kind legislation) as a director who is required to devote substantially the whole of his time to the service of the company in a managerial or technical capacity. The legislation granting interest relief for loans taken out to invest in employee-controlled companies, similarly, contains the provision that (ICTA 1988, s 361(8)):

> 'full-time employee' in relation to a company, means a person who works for the greater part of his time as an employee or director of the company or of a 51% subsidiary of the company.

The provisions governing interest relief for investment in a close company do not use the term 'full-time' employee or director, but refer to an individual who 'has worked for the greater part of his time in the actual management or conduct of the company or of an associated company of the company' (ICTA 1988, s 360(3)(b)). A gloss on this requirement is provided by para 45 of the Inland Revenue booklet IR 11 (1974) 'Tax treatment of interest paid' which states that an individual will normally be regarded as working for the greater part of his time in any period if he works for more than half the normal working day throughout that period apart from normal holidays. In the case where his personal working day comprises less than normal working hours, however, he will not be treated as working more than half his time for the company or companies concerned simply because he spends more than half his own short working hours on their business.

7.48 In the absence of any definition in the relevant provisions, legal certainty as to what constitutes a full-time employee or director cannot be obtained, and each case must be considered on its merits. The examples given above from other legislation, however, serve to illustrate the factors likely to be taken into consideration in any judicial determination of the question.

7.49 The Inland Revenue booklets IR 36, 'Approved profit-sharing schemes' and IR 39, 'Approved savings-related share option schemes' contain no indication as to how the Inland Revenue interprets the term 'full-time', although guidance has been provided in connection with selective share option schemes. An Inland Revenue press release of 13 July 1984 announced an amendment to the provisions relating to approved schemes as they appeared in the 1984 Finance (No 2) Bill, introducing the concept of a 'qualifying employee' (see 6.31). This referred to the change as follows:

> Eligibility of part-time employees to participate in approved schemes: The effect of the Finance Bill as published was that directors and employees were eligible to participate in approved schemes if they worked for their company for at least 25 hours a week [although this was nowhere stated in the Bill]. Eligibility will now also extend to employees (not directors) who work for at least 20 hours a week.

From an examination of the legislation alone it might perhaps have been supposed that, by analogy with qualifying employees, the satisfaction of a 20-hour test would be sufficient to meet the 'full-time' requirement for directors, but the terms of the press release make it clear that the Inland Revenue regards 20 hours as 'part time' rather than full-time employment, so that its previous (arbitrary) definition of 'full-time' as 25 hours per week or more (which was not apparent until the issue of the press release) continues to apply to directors. The introduction of different criteria for the two categories of individual is evidently intentional, although the rationale underlying it is not immediately obvious.

7.50 This Inland Revenue view of what constitutes 'full-time' employment was also indicated in a statement by the Financial Secretary to the Treasury (Mr John Moore) in the course of the Committee Stage debates on the 1984 Finance (No 2) Bill when he said:

> Inland Revenue practice is to regard employment of those contributing at least 25 hours per week as full time for tax purposes.
> HC Official Report, SCA, 22 May 1984, col 520.

This interpretation was endorsed by the Inland Revenue explanatory notes 'Approved Executive share option schemes', which add a further refinement by stating that:

> An individual will be treated as a full-time director if he normally devotes at least 25 hours per week (excluding meal breaks) to the duties of the office.

While given in the context only of the 1984 schemes (and, then, of directors rather than employees), it seems fair to assume that in practice 25 hours per week constitutes the Inland Revenue's general working definition of 'full-time', and that this will apply to both employees and directors under 'profit-sharing' and savings-related schemes.

JUDICIAL REVIEW

7.51 Where the Taxes Acts make no provision for an appeal to the Commissioners, and thence to the courts by way of case stated (see 'Appeals' at 7.1 to 7.5), an alternative remedy may be available by way of an application for 'judicial review' of an administrative decision of the Inland Revenue Department under RSC Ord 53. The remedy may take the form of one of the three 'prerogative orders': mandamus (an order by the court that a certain course of action be followed); prohibition; or certiorari (a declaration as to whether the decision under review is within the jurisdiction of the body making it). Such orders are, however, granted very sparingly: the court will not substitute its own decision for that of the Inland Revenue unless the latter has clearly acted unreasonably; nor will judicial review be granted where an alternative avenue of appeal by way of case stated is available. The foregoing represents only a very broad outline of the procedure, and reference should be made to more detailed legal works as necessary.

LOAN CREDITOR

7.52 The term 'loan creditor' is used in defining a 'participator' in a company for the purposes of ascertaining whether the company is 'close' (see 7.73 to 7.74 and 7.12 to 7.21). A loan creditor is a creditor in respect of any debt incurred by the company (ICTA 1988, s 416(7)):

(a) for any money borrowed or capital assets acquired by the company; or
(b) for any right to receive income created in favour of the company; or
(c) for consideration the value of which to the company was, at the time the debt was incurred, substantially less than the amount of the debt (including any premium thereon); or
(d) in respect of any redeemable loan capital issued by the company.

7.53 Essentially, therefore, a 'loan creditor' is any person who has made a loan, directly or effectively, to the company. In the majority of cases, this will take the form of loan capital within para (d) of 7.52, or a simple loan within para (a). The definition also covers the case where the company makes a purchase of capital assets on credit terms, and the purchase price is left outstanding (for example, in a hire purchase transaction), but does not include a creditor for trade debts, such as revenue expenses or the purchase of trading stock, irrespective of the size of the sums involved. Paragraph (b) of 7.52 covers the unusual circumstances where a debt is incurred not in return for an immediate capital receipt, but in return for a stream of income such as an annuity payable to the company, and para (c) deals with the situation where, for example, a lender indirectly shares in the profits of the company by advancing a sum for a specific project, with the expectation of receiving a much larger sum if the project is successful, and very possibly losing his money altogether if it is not.

7.54 A person carrying on a banking business is not treated as a loan creditor in respect of any loan capital issued, or debt incurred, by the company in respect of money lent to the company in the ordinary course of the banking business. That is not, however, to say that a bona fide banker cannot be a loan creditor in respect of financial transactions outside the normal course of his business (ICTA 1988, s 417(9)).

7.55 A person who is not the creditor in respect of any debt or loan capital described in 7.52 to 7.54, but who nevertheless has a beneficial interest therein, for example as a result of a trust or an equitable assignment, is, to the extent of that interest, treated as a loan creditor in respect of that debt or loan capital (ICTA 1988, s 416(8)).

MARKET VALUE

General

7.56 Market value is defined in the legislation relating to employee share schemes (other than FA 1988, ss 77 to 89: see 2.58) by reference to CGTA 1979, Pt VIII (ss 150 and 152). Essentially, the market value of a share or other asset such as an option is the price which it might reasonably be expected to fetch on a sale in the open market (CGTA 1979, s 150(1)). In estimating such a price, no reduction is made on account of any assumption that the whole of the assets in question is to be put on the market at one time, thus deflating the price (CGTA 1979, s 150(2)).

Quoted securities

7.57 Shares or securities quoted on The Stock Exchange are valued by reference to the prices listed in The Stock Exchange Daily Official List ('SEDOL') except where, as a result of special circumstances, to do so will not give a proper measure of market value (CGTA 1979, s 150(3)). Such special circumstances are most likely to arise where a controlling shareholding is to be valued, and are unlikely to be relevant in the context of employee share arrangements. The fact that directors or shareholders were in possession of information which, if it had been made public, would have affected the quoted price, is not, of itself, a special circumstance, where there is no evidence of impropriety in withholding the information (*Hinchcliffe v Crabtree* [1971] 2 All ER 104, 47 TC 419, HL). Assuming no such special circumstances, the appropriate figure is the lesser of (CGTA 1979, s 150(3)):

(a) the lower of the two prices shown in the SEDOL quotations for the shares or securities on the relevant date, plus a quarter of the difference between those figures (the 'quarter up' basis); or
(b) halfway between the highest and lowest prices at which bargains, other than bargains done at special prices, were recorded in the shares for the relevant date.

If no bargains were recorded for the relevant date, the figure obtained from the application of the 'quarter up' basis is used. In the context of employee share schemes, ABI Investment Committee guidelines (where applicable) require the middle market price (para (b) above),'or similar formula' for executive schemes, to be used where possible (see 5.67 and 6.63).

7.58 If the London trading floor is closed on the relevant date the market value is ascertained by reference to the latest previous date or earliest subsequent date on which it is open, whichever affords the lower market value (CGTA 1979, s 150(3), proviso (ii)).

7.59 These rules do not apply to shares for which The Stock Exchange provides a more active market elsewhere than on the London trading floor. In such a case the general 'open market' principle applies, so that the selling price in that more active market is substituted (CGTA 1979, s 150(3), proviso (i)).

The Unlisted Securities Market

7.60 In the case of shares quoted on the Unlisted Securities Market, the Inland Revenue's statement of practice SP 18/80, 'Securities dealt in on The Stock Exchange Unlisted Securities Market: status and valuation for tax purposes' (see Appendix 9) indicates that such shares are, in general, regarded as unquoted for tax purposes and while the prices at which dealings take place on the USM provide initial evidence of the value of the shares in question, the Inland Revenue reserves the right to consider other factors, such as those which apply in the valuation of unquoted shares in general (see below). Despite this reservation, in the normal case, where dealings on the USM take place with reasonable frequency, it may generally be assumed that, in the absence of special circumstances, the published prices will be used in establishing the value of shares for all tax purposes, including those related to employee share schemes. Although not covered by the statement of practice, similar considerations apply in respect of shares dealt in on 'over the counter' markets, prices for which are published regularly in the press.

Unit trusts

7.61 Where the market value of rights in a unit trust falls to be established, for example where the exemption from the 'growth in value' charge under ICTA 1988, s 138(1)(a) given by s 138(3)(b) and discussed at 2.242 to 2.250 does not apply, then if the buying and selling prices are published regularly by the managers, in the national newspapers or otherwise, the price taken is the lower, or buying, price (the 'bid price') so published on the relevant date, or if no price was published on that date, on the most recent preceding date (CGTA 1979, s 150(4)).

Unquoted shares

7.62 Where unquoted shares fall to be valued, it is assumed that in the open market postulated for the purposes of the general rule in CGTA 1979, s 150(1) (see 7.56) there is available to any prospective purchaser all the information which a prudent purchaser might reasonably require if he were proposing to purchase the shares from a willing vendor by private treaty and at arm's length (CGTA 1979, s 152(1) and (3)). 'Unquoted shares' for this purpose are those which, at the time their value falls to be ascertained, are not quoted on a 'recognised stock exchange' within the definition in 7.83 to 7.86 (ICTA 1988, s 841; CGTA 1979, s 152(2)). Broadly, a 'recognised stock exchange' includes the UK Stock Exchange and any stock exchange outside the UK which is for the time being designated as 'recognised' by an order made by the Board of Inland Revenue (ICTA 1988, s 841(1)).

7.63 The market value will be a matter for negotiation between the company and the Shares Valuation Division of the Capital Taxes Office. The Inland Revenue booklets on approved 'profit-sharing' schemes and savings-related share option schemes, and the Inland Revenue notes on selective share option schemes indicate the information which Shares Valuation Division will require to make a valuation. This is:

(a) copies of the company's accounts for the last three financial years ending prior to the date on which the value is required (unless these have been sent previously in another connection), and any subsequent interim statement or declaration of interim dividend for the company's current financial year;
(b) an estimate of the value placed on the shares, with a brief explanation of how it was arrived at; and
(c) details of any recent arm's length transactions in the shares (including the date on which each occurred, the number of shares sold and the price paid per share).

The Inland Revenue publications indicate that, until the scheme in question has been approved, Shares Valuation Division will normally require prior instructions from Technical Division (Employee Share Schemes) before negotiating a share value. They will also require a copy of the scheme rules, transactions under which may (though only rarely) affect the value of the shares.

Shares quoted on overseas stock exchanges

7.64 The combined effect of the provisions set out in 7.57 to 7.63 is that while there are special rules for shares quoted on the UK Stock Exchange, and special rules for unquoted shares, there are no rules which apply specifically to recognised stock exchanges outside the UK. In practice, valuation varies according to the way in which prices are published by the exchange in question, based on the general principle discussed at 7.56 that it is the selling, rather than the buying price which is relevant.

MATERIAL INTEREST IN A CLOSE COMPANY

Approved share schemes

7.65 Prior to the consolidation of the relevant legislation into ICTA 1988, the general definition of a 'material interest' in a close company was contained in ICTA 1970, s 285(6), which stated that an individual had a 'material interest' in a close company (see 7.12 to 7.21) if:

(a) he, either alone or with one or more associates (see 7.6), beneficially owned or was able, whether directly, or through the medium of other companies, or by any other indirect means, to control (within the definition of ICTA

1988, s 416, then ICTA 1970, s 302: see 7.25 to 7.30) more than 5% of the ordinary share capital of the company; or

(b) such a direct or indirect 5% shareholding was held or controlled by one or more of his associates, even though he personally had no direct or indirect shareholding whatsoever; or

(c) were an apportionment to be made, under the close company 'shortfall' provisions of FA 1972, Sch 16 (now ICTA 1988, ss 423 to 430), of an amount equal to the whole distributable income of the company, more than 5% of that amount could have been apportioned to the individual together with his associates (if any), or to any associate of his, or to any such associates taken together. In straightforward cases, where income was apportioned in accordance with shareholdings, this test would produce the same result as the combined application of (a) and (b) above, but it could also indicate a material interest in other cases where there were different classes of shares with varying voting power and rights to income, or where, for example, income was apportioned to a participator in a close company who was a loan creditor (see 7.52 to 7.55) rather than a shareholder.

7.66 This general definition no longer appears in the consolidated Act (although it would appear to be required; for example, to interpret the term 'material interest' as it appears in ICTA 1988, s 360(2), giving relief on loans taken out to invest in a close company.

7.67 The general definition is adopted, for the purposes of approved 'profit-sharing' and savings-related share option schemes, with the substitution of 25% for 5% in paras (a), (b) and (c) of 7.65; and in the case of selective share option schemes with the substitution of 10%. In the original legislation of FA 1978, FA 1980, and FA 1984 the definition of ICTA 1970, s 285(6) was imported by cross-reference, with provision to substitute the appropriate higher percentage, but in the consolidated legislation of ICTA 1988 the definition is set out in full in its modified form (see 4.144, 5.97 and 6.35). Prior to the change in the definition of 'associate' which took effect from 6 April 1986 (see para (d) of 7.6), corresponding percentages were also substituted in excluding from the definition co-beneficiaries under employee trusts, where the individual in question, with relatives, had an interest of more than 5% in company shares which were held under the trust (see 4.144, 5.97 and 6.35).

7.68 For the purpose of para (a) of 7.65 above (but only as it applies in determining whether an individual has a material interest for the purposes of an approved profit-sharing or share option scheme: FA 1987, s 33(2) and (4)) a right to acquire shares, however arising (including rights under an option scheme) is taken, with effect from 6 April 1987, to be a right to control them (ICTA 1988, Sch 9, para 38(1) and (4), introduced as FA 1987, Sch 4, para 7(1) and (4)). If rights to acquire shares are taken into account in accordance with this provison, and the circumstances are such that, if the rights were exercised, the shares acquired would be shares which were previously unissued, and which the company is contractually bound to issue in the event of the exercise of that right, then an appropriate adjustment is made: in determining before the exercise of that right whether the number of shares which an individual controls or is deemed to control exceeds a particular percentage of the ordinary share capital, that ordinary share capital is taken to be increased by the number of those previously unissued shares (ICTA 1988,

Sch 9, para 38(2) and (3), introduced as FA 1987, Sch 4, para 7(2) and (3), confirming existing published practice; IR press release, 17 March 1987). Thus, if an individual holds options under a formal share option scheme, on the exercise of which new shares will be issued, those shares will enter into both the numerator and the denominator in determining the fraction of the company's capital which he owns. If, however, the arrangements under which he has a right to acquire shares would involve the acquisition of existing shares from a third party, those shares will enter into the numerator (but not the denominator). Similarly, they will only enter into the numerator (and not the denominator) if the company has the choice as to whether to meet the exercise of the option by the issue of new shares or the purchase of shares on the market, as it is not then contractually bound to issue them. Where no consideration has been given for the option, which has been granted under seal (see 1.12), it may also perhaps be questioned whether the company is *contractually* bound to issue the shares, although it is open to doubt whether this point would be taken in practice.

7.69 In determining whether a person has a material interest in a close company for the purpose of any of the three types of Inland Revenue approved employee share scheme (and also in determining whether interest is eligible for relief under the provisions governing loans taken out to invest in a close company: ICTA 1988, s 360(4)(a)), but not for other purposes, there are disregarded (ICTA 1988, Sch 9, para 39):

(a) the interest of the trustees of an approved 'profit-sharing' (share appropriation) scheme in any shares which are held by them in accordance with the scheme, and have not yet been appropriated to an individual; and
(b) any rights (eg, rights to subscribe for other shares, or to control other shares) which are exerciseable by the trustees by virtue of that interest.

It is not clear that this takes such shares out of the denominator in determining the fraction of a company's capital held by any other person (which would make it more likely that any other person would have a material interest), as it is the trustees' interest in the shares, and not the shares themselves, which is to be ignored. It does, however, prevent the trustees being regarded as associates of any participator for this purpose (see 7.6). This provision, inserted by FA 1987, Sch 4, para 8, with effect from 15 May 1987, has effect as respects any time either before or after that date, so also applies (in relation to any matters not determined at that date) to the previous, wider, definition of associate mentioned in 7.6. In practice, the legislation was always operated in this way (IR press release, 17 March 1987).

Benefits in kind

7.70 The same general definition applies for the purpose of establishing whether an individual has a material interest in a company (whether close or not), for the purpose of the benefit in kind rules of ICTA 1988, ss 153 to 168, which exclude from the definition of 'director's or higher paid employment' a director of a non profit-making company with no material interest therein, and not remunerated at a rate of £8,500 pa or more (ICTA 1988, s 167(5): see 7.44). The definition in this context, however, was never expressed by reference to ICTA 1970, s 285(6) but contained in the benefits in kind legislation itself, in what is now ICTA 1988, s 168(11). The test in para (c) of 7.65 only applies, for this purpose, if the company in question is close, and in applying the definition of 'associate' in ICTA 1988, s 417(3) (see 7.6) the term 'relative' is as defined for the purposes of the charge on beneficial loans in ICTA 1988, s 160(6) (see 7.87). This is a wider definition than under ICTA 1988, s 417(4) (see para (a) of 7.6), including, as it does, various relations by marriage in addition to the spouse.

7.71 In addition, for the purpose of the benefits in kind legislation the relevant definition of 'control' in establishing a material interest is that of ICTA 1988, s 840 (see 7.23 and 7.24), rather than (as for a close company) that of ICTA 1988, s 416 (see 7.25 to 7.30) (ICTA 1988, s 168(12)).

ORDINARY SHARE CAPITAL

7.72 'Ordinary share capital', in relation to a company, is defined as all the issued share capital (by whatever name called), other than capital the holders of which have a right to a dividend at a fixed rate, but have no other right to share in the profits of the company (ICTA 1988, s 832(1)). Preference shares carrying a fixed dividend, but also a right to share in profits (as opposed to a simple refund of capital) on liquidation, or with a right to share in profits once they exceed a certain figure, therefore qualify as 'ordinary share capital'. It is understood that in the view of the Inland Revenue shares with no right to dividends fall within this definition.

PARTICIPATOR

7.73 The term 'participator' is used in the context of the close company legislation (see 7.12 to 7.21) to mean, in relation to a company, a person having a share or interest in the capital or income of the company, and in particular, but not exclusively (ICTA 1988, s 417(1)):

(a) a person who possesses share capital or voting rights in the company;
(b) a person who is entitled to acquire share capital or voting rights in the company;
(c) a loan creditor of the company (see 7.52 to 7.55);
(d) a person who has a right to receive or participate in distributions of the company, or to receive or participate in any amounts payable by the company (in cash or in kind) to loan creditors (see 7.52 to 7.55) by way of premium on redemption;
(e) a person entitled to acquire a right of the kind specified in (d) above; and
(f) a person who is entitled to secure that income or assets (whether present or future) of the company will be applied directly or indirectly for his benefit.

7.74 In paras (b), (e), and (f) in 7.73, references to being entitled to acquire or secure anything cover both the case where a person is presently entitled to acquire or secure it at a future date, and the case where he will be so entitled at a future date. A distribution within para (d) of 7.73 is as defined by the general rules of ICTA 1988, s 209 (principally dividends), and does not include amounts treated as distributions only by virtue of ICTA 1988, s 418 dealing with benefits to participators and associates (see 7.6).

PENALTIES

7.75 A failure to comply with various provisions of the Taxes Acts as regards the provision of information to the Inland Revenue in connection with employee share schemes renders the person concerned liable to a penalty not exceeding £50 (TMA 1970, s 98(1)(i)). The circumstances in question are set out at 7.77. Proceedings for the recovery of the penalty may be commenced before the General or Special Commissioners, or in the High Court in England and Wales or Northern Ireland or the Court of Session in Scotland (TMA 1970, s 100(3)). If the failure continues after it has been declared by the court or Commissioners before whom proceedings have been commenced, a further penalty of up to £10 per day may be imposed for so long as the information is not forthcoming (TMA 1970, s 98(1)(ii)). No penalty (not even the initial amount of up to £50) may, however, be imposed if, although the time limit originally specified by the Inland Revenue for the provision of the information is not met, the failure is remedied before penalty proceedings are commenced. The maximum penalty for providing incorrect information through negligence is £250, or, where there is fraudulent intent, £500 and, again, proceedings may be commenced before the General or Special Commissioners, the High Court or the Court of Session (TMA 1970, s 98(2)).

7.76 Where penalty proceedings are commenced before the General or Special Commissioners, an appeal from their decision may be brought before the High Court in England and Wales or Northern Ireland or the Court of Session in Scotland by either party to the proceedings, on a point of law, or by the defendant (defender, in Scotland) against the amount of any penalty awarded, and in the latter case the court may either confirm the decision or reduce or increase the sum awarded (TMA 1970, s 100(6)).

7.77 The information provisions to which the above rules as to penalties apply are:

(a) the requirement for a company which grants an option on which tax may be chargeable under ICTA 1988, s 135, or which allots or transfers any shares on the exercise of such an option, or receives written notice of the assignment of such an option, to deliver written particulars to the Inspector of Taxes within 30 days after the end of the relevant year of assessment (ICTA 1988, s 136(6): see 3.36);

(b) the requirement for a company which, before 26 October 1987, grants shares or an interest in shares to a person in pursuance of a right conferred on him or opportunity offered to him as a director or employee of that or any other company, and not in pursuance of an offer to the public, thus giving rise to the possibility of a 'growth in value' charge under ICTA 1988, s 138(1)(a) (see 2.190 to 2.286) or a 'special benefits' charge under ICTA 1988, s 138(1)(b) (see 2.287 to 2.294), to deliver written particulars of the shares and of the acquisition to the Inspector of Taxes within 30 days of the end of the relevant year of assessment, even where one of the exemptions detailed at 2.228 to 2.275 is available (ICTA 1988, s 139(5): see 2.301);

(c) the requirement to give any information requested by the Inspector of Taxes in connection with a charge under the 'notional loan' provisions of ICTA 1988, s 162 (see 2.303 to 2.339), as discussed at 2.334 to 2.337 (TMA 1970, s 15). See also FA 1974, s 24 re duties performed by a person in the

UK for thirty days or more, under an employment with a non-resident, but for the benefit of a person resident, or carrying on a trade, profession or vocation in the UK.

(d) the requirement for any person on receipt of written notice from the Board of Inland Revenue to furnish it within such time as it may direct (being at least 30 days) with such information as the Board thinks necessary for the performance of its functions in connection with approved profit-sharing schemes (see Chapter 4), and which the person has or can reasonably obtain, including, in particular, information to enable the Board to determine whether to approve a scheme or withdraw approval already given; information in relation to the administration of a scheme and any alteration in its terms; and information to determine the income tax or CGT liability of any participant in an approved profit-sharing scheme (ICTA 1988, Sch 9, para 6: see 4.153 and 4.154);

(e) the requirement for any person, on receipt of written notice, to furnish the Board of Inland Revenue within such time as it may direct (being at least 30 days) with such information as the Board thinks necessary for the performance of its functions in connection with approved savings-related share options schemes (see Chapter 5) and which the person has or can reasonably obtain, including, in particular: information to enable the Board to determine whether to approve a scheme or withdraw an existing approval; information in relation to the administration of a scheme and any alteration of its terms; and information to enable the Board to determine the liability to income tax, or CGT, of any person who has participated in a scheme (ICTA 1988, Sch 9, para 6: see 5.105 and 5.106).

(f) the requirement for any person, on receipt of written notice, to furnish the Board of Inland Revenue, within such time as it may direct, (being at least 30 days) with such information as the Board thinks necessary for the performance of its functions in relation to approved selective share option schemes (see Chapter 6), and which the person has or can reasonably obtain, including, in particular: information to enable the Board to determine whether to approve a scheme or withdraw an existing approval; information required to determine the liability to income tax or CGT of any person who has participated in a scheme; and other information as to the administration of a scheme and any alteration in its terms (ICTA 1988, Sch 9, para 6: see 6.28)

(g) The requirement for a company to give written particulars to the Inspector of Taxes within 30 days of the end of a year of assessment in which a person acquires shares or an interest in shares in the company, on or after 26 October 1987, in pursuance of a right conferred on him or an opportunity offered to him by reason of his office as a director of, or his employment by, that or any other company; and similarly to give details if a person acquires shares or an interest in shares in another company by reason of his office or employment with the first company (FA 1988, s 85(1): see 2.176).

(h) The requirement for such a company, in the case of a variation of rights or restrictions attaching to shares, which constitutes a 'chargeable event' for the purposes of FA 1988, s 78 (see 2.177); or in the case where a person receives a 'special benefit' within FA 1988, s 80(1) in respect of the shares or interest in shares (see 2.177) to give the Inspector of Taxes written particulars within 60 days of that event (FA 1988, s 85(2)).

PREFERENCE SHARES

7.78 'Preference shares' are defined in the provisions governing bonus issues following the repayment of share capital, and this definition is adopted for other purposes. It covers (ICTA 1988, s 210(4)):

(a) shares which do not carry any right to dividends other than at a fixed rate expressed as a percentage of the nominal value of the shares; and
(b) which carry rights in respect of dividends and capital which are comparable with those which are general for fixed-dividend shares quoted on The Stock Exchange.

THE *RAMSAY* PRINCIPLE

7.79 The early 1980s saw a significant change in the attitude of the House of Lords, and thus of the courts in general, to artificial tax avoidance devices. A detailed discussion of the 'new approach' and its implications is beyond the scope of the present work. In summary, however, the *Ramsay* doctrine, first enunciated in *W T Ramsay Ltd v IRC* [1982] AC 300, 54 TC 101, HL, and developed in *IRC v Burmah Oil Co Ltd* [1982] STC 30, 54 TC 200, HL, *Furniss v Dawson* [1984] AC 474, [1984] STC 153, HL and *Craven v White; IRC v Bowater Property Developments Ltd, Baylis v Gregory* [1988] 3 WLR 423, [1988] STC 476, HL is that (to quote Lord Fraser of Tullybelton in *Furniss v Dawson* at 155):

> . . . the fiscal consequences of a preordained series of transactions, intended to operate as such, are generally to be ascertained by considering the result of the series as a whole, and not by dissecting the scheme and considering each transaction separately.

7.80 The limitations of the principle were laid down by Lord Brightman, in the same case (at 166) by reference to the judgment of Lord Diplock in *Burmah*:

> . . . first, there must be a preordained series of transactions or, if one likes, one single composite transaction. This composite transaction may or may not include the achievement of a legitimate commercial (ie business) end . . . Secondly, there must be steps inserted which have no commercial (business) *purpose* [as opposed to a business *effect*, or enduring legal consequences] apart from the avoidance of a liability to tax . . . If those two ingredients exist, the inserted steps are to be disregarded for fiscal purposes. The court must then look at the end result. Precisely how the end result will be taxed will depend on the terms of the taxing statute sought to be applied.

7.81 Lord Brightman's judgment also indicated (again, at 166) that in determining whether a preordained series of transactions existed:

> . . . no distinction is to be drawn for fiscal purposes, because none exists in reality, between (i) a series of steps which are followed through by virtue of an arrangement which falls short of a binding contract, and (ii) a like series of steps which are followed through because the participants are contractually bound to take each step *seriatim*.

7.82 In *Craven v White* (heard together with the *Bowater* and *Baylis v Gregory* appeals) the House of Lords considered three cases where a step was inserted in a series of transactions with a view to minimising the tax on a sale of assets. In each case, however, there was a complete interruption of the series of transactions, or a change of purchaser, or uncertainty as to the identity of the eventual purchaser, before the series was completed. This was sufficient for the House of Lords to decide (in one case, only by a majority) that no 'composite transaction' existed. Lord Jauncey, at page 521, put forward the following as a 'tentative guide, to the approach to be adopted in such cases:

> A step in a linear transaction which has no business purpose apart from the avoidance or deferment of tax liability will be treated as forming part of a preordained series of transactions or of a composite transaction if it was taken at a time when negotiations or arrangements for the carrying through as a continuous process of a subsequent transaction which actually takes place had reached a stage when there was no real likelihood that such subsequent transaction would not take place and if thereafter such negotiations or arrangements were carried through to completion without genuine interruption.

Each case will depend very much upon its particular facts, however, and the possible application of the *Ramsay* principle is a factor to be considered whenever arrangements are entered into with the intention of avoiding liability to tax.

RECOGNISED STOCK EXCHANGE

7.83 In the Corporation Tax Acts, the term 'recognised stock exchange' means the Stock Exchange (i e 'The International Stock Exchange of the United Kingdom and the Republic of Ireland Limited'), and any stock exchange outside the UK which is designated by the Board of Inland Revenue, for the time being, as a recognised stock exchange (ICTA 1988, s 841(1)). This definition was adopted for the purposes of the approved employee share scheme legislation by FA 1986, s 23(6), with effect from 25 July 1986, but in practice it has always had effect. No corresponding provision is required in the consolidated legislation of ICTA 1988, as ICTA 1988, s 841(1) is now expressed to apply for the purposes of the Tax Acts rather than only for the purposes of the Corporation Tax Acts, as was the case with its predecessor, ICTA 1970, s 535(1).

7.84 A designatory order made by the Board may designate a stock exchange by name, or by reference to any class or description of stock exchanges, including a class or description framed by reference to any authority or approval given in a country outside the UK (ICTA 1988, s 841(2)(a)). It may contain any transitional or supplemental provisions which appear to the Board of Inland Revenue to be necessary or expedient (ICTA 1988, s 841(2)(b)) and may be varied or revoked by a subsequent order (ICTA 1988, s 841(2)(c)).

7.85 The following stock exchanges or categories of exchanges have been designated under what is now ICTA 1988, s 841:

(a) by notice in the *London Gazette*, dated 14 December 1970:
- any stock exchange in Australia which is a member of the Australian Associated Stock Exchange, being a prescribed stock exchange within the meaning of Australian law relating to stock exchanges *now revoked—see (g) below*;

- any stock exchange in Austria which is a stock exchange within the meaning of the Austrian law relating to stock exchanges;
- any stock exchange in Belgium which is a stock exchange within the meaning of the Belgian law relating to stock exchanges;
- any stock exchange prescribed for the purposes of the Canadian Income Tax Act;
- any stock exchange set up in France in accordance with the French legislation;
- any stock exchange in the Republic of Ireland which is a stock exchange within the meaning of the law of the Republic of Ireland relating to stock exchanges;
- any stock exchange in Japan which is a stock exchange within the meaning of the Japanese law relating to stock exchanges;
- any stock exchange in the Netherlands which is a stock exchange within the meaning of the Netherlands law relating to stock exchanges;
- any stock exchange in Norway which is a stock exchange within the meaning of the Norwegian law relating to stock exchanges;
- any exchange registered with the Securities and Exchange Commission of the United States as a national securities exchange;
- the Copenhagen Stock Exchange;
- the Helsinki Stock Exchange;
- the Johannesburg Stock Exchange;

(b) by notice in the *London Gazette*, dated 6 April 1971:

- any stock exchange in Hong Kong which is recognised under the Hong Kong Companies Ordinance, s 2A(1);

(c) by notice in the *London Gazette*, dated 16 August 1971:

- any stock exchange approved under the laws relating to stock exchanges in the Federal Republic of Germany;
- any stock exchange in Spain which is a stock exchange within the meaning of the Spanish law relating to stock exchanges;

(d) by notice in the *London Gazette* dated 29 February 1972:

- the Colombo Stock Exchange;
- any stock exchange in Portugal which is a stock exchange within the meaning of the Portuguese law relating to stock exchanges;
- any stock exchange in Luxembourg which is a stock exchange within the meaning of the Luxembourg law relating to stock exchanges;

(e) by notice in the *London Gazette*, dated 3 May 1972 and published on 9 May 1972:

- any stock exchange in Italy which is a stock exchange within the meaning of the Italian law relating to stock exchanges;

(f) by notice in the *London Gazette*, dated 30 June 1977:

- the Singapore Stock Exchange;
- the Zurich Stock Exchange;
- the Basle Stock Exchange;
- the Geneva Stock Exchange;

(g) by notice in the *London Gazette*, dated 22 September 1988 and published on 30 September 1988:

- the New Zealand Stock Exchange;
- the Australian Stock Exchange and any of its stock exchange subsidiaries (revoking the order re Australia in (a) above.

7.86 The stock exchanges in the Republic of Ireland, referred to in para (a) of 7.85 were incorporated into the (UK) Stock Exchange on 25 March 1973.

RELATIVE

7.87 Two definitions of 'relative' are employed in the legislation relating directly or indirectly to employee share schemes. The first is found in ICTA 1988, s 417(4) and is adopted in the definition of 'associate' (see para (a) of 7.6). The second is applicable to the beneficial loan rules of ICTA 1988, s 160 which apply to a loan made to the employee or a relative of his (ICTA 1988, s 160(1): see 2.341), and defines a relative as (ICTA 1988, s 160(6)):

(a) the individual's spouse;
(b) his parents or remoter forebear, child or remoter issue, brother or sister;
(c) his spouse's brothers or sister; or
(d) the spouse of a person falling within (b) or (c).

This latter is a wider definition than that of ICTA 1988, s 417(4), which does not include the categories shown in (c) and (d) above.

SCHEDULE E

General

7.88 Income tax is charged under Schedule E on emoluments from an office or employment under three cases (ICTA 1988, s 19(1), para 1).

Case I

General

7.89 Case I applies where the individual concerned is resident and ordinarily resident in the UK, irrespective of the residence of the employer or the place of performance of the duties (except as described at 7.91).

Foreign emoluments

7.90 Previously, the amount chargeable was reduced if the earnings were 'foreign emoluments'; that is, emoluments of a person not domiciled in the UK from an office or employment with a non-UK resident employer. The reduction was 50% for the first nine years of residence, and thereafter 25% (FA 1974, Sch 2, para 3). With effect from 6 April 1984, however, any such employee who has been resident in the UK for nine out of the previous ten years, and all those newly arrived in the UK, have been taxable on 100% of their emoluments. A measure of relief was retained, temporarily, for those who held a foreign employment in the UK at some time between 6 April 1983 and 13 March 1984 or, alternatively, took up the duties of such an employment before 1 August 1984 under an obligation incurred on or before the date of the 1984 Budget statement on 13 March 1984. Provided they continued to hold such an employment, they were taxable on only 50% of their earnings up to 5 April 1987, unless they exceeded the previous nine-year limit in the meantime. For the years of assessment 1987/88 and 1988/89, they are taxable on 75% of their earnings, and thereafter on the whole amount (FA 1984, s 30(9) to (12) and ICTA 1988, s 192(4)).

7.91 Where foreign emoluments arise in respect of duties which are performed wholly outside the UK, they are excluded from Case I (ICTA 1988, s 192(2)), and therefore fall within Case III (see 7.95). This provision was unaffected by the changes made in FA 1984 and detailed in 7.90.

The 100% deduction

7.92 A 100% deduction is made from Case I emoluments in respect of earnings relating to a period of 365 days or more spent abroad by an individual who does not thereby qualify as non-resident. Certain return trips to the UK within the period are permitted (ICTA 1988, s 193(1) and Sch 12).

The 25% deduction

7.93 Previously, a 25% deduction from overseas earnings was available (where a foreign emoluments deduction as described at 7.90 was not already claimed: FA 1977, s 31(2)) for individuals working abroad for 30 days or more (not necessarily consecutively) in a year of assessment (FA 1977, Sch 7, para 2) and for those who (whether or not they met the 30-day test) performed duties wholly outside the UK for a non-resident employer (FA 1977, Sch 7, para 3). For the year of assessment 1984/85, this deduction was reduced to 12½% and from 6 April 1985 it was abolished (FA 1984, s 30(1), (14) and (15)).

Case II

7.94 Case II of Schedule E applies to an individual who is not resident in the UK, or, if resident, is not ordinarily resident, and brings into charge to tax any emoluments in respect of duties performed in the UK, but not elsewhere (though overseas emoluments may be caught by Case III: see 7.95). The residence status of the employer is irrelevant, unless the employee is not domiciled in the UK and the employer is not resident here, in which case the 'foreign emoluments' deduction described at 7.90 in connection with Case I is available (subject to its expiry as mentioned there).

Case III

7.95 Case III of Schedule E applies to an individual resident in the UK (whether or not ordinarily resident) on emoluments not already taxable under Case I or II (ICTA 1988, s 131(2)) which are actually *received* in the UK (ie a 'remittance basis' rather than an 'earnings basis'). In practice, it can relate only to duties performed overseas, as emoluments in respect of UK duties will always be caught under Case I or II. The charge extends to emoluments which relate either to the year of assessment in which they are received, or to any earlier period in which the individual was resident in the UK, and also applies to payments received in the UK in advance in respect of a year in which the individual was UK-resident, irrespective of whether he was so resident at the time of that earlier receipt. In the last case, the charge is for the year of assessment in which the emoluments are earned, rather than that in which they are received. Foreign emoluments in respect of duties performed wholly outside the UK are also within Case III (see 7.91), but the charge does not in any circumstances extend to remittances of overseas earnings relating to a year of assessment when the individual was not UK-resident.

Summary

7.96 Broadly speaking, therefore, the Schedule E charge arises on individuals who are both resident and ordinarily resident in the UK, irrespective of where their duties are performed (subject to certain deductions); on non-ordinarily UK-resident individuals in respect of duties performed in the UK (subject to one particular deduction); and on UK residents, not otherwise within the charge, in respect of remittances of overseas earnings.

SECURITIES

7.97 'Security' is defined for the purposes of ICTA 1988, Pt VI ('Company distributions, tax credits etc') as including securities not creating or evidencing a charge on assets (such as unsecured loan stock) (ICTA 1988, s 254(1)). This definition is adopted in a number of other contexts in connection with employee share schemes.

SUMS PAID TO A SETTLOR OTHERWISE THAN AS INCOME

7.98 Capital sums paid from a settlement to a settlor are treated as his income, up to the amount of the settlement's undistributed income arising before the payment or up to the end of the tenth subsequent year of assessment thereafter (ICTA 1988, s 677). The same treatment is accorded to a capital sum paid to the settlor by a company connected with the settlement, or an associated company (see 7.10) within five years before or after the receipt by the company of an associated payment from the settlement (ICTA 1988, s 678). A company is connected with a settlement if it is a close company (see 7.12 to 7.21) (or would be but for being non-UK resident) and the participators include the trustees of the settlement, or if it is controlled by such a company, within the definition of 'control' in ICTA 1988, s 840 (see 7.23 and 7.24) (ICTA 1988, s 681(5)).

7.99 The above represents only a very brief summary of the relevant provisions, and for further details reference should be made to the legislation itself.

UNIT HOLDER

7.100 A 'unit holder' is defined as a person entitled to a share of the investments subject to the trusts of a unit trust scheme (ICTA 1988, ss 486(6) and 832(1)). As to an authorised unit trust scheme, see 7.11.

MISCELLANEOUS POINTS

General

Interest in shares

7.101 The Inland Revenue consultative document 'Review of FA 1972, s 79: unapproved employee share schemes', issued on 17 March 1987, made it clear that in the view of the Inland Revenue the term 'interest in shares' does not extend to options over shares (para 8).

Definition of 'associate'

7.102 The provisions set out in 7.8 allow an employee to extricate himself from a situation where, for example, he has as associates the trustees of a major shareholder's family trust, and that trust gives a remote interest to employees in the event of the death of all members of the family. The ability to 'shed' an interest under a discretionary trust not only for the future but for the preceding 12 months enables compliance with the requirement of ICTA 1988, Sch 9, para 8 (see 4.144, 5.97 and 6.35) that an approved profit-sharing or share option scheme may not extend to individuals who have, or have within the preceding 12 months had, a material interest in a relevant close company.

7.103 Prior to the change set out at 7.6, where an individual had as associates any fellow-beneficiaries under a trust, the effect was that their personal shareholdings, as well as any trust holdings, were aggregated with his holding in determining whether he had a material interest, and could also be taken into account in determining whether the company was a close company (see 7.26). An individual with a very remote interest in the company through a trust which included employees in addition to the settlor's family could thus have attributed to him the personal shareholding of a family member with whom he had no significant connection, and so be excluded from participation in an approved scheme.

Capital gains tax

7.104 Where there is an income tax charge on the recipient of shares issued at a discount, under ICTA 1988, s 19, (see 2.13), the base cost of the shares for CGT purposes remains the actual amount given. CGTA 1979, s 29A(1)(b) does not apply to substitute market value, as this is excluded by s 29A(2) (ie there is no corresponding disposal of the shares). By contrast, if the income tax charge arises under the specific statutory provisions of ICTA 1988, ss 135, 162(5) or 185(6), CGTA 1979, s 32A increases the base cost by the amount charged to income tax (see 3.37, 2.315, and 6.17).

Approved 'profit-sharing' schemes

Employees not wishing to participate

7.105 Para 2.9 of IR36 makes the point that if any employee who is eligible to participate in an approved profit-sharing scheme as set out at 4.93 chooses not to participate, that will not be a bar to the approval of the scheme. The same point would presumably apply to savings-related share option schemes.

Acquisition of shares by trustees

7.106 The Inland Revenue booklet IR36 makes it clear (at para 3.1) that the trustees of an approved profit-sharing scheme can acquire shares by subscription; by purchase from existing holders (including scheme participants); by gift; or under a rights or bonus issue, in respect of shares which they have acquired, but not yet appropriated to participants.

Locked-in values

7.107 The Inland Revenue booklet IR36 indicates (at para 8.6) that Inland Revenue Technical Division (Employee Share Schemes) is, where necessary, prepared to help trustees with the recalculation of locked-in values following a capital receipt or a reconstruction.

Savings-related share option schemes

SAYE contracts

7.108 Under an SAYE contract contributions are normally paid by deduction from salary. A participant who leaves his employment may continue to make payments by a different method, on arrangement with the Department for National Savings or the building society concerned.

Cessation of employment

7.109 The Inland Revenue booklet IR39 draws attention (at para 2.29) to the fact that the effect of the provisions set out in 5.38 is that a person is not treated as ceasing to hold the office or employment by virtue of which he is eligible to participate in the scheme merely by virtue of the fact that the employing company has ceased to be a participating company. For the situation where it so ceases because it leaves the group, however, see 5.46.

Selective share option schemes

Relevant emoluments

7.110 The Inland Revenue's notes on approved executive share option schemes point out that 'relevant emoluments' for a year of assessment may include bonuses in respect of that year which are not paid until the following year.

Notional loan charge

7.111 The charge under ICTA 1988, s 160 on a beneficial loan does not apply where interest paid on the loan would be deductible for tax purposes; e g on a loan taken out to defray money applied in acquiring ordinary shares in a close company meeting certain conditions (broadly, a trading company or a member of a trading group) (ICTA 1988, ss 160(4), 353 and 360). It is by no means certain, however, that a notional loan within ICTA 1988, s 162 on the purchase of shares at an undervalue can be said to have been made to an individual 'to defray money applied' in the purchase of those shares.

Appendix 1 Association of British Insurers Investment Committee: Share option and profit-sharing incentive schemes: Revised guidelines to requirements of Insurance Offices as investors

(Reproduced by kind permission of the Association of British Insurers.)

SUMMARY OF REVISION

The Association of British Insurers has reviewed the operation of the guidelines [ie, the Guidelines to Requirements of Insurance Offices as Investors] in the light of developing practice and the recent successes in persuading companies to adopt performance criteria as a condition for the exercise of options. Profit-sharing arrangements are already linked to performance and the Association has sought to devise performance criteria which will require sustained improvement in the underlying performance of a company as a condition for the exercise of all options other than options linked to a savings contract.

The guidelines now make provision for the inclusion in executive share option schemes adopted in the future of a minimum performance requirement that options should only be exercisable if during the option period there has been a real growth in the company's earnings per share. Provision is also made for the grant of options by a company over more than 5% of its ordinary share capital and in excess of four times the annual emoluments of the participant provided that such additional options shall normally be exercisable not earlier than five years from the date of grant and then only if the growth in earnings per share of the company over any five year period following the date of grant has been such as places the company in the top quartile by reference to the growth in earnings per share of the FTSE 100 companies. Arrangements which involve a participant holding options over more than four times emoluments at any one time should require performance of a specified and demanding amount in place of the minimum real growth requirement.

In all cases such arrangements are subject to the overall limit of 10% of a company's ordinary share capital for all employee share schemes in any ten year period with a maximum participation in the same period by any one individual of eight times annual emoluments.

It has been felt sensible to incorporate a provision that in future options should be granted by an independent committee of the board and preferably by a committee of non-executive directors, who will not themselves participate in the options. It will be expected that this committee will satisfy itself with regard to options exercised, that the various performance requirements have been met on a consistent basis, ie the requirements are not achieved by the inclusion of extraordinary items or creative accounting.

In circumstances where the annual remuneration of senior employees already includes a substantial element of performance-related pay, consideration should be given to the inclusion of an overall cap limiting the maximum individual participation in order to avoid an excessive amount of options being granted to any one individual. Details of options granted in any one year should in future be included as a specific item in the report and accounts with a statement of the number of employees participating in a company's scheme.

It is believed that such schemes should provide a clear community of interest between employees and the shareholders and that this is best achieved by the grant of options only over the share capital of the parent equity thus ensuring that any benefit received by the employee is available equally to the shareholders. Arrangements which involve the grant of options over the share capital of a subsidiary company will normally be opposed therefore unless in the case of an overseas susidiary the employee would be precluded by local legislation from participating or, in the case of a UK subsidiary at least 25% of its ordinary share capital is quoted on a recognised exchange and held outside the group.

The guidelines, which replace those issued by the BIA Investment Protection Committee in April 1985, are intended to ensure that where share option arrangements are proposed there will be a real incentive to produce sustained growth in a company's performance, and a community of interest between participants and shareholders. The framework of schemes which are consistent with the spirit of the guidelines should ensure that the share capital earmarked for such schemes will be available to employees as widely as possible and be adequate to meet all reasonable needs of a company in this context. Consideration will of course be given to a situation where the circumstances are not covered by the guidelines.

REVISED GUIDELINES

The guidelines to employee share option schemes have been revised to reflect evolving practice and to incorporate for the first time performance requirements as a condition of the exercise of any option (other than an option granted pursuant to a SAYE scheme which is available to all employees). The requirements set out below outline the restrictions which insurance offices regard as essential under such schemes if excessive appropriation of the equity entitlement of ordinary shareholders is to be avoided.

Insurance Offices have a duty on behalf of policyholders and others on whose behalf they invest to permit only those schemes which make available such an appropriation of the profits and share capital as is felt to be equitable having regard to the finance provided by the proprietors of the company in the past and their reasonable expectations of growth in the future. The Committee believes that the method of providing incentive arrangments in any company is a matter for its management and that the directors will take account of all the interests concerned in formulating the particular schemes proposed which, in all cases involving the issue of equity capital, should be submitted to shareholders for approval. However, as judgement of the incentive effects of particular arrangements involving the equity capital of a company is essentially a matter for its shareholders, observance of all requirements set out below will not necessarily ensure support for schemes which shareholders may feel are inappropriate on other grounds. The guidelines are intended to indicate the basic provisions necessary to give general effect to the principles outlined above in the hope that any scheme proposed which is consistent with the spirit as well as the letter of the requirements will ensure a genuine community of interest between shareholders and scheme beneficiaries. The main objectives of the guidelines are to ensure that over a period of ten years no more than 10% of the shareholders' equity is utilised for schemes of all kinds and that options which are not linked to SAYE savings contracts may be exercised only if there are accompanying and genuine long term benefits to the company. Furthermore, in order to conserve the benefits under such schemes for future participants, no more than 3% of the equity should normally be appropriated for all forms of scheme in any three year period. In order that shareholders may review the effectiveness of option arrangements, schemes should have a life of not more than ten years.

Accordingly, unless there are very exceptional circumstances, insurance offices will be recommended to oppose proposals for the adoption of any scheme which does not satisfy each of the following requirements.

Profit-sharing schemes

(1) The aggregate of the amount of the equity share capital of the proposing company

that may be issued in any calendar year by way of subscription under profit-sharing schemes may not exceed 1% of such share capital in issue on the day preceding the appropriation of profits for the purpose of the scheme as set out under Requirement (3).

(2) The aggregate of the amounts that may be appropriated out of profits in any calendar year for all profit-sharing arrangements involving the acquisition by subscription or purchase of the company's shares may not exceed 5% of that proportion of the profits of the relevant trading period before tax and excluding any exceptional items which, in the opinion of the directors, is attributable to the operation of participating employees. Whenever the amount so appropriated would subscribe at the price calculated in accordance with Requirement (4) more than the amount of share capital permitted under Requirement (1), the balance of such appropriation may be applied in the purchase of shares in the market.

(3) The appropriation of profits for profit-sharing schemes shall be made once only by the directors after announcement of the final results for the trading period in respect of which the appropriation is made and paid over to the trustees of the scheme as soon as practicable.

(4) The price at which shares are subscribed under Requirement (1) shall be the middle market price of the shares of the same class on the dealing day prior to the appropriation of profits under Requirement (3).

(5) On any occasion when part of any appropriation under Requirement (3) is applied in the purchase of shares in the market, the price at which shares are made available to participants under the scheme shall be the average per share of the cost of the shares subscribed under Requirement (4) and the cost including expenses of the shares purchased.

(6) Any monies received by the trustees for the acquisition of shares shall not be retained but shall be applied as far as practicable forthwith in the subscription or purchase of shares for immediate appropriation to the individuals eligible under the scheme.

(7) Any monies received by the trustees by way of dividends on the shares held in trust shall not be retained but shall be distributed immediately to the individual to whom the relevant shares have been appropriated.

(8) On any occasion when the voting rights attached to the shares held in trust fall to be exercised, the trustees shall obtain the instructions of the individuals to whom the relevant shares have been appropriated and exercise the voting rights accordingly.

Option schemes

(9) Except as provided in (10) and (11) below, the amount of ordinary share capital issued or issuable pursuant to all options schemes, other than schemes linked to an SAYE contract, shall be limited to 5% of the ordinary share capital at the time a participation is granted and such options should normally be exercisable only if there has been a real growth in the earnings per share of the company over a three year period following the date of grant. In appropriate circumstances up to a further 5% may be set aside for such schemes provided that any options over shares in excess of 5% of the issued ordinary capital shall be exercisable not earlier than five years from the date of grant and normally then only if the company's growth in earnings per share over a period of at least five years has been such as would place it in the top quartile of the FTSE 100 companies by reference to growth in earnings per share over the same period. The aggregate share capital issued or issuable by the company under all share option or profit sharing schemes within the preceding ten years must not exceed 10% of the ordinary share capital of the company at any time when a participation is granted.

(10) In the case of a company having a market capitalisation of £5m or less, up to 10% of the equity capital when aggregated in accordance with (9) above may be issuable under the scheme provided that the market value of such capital does not exceed £500,000 at the time of the adoption of the scheme.

(11) The market value at the relevant time of the share capital to be appropriated, by allotment or by options granted, to any one participant when aggregated with the market value at the time of appropriation of any share capital appropriated in the preceding ten years to that participant under the proposed or any other share option schemes (other than an SAYE linked option) must not exceed four times the participant's total annual emoluments from the companies within the scheme and there should be a condition that such options will normally be exercisable only if, over any three year period from the date of grant, the company has achieved as a minimum a real growth in earnings per share.

In appropriate cases options having a market value of up to a further four times a participant's annual emoluments may be granted if such additional options are exercisable not earlier than the fifth anniversary from the date of grant and normally then only if the company's growth in earnings per share over a period of at least five years following the date of grant has been such as would place it in the top quartile of the FTSE 100 companies by reference to growth in earnings per share over the same period.

In the case of schemes approved by the Inland Revenue under the Finance Act 1984 [ie, selective schemes, see Chapter 6; in the terms of ICTA 1988, s 185 and Sch 9, 'schemes which are not savings-related share option schemes'] and which do not provide option linking arrangments, options granted up to 1 October 1979 under other schemes may, for the purpose of the individual participation limit, be disregarded and options granted under other schemes after 1 October 1979 but before the adoption of the proposed scheme may be taken into account at one half of the market value of the relevant shares at the date of the grant.

(12) The price at which shares are issued to participants, or at which participants are given an option to subscribe, must not be less than the middle market price of the shares in question (or similar formula) at the time when the participation is granted which must be within a period of 42 days following the date of publication of the results of the grantor company.

(13) No option may be granted for more than ten years or exercised within three years from the date of the grant in the case of those options subject to a real growth in earnings per share requirement or within five years from the date of grant for those options subject to top quartile growth in earnings per share requirements. In the event of a take-over of the grantor company or the death or cessation of employment of the participant options may be exercised or lapse within one year or within three and one-half years from the date of grant, whichever is the later unless arrangements have been made for the option to be converted, in the event of a take-over, into options of the offeror company. No option may be granted within the two years preceding the normal retirement date of the participant either under his contract of employment or otherwise and not later than ten years from the date of the adoption of the schemes.

(14) Participation under the proposed scheme must be restricted to directors or employees who are required to devote substantially the whole of their working time to the business of the grantor company or its subsidiaries and options, which must be non-assignable, may normally be granted only over the share capital of the parent company. As a general rule any arrangement involving the grant of options over a subsidiary company will be opposed unless in the case of an overseas subsidiary where necessitated by local legislation or in appropriate circumstances where at least 25% of the share capital of a subsidiary is quoted on a recognised stock exchange and held outside the group.

Savings-related schemes

(15) The proposed scheme must provide that in the period of ten years commencing at the date of its adoption the total amount of share capital issued or issuable under any savings-related scheme when aggregated with the total amount of share capital issued or issuable under any other profit-sharing or option scheme in the preceding

ten years, whether or not approved under the Finance Acts [now ICTA 1988], shall not exceed 10% of the equity share capital of the company at the time when capital is issued or issuable under the proposed scheme. 'Issuable' share capital includes any share capital in respect of which options have been granted or rights may be exercised.

(16) Participation under the proposed scheme may be granted only within a period of ten years from the date of its adoption.

(17) The price at which participants are given an option to subscribe must not be less than the middle market price of the shares of the class under option at the time when the option is granted unless the scheme has received Inland Revenue approval under statutory provisions relating to contractual savings schemes in which event the option price must be not less than 90% of such middle market price.

(18) No part of the equity share capital may be issued or issuable to participants for subscription out of the proceeds of a contractual savings scheme except as provided under (15) above.

(19) The maximum amount that may be contracted for savings by individual participants under the scheme shall not exceed £150 per calendar month.

General

(20a) To conserve benefits for future participants all schemes must normally provide that not more than 3% of the equity capital may be appropriated for options or subscribed out of profits under all relevant schemes in any year and the two preceding years.

(20b) In the year of introduction of any scheme or schemes otherwise complying with the above requirements and linked to an SAYE contract and available to all employees generally the restriction under (20a) need not be observed provided that the percentage of equity capital appropriated for any options or subscribed out of profits under all relevant schemes in any year and the four preceding years does not exceed 5% and provided that options which are not linked to SAYE arrangements shall remain subject to the limit of 3% as under 20(a).

(21) All options (other than linked to an SAYE contract) should preferably be granted by a committee of non-executive directors of the company or at least by an independent committee of directors who will not themselves participate in the options. This committee will be expected to satisfy itself that prior to the exercise of options, relevant performance criteria have been fully satisfied on a consistent basis, ie they have not been achieved by 'creative accounting' or by the inclusion of inappropriate or extraordinary items and they are accountable to shareholders for such. In appropriate circumstances it would be expected that such a committee will impose an overall cap on the maximum participation under option arrangements by any one individual.

13 July 1987

ADDENDUM TO SHARE OPTION AND PROFIT SHARING SCHEMES GUIDELINES

Following representations by a significant number of the larger companies in the UK, all of whom expressed complete support for the guideline limit of 5% of capital for executive share option schemes, the ABI Investment Committee has agreed to consider a relaxation of guideline (11) in certain circumstances. This would have the effect of allowing the grant following exercise of existing options of replacement options in excess of the guideline limit of four times earnings without requiring satisfaction of the top quartile eps growth provision as a condition for their exercise. Consideration would be given to the amendment of existing schemes to incorporate this revised approach.

This relaxation would be subject to the following minimum conditions:

(1) The scheme must be administered by and the grant of options supervised by a remuneration committee consisting wholly or mainly of non-executive directors.

(2) In the case of an existing scheme the total of options granted within four years from the date of the amendment shall not exceed 2.5% of the issued ordinary share capital of the company with any balance within the overall 5% limit remaining available for the unexpired term of the scheme if any.

In the case of a new scheme it would be envisaged that the 2.5% could be utilised in the first four years of the scheme with the remaining 2.5% being available for the remaining six years.

(3) The remuneration committee must, prior to granting replacement options, be satisfied that there has been a significant improvement in the performance of the company over the two to three years preceding the regrant.

(4) The chairman of a company making any such amendment should emphasise that the 5% limit for the executive share option scheme over a 10 year period is entirely appropriate and adequate for such purposes. He should also address the importance placed by offices as investors on underlying performance by a positive statement that replacement options will be granted having regard to the performance of the company.

In any cases where it is desirable, the yearly basis on which the above limit is calculated may, for the purposes of the scheme, be that of the financial reporting year.

6 May 1988

The following letter from the Secretary of the Association of British Insurers Investment Committee accompanied the above addendum

I enclose a copy of an addendum to the guidelines which has been designed to assist those companies whose usage of options is modest in that no more than 5% of the company's capital will be used in any 10 year period for such purposes and where the options are granted by a remuneration committee, a majority of which comprises non-executive directors.

One of the main objects of the revised guidelines issued last year, was to incorporate in the framework of the guidelines provision for 'super options or replacement options' subject to performance requirements related to the top quartile of the FTSE 100 companies. You will note that the modification in the addendum provides that any performancing requirements shall be imposed by and monitored by the remuneration committee as a condition of regrant. In those cases where companies wish to reserve more than 5% in any 10 year period for share option arrangements or where they do not demonstrate by adopting the alternative arrangements in their entirety that 5% will be adequate for the full 10 year period, then the top quartile earnings per share test remains as set out in the revised guidelines.

It is hoped sincerely that these amendments will be seen as providing the desired flexibility for those companies whose modest usage of share capital for incentivisation is provided for under arrangements which, by limiting participation through options to 5% of the company's capital in any 10 year period enable the framework of general schemes such as SAYE or profit sharing schemes to be made available to employees generally.

11 May 1988

Appendix 2 The National Association of Pension Funds Limited, Investment Committee: Statement on share schemes

(Reproduced by kind permission of the National Association of Pension Funds Ltd.)

The approach of institutional shareholders to the issuing of shares to employees through share schemes has evolved through many years. The NAPF last pronounced on the subject in November 1984. Its statement at that time was in the form of guidelines to potential issuers setting out practices which were not acceptable in general to the membership of the NAPF.

Since 1984 there has been a significant increase in the number of schemes which the NAPF has been asked to consider because in the view of the management, either a particular definition required clarification, or special circumstances justified overriding a particular guideline.

To cope with this increase, and hopefully to move forward the debate in this general area, the NAPF has reappraised its attitude to share schemes. Central to this attitude is the following statement of the NAPF's view of the desirable objective of share schemes:

> The NAPF supports the movement to greater ownership by employees in the company within which they work. It regards this movement as long term in nature, and will support legislation designed to encourage long term ownership of the resulting shares within a fair tolerance of the inevitable dilution effect of its members' interest in those companies.

Against this objective, the use of share schemes solely to achieve tax efficient short-term remuneration is a disappointing development. The NAPF strongly supports profit-related pay, bonuses and other similar remuneration incentives, and regards these as more appropriate short term measures than the use of share schemes with quick exercise rights. Such schemes are deficient in the extent to which sudden fluctuations in share price, well beyond the ability of employees to influence, either enhance or devalue the remuneration aspect. However, this is a risk those using share schemes in this way must be prepared to accept.

With this clear objective as a base from which to proceed, the NAPF states below the principles against which it views such schemes.

(1) The NAPF wishes to encourage the use of share schemes amongst employees to achieve long term employee ownership of companies. Its members recognise that this will result in a dilution of pension funds' equity stakes, but considers that this may be acceptable where it leads to a greater coincidence of interest between shareholders, management and employees.

(2) The NAPF wishes to encourage Boards to permit the widest possible participation in such schemes to the greater overall benefit for the company and the individuals concerned.

(3) Together with the objective of achieving long term employee ownership, the NAPF wishes to encourage the incorporation of an incentive element relating to performance. Share price is, of course, at times a very imprecise measure of the success of companies, but exercise should only be possible at or above the price of the share when the option was granted. Furthermore, when managements wish to introduce share incentive arrangements which would not qualify under the Finance Act 1984 [i e Inland Revenue approved selective share option schemes] for taxation

of the individual benefits at capital gains tax rates, it would expect a highly explicit form of performance criterion to be met.

(4) The NAPF will in general support schemes which result in a 10 year period in a maximum of 10% of ordinary share capital being made available for all share schemes in aggregate, and which in any one year during a 10 year period would result in a maximum of 5% ordinary share capital being made available.

(5) The NAPF supports those companies which give a committee of non-executive Directors responsibility for monitoring and approving the operations of such schemes, and urges all those making use of such schemes to follow this practice.

(6) The NAPF has been associated with a number of initiatives to increase the flow of information available to shareholders through annual reports and accounts. Accordingly, the NAPF urges that annual reports and accounts should provide shareholders with the details of option schemes including information on the number of shares issued and issuable, prices at which options have been granted and the number of participants.

(7) The NAPF urges that in recommending share schemes to their shareholders, Boards comment on the extent to which a particular scheme will operate within these general principles and state that in their opinion:

> 'the scheme is consistent with the general principles for such schemes recommended by the NAPF'.

(8) Where Boards wish to propose a scheme which departs from these general principles, Boards should explain to shareholders the particular reasons why in their opinion shareholders should nevertheless support the scheme.

With the publication of these general principles, the NAPF hopes to encourage share schemes and give relative certainty that schemes conforming to these general principles will be supported.

The NAPF is aware that the Association of British Insurers (ABI) have detailed guidelines on this general subject, about which they consulted the NAPF constructively. That the NAPF has chosen to comment in a different manner should lead no one to see its approach as undermining the stance taken by the ABI.

The NAPF will continue to respond to its members' requests for assistance in respect of share schemes. It will not, as a normal practice, comment as an Association on individual share schemes other than in response to members' requests. The NAPF expects that its members, in carrying out their duties as trustees and shareholders, will examine all share schemes, judging them in the light of these general principles.

This letter supersedes all previous statements made by the NAPF on this subject.

March 1988

Appendix 3 Stock Exchange requirements

(Reproduced by kind permission of the Council of The International Stock Exchange of the United Kingdom and the Republic of Ireland Limited from Section 1, Ch 3, para 9 of 'Admission of Securities to Listing' (the 'Yellow Book') published in November 1984.)

EMPLOYEE SHARE SCHEMES

General

The following provisions apply, with appropriate modifications, to all schemes involving the issue of shares or other securities (including options) by domestic companies to, or for the benefit of, employees. They apply also to schemes of all subsidiaries of listed domestic companies, even if the subsidiary is incorporated and operating abroad.

The Department [ie the Quotations Department of The Stock Exchange] must be consulted on the application of these provisions to schemes intended to apply to employees of associates.

Essential characteristics of an employee share scheme

(a) The scheme, which must be approved by shareholders in general meeting, must contain provisions relating to:
  (i) the persons to whom or for the benefit of whom securities may be issued under the scheme ('participants');
  (ii) the total amount of securities subject to the scheme which must be stated together with the percentage of the issued share capital that it represents at that time;
  (iii) a fixed maximum entitlement for any one participant (if the scheme is subject to any statutory maximum entitlement, that maximum from time to time will be permitted);
  (iv) the amount, if any, payable on application or acceptance and the basis for determining the subscription or option price, the period in or after which payments or calls, or loans to provide the same, may be paid or called; and
  (v) the voting, dividend, transfer and other rights, including those arising on a liquidation of the company, attaching to the securities and to any options (if appropriate). These rights must be drawn to the attention of participants on their joining the scheme.

(b) The scheme or corresponding document, if not circulated to the shareholders, must be available for inspection for at least 14 days in the City of London or such other places as the Committee [ie The Stock Exchange Committee on Quotations] may agree.

(c) The terms of the resolution must approve a specific scheme and refer either to the scheme itself (if circulated to the shareholders) or to a summary of its principal terms included in the circular which must contain all the provisions set out in sub-para (a). Where directors of the company are trustees of the scheme or have an interest direct or indirect in the trustees, the circular must disclose that interest.

(d) (i) Unless the securities subject to the scheme are identical with other listed securities they must be separately designated.

(ii) A scheme may provide for adjustment of the subscription or option price or the number or amount of securities subject to options already granted and to the scheme, in the event of a capitalisation issue, a rights issue, sub-division, consolidation of shares or reduction of capital. Such adjustments should give a participant the same proportion of the equity capital as that to which he was previously entitled.

(iii) The issue of securities as consideration for an acquisition will not be regarded as a circumstance requiring adjustment.

(iv) Adjustments, other than those made on a capitalisation issue, must be confirmed to the directors in writing by the company's auditors to be in their opinion fair and reasonable.

(v) The scheme must provide, or the circular must state, that the provisions relating to the matters contained in (a) and (d) (ii) above cannot be altered to the advantage of participants without the prior approval of shareholders in general meeting.

Appendix 4 Model code for securities transactions by directors of listed companies

(Issued in April 1981, and reproduced by kind permission of the Council of The International Stock Exchange of the United Kingdom and the Republic of Ireland Limited from Section 5, Ch 2, para 45 of 'Admission of Securities to Listing' (the 'Yellow Book'), published in November 1984.)

The Committee [i e The Stock Exchange Committee on Quotations] regards it as highly desirable that directors of listed companies should hold securities in their own companies. Directors wishing to buy and sell such securities must first have regard to the statutory provisions in the Company Securities (Insider Dealing) Act 1985 on insider dealing. [The reference was formerly to Pt V of the Companies Act 1980.] It is regarded as axiomatic that directors of listed companies will not deal in their companies' securities when prohibited from doing so by those statutory provisions. The statutory provisions are not confined to directors of listed companies but concern themselves more widely with individuals 'connected with a company'.

The Committee believes that special considerations apply to directors of listed companies. There are occasions where, even though not expressly prohibited by the statutory provisions, it would be undesirable for a director to buy or sell his company's securities.

These occasions are:

(i) where a director is himself unaware of a price-sensitive matter under discussion (perhaps because it has not yet been made known to the Board) which is likely ultimately to call for an exceptional announcement and where for his own protection he should be told not to deal; and
(ii) the periods prior to the regular announcements of results and dividends.

The purpose of the model code remains primarily to give guidance on these two occasions so as to enable companies to establish an agreed procedure which would provide general protection against misinformed criticism both for the company and for the individual directors, given that, under the statutory provisions, a director might otherwise be free to deal. The Committee sees the model code (including the basic principles set out below) as setting a minimum standard of good practice against which companies should measure their own company codes. The model code should therefore be seen as setting guidelines rather than rigid rules to be followed in every detail.

Two further aspects should be mentioned:

(i) compliance with the model code is not a defence in law and it may therefore be necessary to be satisfied that a proposed dealing would not be in contravention of the statutory provisions. It should not, for example, be assumed that compliance with the procedure set out in basic principle 5 (to establish the time at which an intended acquisition by a company should be deemed price-sensitive information) or that dealing under the extenuating circumstances indicated in rule 3.1 (where a pressing financial commitment has to be met) would necessarily preclude contravention of the statutory provisions. Basic principle 5 and rule 3.1 are intended as guidance for the chairman (or whoever is nominated to receive notification of dealing intentions) as to circumstances where exceptions to the model code may be considered, always assuming that no breach of the statutory provisions would result; and
(ii) the statutory provisions do not specifically relate to other interests of a director, nor

to the position of spouses or infant children. In this respect the model code has broader application than the statutory provisions.

THE BASIC PRINCIPLES

(1) Directors should not deal in their companies' securities on considerations of a short-term nature.

(2) Directors will always be thought to be in possession of more information than can at any particular time be published. Accordingly they must accept that they cannot at all times feel free to deal in their companies' securities, even when the statutory provisions would not prohibit them from doing so.

(3) Notwithstanding this general constraint there must be periods in the year when directors are in principle (but subject to the statutory provisions) to be regarded as free to deal in their companies' securities. The following model rules have been formulated on the basis that:

(i) dealings should not normally take place for a minimum period prior to the announcement of regularly recurring information, particularly profits, dividends and other distributions, whether or not the information is price-sensitive (this period being defined in rule 3.1); and

(ii) dealings should not take place prior to the announcement of matters of an exceptional nature involving unpublished price-sensitive information in relation to the market price of the securities of the company (or where relevant any other listed company).

(4) For the purposes of the model code, the grant to a director of an option to subscribe or purchase his company's securities is to be regarded as a dealing by him, if the price at which such option may be exercised is fixed at the time of such grant. If, however, an option is granted to a director on terms whereby the price at which such option may be exercised is to be fixed at the time of exercise, the dealing is to be regarded as taking place at the time of exercise.

(5) Matters of an exceptional nature cause particular difficulty. A director who has knowledge of the exceptional matter in question will normally be prohibited from dealing by the statutory provisions but even if he is not so prohibited he should nevertheless not deal in the circumstances outlined below. Similarly, a director who has no such knowledge should be advised, when he notifies his intention to deal under rule 2.1 that it would be inappropriate for him to deal where the same circumstances apply. Those circumstances are where:

(i) the matter in question constitutes unpublished price-sensitive information in relation to the company's securities; and

(ii) the proposed dealing would take place after the time when the likelihood of an announcement ultimately being necessary has become a reasonable probability.

An exhaustive definition of price-sensitive information is not possible. Nevertheless it should be assumed for this purpose that the matters referred to in para 10 and paras 14–19 inclusive of Chapter 2 of this Section [of the 'Yellow Book'] are to be so regarded [ie any proposed change in capital structure, including that of the company's listed debt securities; certain major acquisitions or realisations of assets; information required to be disclosed to The Stock Exchange under the City Code on Take-overs and Mergers; in the case of a UK company any information notified to the company under statutory provisions regarding disclosure of interests in shares, and equivalent information for non-UK companies; purchases by the company or group of its listed securities; Board decisions to change the general nature of the business of the company or of the group; and changes in company status for tax purposes under the provisions regarding close companies and approved investment trusts.]

(6) In principle, a director should seek to secure that all dealings in which he is or is

deemed to be interested should be conducted in accordance with the provisions of the model code. Rule 4.1 sets this out as a general proposition. Nevertheless it is recognised that a director's duty in this respect will depend on the particular circumstances. A director who is sole trustee, for example, should follow the same procedure as for any dealings on his own account and should deal only if he would be personally allowed to deal under the code, even if he is excepted from the general prohibitions imposed by the statutory provisions by virtue of the special defences relating to trustees granted by such provisions.

Where a director has co-trustees who are not themselves directors of the company, he may not be able to ensure that the procedure applicable to his personal dealings is followed in respect of dealings on behalf of the trust. The director/trustee has to avoid acting in breach of trust and at the same time to refrain from divulging or abusing confidential information, and it may not therefore always be practicable to expect that trustees will refrain from dealing at a time when one of their number is not personally free to deal.

On the other hand if a director, whether or not himself a trustee, has, as settlor or otherwise, an important influence over the decision of the trustees, the procedure applicable to his personal dealings ought to be followed and the trustees should not deal when he personally is not free to deal. Again, the remoteness of some interests may be such as to make the imposition of any duty under rule 4.1 impracticable or inappropriate. Rules 4.2 and 4.3 indicate certain precautions which should be taken.

It is an overriding principle that under no circumstances should a director deal where prohibited from doing so by the statutory provisions or make any unauthorised disclosure of any confidential information, whether to co-trustees or any other person, or make any use of such information for the advantage of himself or others, even those to whom he owes a fiduciary duty.

(7) When a director places investment funds under professional management, even where discretion is given, the managers should nonetheless be made subject to the same restrictions and procedures as the director himself in respect of proposed dealings in the company's securities.

The following model rules should be used as guidelines for companies in formulating their own codes:

1.1 A director should not deal in any of the securities of the company at any time when he is in possession of unpublished price-sensitive information in relation to those securities.

1.2 The same restrictions should apply to dealings by a director in the securities of any other listed company when by virtue of his position as a director of his own company, he is in possession of unpublished price-sensitive information in relation to those securities.

At any other times, a director WHO IS NOT PROHIBITED FROM DOING SO BY PT V OF THE COMPANY SECURITIES (INSIDER DEALING) ACT 1985 can feel free to deal subject to the provisions of the rules which follow. [The reference was formerly to Pt V of the Companies Act 1980.]

2.1 A director should not deal in any securities of his own company without first notifying the chairman (or other director(s) appointed for the specific purpose), and receiving acknowledgement. In his own case the chairman should first notify the Board at a Board meeting, or alternatively notify the other director(s) appointed for the purpose and receive acknowledgement.

2.2 The procedure established within the company should, as a minimum, provide for there to be a written record maintained by the company that the appropriate notification was given and acknowledged, and for the director concerned to have written confirmation to that effect.

3.1 During the periods of two months immediately preceding the preliminary announcement of the company's annual results and of the announcement of the half-yearly results together with dividends and distributions to be paid or passed, a director should not purchase any securities of the company nor should he deal in securities in the circumstances set out in basic principle 5 above; nor should he sell any such securities unless the circumstances are exceptional, for example, where a pressing financial commitment has to be met. In any event he must comply with the procedure in rule 2 above.

3.2 Companies producing quarterly results should consult the Department [ie the Quotations Department of The Stock Exchange] on the formulation of modified dealing procedures appropriate to their case.

4.1 The restrictions on dealings by a director contained in this code should be regarded as equally applicable to any dealings by the director's spouse or by or on behalf of any infant child and any other dealings in which for the purposes of the Companies Act 1985 he is or is to be treated as interested. [The reference was formerly to the Companies Act 1987.] It is the duty of the director, therefore, to seek to avoid any such dealing at a time when he himself is not free to deal.

4.2 Any director of the company who acts as trustee of a trust should ensure that his co-trustees are aware of the identity of any company of which he is a director so as to enable them to anticipate possible difficulties. A director having funds under management should likewise advise the investment manager.

4.3 Any director who is a beneficiary, but not a trustee, of a trust which deals in securities of the company should endeavour to ensure that the trustees notify him after they have dealt in such securities on behalf of the trust, in order that he in turn may notify the company. For this purpose he should ensure that the trustees are aware of the companies of which he is a director.

5 A list of directors' dealings in the securities of the company since the date of the previous list should be circulated to members of the Board with the board papers; alternatively the register maintained in accordance with s 325 of the Companies Act 1985 should be made available for inspection at every meeting of the Board. [The reference was previously to CA 1967, s 29.]

6 The directors of a company should as a Board and individually endeavour to ensure that any employee of the company or director or employee of a subsidiary company who, because of his office or employment in the company or a subsidiary, is likely to be in possession of unpublished price-sensitive information in relation to the securities of any listed company, deals in those securities in accordance with this model code.

7 References in this code to 'securities' have the meanings ascribed thereto by s 12 of the Company Securities (Insider Dealing) Act 1985 [formerly CA 1980, s 73].

Appendix 5 Specimen trust deed and scheme rules for Inland Revenue approved 'profit sharing' (share appropriation) scheme

(Reproduced by kind permission of the Controller of Her Majesty's Stationery Office.)

The specimen trust deed and scheme rules set out below were issued by the Board of Inland Revenue in February 1987 as part of a supplement to the booklet IR36. Since that time only one legislative change has been made affecting approved 'profit-sharing' schemes, as set out on page 297. The supplement contained the following paragraphs:

'This supplement contains a specimen trust deed and set of rules designed to meet the requirements for approval under FA 1978, Sch 9, para 1 [now ICTA 1988, Sch 9, para 1]. They are intended to illustrate the type of framework which companies might wish to adopt and operate. There is considerable scope for variation to meet the situation of the company or group in question and further provisions may be necessary to comply with the Investment Protection Committees' guidelines [see Appendices 1 and 2]. The provisions in Rule 11 of the Schedule to the deed act as a reminder that these guidelines serve to protect existing shareholders. Rule 11 is not a requirement for approval of the scheme.

At appendix I and II to the schedule draft ancillary documents have been included to assist companies and their advisors in preparing documentation suitable to meet the provisions of the legislation. Companies will wish to consider carefully their plans for communicating, both at the outset of the scheme and subsequently, with employees generally and scheme participants in particular, and the style and tone of the ancillary documents can be tailored to needs, provided the formal legal content is retained.

Companies should consider their own particular needs carefully and be guided by their own professional advisors.'

SPECIMEN TRUST DEED AND RULES OF FINANCE ACT 1978 PROFIT SHARING SCHEME

This Trust Deed is made [date] between [company], whose registered office is at [address] of the one part (hereinafter called 'the Company'), and [names and addresses of trustees] (hereinafter called 'the Trustees' which expression shall where the context so admits include the Trustees or Trustee for the time being of the Scheme) of the other part.

Whereas:

A. The Company wishes to establish a profit sharing scheme known as [name of scheme] (hereinafter called 'the Scheme') complying with the provisions of Chapter III of Part III of the Finance Act 1978 [now ICTA 1988, ss 186 and 187, and Schs 9 and 10] and constituting an employee share scheme for the purpose of providing funds to the Trustees from time to time to enable Shares in the capital of the Company which satisfy the provisions of the Act to be acquired by the Trustees and subsequently to be appropriated by the Trustees to such directors and employees of the Participating Companies (as defined in the Rules hereinafter referred to) as shall be eligible in accordance with the Rules of the Scheme to participate herein.
B. The Scheme is established pursuant to an ordinary resolution of the Company passed on [date].

C. The Trustees have agreed to be the first Trustees of the Scheme.

Now this Deed witnesseth as follows:

1 Definitions

The definitions contained in the Rules as set out in the Schedule hereto or as amended from time to time as therein provided shall apply to this Deed.

2 Trustees' funds

Subject to the further provisions of this Deed and the Rules, the Trustees shall apply the sums of money transferred to them in the acquisition of Scheme Shares or the payment of expenses or other liabilities (as the case may be) in accordance with the Rules, and shall hold the Scheme Shares once appropriated and all other property deriving therefrom upon trust for the Participants to whom those Scheme Shares have been appropriated, and shall apply and deal with the same in accordance with the Rules.

3 Investment

The Trustees shall invest any monies from time to time held by them and not required immediately for the purchase of Scheme Shares in such short-term investments as they may think appropriate. Any income arising on any such short-term investments shall be used for the purpose of acquiring further Scheme Shares or to meet taxation or other liabilities or expenses incurred from time to time in the operation and administration of the scheme.

4 Trustees' obligations

(a) The Trustees shall appropriate the Scheme Shares held by them to Eligible Employees in accordance with the Rules.

(b) As soon as practicable after any Scheme Shares have been appropriated by the Trustees to a Participant in accordance with the Rules the Trustees shall give the Participant notice in writing of the appropriation specifying the number and description of Scheme Shares so appropriate and stating their Initial Market Value and the date on which such Scheme Shares were so appropriated.

(c) The Trustees shall not during the Period of Retention dispose of any Scheme Shares (whether by transfer to the Participant or otherwise) except as mentioned in Section 54(2)(a), (b) or (c) of the Act [now ICTA 1988, Sch 10(1)(a), (b) or (c)].

(d) The Trustees shall not after the end of the Period of Retention and before the Release Date dispose of any Scheme Shares appropriated to a Participant except pursuant to a direction given by or on behalf of the Participant or any person in whom the beneficial interest in his Scheme Shares is for the time being vested and by a transaction which would not involve a breach of the Participant's obligation under paragraphs (c) or (d) of subsection (1) of Section 54 of the Act [now ICTA 1988, Sch 9, para 2(2)(c) and (d)].

(e) The Trustees, subject to their obligations under Section 59 of the Act [now ICTA 1988, Sch 10, para 7] and to any such direction as is referred to in Section 56(3) of the Act [now ICTA 1988, Sch 10, para 4(2)], shall pay over to the Participant any money or money's worth received by them in respect of, or by reference to, any of his Scheme Shares other than money's worth consisting of new shares within the meaning of Section 57 of the Act [now ICTA 1988, Sch 10, para 5] and shall deal only pursuant to a direction given by or on behalf of the Participant or any person in whom the beneficial interest in his shares is for the time being vested with any right conferred in respect of any of his Scheme Shares to be allotted other shares securities or rights of any description.

(f) The Trustees shall maintain such records as may be necessary to enable the Trustees to carry out their obligations under Section 59 of the Act [now ICTA 1988, Sch 10, para 7] and, where the Participant becomes liable to income tax under Schedule E by reason of the occurrence of any event, shall inform him of any facts relevant to determining that liability.

(g) The Trustees shall at all times comply with their obligations to make payments to any of the Participating Companies and to make PAYE deductions contained in Section 59 of the Act [now ICTA 1988, Sch 10, para 7].

(h) The Trustees will take all reasonable steps to notify Participants of the principal terms of any offer, compromise, arrangement or scheme affecting any of a Participant's Appropriated Shares. In the absence of any direction from a Participant concerning how the Trustees should act in respect of his Shares following any offer, compromise, arrangement or scheme the Trustees shall not take any action in respect thereof.

5 Trustees' regulations

(a) The number of Trustees hereof shall be not less than two persons unless a company is appointed as sole Trustee and if at any time the number of the Trustees shall fall below such limits the surviving or continuing Trustee shall have power to act only for the purpose of doing all things necessary to concur in or secure the appointment of a new Trustee or Trustees.

(b) Subject to (a) above any Trustee may at any time resign office by giving notice in writing to the company.

(c) The Company may at any time and without giving any reason therefor by Deed appoint a new or additional Trustee or Trustees or may remove from office any Trustee and appoint a new Trustee or Trustees in the place of any Trustee who is removed from office or whose office is vacated for any reason and any such new or additional Trustee or (as the case may require) the existing Trustees shall thereupon execute such documents and do such things as may be necessary to give proper effect to such appointment or removal.

(d) At all times at least one of the Trustees of the Scheme shall be resident in the United Kingdom.

(e) A person shall not be disqualified from acting as a Trustee of the Scheme by reason of the fact that he is or has been an employee of a Participating Company or is or has been a Participant.

6 The Participating Companies to indemnify the trustees

The Participating Companies hereby covenant with the Trustees that they shall indemnify the Trustees and keep them indemnified against all claims losses expenses and demands whatsoever which may arise out of or in connection with the Scheme other than claims which may arise from their own negligence fraud or misfeasance.

7 Trustees to rely on company information

The Trustees shall be entitled to rely without further enquiry on all information supplied to them by the Participating Companies for the purposes of the Scheme and in particular but without prejudice to the generality of the foregoing any notice given by the Participating Companies to the Trustees in respect of the eligibility of any person to become or remain a Participant in the Scheme shall be conclusive in favour of the Trustees.

8 Trustees' meetings

The Trustees shall meet together at such times as shall be necessary for the administration of the Scheme and all decisions relating to the Scheme made by a majority of the Trustees present at any meeting of the Trustees of which due notice has been given to all the Trustees (and at which at least two of the Trustees shall be present) shall be as effective for all purposes as if such decisions had been the unanimous decisions of all the Trustees. A resolution in writing signed by all the Trustees shall be as effective as any resolution duly passed at a meeting of the Trustees.

9 Trustees exonerated from liability

In the administration of the Scheme no Trustee shall be liable for any loss arising by reason of the negligence or fraud of any agent employed by him or by any of the other Trustees or by reason of any mistake or omission made in good faith by any of the Trustees hereof or by reason of any other matter or thing except negligence fraud or misfeasance on the part of the Trustee who is sought to be made liable.

10 Termination of Scheme

(a) The perpetuity period applicable to this Deed shall be the period of 80 years from the date hereof.

(b) The scheme shall be terminated at the end of the said perpetuity period or if earlier upon the date on which the Board shall resolve to terminate the Scheme.

(c) On the date of termination any unrestricted shares in the Company registered in the names of the Trustees to which any Participant is absolutely entitled shall be immediately transferable to such Participant subject to the requirements of subsections (1) and (2) of Section 54 of the Act [now ICTA 1988, Sch 9, para 2(2) and Sch 10, para 1(1)] relating to the retention and disposal of shares. Any other assets representing the Trust Property shall be paid to the Participating Companies in proportion to the total monies provided by each of them to the Trustees.

11 Subsidiaries

Any company which is for the time being a Subsidiary may with the consent of the Company and the Trustees be and become a party to these presents and the Scheme by entering into a Deed agreeing to be bound in all respects by this Deed and Rules for so long as such company is a Subsidiary.

A company which ceases to be a Subsidiary shall cease forthwith to participate in the Scheme. The Board may also determine that any Subsidiary, which is a Participating Company, shall cease to participate (provided that paragraph 2(3)(a) of Schedule 9 to the Act [now ICTA 1988, Sch 9, para 2(3)(a)] is not thereby breached) and such cessation shall not affect those rights of any Participants employed by such Subsidiary to Shares appropriated before such cessation.

12 Costs and expenses

The costs and expenses of the preparation and execution of this Deed the Rules and all ancillary documentation and of the management and administration of the scheme (including the expenses of any Trustee hereof) shall be borne by the Participating Companies except insofar as the same shall be chargeable to any one or more of the Participants.

13 Amendments

The Company may at any time by Deed modify the trusts of this Deed with the prior approval of the Board of Inland Revenue.

14 This Deed and the Rules shall be governed by and construed in all respects in accordance with English Law.

IN WITNESS whereof the company has hereunto affixed its Common Seal and the Trustees have hereunto set their hands and seals the day and year first before written.

THE COMMON SEAL of
was hereunto
affixed in the presence of:

Director

Secretary

SIGNED SEALED and DELIVERED
by the said
in the presence of:

SIGNED SEALED and DELIVERED
by the said
in the presence of:

THE SCHEDULE above referred to
RULES OF THE [Name of Scheme].

1 Definitions

In the Trust Deed and the Rules:

(a) the following words and expressions bear the following meanings:

"The Act"	The Finance Act 1978 (as amended) [relevant legislation now contained in ICTA 1988, ss 186 and 187 and Schs 9 and 10]
"Announcement Date"	The date on which the Company announces the results for the relevant accounting period.
"Appropriate"	Formally to vest a beneficial interest (subject to the provisions of the Deed) in specific shares in an Eligible Employee pursuant to these Rules.
"Appropriated Shares"	In relation to any Participant, such securities as have been appropriated or are deemed to have been appropriated to him under the Scheme and are for the time being held by the Trustees and, where the context so admits, includes any new Shares within the meaning of Rule 7(c).
"Appropriation Date"	In relation to any Scheme Shares, the date upon which those Scheme Shares are appropriated to a Participant pursuant to the Scheme.
"Approved Scheme"	A profit sharing scheme which is for the time being approved in accordance with Part I of Schedule 9 to the Act [now ICTA 1988, Sch 9, Pt 1].
"The Board"	The Board of Directors of the Company or a duly constituted Committee thereof.
"The Company"	[Name of company setting up this Scheme].
"Eligible Earnings"	In relation to an Eligible Employee on any Appropriation Date, the annual rate of basic salary (excluding any supplements or other emoluments as may be payable in addition to basic salary) payable by

	the Participating Companies on the last day in the Financial Year immediately preceding the Financial Year in which the Appropriation Date falls.
"Eligible Employee"	Any person who is eligible to participate in the scheme in accordance with Rule 2.
"Financial Year"	A financial year of the company as that term is defined in Section 742 of the Companies Act 1985.
"Initial Market Value"	In relation to any Scheme Shares, the market value of those Scheme Shares determined in accordance with Section 150(1) of the Capital Gains Tax Act 1979 as at the Appropriation Date of those Scheme Shares and as agreed in advance between the Trustees and the Shares Valuation Division of the Capital Taxes Office of the Inland Revenue for the purposes of the Scheme. Provided that, if at the Appropriation Date Shares have been admitted to the Official List of The Stock Exchange, the Initial Market Value of a Share shall be taken as the average of the middle market prices as ascertained from the Daily Official List of The Stock Exchange of a Share over the 5 consecutive dealing days ending immediately prior to the relevant Appropriation Date or ending on such earlier date (not being earlier than 25 days preceding such Appropriation Date) as the Trustees may agree in writing with the Board of Inland Revenue.
"Participant"	Any Eligible Employee to whom the Trustees have appropriated Scheme Shares and for whom they hold the Shares on Trust.
"Participating Companies"	The Company and such of the Subsidiaries as, for the time being, are nominated by the Board to be Participating Companies and are bound by the provisions of the Scheme and Trust Deed.
"Period of Retention"	In relation to any of a Participant's Scheme Shares, the period beginning on the Appropriation Date of those Scheme Shares and ending on the second anniversary of that date or, if it is earlier – (i) the date on which the Participant ceases to be an employee or director of the Participating Companies by reason of injury or disability or Redundancy; (ii) the date on which the participant reaches pensionable age (currently 65 years for a man and 60 years for a woman) as defined in Schedule 20 to the Social Security Act 1975; or (iii) the date of the Participant's death (iv) or such other meaning ascribed thereto by Section 54(4) of the Act [now ICTA 1988, Sch 10, para 2].
"Redundancy"	Dismissal by reason of redundancy within the meaning of Part VI of the Employment Protection (Consolidation) Act 1978.
"The Release Date"	In relation to any of a Participant's Scheme Shares, the fifth anniversary of the Appropriation Date of those Scheme Shares or such other meaning ascribed thereto by Section 54(6) of the Act [now ICTA 1988, s 187(2)].

"The Relevant Amount"	The meaning ascribed thereto by Section 61(1) of the Act [now ICTA 1988, s 187(2)].
"The Rules"	The rules set out in this Schedule as amended from time to time in accordance with the provisions herein contained.
"The Scheme"	[Name of Scheme].
"Scheme Shares"	Shares subscribed for or purchased by the Trustees pursuant to the Scheme together with all shares subsequently acquired by the Trustees by virtue of their holding such Shares, exercising any rights attaching thereto or accepting any offer made to the holders of such shares and any reference to a Participant's Scheme Shares is, subject to Rule 7(d), a reference to the Scheme Shares which have been appropriated to him by the Trustees.
"Shares"	Ordinary Shares in the capital of the Company which comply with the conditions set out in Part II of Schedule 9 to the Act [now ICTA 1988, Sch 9, paras 10–12 and 14].
"Subsidiary"	Any company which is for the time being controlled by the company within the meaning of Section 534 of the Income and Corporation Taxes Act 1970 [now ICTA 1988, s 840].
"Trust Property"	Any shares, money and other property from time to time in the name of, transferred to or held by the Trustees or under their control and subject to the terms of this Deed and the Rules.
"The Trustees"	The trustee or trustees for the time being of the Scheme.
"Year of Assessment"	A year beginning on any 6 April and ending on the following 5 April.

(b) Reference to any Act or Part, Chapter or Section thereof (including 'the Act' as herein defined) shall include any statutory modification, amendment or re-enactment thereof for the time being in force.

(c) Words of the masculine gender shall include the feminine and vice versa and words in the singular shall include the plural and vice versa unless, in either case, the context otherwise requires or it is otherwise stated.

2 Eligibility

(a) Any person who fulfills the following conditions, namely:

(i) he is a director or employee of a Participating Company who is required to devote to his duties not less than 25 hours per week (excluding meal breaks), and

(ii) he has completed not less than [period not to exceed five years] of continuous employment as such, and

(iii) he is chargeable to income tax in respect of his employment under Case I of Schedule E.

shall be entitled as of right to participate in the Scheme at an Appropriation Date.

Provided that:

(i) he is not ineligible to have Scheme Shares appropriated to him by virtue of the provisions of Part III of Schedule 9 to the Act [now ICTA 1988, Sch 9, paras 8 and 35]; and

(ii) he has before any Scheme Shares are appropriated to him delivered a contract of participation with the Company in terms which include the observance of the four conditions (a), (b), (c) and (d) set out in Section 54(1) of the Act [now ICTA 1988, Sch 9, para 2(2)] and which is in the form substantially as set out in Appendix I hereto.

(b)(i) As soon as practicable after the Announcement Date the Company shall identify all Eligible Employees who are not then participating in the Scheme and all employees who at the next Appropriation Date are expected to be Eligible Employees and shall communicate in writing with each such person asking whether he wishes to be a Participant.

(ii) Those Eligible Employees who wish to participate in the scheme shall within the period of 14 days after receipt of the notification referred to in (ii) above or such further period as the Company shall allow return to the Company a form of acceptance duly signed agreeing the terms and conditions set out therein and in default thereof they shall not be eligible to participate.

3 Allocation of Funds for Purchase of Shares

(a) The Participating Companies shall allocate funds for the purposes of the scheme on or after each Announcement Date in accordance with the provisions hereof.

(b) The amount of the funds to be allocated as aforesaid shall be such amount (if any) as the Board may determine.

(c) The amount determined as aforesaid shall be notified in writing to the Trustees as soon as it has been determined and shall be paid to the Trustees on the Announcement Date or as soon as possible thereafter by the Participating Companies. The Board shall also notify the Trustees of the number of shares (if any) which are to be made available for subscription by the Trustees and the price at which those shares are to be offered for subscription.

(d) A Participating Company shall only pay to the Trustees such sums as are required in connection with the acquisition of Shares by the Trustees for appropriation to Eligible Employees who are for the time being in the service of that Participating Company.

(e) The Trustees shall on or after the relevant Announcement Date but on on or before the immediately following Appropriation Date apply the amount paid to them under Rule 3(c) above in subscribing for shares if and to the extent that Shares are offered to them and at the price notified to them pursuant to sub-paragraph (c) above and, subject thereto, the balance shall be applied in purchasing Shares from existing shareholders.

4 Appropriation of Scheme Shares

(a) The number of Scheme Shares to be appropriated by the Trustees to each Eligible Employee on any Appropriation Date on which funds have been allocated in accordance with Rule 3 above shall be determined in accordance with the following provisions:

The entitlement of each Eligible Employee under the scheme shall be such amount as the Board shall determine expressed as

(i) a proportion of Eligible Earnings; and/or
(ii) a proportion of Eligible Earnings for each Period of Service; and/or
(iii) a fixed amount determined by the Board; and/or
(iv) a fixed amount determined by the Board for each Period of Service.

Provided that:

(i) in any year the basis of calculation of the entitlement of each Eligible Employee shall be the same;
(ii) fractional amounts of a Scheme Share shall be rounded up or down at the discretion of the Trustees;

(iii) the total of the Initial Market Values of the Scheme Shares appropriated to an Eligible Employee in a Year of Assessment shall not exceed the Relevant Amount.

In the context of this Rule 'Period of Service' shall mean a complete year, or such other complete period as may from time to time be specified, of continuous service as an employee of the Company and/or any Subsidiary.

(b) The Scheme Shares to which each Eligible Employee is entitled as a result of the calculations described above will then be appropriated to him at the aggregate of their Initial Market Value but will be registered in the names of the Trustees on his behalf.

(c) In the event that the Trustees acquire Shares for appropriation on an Appropriation Date and some of those Shares carry a right of any kind which is not carried by every other such share then such Shares as carry such right shall so far as practicable be appropriated pro rata according to the number of Shares appropriated to each Participant on the Appropriation Date.

(d) As soon as practicable after any Scheme Shares have been appropriated by the Trustees to a Participant in accordance with the Rules the Trustees shall give the Participant notice in writing of the appropriation specifying the number and description of Scheme Shares appropriated and stating their Initial Market Value and the date on which such Scheme Shares were appropriated.

5 Rights and Restrictions relating to Scheme Shares

(a) Scheme Shares shall subject to the provisions of the Scheme receive identical treatment and rank pari passu in all respects with all other shares of the same class and in particular in respect of each of the following, where applicable –

(i) the dividend payable (provided that Scheme Shares which have been newly issued may receive, in respect of dividends payable with respect to a period beginning before the date on which such Scheme Shares were issued, treatment which is less favourable than that accorded to Shares issued before that date);

(ii) repayment;

(iii) the restrictions attaching to Shares; and

(iv) any offer of substituted or additional shares, securities or rights of any description in respect of Shares;

but notwithstanding the foregoing, the provisions of Rule 6 shall apply as between the Trustees and the Participants.

(b) While Scheme Shares are held by the Trustees they shall in respect of any matter upon which the Trustees are entitled to exercise any voting right that may attach hereto, seek and comply with any direction from any of the Participants, as to the exercise of such voting rights, and in the absence of such direction refrain from voting.

(c) Subject to the provisions of the Rules and in particular Rule 6 the Trustees shall deal with a Participant's Scheme Shares at all times in accordance with the lawful directions given by or on behalf of that Participant or any person in whom the beneficial interest in his Scheme Shares is for the time being vested.

6 Obligations of Participants

(a) Subject to paragraph (b) of this Rule every Participant shall be bound in contract with the Company –

(i) to permit his Scheme Shares to remain in the hands of the Trustees throughout the Period of Retention, and

(ii) not to assign, charge or otherwise dispose of the beneficial interest in his Scheme Shares during that period, and

(iii) if he directs the Trustees to transfer the ownership of his Scheme Shares to him at any time before the Release Date, to pay to the Trustees before the transfer takes place a sum equal to income tax at the basic rate on the appropriate percentage of the locked-in value of the Scheme Shares at the time of the direction and, for this purpose, 'the appropriate percentage' and 'the locked-in value' shall be as respectively defined in Section 54(7) and Section 55(2) of the Act, [now ICTA 1988, Sch 10, para 3 and s 186(5)], and

(iv) not to direct the Trustees to dispose of his Scheme Shares at any time before the Release Date in any other way except by sale for the best consideration in money that can reasonably be obtained at the time of sale.

(b) Any obligation imposed on a Participant by virtue of paragraph (a) above shall not prevent the Participant from –

(i) directing the Trustees to accept an offer for any of his Scheme Shares (in this Rule referred to as 'the Original Shares'), if the acceptance or agreement will result in a new holding, as defined in Section 77(1)(b) of the Capital Gains Tax Act 1979, being equated with the Original Shares for the purposes of Capital Gains Tax; or

(ii) directing the Trustees to agree to a transaction affecting his Scheme Shares or such of them as are of a particular class, if the transaction would be entered into pursuant to a compromise, arrangement or scheme applicable to or affecting –

(i) all the ordinary share capital of the Company or, as the case may be, all the shares of the class in question, or

(ii) all the shares, or shares of the class in question, which are held by a class of shareholders identified otherwise than by reference to their employment or their participating in an Approved Scheme, or

(iii) directing the Trustees to accept an offer of cash, with or without other assets, for his Scheme Shares if the offer forms part of a general offer which is made to holders of shares of the same class as his or of shares in the Company and which is made in the first instance on a condition such that if it is satisfied the person making the offer will have control of the Company, within the meaning of Section 302 of the Income and Corporation Taxes Act 1970 [now ICTA 1988, s 416], or

(iv) agreeing, after the expiry of the Period of Retention, to sell the beneficial interest in his Scheme Shares to the Trustees for the same consideration as, in accordance with Rule 6(a)(iv), would be required to be obtained for the Scheme Shares themselves.

7 Company Reconstructions, Amalgamations etc

(a) This Rule applies where there occurs in relation to any of a Participant's Scheme Shares (in this rule referred to as 'the Original Holding') a transaction (in this Rule referred to as a 'Company Reconstruction') which results in a New Holding as defined in Section 77(1)(b) of the Capital Gains Tax Act 1979 being equated with the Original Holding for the purpose of capital gains tax and in this Rule 'New Holding' has the meaning aforesaid.

(b) Where shares are issued in the circumstances described in Section 57(2) of the Act [now ICTA 1988, Sch 10, para 5(2)] those shares shall be treated for the purposes of this Rule as not forming part of the New Holding.

(c) In this rule –

(i) 'New Shares' means shares comprised in the New Holding which were issued in respect of or otherwise represent, shares comprised in the Original Holding, and

(ii) 'Corresponding Shares', in relation to any New Shares means those shares in respect of which the New Shares are issued or which the New Shares otherwise represent.

(d) References in the Rules to a Participant's Scheme Shares shall be construed, after the time of the Company Reconstruction, as being or, as the case may be, as including references to any New Shares and for the purpose of the Rules –

(i) a Company Reconstruction shall be treated as not involving a disposal of shares comprised in the Original Holding;
(ii) the date on which any New Shares are to be treated as having been appropriated to the Participant shall be the Appropriation Date of the Corresponding Shares; and
(iii) the New Shares shall be held by the Trustees in accordance with the Scheme as if they had been so appropriated.

(e) In the context of a New Holding any reference in this Rule to shares includes securities or rights of any description which form part of the New Holding for the purposes of Chapter II of Part IV of the Capital Gains Tax Act 1979.

8 Rights Issues

In the event of the Company making an offer to its ordinary shareholders on a rights basis such offer shall be extended to the Trustees in respect of the total number of Scheme Shares. The Trustees shall notify each Participant concerned of the rights which are attributable to his Appropriated Shares. A Participant shall be at liberty to direct the Trustees to accept such offer in respect of all of his Scheme Shares, in which event he shall pay to the Trustees a sum of money before the expiry of the offer sufficient to enable the Trustees to subscribe for that number of Shares in respect of which the direction was made. Alternatively, a Participant may direct the Trustees to sell the whole of the rights attaching to his Scheme Shares, or, if the Trustees so permit, to sell part of such rights in order to enable the Trustees to use the proceeds of such sale to exercise other such rights of the Participant. Any shares subscribed for by the Trustees under this Rule shall be treated as New Shares under Rule 7 in relation to any Participant and any cash arising from the disposal of rights (except insofar as used to accept the offer) shall be accounted for to the Participant entitled thereto (subject to deduction of any tax unless Section 56(6) of the Act [now ICTA 1988, s 186(12)] applies).

9 Release of Shares to Participants

Scheme Shares held by the Trustees on behalf of each Participant on the Release Date shall be transferred to that Participant as soon as reasonably practicable thereafter. In disposing of a Participant's holding of Scheme Shares which comprise Shares appropriated to him at different times Shares appropriated earlier shall, for the purposes of these Rules, be treated as disposed of before those which were appropriated later.

10 Miscellaneous

(a) The Board may alter or add to all or any of the provisions of the Scheme from time to time in any way they think fit.

Provided that

(i) no alteration which would adversely prejudice to a material extent the rights attaching to any Scheme Shares appropriated to Participants shall be made nor shall any alteration be made giving the Participating Companies a beneficial interest in Scheme Shares; and
(ii) if the Scheme is at the time of an amendment or addition approved by the Board

of Inland Revenue in accordance with Part I of Schedule 9 to the Act [now ICTA 1988, Sch 9, Pt I] such amendment or addition to the Scheme shall not take effect unless and until it has been approved by the Board of Inland Revenue in accordance with Part I of Schedule 9 to the Act [now ICTA 1988, Sch 9, Pt I].

(b) Any direction to the Trustees in respect of a Participant's Appropriated Shares must be given in writing by or on behalf of the Participant or any person in whom the beneficial interest in his Shares is for the time being vested. Any notification, document, payment or other communication to a Participant shall be delivered personally or sent by post to the Participant at the address which he shall give to the Company for the purpose, or failing any such address to his last known place of abode.

(c) The Company will provide Participants with copies of the annual report and accounts and all notices and circulars sent to the holders of Shares of the Company.

(d) Any stamp duty payable on a transfer of a Participant's Appropriated Shares to him shall be paid by the Trustees.

11 Limitation upon number of Shares available to the Scheme

(a) The aggregate nominal amount of all Scheme Shares issued by the Company to the Trustees and appropriated by them under the provisions of this Scheme shall not exceed [£] and in any event shall not, in any one calendar year, exceed one per cent of the issued share capital of the Company provided always that in the event of an issue of ordinary shares

(1) credited as fully paid up by way of capitalisation of profits or reserves; or
(2) by way of rights

such limitation shall be adjusted as the Auditors for the time being of the Company shall confirm in writing to be appropriate in their opinion in order to maintain the same as a constant percentage of the issued ordinary share capital of the Company.

(b) The Initial Market Value of all Scheme Shares subscribed by the Trustees and appropriated to all Eligible Employees in respect of any Financial Year of the Company shall not exceed five per centum of the profits (before taxation and extraordinary items) for the Company and its Subsidiaries for that Financial Year.

APPENDIX I TO THE SCHEDULE

Offer of Participation in the Employee Share Scheme

This letter formally offers you participation in the [name of scheme] which is approved by the Inland Revenue under the Finance Act 1978 [now ICTA 1988]. Your acceptance will entitle you to participate in the scheme for the year ended [ ] and for future years so long as the scheme remains in operation and approved by the Board of Inland Revenue and so long as you remain eligible to participate under the Rules of the Scheme. You may withdraw from participation at any time in accordance with the Rules of the Scheme.

Under the provisions of Section 54(1) of the Finance Act 1978 [now ICTA 1988, Sch 9, para 2(2)], a copy of which is attached to this letter [but not reproduced here], participants who have been appropriated shares under the Scheme are subject to certain restrictions mainly concerning disposals and taxation. An eligible employee is also required by the Act to bind himself in contract with the company to permit his shares to remain with the Trustees of the Scheme for a two year period of retention on the terms set out in Section 54(1) [now ICTA 1988, Sch 9, para 2(2)], before he can participate in the scheme.

A copy of the Trust Deed and of the Rules of the Scheme is available for your inspection at [ ] and will remain so available during the operation of the scheme. If you participate in the scheme you will be bound by the terms of the Trust Deed and the Rules.

The formal contract required by Section 54(1) [now ICTA 1988, Sch 9, para 2(2)] consists of this notice and the enclosed form of acceptance. If you wish to participate in the Scheme please complete sign and date the form of acceptance and return it to the Company Secretary to arrive not later than [ ]. You should retain the duplicate copy.

By order of the Board

Secretary

Date

FORM OF ACCEPTANCE AND CONTRACT OF PARTICIPATION IN [NAME OF SCHEME]
TO: The Company Secretary
[Name of Company]

I accept the offer of participation in the above scheme contained in the company's letter dated [ ]. Subject to and in consideration of my being allowed to participate in the scheme I agree to accept such shares as are appropriated to me under the Scheme on and subject to the terms of Section 54(1) of the Finance Act 1978 [now ICTA 1988, Sch 9, para 2(2)] (set out overleaf) [but not reproduced here] and to be bound in contract with [name of company] in respect of all such shares in the terms set out in the said Section 54(1) [now ICTA 1988, Sch 9, para 2(2)]. I further agree to be bound by the terms of the Trust Deed and the Rules.

Signed .... Date ....
Full name (in block capitals) of signatory ....
Private Address (in block capitals) ....
....
....
....
Postcode ....

APPENDIX II TO THE SCHEDULE

Share Appropriation Notice and Certificate of Beneficial Ownership

Date

(Name of Scheme)

This is to certify that [Name of Participant] ('the Participant') is the beneficial owner of [ ] Ordinary Shares of [p] each in [name of company] and that the shares were appropriated to the Participant at an Initial Market Value of [ ] on [ ] and are held for the Participant by the Trustees of [name of scheme] and are subject to a valid contract under Section 54(1) of the Finance Act 1978 [now ICTA 1988, Sch 9, para 2(2)]

Signed

For and on behalf of the Trustees of the [Name of Scheme]

LEGISLATIVE CHANGES

Since the above trust deed and scheme rules were issued by the Inland Revenue, FA 1987, s 33(2) & (4) and Sch 4, paras 6 to 8 (now ICTA 1988, s 187(4) and Sch 9, paras 37 to 39) have introduced changes in the definition of 'material interest' in a close company, as it applies for the purposes of the employee share schemes legislation (see 7.68 and 7.69). This has no effect upon the wording of the above documentation.

Appendix 6 Specimen scheme rules for Inland Revenue approved savings-related share option scheme

The specimen scheme rules set out below were issued by the Board of Inland Revenue in August 1986 as a supplement to the booklet IR 39. Since that time, various legislative changes have been made, as set out on page 304. The introduction to the supplement contained the following paragraphs:

'This supplement contains a set of scheme rules designed to meet the requirements for approval under Schedule 10 to the Finance Act 1980 [now ICTA 1988, Sch 9]. It is intended as an illustration of the type of framework which companies might wish to adopt and to assist in drafting certain provisions which frequently cause difficulty. There is scope for varying the scheme rules, especially those which are not essential for Inland Revenue approval; companies should consider their particular needs carefully and obtain professional advice where necessary.

In addition to a set of rules, a workable scheme will require ancillary documents such as a letter of invitation, application form, option certificate and notice of exercise. It will be essential to ensure that the company's proposed administrative arrangements are compatible with those of the savings body with whom the savings contracts are to be entered into and consultation should be undertaken at an early stage.

This supplement should be read in conjunction with Inland Revenue booklet IR 39 and regarded as part thereof.'

RULES OF THE [ ][1] SAVINGS-RELATED SHARE OPTION SCHEME

1.1 Definitions

In these Rules the following words and expressions shall have the following meanings:

"Adoption Date"	the date on which the Scheme is adopted by the Company in general meeting
"Announcement Date"	the date on which the annual or half yearly results of the Company are announced
"Associated Company"	the meaning that the expression bears in Paragraph 12 of Schedule 10 by virtue of Paragraph 26(1) thereof [now ICTA 1988, Sch 9, para 23 and s 187(2)]
"Auditors"	the auditors for the time being of the Company (acting as experts, not as arbitrators)
"Board"	the board of directors of the Company or, except in Rule 10.4, a duly constituted committee thereof
"Bonus Date"	either (i) where pursuant to Rules 2 and 3 the repayment under the Savings Contract is taken as including the maximum bonus, the earliest date on which the maximum bonus is payable or (ii) in any other case, the earliest date on which a bonus (the 'standard bonus') is payable under the Savings Contract

"Company"	[ ][1]
"Control"	has the same meaning as in Section 534 of the Income and Corporation Taxes Act 1970 [now ICTA 1988, s 840]
"Date of Grant"	the date on which an application for an Option is, was or may be accepted in accordance with Rule 4
"Eligible Employee"	any director or employee of any Participating Company who normally devotes to his duties 25 hours or more per week, had on the day preceding the date of issue of the relevant invitations pursuant to rule 2.1 been such a director or employee for [three][6] or more years and is chargeable to tax in respect of his office or employment under Case I of Schedule E and any other director or employee of any Participating Company nominated by the Board to be an Eligible Employee
"Market Value"	[on any day the average of the middle market quotations of a Share as derived from The Stock Exchange Daily Official List for the three immediately preceding dealing days][2] [on any day the market value of a Share determined in accordance with the provisions of Part VIII of the Capital Gains Tax Act 1979 and agreed for the purposes of the Scheme with the Inland Revenue Shares Valuation Division][3]
"Option"	a right to subscribe for shares granted (or to be granted) in accordance with the rules of this Scheme
"Participating Company"	the Company and any other company of which the Company has control and which has been nominated by the Board as a Participating Company
"Savings Contract"	a contract under a certified contractual savings scheme, within the meaning of Section 415 of the Income and Corporation Taxes Act 1970 [now ICTA 1988, s 326] and which has been approved by the Board of Inland Revenue for the purposes of Schedule 10 [now ICTA 1988, Sch 9]
"Schedule 10"	Schedule 10 to the Finance Act 1980 [now ICTA 1988, Sch 9]
"the Scheme"	the savings-related share option scheme constituted and governed by these rules as from time to time amended
"Share"	an ordinary share in the capital of the Company which satisfies the conditions specified in Paragraphs 15 to 19 inclusive of Schedule 10 [now ICTA 1988, Sch 9, paras 10 to 14]
"Subscription Price"	the price at which each Share subject to an Option may be acquired on the exercise of that Option being, subject to Rule 8, the higher of (i) the nominal value of a Share and (ii) 90% of the Market Value of a Share on the day the invitation to apply for that Option was issued pursuant to Rule 2
"Subsisting Option"	an Option which has neither lapsed nor been exercised

1.2 Interpretation

In this Scheme, except insofar as the context otherwise requires:

(i) words denoting the singular shall include the plural and vice versa
(ii) words denoting the masculine gender shall include the feminine gender
(iii) reference to any enactment shall be construed as a reference to that enactment as from time to time amended, extended or re-enacted

2 Invitations to apply for options

2.1 The Board may invite every Eligible Employee to apply for the grant of an option to acquire Shares in the Company on any one occasion within each of the following periods:

(i) a period of four weeks commencing four weeks following the approval of the Scheme by the Board of Inland Revenue pursuant to Schedule 10 [now ICTA 1988, Sch 9]
(ii) a period of four weeks commencing two weeks after each Announcement Date provided that no invitation may be made after the tenth anniversary of the Adoption Date.

2.2 Each invitation shall specify:

(i) the date, being 14 days after the issue of the invitation, by which an application must be made
(ii) the Subscription Price at which Shares may be acquired on the exercise of any Option granted in response to the application and
(iii) the maximum permitted aggregate monthly savings contribution, being the lesser of the maximum specified in Paragraph 13 of Schedule 10 [now ICTA 1988, Sch 9, para 24] and such sum (being a multiple of £1 and not less than £10) as the Board decides shall apply to every Eligible Employee in respect of that invitation.

2.3 Each invitation shall be accompanied by a proposal form for a Savings Contract and an application form which shall provide for the applicant to state:

(i) the monthly savings contribution (being a multiple of £1 and not less than £10) which he wishes to make under the related Savings Contract
(ii) that his proposed monthly savings contribution, when added to any monthly savings contributions then being made under any other Savings Contract linked to an option granted under the Scheme or any other scheme approved under Schedule 10 [now ICTA 1988, Sch 9], will not exceed the maximum permitted aggregate monthly savings contribution specified in the invitation
(iii) whether, for the purpose of determining the number of Shares over which an Option is to be granted, the repayment under the Savings Contract is to be taken as including the maximum bonus, the standard or no bonus,

and to authorise the Board to enter on the Savings Contract proposal form such monthly savings contribution, not exceeding the maximum stated on the application form, as shall be determined pursuant to Rule 3 below.

2.4 Each application shall be deemed to be for an Option over the largest whole number of Shares which can be bought at the Subscription Price with the expected repayment under the related savings contract at the appropriate Bonus Date.

3 Scaling down

If the Board receives valid applications for Options over an aggregate number of Shares which exceeds the limit determined pursuant to Rule 5.2 below in respect of that invitation, then the following steps shall be carried out successively to the extent necessary to eliminate the excess:

(i) the excess over £10 of the monthly savings contribution chosen by each applicant shall be reduced pro rata to the extent necessary;

(ii) each election for the maximum bonus to be included in the repayment under the Savings Contract shall be deemed to be an election for only the standard bonus to be so included;
(iii) each election for a bonus to be included in the repayment under the Savings Contract shall be deemed to be an election for no bonus to be so included;
(iv) applications will be selected by lot, each based on a monthly savings contribution of £10 and the inclusion of no bonus in the repayment under the Savings Contract.

Each application shall be deemed to have been modified or withdrawn in accordance with the application of the foregoing provisions and the Board shall complete each Savings Contract proposal form to reflect any reduction in monthly savings contributions resulting therefrom.

4 Grant of options

Not later than the thirtieth day following [the earliest of the three dealing days referred to in the definition of Market Value][2] [the day on which invitations were issued pursuant to Rule 2][3] the Board shall grant to each applicant who is still an Eligible Employee and is not precluded from participation in the Scheme by virtue of Paragraph 23 of Schedule 10 [now ICTA 1988, Sch 9, para 8] an Option over the number of Shares for which, pursuant to Rule 2.4 and subject to Rule 3, he is deemed to have applied.

As soon as possible after Options have been granted the Board shall issue a certificate of option in respect of each Option in such form, not inconsistent with these Rules, as the Board may determine.

No Option may be transferred, assigned or charged and any purported transfer, assignment or charge shall cause the Option to lapse forthwith. Each option certificate shall carry a statement to this effect.

5 Limitation on grants

[5.1 No Option shall be granted pursuant to Rule 4 above if such grant would result in the aggregate of

(i) the number of Shares over which Subsisting Options have been granted under this Scheme and
(ii) the number of Shares which have been issued on the exercise of Options granted under this Scheme and
(iii) the number of Shares over which subsisting options have been granted under any other share option scheme during the period of 10 years ending on the relevant Date of Grant and
(iv) the number of Shares which have been issued pursuant to any other employee share scheme (including a share option scheme) during the period of 10 years ending on the relevant Date of Grant

exceeding 5% of the number of Shares then in issue][4]

5.2 The Board may, before issuing invitations on any occasion, determine a limit on the number of Shares which are to be available in respect of that invitation in order to ensure that Shares remain available for subsequent invitations.

5.3 No Option shall be granted to an Eligible Employee if the monthly savings contribution under the related Savings Contract, when added to the monthly savings contributions then being made under any other Savings Contract would exceed the maximum specified in Paragraph 13 of Schedule 10 [now ICTA 1988, Sch 9, para 24].

6 Exercise of options

6.1 Subject to Rule 9 below any Subsisting Option may be exercised in whole or in part at any time following the earliest of the following events:

(i) the relevant Bonus Date
(ii) the death of the Option holder
(iii) the Option holder ceasing to be a director or employee of any Participating Company by reason of injury, disability, redundancy within the meaning of the Employment Protection (Consolidation) Act 1978 or retirement on reaching pensionable age within the meaning of Schedule 20 to the Social Security Act 1975 or any other age at which he is bound to retire in accordance with the terms of his contract of employment
(iv) the Option holder ceasing to be a director or employee of any Participating Company by reason only that—
  (a) that office or employment is in a company of which the Company ceases to have Control, or
  (b) that office or employment relates to a business or part of a business which is transferred to a person who is neither an Associated Company nor a company of which the Company has Control
(v) the Option holder ceasing to be a director or employee of any Participating Company more than three years after the Date of Grant of the relative Option by reason of [. . . . . .][5]

6.2 An Option shall lapse on the earliest of the following events:

(i) except where the Option holder has died, the expiry of six months following the Bonus Date
(ii) where the Option holder died during the six months following the Bonus Date, the first anniversary of the Bonus Date
(iii) where the Option holder has died before the Bonus Date, the first anniversary of his death
(iv) unless the Option holder has died, the expiry of six months after the Option has become exercisable by virtue of Paragraph (iii) of Rule 6.1
(v) the expiry of six months after the Option has become exercisable by virtue of Paragraph (iv) or (v) of Rule 6.1 or in accordance with Rule 7
(vi) the Option holder ceasing to be a director or employee of any Participating Company in circumstances in which the Option does not become exercisable
(vii) the Option holder being adjudicated bankrupt.

6.3 If an Option holder continues to be employed by a Participating Company after the date on which he reaches pensionable age within the meaning of Schedule 20 to the Social Security Act 1975 he may exercise any Subsisting Option within six months following that date.

6.4 No person shall be treated for the purposes of this Rule 6 as ceasing to be employed by any Participating Company until he is no longer employed by the Company, any Associated Company or company of which the Company has Control.

7 Takeovers and liquidations

7.1 If any person obtains Control of the Company as a result of making –

(i) a general offer to acquire the whole of the issued ordinary share capital of the Company which is made on a condition such that if it is satisfied the person making the offer will have Control of the Company or
(ii) a general offer to acquire all the shares in the Company which are of the same class as the Shares

then any Subsisting Option may be exercised within six months of the time when the person making the offer has obtained Control of the Company and any condition subject to which the offer is made has been satisfied.

7.2 If under Section 425 of the Companies Act 1985 the Court sanctions a compromise or arrangement proposed for the purposes of or in connection with a scheme for the reconstruction of the Company or its amalgamation with any other company or companies, any Subsisting Option may be exercised within six months of the Court sanctioning the compromise or arrangement.

7.3 If any person becomes bound or entitled to acquire shares in the Company under Section 428 or 429 of the said Act of 1985 any Subsisting Option may be exercised at any time when the person remains so bound or entitled.

7.4 If the Company passes a resolution for voluntary winding up, any Subsisting Option may be exercised within six months of the passing of the resolution.

7.5 For the purposes of this Rule 7 a person shall be deemed to have obtained Control of a Company if he and others acting in concert with him have together obtained Control of it.

7.6 The exercise of an Option pursuant to the preceding provisions of this Rule 7 shall be subject to the provisions of Rule 9 below.

8 Variation of share capital

In the event of any capitalisation or rights issue or any consolidation, sub-division or reduction of capital by the Company, the number of Shares subject to any Option and the Subscription Price for each of those Shares shall be adjusted in such manner as the Auditors confirm to be fair and reasonable provided that:

(i) the aggregate amount payable on the exercise of an Option in full is neither materially changed nor increased beyond the expected repayment under the Savings Contract at the appropriate Bonus Date
(ii) the Subscription Price for a Share is not reduced below its nominal value
(iii) no adjustment shall be made without the prior approval of the Board of Inland Revenue and
(iv) following the adjustment the Shares continue to satisfy the conditions specified in Paragraphs 15 to 19 inclusive of Schedule 10 [now ICTA 1988, Sch 9, paras 10 to 14].

9 Manner of exercise of options

9.1 No Option may be exercised by an individual at any time when he is, or by the personal representatives of an individual who at the date of his death was, precluded by Paragraph 23 of Schedule 10 [now ICTA 1988, Sch 9, para 8] from participating in the Scheme.

9.2 No Option may be exercised at any time when the shares which may thereby be acquired are not Shares as defined in Rule 1.1.

9.3 An Option may only be exercised over the number of shares which may be purchased with the sum obtained by way of repayment under the related Savings Contract.

9.4 An Option shall be exercised by the Option holder, or as the case may be his personal representatives, giving notice to the Company in writing of the number of Shares in respect of which he wishes to exercise the Option accompanied by the appropriate payment (which shall not exceed the sum obtained by way of repayment under the related Savings Contract) and the relevant option certificate and shall be effective on the date of its receipt by the Company.

9.5 Shares shall be allotted and issued pursuant to a notice of exercise within 30 days of the date of exercise. Save for any rights determined by reference to a date preceding the date of allotment, such Shares shall rank pari passu with the other Shares of the same class in issue at the date of allotment.

9.6 When an Option is exercised only in part, it shall lapse to the extent of the unexercised balance.

9.7 For the purposes of Rules 9.3 and 9.4 above, any repayment under the Savings Contract shall exclude the repayment of any contribution the due date for payment of which falls more than one month after the date on which repayment is made.

10 Administration and amendment

10.1 The Scheme shall be administered by the Board whose decision on all disputes shall be final.

10.2 The Board may from time to time amend these Rules provided that:

(i) no amendment may materially affect an Option holder as regards an Option granted prior to the amendment being made
(ii) no amendment may be made which would make the terms on which Options may be granted materially more generous or would increase the limit specified in Rule 5.1 without the prior approval of the Company in general meeting and
(iii) no amendment shall have effect until approved by the Board of Inland Revenue.

10.3 The cost of establishing and operating the Scheme shall be borne by the Participating Companies in such proportions as the Board shall determine.

10.4 The Board may establish a Committee consisting of not less than three members to whom any or all of its powers in relation to the Scheme may be delegated. The Board may at any time dissolve the Committee, alter its constitution or direct the manner in which it shall act.

10.5 Any notice or other communication under or in connection with the Scheme may be given by the Company either personally or by post and to the Company either personally or by post to the secretary; items sent by post shall be pre-paid and shall be deemed to have been received 72 hours after posting.

10.6 The Company shall at all times keep available sufficient authorised and unissued Shares to satisfy the exercise to the full extent still possible of all Options which have neither lapsed nor been fully exercised, taking account of any other obligations of the Company to issue unissued Shares.

Notes

1. Insert name of company.
2. Appropriate only where the scheme shares are listed in The Stock Exchange Daily Official List.
3. Appropriate where the scheme shares are not listed in The Stock Exchange Daily Official List.
4. These provisions are not required for Inland Revenue approval. They are designed to protect existing shareholders and each company must decide for itself what, if any, limits should be imposed.
5. If an option holder leaves employment for reasons other than those specified in Rule 6.1(iii), any option which has been held for more than three years at the date of leaving may be exercised if the rules so allow. The company should decide in what circumstances, if any, such exercise should be permitted and specify these in Rule 6.1(v).
6. Any period not longer than 4 years 334 days may be chosen here so that the interval between the beginning of the period and the date of grant does not exceed 5 years.

LEGISLATIVE CHANGES

The following legislative provisions have been introduced since the above specimen rules were issued by the Inland Revenue:

1. FA 1987, s 33(1) and Sch 4, paras 1, 3, and 4 and F(No 2)A 1987, s 59(1) and (2) (now ICTA 1988, Sch 9, para 15; CGTA 1979, s 144A(4): release of options in consideration of grant of new options on takeovers, etc (see 5.51 to 5.61). This necessitates the inclusion of new provisions in the rules if advantage is to be taken of the statutory change.
2. FA 1987, s 33(2) and Sch 4, paras 6 to 8 (now ICTA 1988, s 187(4) and Sch 9, para 37): changes to definition of 'material interest' in a close company (see 7.68 and 7.69). This has no effect on the wording of the above rules.

Appendix 7 Specimen rules for approved executive ('selective') share option scheme

(Reproduced by kind permission of the Controller of Her Majesty's Stationery Office.)

The scheme rules set out below form an appendix to the Inland Revenue notes on approved executive share option schemes first published on 19 December 1984 and last reprinted, with revisions, in June 1988. The text of those notes contains the following passage (at paragraph 1.11):

> [The appendix] contains a set of scheme rules designed to meet the requirements for approval. It is intended only as an illustration of the type of framework which companies might wish to adopt. There is considerable scope for varying the scheme rules, especially those which are not essential for Inland Revenue approval. Companies should consider their own particular needs carefully and obtain professional advice where necessary.

Where indicated, reference should be made to the numbered notes at the end of this appendix.

RULES OF THE [............................] EMPLOYEE SHARE OPTION SCHEME

1.1 Definitions

In these Rules the following words and expressions shall have the following meanings:

"Announcement date"	the date on which the annual or half-yearly results of the Company are announced.
"Appropriate period"	the meaning given in paragraph 15(2) of Schedule 9
"Approval date"	the date on which the Scheme is approved by the Board of Inland Revenue under Schedule 9
"Associated company"	has the same meaning as in s 416 of ICTA 1988.
"Auditors"	the auditors for the time being of the Company (acting as experts and not as arbitrators).
"Board"	the Board of Directors of the Company or, except in Rule 10.4, a duly constituted committee thereof.
"Company"	[.....................][1]
"Control"	has the same meaning as in s 840 of ICTA 1988.
"Dealing day"	[a day on which The Stock Exchange is open for the transaction of business.][2]
"Date of grant"	the date on which an Option is, was, or is to be granted under the scheme.
"Eligible Employee"	any director or employee of any Participating Company who is required to devote to his duties not less than 25 hours (or, in the case of an employee who is not a director of any Participating Company, 20 hours) per week (excluding meal breaks) and is not precluded by para 8 of Sch 9 from participating in the Scheme.
"Market Value"	[on any day the average of the middle market quotations of a Share as derived from the Daily

Official List of The Stock Exchange for the three immediately preceding Dealing Days. (Provided that if the Dealing Days do not fall within the period specified in Rule 2, only such days as do fall within that period will be taken into account in arriving at the Market Value.)][3]

[on any day the market value of a Share determined in accordance with the provisions of Pt VIII of CGTA 1979 and agreed for the purposes of the Scheme with the Inland Revenue Shares Valuation Division on or before that day.][4]

"Option" — a right to subscribe for Shares granted (or to be granted) in accordance with the Rules of this Scheme.

"Option Holder" — an individual to whom an Option has been granted or his personal representatives.

"Participating Company" — the Company and any other company of which the Company has Control and which is for the time being nominated by the Board to be a Participating Company.

"Relevant Emoluments" — the meaning which the term bears in sub-para (2) of para 28 of Sch 9 by virtue of sub-para (4) of that paragraph.

"Schedule 9" — Schedule 9 to ICTA 1988.

"Scheme" — the employee share option scheme constituted and governed by these rules as from time to time amended.

"Share" — An [ordinary][5] share in the capital of the company which satisfies the conditions specified in paragraphs 10 to 14 inclusive of Sch 9.

"Subscription Price" — the price at which each Share subject to an Option may be acquired on the exercise of that Option being, subject to Rule 8, the higher of
- (i) the nominal value of a Share and
- (ii) the Market Value of a Share on the day the invitation to apply for that Option was issued pursuant to Rule 2.

"Subsisting Option" — an Option which has neither lapsed nor been exercised.

"Year of Assessment" — a year beginning on any 6 April and ending on the following 5 April.

1.2 Where the context so admits the singular shall include the plural and vice versa and the masculine shall include the feminine.

1.3 Any reference in the Scheme to any enactment includes a reference to that enactment as from time to time modified, extended or re-enacted.

2 Invitation to apply for options

At any time or times within a period of four weeks after an Announcement Date or the Approval Date, and in any case not earlier than the Approval Date nor later than the tenth anniversary thereof, the Board may in its absolute discretion select any number of individuals who may at the intended Date of Grant be Eligible Employees and invite them to apply for the grant of Options to acquire Shares in the Company. Each invitation shall specify:

(i) the date (being neither earlier than 7 nor later than 14 days after the issue of the invitation) by which an application must be made,
(ii) the maximum number of Shares over which that individual may on that occasion apply for an Option, being determined at the absolute discretion of the Board save that it shall not be so large that the grant of an option over that number of shares would cause the limit specified in Rule 5.2 to be exceeded, and
(iii) the Subscription Price at which Shares may be acquired on the exercise of any Option granted in response to the application.

Each invitation shall be accompanied by an application in such form, not inconsistent with these Rules, as the Board may determine.

3 Applications for options

Not later than the date specified in the invitation each Eligible Employee to whom an invitation has been issued in accordance with Rule 2 above may apply to the Board, using the application form supplied, for an Option over a number of Shares not exceeding the number specified in the invitation.

[Each application shall be accompanied by a payment of £1 in consideration for the Option to be granted.][6]

4 Grant of options

4.1 Not later than the twenty-first day following the issue of invitations the Board may grant to each applicant who is still an Eligible Employee an Option over the number of Shares specified in his application.

4.2 As soon as possible after Options have been granted the Board shall issue a certificate of option in respect of each Option in such form, not inconsistent with these Rules, as the Board may determine.

4.3 No Option may be transferred, assigned or charged and any purported transfer, assignment or charge shall cause the Option to lapse forthwith. Each option certificate shall carry a statement to this effect.

5 Limitations on grants

[**5.1** No option shall be granted pursuant to Rule 4 above if such grant would result in the aggregate of:

(i) the number of Shares over which Subsisting Options have been granted under this Scheme and
(ii) the number of Shares which have been issued on the exercise of Options granted under this Scheme and
(iii) the number of Shares over which subsisting options have been granted under any other share option scheme during the period of ten years ending on the relevant Date of Grant and
(iv) the number of Shares which have been issued pursuant to any other employee share scheme (including a share option scheme) during the period of ten years ending on the relevant Date of Grant

exceeding (X%) of the number of shares then in issue.][7]

5.2 No Option shall be granted to an Eligible Employee if immediately following such grant he would hold Subsisting Options over Shares with an aggregate Subscription Price exceeding the greater of:

(i) £100,000 or
(ii) four times the amount of the Eligible Employee's Relevant Emoluments for the current or preceding Year of Assessment (whichever of those years gives the greater amount) or, if there were no Relevant Emoluments for the preceding Year of Assessment, four times the amount of the Relevant Emoluments for the period of twelve months beginning with the first day during the current Year of Assessment in respect of which there are Relevant Emoluments.

For the purposes of this Rule 5.2 Options shall include all Options granted under this Scheme and all options granted under any other scheme, not being a savings-related share option scheme, approved under Schedule 9 and established by the Company or any Associated Company thereof.

6 Exercise of options

6.1 Subject to Rule 9 below any Option which has not lapsed may be exercised in whole or in part at any time following the earliest of the following events:

(i) the third anniversary of the Date of Grant
(ii) the death of the Option holder
(iii) the Option holder ceasing to be a director or employee of any Participating Company by reason of injury, disability, redundancy or retirement [or for such other reasons as are specified in the rules].

6.2 An Option shall lapse on the earliest of the following events:

(i) the tenth anniversary of the date of the grant
(ii) the first anniversary of the Option holder's death
(iii) six months following the Option holder ceasing to be a director or employee of any Participating Company, other than by reason of his death
(iv) unless a release has been effected under Rule 7.4, six months after the Option has become exercisable in accordance with Rule 7
(v) the Option holder being adjudicated bankrupt.

7 Takeovers and liquidations

7.1 If any person obtains control of the company as a result of making:

(i) a general offer to acquire the whole of the issued share capital of the Company which is made on a condition such that if it is satisfied the person making the offer will have Control of the Company or
(ii) a general offer to acquire all the shares in the Company which are of the same class as the Shares

then any Subsisting Option may subject to Rule 7.4 below be exercised within six months of the time when the person making the offer has obtained Control of the Company and any condition subject to which the offer is made has been satisfied.

7.2 If under [s 425 of the Companies Act 1985 or Art 418 of the Companies (Northern Ireland) Order 1986][8] the Court sanctions a compromise or arrangement proposed for the purposes of or in connection with a scheme for the reconstruction of the Company or its amalgamation with any other company or companies, any Subsisting Option may, subject to Rule 7.4 below, be exercised within six months of the Court sanctioning the compromise or arrangement.

7.3 If any person becomes bound or entitled to acquire shares in the Company under [ss 428 to 430 of the said Act of 1985 or Arts 421 to 423 of the said Order of 1986][8] any Subsisting Option may, subject to Rule 7.4 below, be exercised at any time when that person remains so bound or entitled.

7.4 If as a result of the events specified in Rules 7.1 or 7.2 a company has obtained Control of the Company, or if a company has become bound or entitled as mentioned in Rule 7.3, the Option Holder may, by agreement with that other company (the 'Acquiring Company'), within the Appropriate Period, release each Subsisting Option (the 'Old Option') for an option (the 'New Option') which satisfies the conditions that it:

(i) is over shares in the Acquiring Company or some other company falling within para (b) or para (c) of Para 10, Schedule 9, which satisfy the conditions specified in Paras 10 to 14 inclusive of Schedule 9;
(ii) is a right to acquire such number of such Shares as has on acquisition of the new option an aggregate Market Value equal to the aggregate Market Value of the shares subject to the Old Option on its release;
(iii) has a subscription price per Share such that the aggregate price payable on the complete exercise equals the aggregate price which would have been payable on complete exercise of the Old Option; and
(iv) is otherwise identical in terms to the Old Option.

The New Option shall, for all other purposes of this Scheme, be treated as having been acquired at the same time as the Old Option.

Where any New Options are granted pursuant to this clause 7.4, Rules 4.3, 6, 7, 8, 9, 10.1, and 10.3 to 10.6 shall, in relation to the New Options, be construed as if references to the Company and to the Shares were references to the Acquiring Company, or as the case may be, to the other company to whose shares the New Options relate, and to the shares in that other company, but references to Participating Company shall continue to be construed as if references to the Company were references to [.........................][1]

7.5 If the Company passes a resolution for voluntary winding up, any Subsisting Option may be exercised within six months of the passing of the resolution.

7.6 For the purposes of this Rule 7 other than Rule 7.4 a person shall be deemed to have obtained Control of a Company if he and others acting in concert with him have together obtained Control of it.

7.7 The exercise of an Option pursuant to the preceding provisions of this Rule 7 shall be subject to the provisions of Rule 9 below.

8 Variation of share capital

In the event of any capitalisation or rights issue or any consolidation, subdivision or reduction of capital by the Company, the number of Shares subject to any Option and the Subscription Price for each of those Shares shall be adjusted in such manner as the Auditors confirm to be fair and reasonable provided that:

(i) the aggregate amount payable on the exercise of an Option in full is not increased
(ii) the Subscription Price for a Share is not reduced below its nominal value
(iii) no adjustment shall be made without the prior approval of the Board of Inland Revenue and
(iv) following the adjustment the Shares continue to satisfy the conditions specified in paras 10 to 14 inclusive of Schedule 9.

9 Manner of exercise of options

9.1 No Option may be exercised by an individual at any time when he is precluded by para 8 of Schedule 9 from participating in the Scheme.

9.2 No Option may be exercised at any time when the shares which may be thereby acquired are not Shares as defined in Rule 1.1.

9.3 An Option shall be exercised by the Option Holder giving notice to the Company in writing of the number of Shares in respect of which he wishes to exercise the Option accompanied by the appropriate payment and the relevant option certificate and shall be effective on the date of its receipt by the Company.

9.4 Shares shall be allotted and issued pursuant to a notice of exercise within 30 days of the date of exercise and a definitive share certificate issued to the Option Holder in respect thereof. Save for any rights determined by reference to a date preceding the date of allotment, such Shares shall rank pari passu with the other shares of the same class in issue at the date of allotment.

9.5 When an option is exercised only in part, the balance shall remain exercisable on the same terms as originally applied to the whole Option and a new option certificate shall be issued accordingly by the Company as soon as possible after the partial exercise.

10 Administration and amendment

10.1 The scheme shall be administered by the Board whose decision on all disputes shall be final.

10.2 The Board may from time to time amend these Rules provided that:

(i) no amendment may materially affect an Option holder as regards an Option granted prior to the amendment being made

(ii) no amendment may be made which would make the terms on which Options may be granted materially more generous or would increase the limit specified in Rule 5.1 without the prior approval of the Company in general meeting and

(iii) no amendment shall have effect until approved by the Board of Inland Revenue.

10.3 The cost of establishing and operating the Scheme shall be borne by the Participating Companies in such proportions as the Board shall determine.

10.4 The Board may establish a committee consisting of not less than three Board members to whom any or all of its powers in relation to the Scheme may be delegated. The Board may at any time dissolve the Committee, alter its constitution or direct the manner in which it shall act.

10.5 Any notice or other communication under or in connection with the Scheme may be given by the Company either personally or by post and to the Company either personally or by post to the secretary; items sent by post shall be prepaid and shall be deemed to have been received 72 hours after posting.

10.6 The company shall at all times keep available sufficient authorised and unissued Shares to satisfy the exercise to the full extent still possible of all Options which have neither lapsed nor been fully exercised, taking account of any other obligations of the company to issue unissued shares.

Notes

1 Insert name of company.
2 This definition is of use only if the scheme shares are quoted on The Stock Exchange.
3 Appropriate only where the scheme shares are quoted on The Stock Exchange.
4 Appropriate only where the scheme shares are not quoted on The Stock Exchange.
5 The description of the scheme shares should be inserted here.
6 This sentence may be omitted if provision is made in the Rules for options to be granted under seal. This is to ensure that the option holder has an enforceable right.
7 These provisions are not required for Inland Revenue approval. They are designed to protect existing shareholders and each company must decide for itself what, if any, limits it needs to impose.
8 The provision appropriate to the company should be chosen.

Appendix 8 Inland Revenue Statement of Practice SP 18/80, 23 December 1980: Securities dealt in on The Stock Exchange Unlisted Securities Market: status and valuation for tax purposes

The Stock Exchange introduced an organised market in unlisted securities—the Unlisted Securities Market—on 10 November 1980.

In the view of the Inland Revenue securities dealt in on the Unlisted Securities Market will not fall to be treated as 'listed' or 'quoted' for the purposes of those sections of the Taxes Acts which use these terms in relation to securities. The securities will, however, satisfy the tests of being 'authorised to be dealt in' and 'dealt in (regularly or from time to time)' on a recognised stock exchange.

Where it is necessary for tax purposes to agree the open market value of such securities on a given date, initial evidence of their value will be suggested by the details of the bargains done at or near the relevant date. However other factors may also be relevant and the Shares Valuation Division of the Capital Taxes Office will consider whether a value offered on the basis of those bargains can be accepted as an adequate reflection of the open market value.

Appendix 9 Inland Revenue Press Release of 11 June 1985: Approved employee share option schemes: Revenue revise practice on some share restrictions

Following legal advice the Inland Revenue have revised their practice concerning the admissibility of employee share options schemes under FA 1980 and FA 1984 [now ICTA 1988, Sch 9], where the shares are subject to a directors' discretionary veto on share transfer. In future, if a company declares that the discretionary power will not be used to discriminate against the transfer of shares acquired under the scheme, the scheme will be approved provided the other statutory conditions are met. Otherwise the Revenue's practice on approving employee share option schemes is unchanged.

(1) Under the approved share option provisions the shares which a company uses in its scheme must not be subject to restrictions other than restrictions which attach to all shares of the same class. The Revenue have in the past refused to give approval to a share option scheme if the shares in question are subject either to a directors' discretionary veto on share transfer or to employee pre-emption arrangements.

(2) On the question of discretionary veto, the Revenue are modifying their interpretation of the legislation. In future, it will therefore be acceptable for a company to have in its articles of association a provision authorising the directors to refuse to register a transfer of shares. However, since their legal advice is that the exercise of such a veto in a discriminatory way could offend the statutory requirement, the Revenue will be asking any company whose articles contain such a provision to complete a declaration. The declaration should confirm that the discretionary power of the directors will not be exercised so as to discriminate against the transfer of shares acquired under the scheme and its existence should be made known to employees participating in the scheme.

(3) On the question of employee pre-emption arrangements, the Revenue confirm their current interpretation of the law. In consequence, they will continue to refuse approval to any share option scheme where a company could compel an employee who leaves his job to sell his shares to another shareholder. [Statutory provisions in ICTA 1988, Sch 9, para 12(1)(c), (2) and (3) now permit such restrictions in certain circumstances. See 5.80 to 5.81 and 6.53 to 6.54].

Notes

(1) Under FA 1980 a company can set up a savings-related share option scheme which attracts relief from the normal income tax Schedule E charge for employees who participate in the scheme. An employee granted an option over shares under one of these schemes will be liable to CGT when he disposes of his shares, on the gain over the option price. (There would otherwise be liability to income tax on the gain as soon as the option was exercised.) To qualify for this treatment the scheme must be approved by the Board of Inland Revenue and the shares must be purchased out of the proceeds of savings derived from a special SAYE contract with either the Department for National Savings or a building society. The current upper limit on monthly contributions is £100.

(2) A share option scheme approved by the Revenue under FA 1984 gives similar CGT treatment to participating employees, provided certain conditions are satisfied, but differs from a scheme approved under FA 1980 in a number of important respects.

For example, it may be approved without the necessity for it to be open to all employees and it need not depend on participants taking out SAYE contracts to fund the eventual exercise of options.

(3) Before giving approval to a share option scheme either under FA 1980 or under FA 1984 the Revenue must be sure that certain statutory requirements, relating, for example, to the scheme shares, are met. Inter alia, the provisions stipulate that any restrictions attaching to the scheme shares must also attach to all the other shares of the same class [subject to the subsequent statutory modification referred to in 5.80 to 5.81 and 6.53 to 6.54].

(4) As a separate matter, the wording of FA 1978, which provides relief from income tax for approved profit-sharing schemes, is less specific about what constitutes a restriction. The Revenue's view has always been that a more liberal interpretation is therefore possible. They have therefore accepted, and will continue to accept, that under the FA 1978 legislation a company's articles of association can require an employee who has ceased to work for the company to transfer his shares, but only after their legal ownership has passed to him from the scheme trustees. This will be either at the specific and voluntary direction of the employee concerned or after the period during which shares are held in trust has expired. (This period is currently seven years but a [1985] Budget proposal reduces it to five years.) [This point is now covered by ICTA 1988, Sch 9, para 12. See 4.127]

Appendix 10 Inland Revenue Statement of Practice SP 4/83: Approved savings-related share option schemes: Rights of certain employees to exercise options: FA 1980, Sch 10, para 8

(1) Schedule 10 to FA 1980 [now ICTA 1988, Sch 9] provides that [savings-related] share option schemes approved by the Inland Revenue should not normally permit employees to exercise their option rights to acquire shares before the earliest date on which repayments under the associated SAYE contract are due (para 6) [now ICTA 1988, Sch 9, para 17].

(2) Approved schemes are allowed to provide for the earlier exercise of options only in certain circumstances, including the following:

(a) if the participant ceases employment owing to injury, disability, redundancy or retirement on reaching normal retirement age (para 8) [now ICTA 1988, Sch 9, para 19]; or

(b) if he ceases employment for any other reason having held the option rights for more than three years (para 8) [now ICTA 1988, Sch 9, para 19].

(3) Where the conditions of (a) and (b) above are satisfied, para 8 [now ICTA 1988, Sch 9, para 19] requires that in either case the options must be exercisable, if at all, within six months of the participant ceasing employment. Where employment has ceased before the maturity date of the SAYE contract and the conditions of para 8 [now ICTA 1988, Sch 9, para 19] are not satisfied the participant will not be permitted to exercise them at all.

(4) A participant is regarded as having ceased to be employed for the purposes of the para 8 [now ICTA 1988, Sch 9, para 19] conditions described above only when he is no longer employed by the company which established the scheme or any of its associated or controlled companies.

(5) Some doubt has arisen as to whether the terms of para 8 [now ICTA 1988, Sch 9, para 19] allow employees to exercise their option if the company employing them has left the group and consequently ceased to be a participating company in the scheme. It could be argued that if the employees concerned have not actually ceased to hold employment with that company, they would fail to satisfy the conditions of para 8 [now ICTA 1988, Sch 9, para 19].

(6) Originally the Inland Revenue took the view that such employees were precluded by the terms of Sch 10 [now ICTA 1988, Sch 9] from exercising their options at all, even if they had held them for more than three years. However, it is now accepted on the basis of legal advice that this interpretation of the legislation was not correct.

(7) The position now is that, if the scheme rules permit and if the rights have been held for more than three years, the Inland Revenue accept that an employee may exercise his option rights within the normal period of six months from the time when his employing company left the control of its parent company. It is up to the company establishing the scheme to decide whether it wants to include such a provision in its scheme.

(8) In this connection it should be noted that s 40(8) of FA 1982 has amended the definition of 'associated company' in FA 1980, Sch 10, para 26 [now ICTA 1988, s 187(2)]. This ensures that where the conditions at para (7) above are satisfied an option can be exercised by a scheme participant as soon as a subsidiary leaves the control of its parent company.

[This practice was given statutory effect, from 25 July 1986, by FA 1986, s 25(4), introducing what is now ICTA 1988, Sch 9, para 21(1)(e)].

Appendix 11 Inland Revenue Extrastatutory Concession B 27: Approved employee share schemes—jointly owned companies

(Reproduced by kind permission of the Controller of Her Majesty's Stationery Office from the Inland Revenue booklet IR1, 'Extrastatutory Concessions' as at June 1985.)

A jointly owned company cannot strictly participate in an approved employee share scheme run by either of its joint owners because it will not be controlled by a single company operating a scheme as the legislation requires (FA 1978, Sch 9, para 1(2); FA 1980, Sch 10, para 1(3) and FA 1984, Sch 10, para 1(3) [now ICTA 1988, Sch 9, para 1(3)]). By concession, the Revenue will normally admit such a company as a participating company in an approved scheme where:

(a) the company is to participate in only one group scheme under the particular legislation in question [ie, one 'profit-sharing scheme', one savings-related share option scheme, and one selective share option scheme];
(b) it is not under the control of any single person (within the definition in ICTA 1970, s 534) [now ICTA 1988, s 840];
(c) two persons between them control it and one of them is a company operating the relevant approved scheme; and
(d) an undertaking is given to notify the Revenue of any changes in the ownership or control of the company itself, the company operating the scheme or the other joint owners as soon as any such change occurs.

The Revenue will consider each request for a concession on the merits of the particular circumstances. Once a concession has been granted if a change in ownership does occur they retain the right to withdraw it.

Appendix 12 Inland Revenue Press Release of 14 April 1988: Unapproved employee share schemes

The Chancellor announced in his Budget major changes to the rules – in FA 1929 s 79 [now ITCA 1988, s 138] – which apply to certain shares acquired by employees outside an approved scheme. These changes are contained in clauses 72 to 84 of the Finance Bill, published today [now FA 1988, ss 77 to 89].

The changes are designed to help companies and employees by targeting the provisions much more narrowly on the particular kinds of abuse at which they are aimed. This relaxation will also apply where the shares are those in a qualifying subsidiary company.

The proposals are substantially the same as those that were announced on 26 October 1987 and published in the form of draft clauses for consultation. These were generally welcomed as a significant improvement on the existing provisions. However, some minor, technical changes to the earlier draft clauses have been made, to help ensure that they achieve the result intended and to meet various points made in representations.

The main changes to the earlier draft clauses are –

(a) subject to certain safeguards, a company which is a subsidiary will not be deemed to be a 'non-qualifying' subsidiary solely by virtue of having subsidiaries of its own (clause 81(2)) [now FA 1988, s 86(2)];
(b) any payments to a company concerned in respect of group relief will be excluded from the definition of 'intra-group' transactions (clause 81(3)) [now FA 1988, s 86(3)];
(c) shares in a subsidiary company may still qualify for the new treatment even if the 'majority test' in clause 73(6) [now FA 1988, s 88(6)] is not satisfied, provided that the company has only a single class of shares;
(d) amendments have been made to clarify how relief for income tax charged under these provisions will be given in capital gains tax computations where company reorganisations occur or there are transactions with 'connected' persons;
(e) for shares acquired before 26 October 1987 which at the time of acquisition had attached to them a restriction previously exempt under the provisions of FA 1973 Sch 8 para 7 [now ICTA 1988, s 139(9)], the lifting of any such restriction shall not count as a chargeable event under the new provisions;
(f) certain of the time limits (in clause 80(2) and 81(1)) [now ICTA 1988, ss 85(2) and 86(1)] relating to the furnishing of returns have been relaxed.

Performance-related rights or restrictions

Under the proposed new regime there will in most cases be a charge only if, when and to the extent that value is actually shifted preferentially into the employee shares as a result of manipulation of rights or restrictions attaching to the shares. There was concern in some representations, however, that this might also catch certain kinds of performance-related right or restriction (sometimes known as 'equity ratchets') which are commonly to be found in management buy-outs, and under which the portion of the company's equity represented by the managers' shares is increased on some predetermined basis by reference to the company's performance.

Subject to the precise facts in each particular case, the Revenue agree that a charge should not normally arise on the triggering of such a right or restriction on achievement of the predetermined performance level, where the right or restriction attached to the shares from the outset. Obviously, the Revenue will still, for normal Schedule E purposes, need to ensure that the price paid for the shares reflects their true value including the effect of any such rights relating to them.

Notes

(1) FA 1972 s 79 [now ICTA 1988, s 138] contains wide-ranging anti-avoidance provisions relating to unapproved employee share schemes. The main effect is to apply a charge to income tax on the whole of any increase in the value of shares acquired by employees in that capacity outside an approved scheme, where the shares are subject to certain kinds of restriction or where certain other conditions are not satisfied.

(2) The aim is to prevent companies from passing to their employees share-related benefits which in reality are part of the employee's remuneration, but which, because they are in 'capital' form, avoid a charge to income tax on that remuneration. This might be done in a number of ways – for example, by subjecting the employee shares (prior to acquisition) to special restrictions of one kind or another which depress their value and then, after acquisition, removing those restrictions, thus restoring the value of the shares to that of the company's shares in general issue, and thereby giving the employees an essentially artificial benefit.

(3) FA 1972 s 79 [now ICTA 1988, s 138] has increasingly been criticised for being too wide-ranging in its effect. For example, the growth in value charge can apply even if there is no actual manipulation of the restrictions concerned. The detailed provisions are also such that FA 1972 s 79 [now ICTA 1988, s 138] will nearly always apply where the shares are those in a subsidiary company, again whether or not abuse actually occurs.

(4) A review of FA 1972 s 79 [now ICTA 1988, s 138] was announced by the Chancellor of the Exchequer on 17 March 1987, when a consultative document was also issued by the Revenue and views were invited on ways of simplifying and improving the provisions, consistent with their underlying purpose. The review was undertaken by the Revenue, with the assistance of a small informal working group of outside practitioners who have expertise in this area.

(5) Following completion of the review and consideration of the group's report, the government announced last October its intention to introduce major changes, designed to help companies and their employees by targeting the provisions as narrowly as possible on the particular kinds of abuse at which this legislation is aimed. In most cases, the present growth in value charge is to be replaced with a new, more narrowly targeted charge that will arise only if and to the extent that value is actually shifted preferentially into the employee shares as a result of manipulation. This relaxation will also apply to shares in 'qualifying' subsidiaries.

(6) The proposed changes will take effect from 26 October 1987 when draft clauses incorporating them were published for consultation. Shares acquired before 26 October 1987 and at present subject to FA 1972 s 79 [now ICTA 1988, s 138] will also be able to get the benefit of the new more relaxed rule with effect from that date, provided that the qualifying conditions are satisfied.

Appendix 13 Inland Revenue Press Release of 11 October 1988: Taxation of employee priority shares in a public offer

Last year the government announced that an income tax exemption would be introduced for the benefit which an employee may derive from being given priority rights – as compared with members of the public – to shares in a public offer of shares.

The government has today announced some technical improvements to the legislation which was included in this year's Finance Act. Their effect will be that

- the exemption for the benefit from priority will be extended to apply in addition where employees are allocated priority shares at a discount to the price at which they are offered to the public (but the discount itself will remain taxable);
- where a single public offer of shares consists of several elements (e g shares offered at one or more fixed prices, by tender, or through placings) and employee priority is not given for every element in the offer it will be possible to allocate a larger number of shares to employees in priority without loss of the tax exemption.

The changes in detail

(a) *Background*

(1) Where a company is making a public offer of shares, employees are often given priority rights, as compared with members of the public, to the shares on offer. Essentially this means that, if the offer is over-subscribed, the employees will nevertheless still be entitled to receive their full allocation of shares, or, if there is scaling down, to receive more shares than a member of the public who has applied for the same number of shares.

(2) If, at the time the shares are allocated to the employee, they are worth more than the price paid then, as compared with a member of the public, the employee receives an extra benefit through his employment, to the extent that he has received more shares. Under the rules for taxing employees, that benefit was taxable prior to the relief introduced in the 1988 Finance Act.

(3) As part of its policy for encouraging the spread of wider share ownership, and the holding by employees of shares in the companies for which they work, the government last year announced its intention to introduce legislation exempting this benefit from income tax where the offer was primarily an offer to the public of which the priority allocation to the employees formed only a small part. The government's intention was (and remains), however, to charge to tax any benefit an employee receives through being entitled to buy shares at a lower price than paid by ordinary members of the public.

(b) *Shares where employees are entitled both to priority and discount*

(4) The legislation introduced this year (as FA 1988, s 68) provides an exemption where shares carry only priority rights. But in some circumstances employees will be entitled to shares which carry both priority and discount rights. In these cases, at present, both the priority and discount benefits are taxable. One of the

improvements proposed is that in such cases the priority benefit will be exempted (if the necessary conditions are met) while the discount remains taxable.

(5) The following example illustrates the effect of the proposed new relief:

– price paid per share by employees	90p
– price paid per share by the public	100p
– market value of shares when allocated to employees	120p

At present the employee is taxable on the 30 pence difference between the market value of the shares and the price paid.

The intention is that the employee will be exempt from income tax on the *priority gain*, ie the 20p gain (120p market value minus 100p price paid by the public), in relation to the *extra* shares he receives as a result of his priority as compared with a member of the public. The 10p *discount gain* (price to the public 100p less price to employee 90p) will remain taxable in relation to *all* the shares the employee receives with the benefit of the discount.

(c) *Limit on priority shares granted to employees*

(6) The present exemption applies only where no more than 10% of the shares on offer are allocated in priority to employees. Most offers to the public consist of only one element (eg the whole of the shares are offered at a fixed price) and in these cases this rule causes no difficulty. But where the offer contains a number of different elements, and the employees are entitled to priority in only one of them, the total shares which can be offered to employees in priority can be reduced well below 10% of the whole offer. This is because the condition applies *separately* to each separate element of the total public offer.

(7) To avoid this rule unduly restricting the scope for giving employees priority rights in more complicated public offers, the government proposes to establish separate limits. For the offer as a whole, the limit will remain at 10% of the total of the ordinary shares comprised in the whole offer. This is in line with the government's intention (see paragraph (3)) that relief should be available only where employee priority shares are a small part of the whole offer. But for an offer consisting of more than one element, the limit *in each element* will be increased to 40%, subject of course to the overall limit test outlined above.

(8) This change will in no case reduce the amount of relief available at present. The 40% limit will enable a substantially greater number of priority shares to be allocated to employees in more complicated public offers, while the 10% limit on the total offer will maintain, for all such offers, the requirement that employee priority shares which can qualify for tax relief are only a small part of a genuine offer to the public.

(9) For the purposes of any capital gains tax computation on a subsequent disposal, the shares will be treated as acquired at the price paid by the employee where he paid the same price as members of the public. Where the employee purchased his shares at a discount to the price paid by members of the public, the shares will be treated as acquired at the price paid by him plus the amount of the discount chargeable to income tax. For shares that exceed the proposed limit, there will be an adjustment to exclude from the capital gains tax computation any amounts that were chargeable to income tax.

(d) *Starting date*

(10) The Government propose that these improvements in the relief should apply to any public offer of shares made on or after today.

(e) *Legislation*

(11) Legislation to this effect will be included in the 1989 Finance Bill. The government intend to publish draft legislation as soon as it is available.

Notes

(1) Under the present legislation (FA 1988, s 68) where certain conditions are met there is no income tax charge on the benefit which can arise to employees from priority in a public offer of shares where the employees pay the same price for their shares as members of the public. Where, however, employees acquire the shares in priority at a discounted price, they do not qualify for the exemption provided by the legislation.

(2) The benefit of priority in such cases is taxable as income and is determined by reference to both the extra number of shares received by the employee under the priority allocation compared to a member of the public who had applied for the same number, and the difference between the value of the shares at the date they were allocated and what he paid for them. In practice, the benefit, if any, will often be difficult to determine and small and could not be foreseen with certainty at the time the employee applied for shares. Having regard to these factors, and its policy of encouraging wider share ownership, the government believe it is right that there should (where appropriate conditions are met) be no income tax charge arising from employee priority shares.

(3) The changes now proposed are designed to give improved expression to the government's intentions with regard to the taxation of employee 'priority' allocations of shares in cases of more complicated public offers of shares comprising a variety of different elements.

Index